The History of
Auchinleck
Village & Parish

Other books by Dane Love:

Scottish Kirkyards	Robert Hale
Pictorial History of Cumnock	Alloway Publishing
Pictorial History of Ayr	Alloway Publishing
Scottish Ghosts	Robert Hale
Scottish Ghosts	Barnes & Noble
The Auld Inns of Scotland	Robert Hale
Guide to Scottish Castles	Lomond Books
Tales of the Clan Chiefs	Robert Hale
Scottish Covenanter Stories	Neil Wilson
Ayr Stories	Fort Publishing
Ayrshire Coast	Fort Publishing
Scottish Spectres	Robert Hale
Scottish Spectres	Ulverston Large Print
Ayrshire: Discovering a County	Fort Publishing
Ayr Past and Present	Sutton Publishing
Lost Ayrshire	Birlinn
The River Ayr Way	Carn Publishing
Ayr – the Way We Were	Fort Publishing
The Man Who Sold Nelson's Column	Birlinn
Jacobite Stories	Neil Wilson
The History of Sorn – Village & Parish	Carn Publishing
Legendary Ayrshire	Carn Publishing
The Covenanter Encyclopaedia	Fort Publishing
Scottish Ghosts	Amberley Publishing
Scottish Kirkyards	Amberley Publishing
A Look Back at Cumnock	Carn Publishing
A Look Back at Girvan	Carn Publishing
A Look Back at Ayrshire Farming	Carn Publishing
Ayr Then and Now	The History Press
Ayrshire Then and Now	The History Press
The History of Mauchline - Village & Parish	Carn Publishing
The Galloway Highlands	Carn Publishing
Scottish Castles	Pocket Mountains

www.dane-love.co.uk

The History of
Auchinleck

Village & Parish

Dane Love

CARN PUBLISHING

© Dane Love, 2015.
First Published in Great Britain, 1991.
Second, expanded edition, published 2015.

ISBN - 978 0 9567550 9 4

Published by Carn Publishing,
Lochnoran House,
Auchinleck, Ayrshire, KA18 3JW.

Printed by Bell & Bain Ltd,
Glasgow, G46 7UQ.

The right of the author to be identified as the author of this work has been asserted by him in accordance with the Copyright, Designs and Patents Act 1988.

All rights reserved. No part of this publication may be reproduced, stored, or transmitted in any form, or by any means, electronic, mechanical or photocopying, recording or otherwise, without the express written permission of the publisher.

Contents

List of Illustrations	6
Introduction	9
1 Early Times (Before 1504)	11
2 Sixteenth Century (1504-1600)	29
3 Seventeenth Century (1600-1689)	37
4 Planned Village and Rural Advancement (1689-1840)	60
5 Industrial Growth (1840-1901)	121
6 War and Depression (1901-1945)	169
7 The Golden Years (1945-2000)	247
8 Twenty-First Century	299
Appendix I: Farms and Small Lairdships	307
Appendix II: Mines	327
Bibliography	331
Index	337

List of Illustrations

1.1	Bronze Age finger ring, found in Wardlaw cairn *(Author's Collection)*	13
1.2	Rocking Stone at Lugar *(Dane Love)*	14
1.3	Plan of Dornal Moat, drawn in 1893 *(Author's Collection)*	17
1.4	Auchinleck Castle, as drawn by Francis Grose, 1791 *(Author's Collection)*	18
1.5	Auchinleck Castle (plan) *(Dane Love)*	19
1.6	Kyle Castle (plan) *(Dane Love)*	25
1.7	Kyle Castle *(Dane Love)*	26
1.8	Templar's Gravestone *(Dane Love)*	28
3.1	West part of parish as shown on Timothy Pont's *Coila Provincia* (1654)	38
3.2	Old Place of Auchinleck from MacGibbon & Ross *(Author's Collection)*	40
3.3	Old Place of Auchinleck (plan) *(Dane Love)*	41
3.4	Old Place of Auchinleck from west *(Dane Love)*	42
3.5	James Wallace of Wallaceton's tombstone *(Dane Love)*	46
3.6	Cameron's Stone, Airds Moss *(Dane Love)*	54
3.7	Memorial marking Covenanter skirmish at Bello Path *(Dane Love)*	57
4.1	Auchinleck Parish from Armstrong's *Map of Ayrshire* (1775)	61
4.2	Bridgend Mill *(Author's Collection)*	63
4.3	Auchinleck House in 2015 *(Dane Love)*	65
4.4	James Boswell *(Author's Collection)*	70
4.5	James Boswell *(Author's Collection)*	72
4.6	Boswell Arms *(Dane Love)*	77
4.7	Boswell family burial vaults, Auchinleck *(Dane Love)*	82
4.8	The Boswell Mausoleum (Dane Love)	85
4.9	Communion Tokens (a-c Parish Church; d Associate Church) *(Author's Collection)*	89
4.10	Old Parish Church *(Dane Love)*	90
4.11	John Dun's *Sermon upon Occasion of the Death of Lady Auchinleck* (1766) *(Author's Collection)*	91
4.12	William Halbert's *The Practical Figurer* (1789) *(Author's Collection)*	98
4.13	Tarrioch as shown on Ordnance Survey Six Inch Map of 1860	100
4.14	Glenmuir Limeworks in 1990 *(Dane Love)*	102
4.15	Rigg Toll Cottage *(Dane Love)*	108
4.16	The Temple, Dumfries House Estate *(Author's Collection)*	111
4.17	Bello Mill in 1954 *(Author's Collection)*	112
4.18	Murdoch's Cave and Bello Mill *(Author's Collection)*	114
5.1	Town Hall, Auchinleck *(Author's Collection)*	123
5.2	Lugar *(Author's Collection)*	125
5.3	Weir Institute, Lugar *(Author's Collection)*	126
5.4	Gasswater *(Author's Collection)*	127
5.5	Commondyke *(Author's Collection)*	128
5.6	Boswell coat of arms from Burial Aisle *(Dane Love)*	131
5.7	Dumfries House Gardens Cottage *(Author's Collection)*	132
5.8	Parish Church *(Dane Love)*	134
5.9	Auchinleck Manse *(Author's Collection)*	135
5.10	Lugar Parish Church *(Dane Love)*	136
5.11	Darnconner Parish Church *(Author's Collection)*	137
5.12	Our Lady & St Patrick's Chapel, Birnieknowe *(Author's Collection)*	139
5.13	Rev Sister Laurienne's Cross *(Dane Love)*	141
5.14	Lugar Ironworks on O.S. Map of 1911 *(Author's Collection)*	148

5.15	High Dalbair lime kiln *(Dane Love)*	156
5.16	Clydesdale and North of Scotland Bank *(Author's Collection)*	159
5.17	Mauchline Road, with Toll Cottage to left *(Author's Collection)*	161
5.18	Rev Alexander Kennedy Hutchison Boyd *(Author's Collection)*	165
5.19	Auchinleck Notables' Monument *(Dane Love)*	167
6.1	Auchinleck around 1900 *(Dane Love)*	170
6.2	Highhouse Rows *(Author's Collection)*	173
6.3	William Murdoch's plaque, Bello Mill *(Dane Love)*	175
6.4	Invitation to unveiling of Murdoch plaque *(Author's Collection)*	176
6.5	Men filling in Churchhill Quarry *(Author's Collection)*	177
6.6	Lugar around 1900 *(Dane Love)*	179
6.7	Cronberry *(Author's Collection)*	180
6.8	Darnconner *(Author's Collection)*	183
6.9	Darnconner and Commondyke around 1900 *(Dane Love)*	184
6.10	Lugar Armistice Celebrations, 1918 *(Author's Collection)*	187
6.11	Auchinleck War Memorial *(Dane Love)*	189
6.12	Lugar War Memorial *(Dane Love)*	197
6.13	John Douglas Boswell of Garrallan and Auchinleck *(Author's Collection)*	202
6.14	Our Lady & St Patrick's Chapel, Birnieknowe (interior) *(Author's Collection)*	209
6.15	Public School – building erected in 1903 *(Dane Love)*	210
6.16	Public School – new building in School Road *(Dane Love)*	210
6.17	Darnconner School, 1906 *(Author's Collection)*	212
6.18	Darnconner School – class photograph *(Author's Collection)*	213
6.19	Highhouse Colliery *(Author's Collection)*	219
6.20	Mines Rescue Station in 1990 *(Dane Love)*	222
6.21	Auchinleck Co-Operative Society Parade, 1932 *(Author's Collection)*	227
6.22	Auchinleck Post Office *(Author's Collection)*	228
6.23	Townhead of Auchinleck farm *(Author's Collection)*	231
6.24	Auchinleck Curling Club, Eglinton Jug Winners, 1927 *(Neil Sands)*	238
6.25	Auchinleck Picture House *(Author's Collection)*	240
7.1	Parish Church and Boswell Mausoleum in 1990 *(Dane Love)*	256
7.2	Former Peden Church in 2015 *(Dane Love)*	258
7.3	St Patrick's Primary class, *c.* 1961 *(Moira Frize)*	265
7.4	Auchinleck Academy in 2015 *(Dane Love)*	267
7.5	Barony Colliery from the air *(Author's Collection)*	269
7.6	Gasswater Barytes Mine *(Author's Collection)*	273
7.7	Gasswater Barytes Treatment Works *(Author's Collection)*	274
7.8	Barony Power Station and Barony Colliery *(Dane Love)*	275
7.9	Barony Power Station *(Author's Collection)*	276
7.10	Selection of different bottles produced by Currie's of Auchinleck *(Dane Love)*	278
8.1	Millennium Clock *(Dane Love)*	291
8.2	Barony A Frame *(Dane Love)*	292
8.3	Barony Winding Wheels *(Dane Love)*	293
8.4	The Boswell Centre *(Dane Love)*	294
8.5	Knockroon *(Dane Love)*	295
8.6	The Queen Elizabeth Garden, Dumfries House Estate *(Dane Love)*	296
8.7	Interior of Parish Church *(Dane Love)*	298
8.8	Auchinleck Primary School *(Dane Love)*	300
8.9	Auchinleck Talbot Scottish Junior Champions, 2011 *(Hazel Love)*	304
8.10	Boswell coat of arms – David Rutherford Boswell *(Author's Collection)*	306

Introduction

Writing in the first edition of this book, published in 1991, I noted that it was almost a century since the last history of Auchinleck had been written. It is now a further 24 years since the first edition of my own book was published and, as it is now out of print, I felt that an up-dated and expanded edition was now due. The first edition of *The History of Auchinleck – Village and Parish* was a local success, and I am pleased to report that it was well received and highly regarded as being the standard history of the parish. Now, having written almost thirty books, I realise that the book was not as comprehensive as the current one, and I am hoping that the present work is as well received as the original.

Progress in digitising early rersources, census information, and other official records has meant that much more is readily available for researchers. The internet has opened up opportunities for wider and deeper investigations, and there is much more to be discovered than what can be included in this volume.

How has Auchinleck changed over the last quarter of a century? Some say nothing changes, it all stays the same. This is true to some extent, but progress is never-ending, and the final chapter has been added to give a flavour of what is happening in Auchinleck parish today. The village is fairly static in size, the population remaining much the same, if not declining. Industry and employment is not as great as it was when the mines were in full production, and today Auchinleck is more of a commuter community, residents having to travel to find employment.

But Auchinleck folk are keen on their community, supporting Talbot and defending their heritage, be it mining, Boswell or Covenanter.

Writing in the original Introduction, I noted that the book wasn't too bad an effort for a Cumnockian. Some may say that I have now seen the light, for since that book was published I have built my own home within the parish, and my two children are proud to call themselves Auchinleckites.

Dane Love
Auchinleck, 2015.

Acknowledgments

Many people assisted in various ways to make this book, as well as the first edition of it, possible. Those most deserving a mention, though some have since passed away, are:

Sheena Andrew, Robert Duncan; William Girvan; Eric Hodgson; Alexander Hunter; John Laurenson; John McCombe; Alexander Morrison; John Park; Neil Sands; John Stirling; James Tanner; James Templeton; John Withers. I must also acknowledge the assistance and support of my wife, Hazel, who has checked a number of facts for me, particularcly in genealogical areas, as well as commenting on the original manuscript.

CHAPTER ONE

EARLY TIMES (before 1504)

DESCRIPTION OF PARISH
The parish of Auchinleck lies in the central part of Ayrshire, called Kyle, and within that half of Kyle named Kyle-Stewart, from it having been under the jurisdiction of a steward, as opposed to the southern half, called King's Kyle, which came under the direct jurisdiction of the Crown. The parish extends to 24,273 acres, located on the north side of the Lugar and Guelt waters, surrounded by the parishes of Kirkconnel (Dumfriesshire), Old and New Cumnock to the south, Ochiltree to the south and west, Mauchline, Sorn and Muirkirk to the north, and to the east by Crawfordjohn, in the county of Lanark. The parish is rather elongated, being about sixteen miles in extent from Auchinleck Castle in the west to the Threeshire Stone in the east. From north to south the width varies from about one mile at Auchinleck to four miles between Tarrioch and Dalblair.

Much of the parish comprises moorland, a considerable portion of Airds (or Airs, from 'Ayr's') Moss being within it, as well as Boghead Moor and the Glenmuir grouse moors. This moorland portion is drained by the Guelt, Glenmuir, Gass and Bello waters which merge at Bello Mill to form the Lugar Water, which marks the southern boundary of the parish for seven miles westwards. The northern part of the west end of the parish is drained by the Dippol Burn, a tributary of the Lugar. At Tarrioch the River Ayr forms the boundary for two miles. The only other watercourse of note is the Auchinleck Burn, which rises on the moss at Templandshaw and meets the Lugar below Knockroon farm. On old maps it is called the Kirk Burn, but locally it is also known as the Miller's Burn.

The western half of the parish comprises reasonable agricultural land, more suited to dairying than crop-growing, although over the years various harvests have been taken from the fields. The *Statistical Account* (1792) notes that oats, bere (a type of barley), barley proper, clover and rye-grass were much cultivated, but that pease and turnips did not grow well. Only on ground owned by the Earl of Dumfries (Waterside) was wheat grown. As one travels further east the soil becomes thinner, the grassland rougher, and the ground higher, before merging into the rough countryside of Airds Moss, Gass, and Glenmuir. Here sheep graze (around

8,500 in 1792) and the heather moors are tended for sporting purposes. There are just two significant hills in the parish, both of which are found on the border (Wardlaw Hill – 1,631 feet; and Stony Hill – 1,843 feet), as well as a number of lesser heights, including Auchtitench Hill, Foredibban Hill, Benalt, and Threeshire Hill, on which summit stands a boulder at the junction of three counties - Ayr, Lanark and Dumfries.

Below the soil the rocks have been good to the parish, for were it not for the seams of coal and ironstone the district would today be far less populous and be more of a rural community. Other rocks and minerals have been worked over the centuries - at Wallaceton there was a quarry for a black fire-proof stone, in demand for building ovens. Limestone has been quarried throughout much of the parish, fireclay at Gasswater, barium sulphate or barytes in the upper Gass valley, freestone for building at Auchinleck and elsewhere, and lead was noted at Bell's Park, but which was never worked.

The name Auchinleck has been variously spelled over the years but most authorities agree that it derives from the Gaelic *Achadh na Leac*, which means 'field of the flagstone'. The place to which this description applies is the area around the old castle, at the west end of the parish, where the sandstone rock protrudes through the earth. Spellings over the years include Achinlek, Achenlek, Auchinlacke, Auchinlek and Achirsek, the latter probably an error, for on the same map (in Blaeu's *Atlas Novus*) Achinlek is also listed.

The name 'Affleck' is also associated with the parish, being a version of the name. This appeared on some older documents, communion tokens, and in the name Mill Affleck. The name Auchinleck became the more recognised way in which to describe the place, but the Boswell family often referred to the area as Affleck, in the 1820s, Sir Alexander and his family preferring to call the parish that way.

STONE AND BRONZE AGES

The Ayrshire Victorian antiquary, John Smith, who lived in Lugar for a time, noted in *Prehistoric Man in Ayrshire* that 'there are but few remnants of antiquity' in the parish. He wrote this in 1895, and few examples of prehistoric remains have been discovered since then.

Following the retreat of the last Ice Age, which occurred around 8000 BC, the first men and women arrived in Ayrshire, either overland from England, or else by small coracle-type boats from Ireland. This was in the early Stone Age, or Mesolithic period, but they do not seem to have settled in what is now Auchinleck parish. However, the Mesolithic people, who were hunters and food-gatherers, no doubt passed through the area, for finds from that period have been obtained on locations surrounding the district - in Glengavel, Loch Doon, and along the Ayrshire coast.

By Neolithic times (the New Stone Age, c. 3000-2000 BC) some hunters seem to have settled in this parish, for remains of their pottery were found on Airds Moss near Cameron's Stone. These were discovered at the beginning of the twentieth century and were presented to the National Museum of Antiquities in Edinburgh in 1945 by the finder, Archibald Fairbairn.

A stone axe hammer-head was discovered when work was taking place at Pennylands in 1970. The hammer head was unfinished, but was in the process of being made from a granitic stone, identified as Essexite. It was presented to Glasgow Kelvingrove Museum.

The men of the Bronze Age left a number of monuments and other fragments which have been discovered over the years. A number of burial cairns can still be made out on the ground, most notably in the eastern half of the parish, where the moors have been less disturbed by the hand of man over the intervening centuries.

The most significant Bronze Age remnant to be seen today is the burial cairn on the summit of Wardlaw Hill, located on the parish border with Muirkirk. On the highest point of the hill is a circular ring of stones, 30 feet in diameter, infilled with numerous smaller stones. This is all that survives of a round cairn which was plundered of stone in 1917 in order to build the memorial cairn to Colonel John George Alexander Baird of Wellwood (1854-1917), which stands a few yards to the east.

Wardlaw cairn was excavated in the 1920s by Archibald Fairbairn. He discovered that the centre of the cairn had been used as a beacon site, perhaps for centuries. No remains were discovered, but under a marginal boulder, outwith the fire-marked area, was found a massive late Celtic finger-ring of bronze, varying from 1.19 inches to 1.94 inches in diameter. This ring is now preserved in the National Museum of Scotland. Other possible burial cairn remains exist further east on the summit plateau.

1.1 Bronze Age finger ring, found in Wardlaw cairn
(Author's Collection)

A further bronze-age burial cairn in the parish exists on Airds Moss, 430 yards east of Cameron's Stone. This cairn measures 25 feet in diameter and seems to be part of a group of such cairns in the Wellwood area. During the period 1913-27, J. G. A. Baird of Wellwood (until his death) and Archibald Fairbairn carried out a number of excavations of the antiquities around Muirkirk, this cairn being one of those investigated. The central area was explored to a depth of three feet at which point much oak charcoal in small fragments was found, mixed with a dark soil. Although no evidence of sepulchral rites was found, an unmarked flake of flint was discovered. To the east of this cairn, on a low knoll of drier ground, three boulders were observed projecting through the grass. Thinking it may have been a stone circle of sorts, it was stripped of turf to reveal the floor of a circular hut, measuring fourteen feet in diameter. The hearth was discovered slightly south of the centre, with the remnants of the red burnt embers still in it. Two kinds of pottery were found on the site, one a fairly thick buff-coloured and wheel-turned kind, with a thin fringe of green glaze, the other a thin and unglazed pottery of light-red colour. Also discovered were some fragments of chert (a flint-like stone), some unworked flakes of flint and a small piece of 'keel' (a primitive drawing substance) showing several facets of wear.

On the farm of Whiteholm of Dornal a cist was discovered sometime in the nineteenth century by the farmer who was constructing a new road down to a lower field. It comprised a coffin constructed of stone slabs, covered over by another slab. The farmer found it to be empty. Located in the slope of a river terrace, the cist was without its usual covering mound of earth or stones. The slabs were later used on the farm as flagstones.

Other possible sites of burials existed on the farm of Wallaceton where a small 'urn' was found, measuring 4½ inches by 3¾ inches. This was probably a food vessel.

At the Chapel Knowe in Lugar, whilst excavations were taking place for the Iron Works (around 1845) the workmen unearthed a small, rude urn which contained bones, indicating that the Chapel Knowe had probably been a burial

1.2 Rocking Stone at Lugar *(Dane Love)*

cairn. Also from Lugar a battle-axe was found, of the Wilsford type, dating from around 1000 BC, now located in the National Museum of Scotland in Edinburgh. Slightly older (c. 1600 BC) is a midrib dagger found on Airds Moss, near to Cameron's Stone, by the Scottish antiquary, A. Henderson Bishop. It was presented to the Hunterian Museum of Glasgow University in 1914.

Two stone axe-hammers were found in a gravel bank of the Lugar water, just below the mouth of the Cottertax Burn. These are believed to date from the early Bronze Age period and one of them is preserved in the Glasgow Museum and Art Gallery, the other in the National Museum of Scotland in Edinburgh.

From a similar period is the Rocking Stone at Bello Path, east of Lugar. Here a large boulder of some tons in weight was set on top of two other rocks, lesser stones marking an arc around it. The uppermost boulder is about six feet long, five feet tall, and three feet wide. The arc comprises six stones of around two feet square.

What purpose these stones formed is not known, but the Rocking Stone no doubt was a significant location to the Bronze Age people. Its most probable function was as a chambered cairn, its upper mound of stones robbed over the centuries for building material. The stone lost its ability to rock sometime around 1800 when its equilibrium was destroyed.

There are two prominent stones located on the moors of the eastern half of the parish which may have at one time formed part of an ancient stone circle or burial cairn. Significantly, both stand on eminences known as Cairn Hill, hinting that the latter theory may be more likely. The first is located by the fence crossing the low knowe of Cairn Hill, near Stonebriggs, from which Cairnhill pit got its name. It has a modern, though crude, inscription on it commemorating a rabbit killed in an air raid.

The second is located by the dike along the western ridge of Wardlaw Hill, known as Cairn Hill, on the border with Muirkirk parish. This stone, situated 1,300 feet above sea-level, is known as the Greymare Stone, and is associated in legend as marking the site of the massacre of the Plain of Gass in AD 655.

On Connor Hill, above the March Burn, at the east end of the parish, are the remnants of a prehistoric enclosure. Little on the ground can be seen, but from overhead the remains describe an almost perfect circle on the ground, around 75 feet in diameter. The site has not been excavated, but it has been speculated that this may have been a henge or some form of ritual site. The enclosure contains an inner bank, berm and palisade trench. There are indications of an entrance through the ditch on the western side.

Near to Glenmuirshaw, the diminutive Thorter Burn flows into the Polwhannan Burn. By the side of the Thorter Burn archaeologists have discovered the remains of a Mesolithic chipping floor. The microliths were used as blades, and there are many fragments of flaking waste in the vicinity. The stone used was agate which can be found in the stream hereabouts.

ROMAN TIMES

Sometime around the year 150 AD the Romans pushed northwards over Hadrian's Wall and established a new frontier across the waist of Scotland. Built by Lollius Urbicus it was named the Antonine Wall in honour of the reigning caesar, Antoninus Pious. A number of roads and forts were built between the walls, in the district notably the roadway up Nithsdale to Durisdeer and thence by the Well Path to Clydesdale, and the roadway west from Clydesdale passing Strathaven to a fort below Loudoun Hill. A linking roadway is believed to have gone by way of the old Sanquhar to Muirkirk road and Strathaven Moor. West of this Roman remains are far less obvious on the ground, and it is not known if they got round to building roads or forts in the rest of Ayrshire. No doubt parties of soldiers did make some reconnaissance trips and one of these may have dropped a coin as it made its way through what became Auchinleck. In November 1953 someone digging in the garden of a house in Main Street found an old worn coin about one foot below ground level. It was cleaned up and on inspection was found to be a bronze coin minted at Antioch during the reign of Constans Caesar (c. 50 AD). It was presented to the National Museum of Antiquities in Edinburgh.

DORNAL MOAT

One of the most intriguing antiquities in the parish is the mound and moat on Dornal farm, in the Glenmuir. Some authorities dismiss it as purely natural, the mound a glacial moraine, the moat a dried up water course, but its layout is such that it was probably man-made, or at least an adaption of natural features. If this was so, then it was most probably a moated homestead. In 1893, D. Christison made a short reference to it in a paper within the *Proceedings of the Society of Antiquaries of Scotland*. He wrote that it had 'a unique plan, unintelligible without explanation.'

Writing in 1895, John Smith described the mound:

> At Dornal there is a natural eminence called The Moat, and the people of the district have a tradition to the effect that it was at one time occupied as a fort. I examined it carefully, and found that its sides are very steep, and look as if they had been scraped. It lies in a low meadow beside the Glenmore Water, and the farmer told me that it was at one time surrounded by water, and when so, it must have formed a pretty safe retreat. I think there can be no doubt but that it was a *natural* island, carved out of the boulder clay by the action of the river. It occurs as a ridge parallel with the valley, and measures along its summit 52 paces in length, by 5 to 6 paces in breadth, the height above the meadow being 15 feet 6 inches.

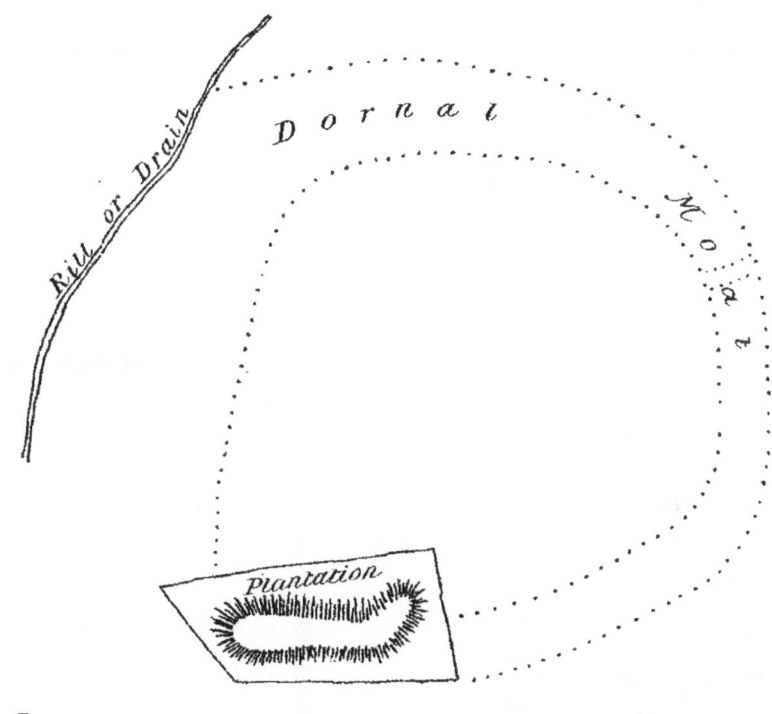

1.3 Plan of Dornal Moat, drawn in 1893 *(Author's Collection)*

The mound measures about 160 feet along its summit, by about 23 feet wide and rises fifteen feet six inches above the surrounding field. It has steep sides but does not have the usual characteristics of a Norman motte-hill. To the north of the mound, forming a large circular shape about 450 feet in diameter, are the remains of a moat, 60 feet wide and up to a maximum depth of four feet, best preserved on the eastern half. In winter months this is often filled with water, but at other times of the year is quite dry. No remains of building foundations or earthworks have been discovered in the moated area, though it has been repeatedly ploughed over the centuries. The site, if it was a moated homestead, probably had timber dwellings in it, and would date to sometime in the first or second centuries AD. Dwellings of this period were generally circular in plan, about 25 feet in diameter. There would have been a tall central pole of timber, surrounded by a ring of lower supports, holding aloft a conical roof of thatch.

The average house in these times was much smaller and less refined, of course. Homes were simple buildings with rubble or turf walls, roofed over in thatch. A mediaeval turf house of this type was discovered on the moor near to Cronberry prior to excavation for coal. The building was totally excavated by Headland Archaeology in the last years of the twentieth century. They discovered a turf building and enclosure. The building was a sub-rectangular structure, the walls constructed of turf and soil. Within was found a stone hearth, and some of the floor had remnants of stone paving. Some charcoal and burnt objects discovered within the excavated area led the archaeologists to think that the building was very old, and had been rebuilt over the years. The most modern dating evidence found was some pottery which belonged to no later than the sixteenth century. The enclosure, which was no doubt for cattle or sheep, was also constructed of turf walls.

LANDOWNERS - AUCHINLECK CASTLE

The ancient castle of Auchinleck stood on a rocky eminence in the angle between the Lugar Water and the Dippol Burn. According to Rev John Dun, who wrote the contribution on Auchinleck for the *Statistical Account*, of its age 'there is not the smallest account to be found.' Only fragmentary remains of it survive; the zigzag pathway to the main entrance distinguishable on the ground.

1.4 Auchinleck Castle, as drawn by Francis Grose, 1791 *(Author's Collection)*

One corner of dressed masonry survives, perched precariously one hundred feet above the level of the Dippol Burn. This was the north-east corner of the building. From the plan we find that the building must have been a rather elongated structure, around 115 feet long internally, twenty feet wide at the eastern end, the west only fourteen feet wide. From the western end a winding path descends to an otherwise inaccessible point of rock between the Lugar and Dippol, probably indicating a small gateway here, giving access for water. Centrally placed on the south front was the main gateway, probably protected on the left by a tower of around fourteen feet square internally. This is reached by an ascending slope just wide enough for one man or a horse. Due south of the castle is an old well, reached by descending 37 steps. Some of the internal walls of the castle must have been formed by natural rock faces.

According to Paterson, writing in 1852, a few arches were then discernible. Some accounts place the date of erection of the castle to sometime in the fourteenth century, which is not unlikely, a wooden structure probably having existed before then. According to Dr Johnson, though on what authority he based his observations is not known, the castle was at one time surrounded by a moat, and a drawbridge crossed from the castle to a nearby rock. A view of the ruins was drawn in 1791 and published in Francis Grose's *Antiquities of Scotland*. Even at that time only a fragment of ruined wall, containing an arched window, and a tall tower of masonry, perhaps a chimney, existed.

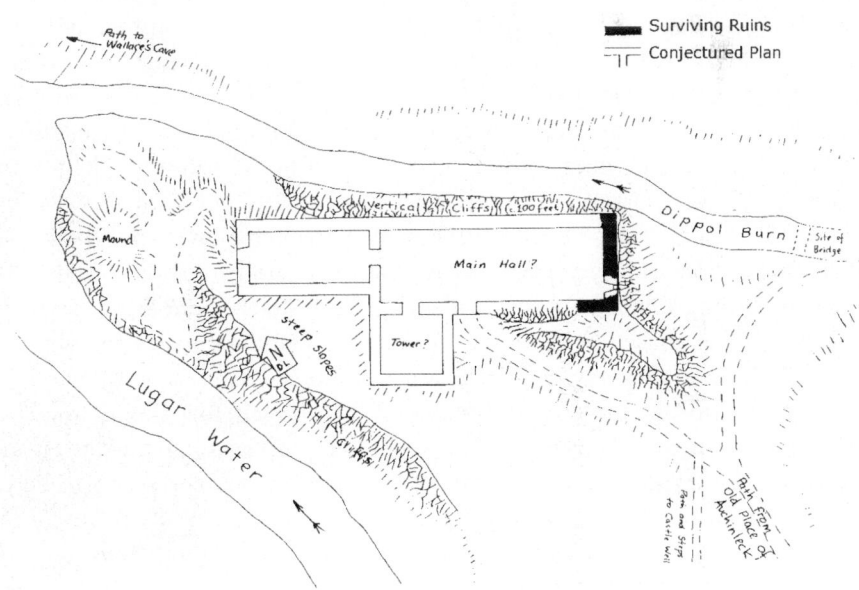

1.5 Auchinleck Castle (plan) *(Dane Love)*

Associated with this castle was an old postern gateway, one half of which survives, having been hewn from the natural rock. It is located between the old and new castles. Through it one could descend to the Dippol Burn, and on to Wallace's Cave, a man-made cavern in the sandstone cliff adjacent to the Lugar Water. Carved from the solid rock, internally the cave measures fourteen feet wide, by twelve feet deep. In the four corners are stone ribs, again carved from the parent rock, rising up to form diagonals across the ceiling, forming either a saltire or cross. At its maximum, the ceiling is ten feet tall. Complete with gothic-arched window and door, the latter three feet wide and seven feet to the apex, this cave is believed to have been constructed as early as the thirteenth century. There is no known connection with it and the great Scots patriot of the time. The cave is actually beyond the parish boundary, being within Mauchline parish.

AUCHINLECK OF THAT ILK
As with many places in Scotland, the original owners and occupiers of the lands adopted the district name as their surname, when surnames came into fashion. Thus the owners of Auchinleck took that name as their second name, though it was spelled in numerous ways over the years. Similarly, in the county of Angus, another family took the surname Auchinleck also, from lands there known variously as Auchinleck or Affleck. For their coat of arms, the Auchinlecks of that Ilk (in Ayrshire) were granted Argent, three bars sable, which still appears in the arms of the Boswell successors.

The earliest Auchinleck recorded in history was one Nicol de Achethlec who is named in the Ragman Roll, which is a list of those who submitted and swore fealty to King Edward of England between 1292 and 1297. Two thousand Scots lairds signed this oath of allegiance to the king, but many were forced into it and did so under threat. Nichol Auchinleck was one of these, for he is noted in history as a zealous patriot who did much for the cause of freedom. According to the fifteenth century poet, 'Blind' Harry the Minstrel, author of *The Acts and Deeds of Sir William Wallace*, Auchinleck was a blood-relation of Wallace, being his uncle. The English soldiers at one time held a garrison in Glasgow's castle, under Bishop Anthony Beik of Durham. Riding at first from Ayr, William Wallace attacked the castle around the year 1300 but was chased by the English soldiers down the town's High Street. At the Bell o' the Brae they stopped flight and were joined by a second force of 140 men led by Nichol Auchinleck, advancing up the Drygait, and thus attacked the English from their rear. At the arrival of Auchinleck's division, during the ensuing confusion of the English forces, William Wallace ran forward and split Earl Percy's head in two by a single stroke of his broad sword. The English forces were forced to retreat, fleeing to Bothwell, where they joined another English army which checked the further advances of Wallace's men.

Blind Harry's version runs:

> The Bishop Beik and Piercie that were wight,
> A thousand led of men in armour bright,
> Wallace saw well what number sembled there,
> He made his men in two parts for to fare,
> Graithed them well without the town's end,
> He called Auchinleck for he the passage kend,
> Uncle, he said, be busy into wear,
> Whether will ye the Bishop's tail upbear,
> Or pass before, and take his beneson.
>
> ---
>
> Auchinleck said, 'We shall do all we may,
> We would like ill to bide ought lang away;
> A boutteous ttail betwixt us soon must be,
> But to the right Almighty God have eye.'
> Adam Wallace and Auchinleck were bown,
> Sevenscore with them on the back-side of the town;
> Right fast they yeed, while they were out of sight,
> The other part arrayed them full right.
>
> ---
>
> Adam Wallace and Auchinleck came in,
> And parted Southeron right suddenly in twin,
> Return'd to them as noble men in wear,
> The Scots got room, and may down they bear.

JOHN AUCHINLECK OF THAT ILK

After Nichol Auchinleck, the next member of the family recorded in history is John Auchinleck of that Ilk. He is mentioned in the Chartularies of Paisley Abbey, dated 10 May 1385. Written in Latin, the document styles him 'Johannes de Auchinleck, dominus ejusdem, miles', meaning 'John Auchinleck, Lord of that Ilk, soldier'. It goes on to record: 'pro contemptu et violatione iis factis cuidam monacho ipsius monasterii, vasa sua seminaria amputando, per me et complices meos, viginti solidos Sterlingorum, de terris et proventibus firmarum terrarium mearum, ad duos anni terminos.'

According to tradition, as noted by Alexander Nisbet in *A System of Heraldry*, John Auchinleck found the monk lying with his daughter, and so felt he had to take revenge in some way. On catching the monk he emasculated him. The mortification of the Convent of Paisley was confirmed in 1392, by 'Johannes Auchinleck, dominus ejusdem' probably the perpetrator's son, as he is not designated 'miles', though this is unconfirmed. It may be that the first John died around 1392, hence the new Charter of Confirmation. A further confirmatory charter was written up on 10 February 1404. The fine of twenty pounds Sterling had to be paid twice yearly, at Whitsunday and Martinmas, and John Auchinleck had to give security that the rental would continue to be paid in all time coming by his heirs and successors.

JAMES AUCHINLECK OF THAT ILK (I) AND THE FEUD

John Auchinleck was succeeded by his son, James Auchinleck of that Ilk, sometime in the first half of the fifteenth century. James married the daughter and co-heiress of Alexander Melville of Glenbervie, and thus acquired that barony, which is located seven miles west of Stonehaven, in the county of Kincardine. His wife predeceased him and he married Christian Douglas, widow of David Wemyss of that Ilk, sometime after 1430. James Auchinleck received a charter under the Great Seal of James II on 26 March 1446 which records some of his properties:

> Apud Strivelin. Rex confirmavit Jacobo de Achinlek de eodem militi, et herebus ejus, - terras de Achenlek, Rogerstoun, Kethstoun, Crakistoune, le Bannachtinis Yardis, et de la Tempilland, in le Kyle-Stewart, vic. Ayr:- quas idem Jac. resignavit;- et quas rex in unam liberam baroniam de Achinlek creavit et incorporavit.

During the life of James, the Auchinleck family became friendly with their near neighbours, the Colvils of Ochiltree Castle. Auchinleck Castle and Ochiltree Castle stood on cliff-tops on either side of the Lugar Water, the latter a little bit further downstream. To save the two families the trouble of crossing the ravine and often deep waters of the Lugar, they had a rope joining the two buildings, along which messages could be sent by means of a basket. Something caused a misunderstanding between James and Robert Colvil of Ochiltree, so Auchinleck sent over the bare bones of a sheep's skull in the basket, well wrapped up. Colvil, thinking that the gift was an act of repentance by Auchinleck, had the basket brought to his main hall and opened before him. When he saw the disgusting remains of the sheep his temper grew and he vowed to get his own back. He managed to force an entrance into Auchinleck Castle and kill the laird. The rest of the family escaped and enlisted the help of the Douglas clan who attacked the castle of Ochiltree and set it alight. This fact was confirmed by the finding of pieces of charred oak where the castle stood, believed to have come from the roof timbers. Colvil escaped from the building and tradition states that he and his sons were slain by Douglas at Polshill Burn, in the parish of New Cumnock, within a few days of Auchinleck's murder. The year of this feud was 1449.

SIR JOHN AUCHINLECK OF THAT ILK (I)
Following the murder of James Auchinleck, his son John succeeded as Auchinleck of that Ilk. Little is known about him, but he is listed as sitting in the Scots parliament of 1469, during the minority of King James. It was probably for his work in the parliament that he was knighted, for he is listed as Sir John Auchinleck in later documents. Sir John had at least two sons, James, who succeeded, and one whose name is not known, founder of the family of Auchinleck of Balmanno Castle, near Dron, in Perthshire.

JAMES AUCHINLECK OF THAT ILK (II)
James succeeded Sir John to the lands of Auchinleck. He had married Egidia, daughter of John, Lord Ross of Hawkhead, near Paisley, by whom he had just one child, a girl, heiress of line of her grandfather. Prior to the wedding of James and Egidia, she resigned all rights to the lands of Auchinleck in a paper dated 1481. This makes interesting reading, for it details a number of tenant farmers living on the estate at that time:

> Be it kend, etc. . . . me Gelis [Egidia] the Ros, douchter of Schir Johnne the Ros of Halkhed, Knicht, to be bunden and oblist . . . til Schyr Johnne Auchinlek of that Ilk, Knycht, and to his airis, that I sall resigne and be thir present lettres resignes and overgefis thair landis quhilk I am in undirwritten, that is to say;- 6 merkis worth of the lands of Nethircrokstoun, 4 merkis worth of land of the Pennyland that Andro Ralestoun and his two sonnis duellis in; 2 merkis worth of the samyn land that Gib. Clerk duellis in; 2 merkis worth of the same land that Adam Auchinlek duellis in; and 4 merkis worth of land of the thrid part lyand next the halfpennyland that Finlaw Johnestoun, Rob. of Libertoun and Mathe Walkar duellis in, within the schyrefdome of Air and Barony of Auchinlek, - that quat time and how sone the mariage beis made lauchfull betuix James Auchinlek, sone and apparend are to the said Schyr Johne, and me the said Gelis, than I resigne all the forenemit landis;- and gife it happenis me to part with the said James or the dispensatione cum hame in my default, than likewise I resigne. . . the said landis . . . or gife it sall happin me, eftir the dispensation cum hame to part with the said James and will nocht marry him agane efter the tenour of the said dispensatioun, than I resignis the said landis. . . . In witnes, etc. . . . I have set to my sele at Halkhead, 3 Mar 1480.

SIR JOHN AUCHINLECK OF THAT ILK (II)

The family tree of the Auchinleck family becomes confused following the death of James Auchinleck. Whilst he still lived, Eugenius Achlek was one of the Privy Council in 1475. He is believed to be the son of the Auchinleck who founded the Balmanno branch, and nephew of the above James. Eugenius succeeded to the Barony of Auchinleck on the death of James, and he is known to have sat in the Scots parliaments of 1478 and 1487.

Eugenius seems to have been succeeded by Sir John Auchinleck of that Ilk. In 1499 the Barony of Auchinleck passed from Sir John to his eldest daughter, Marion Auchinleck, who had married William Cunningham of Craigends (near Houston, Renfrewshire). The following six years are most confusing for historians, and just what happened up to the arrival of the Boswells in 1504 is not fully known. Many accounts of the change of ownership state that Sir John Auchinleck disponed the estate to his eldest daughter without the consent of his superior, namely King James IV. Thus the barony 'recognosced', or was returned to its superior, who granted it to another, in this case Thomas Boswell, a younger son of the Boswells of Balmuto. This theory is subscribed to by Paterson in his *History of the County of Ayr* and by Nisbet in *A System of Heraldry*.

However, the person supposedly chosen by the king was no stranger to the lands and family of Auchinleck, for he was married to Annabel Campbell, daughter of Sir Malcolm Campbell of Loudoun, the second husband of Marion Auchinleck. It was also the case that the king had previously issued a charter to Marion Auchinleck and William Cunningham in 1501. This implies that Sir John Auchinleck could not have transferred the ownership of Auchinleck to Marion without the king being aware of the situation. The king's charter follows one of 23 May 1499:

> Johannes Auchinleck, baro baronie de Auchinleck, vendidit, &c, Willelmo Cunnynghame de Craganis et Mariote Auchinlek sponse ejus, filie dicti Joh. et heredibus eorun masculis legitime procreandis utentibus cognomine Auchinlek,- baronian de Auchinlek et terras ejusdem, viz. terras de Crakistoun, Ovir et Nethir Kethistoun et Rogertoun, umacum castro, fortalicio, tenandis, tenandriis et servitiis liberetenentium ejusdem, vic. Are;- pro certa summa pecunie sibi in sua urgente necessitae per prefat. Wil. et Mar. soluta:- Tenend. dictam baroniam, &c. a dict. Joh. de supremo domino rege tanquam Senescallo Scotie, dictis Wil. et Mar. et eorum alteri diutius viventiet eorum heredibus prenotatis:- Reddend. unum derarium argenti nomine albe firme:- Test. Jac. Douglas, Joh. Cunynghame, Joh. Glen, Tho. Smyth.

Sir John Auchinleck's second daughter, Dame Elizabeth Auchinleck was given the Barony of Glenbervie. She married Sir William Douglas, son of the Earl of Angus, taking Glenbervie to that family.

KYLE CASTLE

Sometime at the beginning of the fifteenth century a castle was erected at the junction of the Glenmuir and Guelt waters. Known as Kyle Castle, its history is at best fragmentary, but it is associated in legend with King Coilus, the 'Old King Cole' of the nursery rhyme. Having the same name as the province of Kyle (central Ayrshire), one would assume that the castle had a prominent place in local history, but no reference to connect it with the greater lands survives.

Like its history, the remains are scanty, the most obvious fragment being the surviving section of wall. This rises eighteen feet in height, and is six feet six inches thick. This formed the north side of a keep which measured around 40 feet by 26 feet externally. Internally, the tower had a great hall that measured around 26 feet by 15 feet. The wall is built of coursed ashlar masonry, typical of the fifteenth century, and is 6 feet 6 inches in thickness. On either end of the surviving masonry are remnants of the splayed windows that once lit the hall, the interior sills being three feet above the old floor line. This must have been a timber floor, there being no sign of vaulting, and square holes in the masonry hint that beams were once bedded there. It is no longer possible to determine where other windows and doors were located, or where the stairway was positioned.

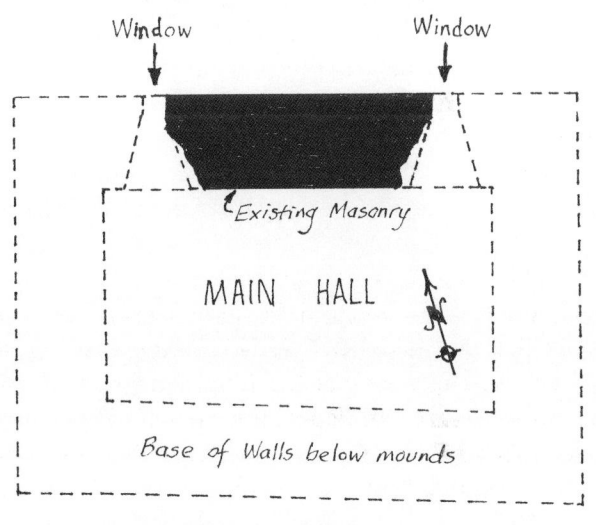

1.6 Kyle Castle (plan) *(Dane Love)*

The remains are situated on a flat-topped spur of land, and there was probably a courtyard to the north and west of the keep, there being low mounds indicating the line of former walling. At the west end of the promontory is a narrow 'covered way' which meanders up the hillside to the curtain wall. This, however, may have

1.7 Kyle Castle *(Dane Love)*

been a later construction. North-east of the tower, on a level section of ground halfway down to the river, is what has been claimed to have been the castle garden, reached by a ramp from the top of the hill.

In 1445 the commendator of Melrose Abbey issued a charter of the lands of Castle 'Cavil' to John Farquhar of Gilmilnscroft, near Sorn. On Pont's map of Kyle, dated 1654, the building is named 'Castel Keyil.'

EARLY CHURCH HISTORY
Probably the first building to be constructed in what is now the village of Auchinleck was a *cille*, or cell, a place of study where early Celtic Christians could study the Scriptures. These *cilles* were built throughout Scotland by the missionaries of the time, and were usually dedicated to some saint. Few of them survive, but a number are known to have existed because of their incorporation in place-names, such as Kilmarnock (Cille of St. Marnock), Kilmaurs (Cille of St. Maurs) or Kilwinning (Cille of St. Winning). Cilles were stone structures, usually with a vaulted roof, and were often partly subterranean. To which saint the *cille* at Auchinleck was dedicated has long since been forgotten. However it has been surmised that the place of worship was used by the Holy Duncans of the Moor, one of whom, Crinan, became Abbot of Dunkeld and was grandfather of David I, King of Scotland (reigned 1034-1040). The Holy Duncans are commemorated to this day in the farm name, Duncanziemere, pronounced 'duncan-yoo-mer', where 'yoo' is the Gaelic, *naomh* or 'holy'.

In 1147 Walter Fitzalan became the High Steward of Scotland, which honour he held until his death in 1177, being succeeded by his son, Alan, followed by his grandson Walter. Further descendants continued until Robert, 7th High Steward, succeeded to the Scottish throne as King Robert II, being son of Marjorie Bruce, daughter of King Robert the Bruce. The Stewards (or Stewarts as they became) were originally from Brittany in France, Walter arriving in Scotland in 1141 under David 1. In 1163 Walter, 1st Steward of Scotland, established the Cluniacensian priory of the Gilbertine order at Paisley, to replace a smaller monastery which had existed from around 1140. He is also believed to have enlarged the *cille* at Auchinleck around the same time (between 1145 and 1165) creating a small church, this being located on lands which belonged to him. During the late twelfth and early thirteenth centuries it was common for the lairds to gift the church lands to various abbeys in order to support the monks who in turn supplied readers to take the parish services. Thus Walter Fitzalan, grandson of Walter, 1st Steward, gifted the church of Auchinleck with all its pertinents, to the monks of Paisley Abbey, in pure alms, in 1238. The monks collected the tithes (tenth-part of the landowners' incomes and tenants' produce) and other revenues for over three hundred years thereafter and provided a chaplain to serve the parishioners. Confirmation was made in 1239 to the service of the Abbey by William, Bishop of Glasgow, with provision made for a vicarage perpetual, the parsonage thereafter remaining so annexed. Walter, 3rd Steward, went on to found Crossraguel Abbey as an independent Cluniac house in 1244 (it had been granted to Paisley around 1214), with its own group of churches, but Auchinleck remained under the control of Paisley. In 1265 Pope Clement IV issued a Papal Bull which listed the extent of the Patronage of the Abbot of Paisley, and included within it was mention of the parish of Auchinleck.

1.8 Templar's Gravestone *(Dane Love)*

The church of Auchinleck was not the only place of worship in the parish at this early date. Near the castle of Auchinleck stood another kirk, dedicated to St Vincent. This was located due south of the castle, above the Lugar Water, near to a small stream which passed Greenfoot. According to James Boswell, St Vincent's Chapel was the original burial site of the Boswell family and their Auchinleck ancestors. Traditionally the stones from the church were used when the new castle was built in the early seventeenth century.

An old grave slab was formerly located in a burial ground surrounding this chapel, latterly moved beside the castle, but which is now built into the internal gable of the Boswell Museum. This slab is devoid of any inscription, but has a sword and Maltese cross inscribed upon it, indicative of a thirteenth to fourteenth century date. The slab measures around four feet six inches long, two feet wide and around six inches thick. In style, the grave slab has been associated with the Crusaders, who journeyed to the Holy Land from 1118 to 1291 to take part in the Holy Wars there. The gravestone most probably commemorated one of the John Auchinlecks, though there is no reference to either of them taking part in the military expeditions.

CHAPTER TWO

SIXTEENTH CENTURY (1504-1600)

VILLAGE LIFE

Life in Auchinleck for those who did not hold their own land, or serve the church, was difficult and hard. There was no village as such, other than a few cottages near to the kirk, and residents of the parish would spend most of their time making a living from the land. Little survives to indicate how the parishioners lived, but excavations of a dwelling on the edge of the moor near to Gasswater, prior to open cast workings, unearthed a sixteenth century hut and possible enclosure. This would have been fairly typical of all of the dwellings across the parish – simply built using local timber, clay and thatch. Around it were a few lazybeds where basic vegetables were grown, and a few cattle and sheep were reared on the few acres that were allocated to the resident.

A few traditional tales from the sixteenth century survive. In 1568, after Mary Queen of Scots' defeat at the Battle of Langside, near Glasgow, she is supposed to have passed near to Lugar on her flight south. At Braehead farm her horse is supposed to have stumbled whilst crossing a ditch. It is not known if the queen fell from her mount, but she is supposed to have lost a shoe in the incident. The spot where the horse stumbled has been known as the 'Queen's Sheuch' ever since. The queen is also said to have either spent the night, or at least rested, at Kyle Castle on the same journey.

LANDOWNERS – THOMAS BOSWELL OF AUCHINLECK (I)

In 1504 the family of Boswell became associated through ownership with the parish of Auchinleck for the first time. The Boswells, or Bosvilles, were of Norman extraction, possibly taking their name from Beuzeville-la-Gifford, a small town in northern France. The first of them, Sieur de Bosville, arrived in Britain with William the Conqueror, under whom he had a considerable command at the Battle of Hastings in 1066. His descendants settled at first in England, then at Oxmuir in Berwickshire.

A further descendant, Roger de Bosvil, established the Boswells in Fife around 1320. His great-grandson, Sir John Boswell established the Boswells of Balmuto in that county. Sir John's grandson, David Boswell, was married twice, and by his second wife, Lady Margaret Sinclair, daughter of the 1st Earl of Caithness, had a son Thomas Boswell, born around 1487. This Thomas married Annabel, daughter of Sir Hugh Campbell of Loudoun. Thomas Boswell was a friend of King James IV and it is known that James IV bought Boswell 'daunsing gere' or dancing clothes, the monarch being noted in history for socialising with 'familiars'. The king granted Thomas a charter of the lands of Auchinleck, which he had acquired through marriage. This charter, issued from Edinburgh on 20th November 1504, reads:

> Rex, pro servitio sibi impenso, concessit familiari suo Thome Boswell, - terras et baroniam de Auchinlek, cum castro, fortalicio et molendino, tenentibus, &c. advocationibus et donationibus ecclesiarum et capellaniarum, vic. Aire.

On 16 June 1505 James IV visited Ayr, from where he issued a second charter to Thomas Boswell. This charter granted him further lands, namely Craigston, Over and Nether Keithstoun, and Rogerton, with the castle, fortalice, mill and buildings thereof. Whether or not the king visited Auchinleck whilst he was in the county is not recorded.

Three years after James IV granted Thomas Boswell the lands of Auchinleck he gifted him a further charter, dated 27 May 1507, founding the Burgh of Auchinleck, or the Free Burgh in Barony of Keithstoun, as it was named in the charter. This allowed Thomas to establish a market at the small clachan round the church, but there is considerable doubt as to whether the charter was put into practice, for no references to Auchinleck as a market centre exist from that time. It may have been the case, however, that a market was established in 1507, only to die out within a few years after the formation of the Burgh of Cumnock in 1509, where the fair was successful, perhaps due to when it was held (St. Matthew's Day), or else due to its location at a road junction. Another theory is that Auchinleck was created as a Burgh in Barony just as a mark of social prestige for Thomas Boswell, he being in a position to persuade the king to confer this honour. Most burgh charters state that the burgess can erect a market cross within the town, but there is no reference in history to there having been one in Auchinleck. Thus Auchinleck seems to have been an example of a 'parchment burgh', or a burgh which existed on paper only.

The precept of the charter for erection as a Burgh of Barony is as follows:

> Apud Edinburgh, 27 Maii [1507].
> Preceptum carte Thome Boswell de Auchinlek, - creando villam et terras de Keithstoun, cum pertinen., jacen. in baronia sua de Auchinlek, et infra vic. de Aire, liberum burgum in baronia pro perpetuo: Concedendo etiam inhabitantibus dictum burgum et

imposterum inhabituris, potestatem emendi et vendendi in ipso burgo vina, ceram, pannum laneum et lineum, latum et artum, aliaque mercimonia quecunque; cum libertate habendi et tenendi pistores, brasitores, carnifices et tam carnium quam piscium macellarios, omnesque alios artium operarios ad libertatem burgi in baronia spectantes, etiam [quod] sint burgenses in dicto burgo, et quod idem potestatem habeant temporibus affuturis, eligendi annuatim ballivos aliosque officiarios pro gubernatione ejusdem necessarios, et [quod] possideant in eadem crucem foralem et forum die Sabbati singulis ebdomadis, et nundinas publicas singulis annis die festivitatis beatorum Petri et Pauli apostolorum, ett SS. Symonis et Jude, et per octavas eorundem, cum theoloneis et omnibus libertatibus ad hujusmodi nundinas spectantibus: Tenend. etc., predictas villam et terras de Keithstoun cum bondis et petinentiis earundem, etc., in merum burgum in baronia cum suprascriptis privilegiis, etc. Per Signetum.

Being a close friend of King James IV, it was natural that Thomas Boswell would wish to fight with him against the English. Many Scots lairds joined the king, Boswell being accompanied by Robert Colville of Ochiltree and Sir David Dunbar of Cumnock from the district. James IV led an army of about 20,000 men south into Northumberland, along with seventeen cannon, 'as goodly guns as have been seen in any realme'. The two sides met at Branxton Hill, north-west of the village of Flodden, in the afternoon of 9 September 1513. The Scots left-hand side, led by Lord Hume, managed to disperse their opponents, but the right, led by the earls of Argyll and Lennox, were routed and fled. The middle battalion, under the direct command of the king, forced its way into the English troops, James coming close to defeating the opposite leader, the Earl of Surrey. However, an English soldier managed to kill the king. Some of the remaining Scots fought on until night-fall, only prolonging the defeat. The king lay dead on the field, along with eight of the 22 Scots earls, and numerous bonnet-lairds. Among these were Thomas Boswell of Auchinleck and his elder half-brother, Sir Alexander Boswell of Balmuto.

DAVID BOSWELL (II)

Thomas Boswell was succeeded by his only son, David Boswell, 2nd of Auchinleck, who must have been a minor of around ten years at that time. The estate would have been held in trust for him by his mother, who seems even to have outlived her son for she is listed in the parliamentary records as being alive in 1586. David obtained a charter confirming his right to the barony of Auchinleck from James V in 1514. He was married in 1531, the following note being recorded: 'At Linlithgow, at eight in the evening of 13 February 1531, David Boswale of Auchynflek, and Janet

Hammyltoun, daughter of the late James, Earl of Arrane'. Janet was also referred to as Lady Jane Hamilton, daughter of the 2nd Earl of Arran. Soon after this he obtained a revisionary charter of the barony in favour of himself and his wife.

The *Protocol Book* of John Foular notes that on 14 February 1532 sasine was given to 'David Boiswell of Afflek, as heir of the late Master John Boiswell, his uncle, on his cognition by Edward Kincaid, baillie, of a land of Master John Boiswell, built and waste, lying below the Netherbow, on the south side of the High Street [Edinburgh], within a tenement of the late Martin Huntar. . . Which land David Boswell resigned in the hands of the baillie, who gave sasine thereof to Patrick Boiswell, his heirs and assignees'. What connection Patrick was to David is unknown.

The first half of the sixteenth century was a time of inter-clan feuding in Ayrshire, Patrick Dunbar being murdered in Cumnock kirk in 1512, Lord Cassillis killed at Prestwick in 1526 and John Sampson having his right thumb mutilated in 1537. This latter deed was performed in part by David Boswell, along with Cuninghame of Caprington and several others. They were fined for their part in the feud. David seems to have followed the side of the law thereafter, for we find him appearing in the jury of assize in 1554 which judged the fate of George Crawford of Leifnoreis Castle (Old Cumnock) for intercommunicating with the Laird of Ballagan. David Boswell died around 1562, his widow remarrying, firstly to John Hamilton of Auchingemmill, who must have died soon thereafter, and secondly to John Crawfurd in Shaw, sometime in late 1563. David and Janet seem to have had two sons at least, John who succeeded, and James, who appears in the jury of the trial of James Kirkcaldy, charged with treason in 1573.

JOHN BOSWELL (III)

John Boswell, 3rd of Auchinleck, seems to have fallen out with his step-father 'Johnne Crawfurd of the Schaw' for in 1577 he was pursuer, before the criminal court, against Crawfurd. The latter was charged with arson, having set a byre on fire and other crimes. He married Christian, daughter of Robert Dalzell of that Ilk and of Glenae, progenitor of the Earls of Carnwath, on 21 August 1562. By her he had three sons, James who succeeded, John who was granted Duncanziemere, and Robert. Christian seems to have predeceased John, for he married again, to Agnes, daughter of the 2nd Lord Stewart of Ochiltree. By her he had a fourth son, William, who was granted the estate of Knockroon.

In 1568 John Boswell took part in the Battle of Langside. On 5 March 1591 Boswell fell foul of the Privy Council, from whose records we find that he 'not onlie hes oft and divers tymes consultit with witchis, bot alsua be himselff practized witchecraft, sorcerie, inchantment and uthiris divilishe practizeis, to the dishonnour of God, sklender of his worde, and grite contempt of his Hienes, his authoritie and lawis.' He was ordained to appear before the Privy Council, but failed to turn up, whereupon he was denounced a rebel. The principal witness in the case, Ritchie Graham, who was also the sorcerer that Boswell was supposed to have consulted, confessed in 1592 that he had raised the devil in Boswell's house, probably his town house in the capital. On 28 February 1592, Graham was burned at the Cross of Edinburgh. John Boswell died in 1609.

OTHER LANDOWNERS

The lands of Pennyland at this time formed a small estate, worth two merks in value, a merk being 13½ old pence. On 27 November 1504 King James IV issued a charter of these lands to James Douglas:

> Rex, pro servitio sibi impenso, concessit familiari suo in camera servitori Jacobo Dowglace, et heredibus ejus - 2 mercatas terrarum antiqui extentus de le Pennyland, tunc per ipsum Jac. occupatus, in baroniam de Auchinleck, vic. Aire.

In 1537 we find notice of George Douglas of Pennyland who had to find security, along with Cuninghame of Caprington Castle, David Boswell, 2nd of Auchinleck, and others, to adhere to the law, following their part in the mutilation of John Sampson's right thumb. Two years later the same George Douglas is listed as one of the securities (along with Lord Morton), for the wardship of the natural son of Douglas of Parkhead. From these connections the historian Paterson implies that Douglas of Pennyland was a branch of the noble house of Douglas of that Ilk, which is not unlikely. George Douglas died in 1547 and was succeeded by his son, Adam. From J. Mason's *Notorial Records* we find reference to his son: 'Nov 17, 1578 - William Wallace in Achindonane . . . gaif heretabill stait and sesing to George Douglas, zounger of Pennyland, and Margaret Douglas his spous, personalie present, of all and haill his xx s. [twenty shilling] land of Ovir Barnweill.' Sometime after, Pennyland passed to David Reid, whose daughter, Agnes, is mentioned in 1587 as acquiring the lands of Spittelboig from Hew Campbell of Terringzean Castle.

A second barony existed within Auchinleck parish, that of Glenmuir, part of which extended into Old Cumnock parish. The location of the caput, or seat of the barony, is unknown. It may have been at Laigh Glenmuir, where stood a house known as Hallglenmuir, between the old school and the Red Bridge. This was previously known as Whitestoneburn, but has long since been demolished. The earliest known owner was George Schaw of Glenmuir, who married Margaret Wallace, daughter of John Wallace of Monktonhill. The Schaws were given the lands of Monktonhill in November 1585. In 1600 George Schaw and his brother, Adam Schaw in Castle-Kyle, were charged before the criminal court 'for bering, wering, and schuting of pistolettis, and hurting and wounding of George Campbell of

Horscleuch in the right arm.' George Schaw was remitted by the king on payment of five hundred merks, but Adam was put to the horn for not appearing.

Parts of Glenmure (as it was spelled) were owned by Sir William Hamilton of Newton Castle, Ayr, in the mid-sixteenth century. Hamilton was the alderman and Provost of Ayr a number of times from 1539-1559. He was granted a Barony of Sanquhar (St Quivox) in 1530, and acquired considerable property thereafter. In 1582 Hamilton sold the lands to William Cunninghame of Caprington. A charter under the Great Seal lists the properties as:

> Tres quartas partes et 40 denariat. terrarium de Glenmure, tam proprietatem quam tenandris, cum molendinis, viz. 2 marcatas terrarium de Banbrek (sive Panbrek) [Penbreck], 40 sol. de Paperthill, 4 marcat. de Schaw, 6 marcant. de Dalblairis et Constabillmark, 5 marcat. de Castelcauill, 2½ marcat. de Dornell, 1 marcatam de Auchtitanche [Auchtitench]…

The lands of Boghead and Tarrioch, at the north-east end of the parish, were in the early sixteenth century owned by Ninian Bannatyne of Kames. James V issued a charter of 20 July 1537 from Edinburgh as follows, which lists the lands and mentions some of the early occupiers of the farms:

> Rex confirmavit cartam Niniani Banotyne de Camis - [qua, pro summa pecunie sibi persoluta, venditit Johanni Reid in Rogertoun, heredibus ejus et assignatis - marcatam terrarum de Bannotinis-yardis (per dictum Joh. et Joh. Richart inhabitatam), ac marcat. de Torreachis et Bogheid, (inhabitat. per Gilbertum Wallance, Jac. Wilsoun, relictam Johannis Patersoun) antiqui extentus, in balliatu de Kile-stewart, vic. Air.]

CHURCHES

The ministers or priest who came to Auchinleck from Paisley to preach had an assistant in each parish, known as a parish clerk, a person who looked after the kirk's business in its locale. At the turn of the sixteenth century the clerk of Auchinleck was one John Lekprevick, or Lapraik as it was later spelled. In 1527 he was succeeded by his son, also John Lekprevick, a minor, 'by suffragan'.

The Knights of St John of Jerusalem, known also as the Knights Hospitallers, who had their Scottish headquarters at Torphichen Preceptory in West Lothian, held lands in Auchinleck parish. These religious men dispensed justice and treated people who were ill. Where they were based in the parish is unknown, one possible site of their chapel being at Lugar, preserved in the name Chapel Knowe, location of the present church. This is all the more possible when we realise that the Chapel

Knowe is located between the two surviving 'Temple-land' place-names - Templand Mains and Templandshaw. Alternatively the old parish kirk may occupy the temple site, for it is not too far from the spot where stood the croft of Templeton, at the west end of Mauchline Road. The third ancient chapel site in the parish, St Vincent's Chapel, near Auchinleck Castle, is another contender, for here was found the old coffin slab known as the Templar's Stone. However, Lugar probably has the greatest claim to the Knight's Temple. In 1540 it is known that the rental of these lands was 18 pence and that they were leased to Patrick Black, for in a list of temple lands it is noted: 'Tempill auchinlek patrik blak xviijd.' In 1588 the owner of 'Tempilland-Auchinleck' was Hew Craufurd. According to the chartulary of Torphichen, 'Temple Schaw', or Templandshaw, was leased by George Sinclair in 1598, indicating that it formed part of the temple lands of Auchinleck.

REFORMATION

In the first half of the sixteenth century the earliest rumblings of dissatisfaction with the Roman Catholic faith took place in Scotland. Andrew Stewart of Ochiltree was taken before the Bishop of Glasgow in 1533 for casting down images in Ochiltree kirk. George Wishart, on his return to Scotland, preached at Mauchline in 1544, sowing the seeds of reformation. He was later burned at St Andrews in 1546. The great John Knox preached at various nearby castles on his tour of Ayrshire in 1556. Two thousand Ayrshire men marched to Perth in 1559 to form the Lords of the Congregation and the revolt against papal domination began. By August 1560 Parliament had authorised the Confession of Faith, a statement of reformed doctrine. Auchinleck church seems to have been one of the first churches in the country in which the reformed doctrine was taught, for it is recorded that the kirk here was 'statedly anathematised by the Pope'. The appearance of heresy in the preaching within Auchinleck kirk was first noted in 1562. Around this time Sir John Reid was curate of the parish and Adam Landells (or Landless) was the notary and chaplain in 1548-51.

Landells was recommended as fit to be a reader at the General Assembly in 1560. He acted as exhorter to Ochiltree, Auchinleck and Cumnock from 1567 until around 1570. Landells had died by 1571.

Landells was probably replaced as reader by John Gemmill, who is referred to in 1574. He appears to have remained until at least 1601. The rental of Auchinleck church in 1562 was worth £66 13s 4d per annum.

After the Reformation the patronage of the churches in Scotland was transferred to secular persons, though in many cases former commendators of the abbeys received them. This happened in the case of Auchinleck, the former commendator of Paisley, Lord Claud Hamilton, receiving the patronage. A charter was issued in 1587 confirming this, granting the patronage, tithes and church lands to Hamilton and his heirs. He died in 1621 and the patronage passed to his grandson, James, 2nd Earl of Abercorn. However, John, 1st Lord Loudoun, seems to have obtained the patronage of Auchinleck Kirk in March 1620, this being ratified in parliament in 1633. On 14 November 1656 the Protectorate issued a charter to John Sempill of these lands, which lists their extent, namely: 'The lands called the Twa Tirrochis, pertinents, &c, thereof, in the parish of Auchinlacke . . . the teind sheaves great and small, fruits, rents, manse, glebe, emoluments, &c, whatsoever of the Kirk of Auchinlacke, not disponed already to the heritors in the parish nor allocated to the minister's stipend.' The kirk lands quickly passed through a series of owners thereafter to William Reid, merchant burgess of Edinburgh, in 1653. James Reid, his heir, was retoured in the lands of the 'Terriochies' and church lands in 1666. The patronage was halved sometime after this, being owned at times by Campbell of Cessnock (1691), James Carmichael (1692) and John Dalrymple, 2nd Viscount Stair (1698). Soon after this the patronage was acquired by the Boswells, in whose hands it remained until patronage was abolished in 1874.

FIRST PROTESTANT MINISTER

It seems to have taken around fourteen years from the date of the Reformation until a minister of the Protestant faith came to Auchinleck. At least there is no reference to anyone before Rev John Inglis, who was translated from Ochiltree, to Auchinleck in 1574. Previously he had served the three parishes of Ochiltree (from 1567), Auchinleck and Old Cumnock, the latter until 1572. He remained for just six years, returning to Ochiltree. However, he may have served Auchinleck jointly after 1580, for during his time in Auchinleck he also served Ochiltree. He had a stipend of £10 per year, with the kirk lands of both parishes.

John Inglis studied at St Andrews University, where reference to him is found between 1540 and 1557. He was married to Agnes Grosar, by whom he had five sons. These were John, who was apprenticed to Robert Skinner, flesher, on 20 January 1587; Joseph, apprenticed to Robert Graham, tailor on 25 February 1590; Daniel, apprenticed to John Skinner, 1 April 1607; Samuel, apprenticed to Patrick Hepburn, apothecary, 26 December 1610; and William, apprenticed to Thomas Finnie, tailor, 8 September 1613. All of these apprenticeships took place in Edinburgh.

CHAPTER THREE

SEVENTEENTH CENTURY (1600-1689)

VILLAGE LIFE

In 1691 a one-off tax on landowners and tenants was charged on households across Scotland. This was agreed by parliament in 1690, and the tax of 14 shillings per hearth was payable on Candlemas (2 February) 1691. The poor were exempt from paying this tax, which was primarily introduced to help recoup arrears in the army and repay loans made to parliament by various burghs and counties. The tax was collected locally by David Craufurd of Drumsuie (Coylton parish) and took a few years to gather.

In Auchinleck parish, according to the returns, there were 212 households in the parish that had hearths, although a fair number of larger houses had more than one hearth. Auchinleck Castle, for example, had fifteen hearths within it. The next largest houses appear to be Boghead with seven hearths, Walstounburn (Whitestoneburn) and Dornal with six each, and Duncanziemere with five. The number of households that paid the tax was 183. It was noted that nine households had failed to pay, and twenty were not liable to pay as the house was occupied by the poor.

The list of tax-payers gives us an insight into some of the residents of the parish at the end of the seventeenth century. Many of the surnames are popular in the district today, whereas others have died out. The twenty poor were: John Shaw, William Duncan, Margaret Bigg, James Wilson, Isobel Rid, Isabell Aird, Little Whier, Abraham Murdoch, Hugh Calder, Marrie Miller, Isobel Dalrymple, Janet Manson, John Ronald, Janet Reid, George McCaw, Christain Rea, John Nicoll, Christain Hendry and Janet Barber. Other names of Auchinleckites who paid the tax include Hew Crawford, Allan MacCarra, William Logan, John Black, John Mackora, David Muidie, William Renton, George Thomson, Andrew Johnkin, Christian Rid, Janet Smith, James Wight, Thomas Gibson, William McGanie, James Wilson, Isobel Murdoch, Robert Clayton, John Cortonse, James Hair, Hew McOuan, John Olister, William Broun, John McCaulne, James Wilson, Gawen Wilson, Alexander Wallance, George Wallance, William Paterson, John Murdoch, Hew Gibson, William Alexander, George Maxwell, Thomas Stodart, James

Murdoch, Martin Mathie, John Johnstone, John Campbell, John Dalrymple, Hew McOuan, John Strachan, Hew Steven, John Reid, Adam Steill, Hew Lamon, Andrew Allan, James Richmount, James McGanno, and Matthew Hodge.

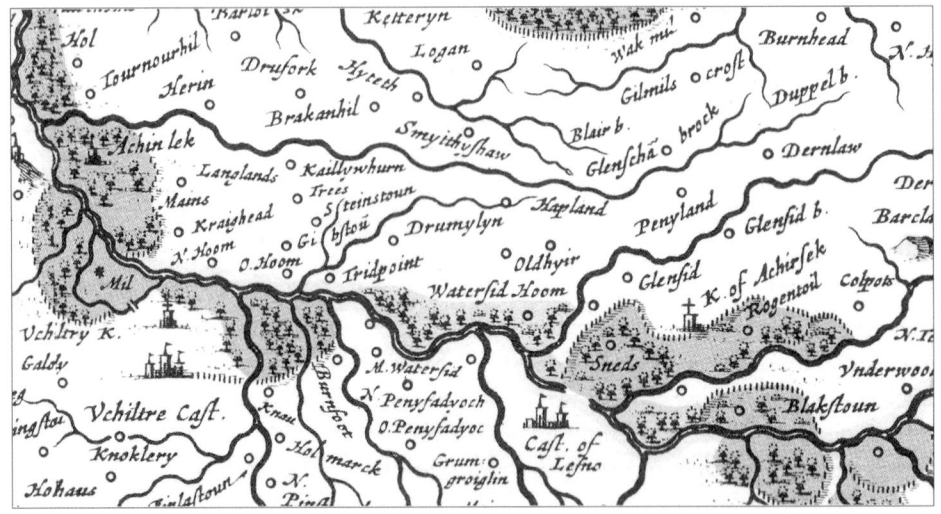

3.1 West part of parish as shown on Timothy Pont's Coila Provincia (1654)

LANDOWNERS – JAMES BOSWELL (IV)

James Boswell succeeded as 4th of Auchinleck in 1609. He married Marion Crawfurd of Kerse and had a numerous family. The eldest son, David, succeeded as 5th of Auchinleck, the second, James, married Margaret, the daughter of James Cunningham of Glengarnock. The third son, Captain John Boswell, was killed in England during the wars of the time of Charles I. James' three youngest sons entered the army of Gustavus Adolphus, King of Sweden, in which country they settled, establishing a Boswell sept there. Before succeeding to the barony, James Boswell was charged with abiding from the Raid of Dumfries, along with his brother, John, in July 1600. In the document relating to this, they are named as 'James Boiswell, feare [younger] of Auchinleck, Johnne Boiswell of Duntrinezemen [Duncanziemere].' In this case a number of parties were fined, others being discharged. In 1602 James acted as one of the 'Preloquutouris" [prolocutors] or counsel, for John Mure of Auchindrane, who was placed on trial for the murder of Sir Thomas Kennedy of Culzean, on 24 June. This was the famous *Auchindrane Tragedy*, written about in verse by Sir Walter Scott. Captain John Boswell was a member of the jury at the trial of Thomas MacAlexander of Drummochreen in 1601, charged, with others, with forging and spending counterfeit coins.

In September 1615 there occurred an insurrection in the southern Hebrides when Sir James MacDonald escaped from prison and caused disruption to the king. James VI sent the Earl of Argyll and several battalions to the islands in an attempt to achieve the final pacification of the Hebrides. James Boswell, 4th of Auchinleck, led one of the two main battalions. They left from Duntrune Castle on the shores of Loch Crinan (Argyll) to attack MacDonald's camp on the western shore of Kintyre, opposite the island of Cara. Between seven and eight hundred of Argyll's men left in ships for the camp, Argyll leading the two battalions across the peninsula on foot and horseback. Robert Campbell, Captain of Dunoon, and James Boswell both led a battalion. Word reached MacDonald of the advancing soldiers and he escaped to Rathlin Island in Northern Ireland, though not before some of his men suffered death. MacDonald and his men returned to Islay where they encamped on the Rhins. Argyll sent Boswell and Campbell of Cawdor with 1,000 troops under the cover of darkness to the island. MacDonald again received some warning of attack, and he made his escape to Inchdaholl, another Irish island, never again returning to Scotland. His second-in-command, Coll MacGillespick, surrendered the camps at Dunivaig and Lochgorm to Boswell and Campbell, swapping sides to join the fight against the rebels. MacDonald fled further to Spain, and as W. D. Lamont wrote in his *The Early History of Islay*, 'left the honour of dying to those whom he abandoned when they could no longer serve his ambition.'

James Boswell died in February 1618, a few days after making his will. This is preserved in the Glasgow Commissary Court Records, having been witnessed by Rev George Walker, minister of the parish, and confirmed on 25 August 1618. From it we find the following:

> Legacie – At Auchinleck, the 20 day of Februar, the yeir of God 1618, the quhilk day James Boswall makis his testament as followis, quha nominat and constitute Mareoun Crawfuird, his spous, Margaret, Jeane and Issobell Boswallis, his dochteris, his executoris and only intromitoris, &c., and ordainis Dame Grissall Boswall, spous to ane reverend father in God, James, Archbishop of Glasgow, David Boswell in Auchinleck, his sone and appeirand air, to be overisman and oursear to thame, that ilk ane do thair dewtie to utheris. Item, he ordains also Johne, Robert, and William Boswallis, his brethir, also overismen with the said David, to the effect afoirsaid. Item, he levis Mathow his son naturail, thrie of the best ky in the [byre]. Item, he levis to Margarat [sic] Crawfurd, his spous, the stand bed in the young lairdis chalmer, that he lyis in, with ane laich bed nerrest the window in the auld lairdis chalmer, &c. And ordains James, William, George and Johne Boswallis, my sones, to quyt claim and discharge utheris portiones and partis of the guidis. . .

In 1612 James Boswell, 4th of Auchinleck, built for himself a new castle near to the ancient tower of Auchinleck. This new building was a typical Scots tower house of

3.2 Old Place of Auchinleck from MacGibbon & Ross *(Author's Collection)*

the period, but a rather grand version of such, with some unusual decorative features. The tower was basically of the L-plan, with a square stair tower in the re-entrant, also containing the entrance doorway. One arm of the 'L' was probably a later extension, the castle previously having a 'T' shaped plan. Reduced to this size, the castle would have resembled the newer half of the Old Place of Mochrum in Wigtownshire, which has been dated to the late sixteenth century. The ground floor of the castle contained three vaulted rooms in the old section, one larger than the other two (about 17 feet by 11 feet 9 inches compared with 12 feet by 7 feet 9 inches). Narrow slit windows passed through the north wall of these. By ascending the spiral staircase one reached the first floor, probably containing the great hall, which must have measured about 32 feet by 18 feet internally. The main block was three and a half storeys tall, the stair tower rising higher, being corbelled out, and containing a look-out post. The roof was saddle-backed, the gables having corbie-steps. Over the doorway a defensive projection allowed the castle's occupants to attack anyone forcing the door. In the angle between the tower and the east wing was an unusual corbelled projection, probably containing a passage from the stair to the room in the wing. The castle was surrounded by a high wall and some lesser wings, probably containing stables and the like, though the west wing is believed to have formed a chapel, similar to the chapel in the wing at Traquair House today. At the southern side of the castle was the old home farm, known as Greenfoot, and a gardener's cottage. The gardens were laid out to the east of the castle. Where the buildings of Greenfoot stood there survives an old well. When it became superseded by the present mansion, the 1612 building became known as Auchinleck Old House, or the Place of Auchinleck.

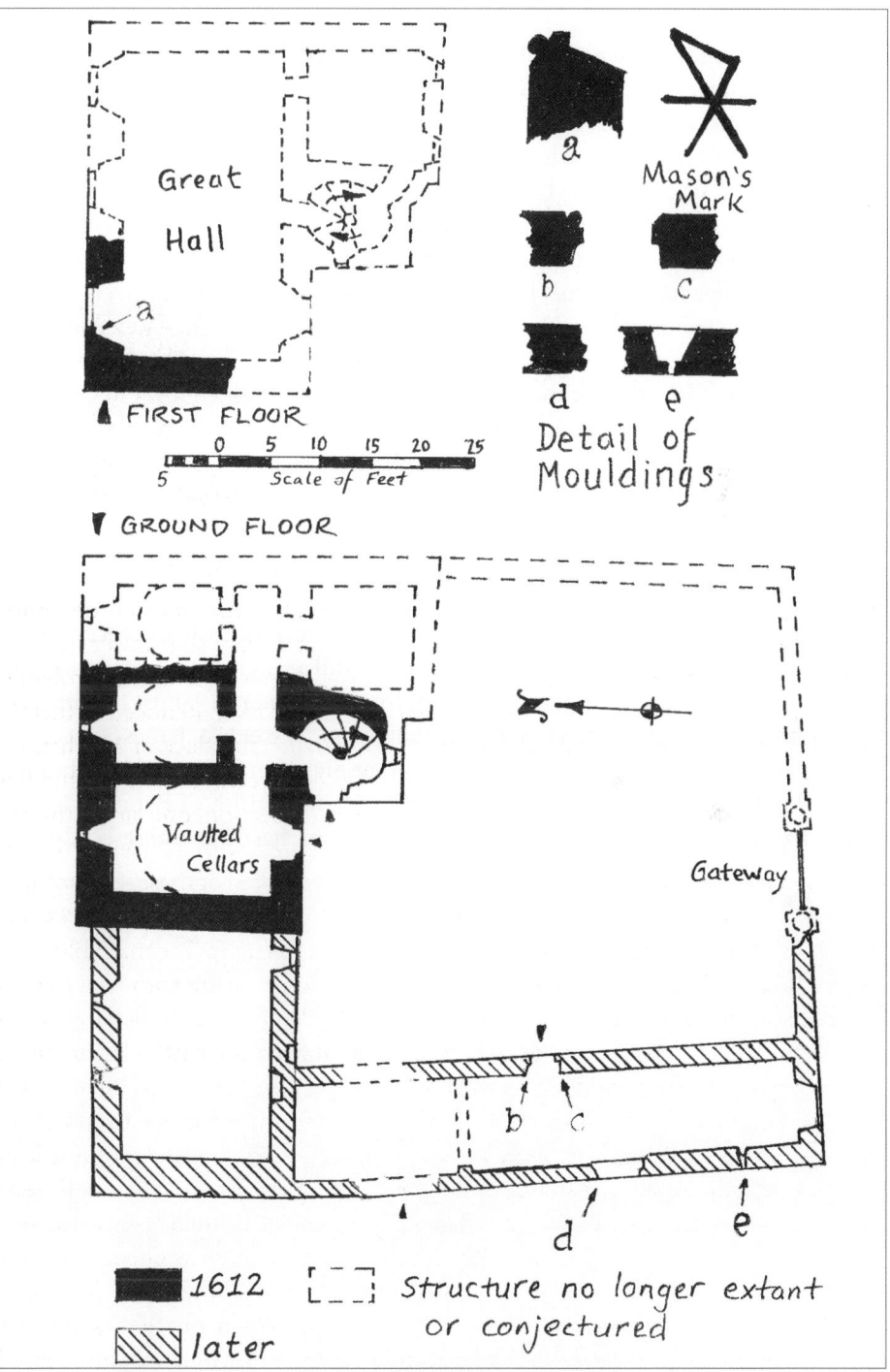

3.3 Old Place of Auchinleck (plan) *(Dane Love)*

DAVID BOSWELL (V)

David Boswell succeeded as 5th Boswell of Auchinleck in 1618. He had previously obtained a charter under the Great Seal in 1609 of the lands of Cromderrie (Cronberry) and Bogside. He was married twice, firstly to Isobel, daughter of Sir John Wallace of Carnell, by whom he had four daughters - Marion, who married the 6th Lord Cathcart; Isobel, who married John Shaw of Sornbeg; Jean who married John Gordon, younger of Earlstoun; and Margaret, who married David Blair of Adamton. His second wife was Margaret, daughter of Sir Archibald Stewart of Blackhall. They had no issue. David Boswell, from his marital connections with the Wallaces, acted as creditor in the will of Sibilla Wallace, wife of Rev Alexander Wallace of Galston, in 1643.

During the time of the Covenant, David Boswell remained loyal to Charles I, and he is reported to have paid a heavy fine, rather than subscribe to the Covenant.

David Boswell died in 1661 and, having no sons, the estate passed to his nephew, also called David, son of James Boswell and Margaret Cuninghame, daughter of Sir James Cuninghame of Glengarnock.

DAVID BOSWELL (VI)

David Boswell, 6th Boswell laird of Auchinleck, was born in 1640 and succeeded to the barony at the age of twenty-one. He was then still a single man, not getting wed until 24 July 1666 when he married Anne, third daughter of James Hamilton of Dalzell. By her he had two sons and three daughters. The eldest, James, succeeded.

The second son, John, became a Writer to the Signet in Edinburgh and built up a considerable fortune. In 1722, when Andrew Boswell, 10th of Balmuto in Fife, placed Balmuto Castle and estate up for sale, John purchased it, and re-established

3.4 Old Place of Auchinleck from west *(Dane Love)*

a Boswell connection with that seat. He married a fellow Writer's daughter and his eldest son, Claude Irvine-Boswell (1742-1828) succeeded, being noted in history as Lord Balmuto of the College of Justice.

David Boswell's three daughters were Jean, who married John Campbell, 8th of Horsecleugh (Cumnock), on 10 November 1697; Margaret, who married Captain Hugh Campbell of Barquharrie (Ochiltree), third son of Sir Hugh Campbell of Cessnock; and Anne, who married George Campbell, 2nd of Treesbank (Riccarton). In 1672, David Boswell, 6th of Auchinleck, received notice of ratification of the lands of Auchinleck, with the exception of those parts disponed by himself to William, Earl of Dundonald, in liferent, to Dundonald's only son and to Sir John Cochrane of Ochiltree, in fee. In 1692 Boswell was the commissioner from Ochiltree parish to Ayr Presbytery. David Boswell died in 1712, his wife surviving until the following year.

SMALLER ESTATES

The estate of Waterside occupied the lands north of the Lugar Water and to the west of Pennyland. Waterside House was situated in a field at one time known as 'The Damilonians', the site of it now occupied by Dumfries House's walled garden. Waterside and Pennyland formed a single estate at one time, Waterside being formerly known as Nether Pennyland. The earliest reference to the name Waterside is in 1612, at which time it was owned by George Douglas of Pennyland. James VI issued a charter on 31 December 1612 confirming the sale of the lands by George Douglas, junior of Pennyland, to William Reid, merchant burgess in Edinburgh. From this charter we find that the 2 merk lands of Pennyland have been halved, and contained a fortalice, or tower house. The occupiers and tenants on the estate were George Douglas senior, Adam Brown, Michael and George Swann. George Douglas, younger of Waterside, is mentioned as a debtor in the testament of George Crauford of Auchincross in 1617. In 1631 a further charter of Nether Pennyland, or 'the Wattersyd', lists Dalsallochhill as part of the estate. Waterside was sold sometime after 1640 to Sir John Cochrane of Ochiltree, who gifted it to John, his second son, a notable Covenanter.

John Cochrane of Waterside was born in 1662 and baptised on 30 June that year. He took part in the Battle of Bothwell Bridge on 22 June 1679, fighting for the Covenanters, even though he was just seventeen years old. He subsequently fled to Holland with his father but returned in 1685 when he was active in the Monmouth and Argyll insurrection. In 1684 he was forfeited of his lands for his part at Bothwell, but after the revolution he and his father both were granted pardons by the king. John Cochrane married Hannah de Worth, from London, on 14 September 1687, by whom he fathered eight sons and seven daughters, and died around 1734.

Waterside was then owned by his son, also John of Waterside. John Cochrane was drowned on 23 November 1752. His widow, whom he married on 11 August 1733, was Elizabeth Cairns, grand-daughter of James Cairns of Minniebuies. She lived for a further 25 years and died on 4 January 1777.

John of Waterside's second son was James Cochrane, who became a Judge Advocate. He was married in January 1731 to Cecilia, daughter of George Oliphant of Edinburgh. James died on 29 August 1762, leaving a son, William Cochrane, who succeeded his father as Judge Advocate. William Cochrane died on 20 January 1766.

Around the middle of the eighteenth century the Cochranes sold the estate, it being acquired by the Earl of Dumfries. In the spring of 1763 the old house was demolished, the stone being used for other building work where possible. There survives an account, presented to the Dumfries family by John Thomson, quarrier, 'for taking off the roof and throwing down the old house at Wattersyde and carrying out the buildable stones.' He also refers 'to throwing down the old vault and other stones at Waterside.' The latter comment probably indicates that the lower floor of the house was vaulted, typical of old Scots tower houses.

The lands of (Over) Pennyland were owned by the Reids at the beginning of the seventeenth century. David Reid was probably succeeded by James Reid, mentioned as a debtor in the testament of Margaret Wilson, wife of John Reid, merchant burgess in Glasgow, dated January 1618. He was still alive in 1648, for his name appears in the testament of William Gemmill of Templand, as does that of his son, John Reid. Within a few years the two merk lands of Pennyland were sold to David Boswell, 5th of Auchinleck, whose son, also David, sold them to the Earl of Dundonald. This family retained Pennyland until the end of the eighteenth century when it was acquired by the Earl of Dumfries.

At Tarrioch and Cronberry the lands were owned by John Reid, who received a charter under the Great Seal in 1607. This describes him as John Reid, then in Rogerton, heir of John Reid of Rogerton. The lands mentioned in the charter were the two Bannatyneyards, the two Tarriochs, Boghead, and Cronberry ('Crondarrie'), formerly owned by Hector Bannatyne of Kames.

Gass and Welltrees formed a five merk-worth of land and in 1602 were held by Josie Stewart of Wester Polquhairn. A charter under the Great Seal was issued to him in respect of these lands at that time.

The lands of Knockroon were granted by John Boswell (3rd of Auchinleck) to his fourth son (and first by his second marriage) William, around 1600. Little is known about this William, or even about his son William, 2nd of Knockroon. The younger William married Margaret Montgomerie of Bridgend Castle, Alloway (now Doonside), a descendant of the Montgomeries of Lainshaw. By her he had an heir, also William, who died without issue, so the estate of Knockroon passed to his eldest sister Elizabeth, wife of John Fergusson, of the Kilkerran family. Of the younger sister, Agnes, little is known.

Hew Craufurd of Templand was succeeded by William Craufurd, mentioned in a testament of 1615 as creditor 'for the ferme of Blakistoun'. He died in 1622 when Templand passed to Hugh Nisbet of Knevocklaw (near Darvel), grandson of Hugh Nisbet of Hage. Hugh's charter notes that it was the five-pound lands of Templand, also known as Templand-Auchinleck. A charter under the Great Seal of 30 August 1662 gives some interesting details on the lands of Templand:

> Charter of apprising to Mr Thomas Wallace of Craigie, advocate, his heirs and assignees, - of the £5 lands of Tempilland of old extent, with manor-place etc., with salmon, and other fishings in the water of Lugar, lying in the parish of Auchinleck, sheriffdom of Air; - also those four acres of land or thereabout called *the Fald* and *Bank*, near that called the *Viccars Bank* and *Dyron* [sic], and that acre of land called the *Wrutting Aickere*, lying near the said Fauld and Bank, and similarly that part and particular land called the hundredth merk land, lying near the said *Wrytting Aiker*, on the south side of the water of Lugar, in the parish of Cumnock, the Kingskyll, and in the sheriffdom of Air, with teind sheaves, etc.; - which lands formerly belonged to the late William Gemill of Tempilland, and were apprised at Edinburgh, 31st January 1656, from Euphame Gemill, lawful daughter of the said William, as charged to enter heir, and the said Mr Thomas Wallace, called younger of Failfurde, her husband, at the instance of William Mitchell, younger of Baramuir, in payment to him as assignee of a sum, principal annual rents and expenses, amounting in all to the sum of £17,813 13s 4d as principal, and the sum of £890 10s 4d sheriff's fee, 8th February 1656, which said William Mitchell, in May 1656, assigned the said Mr Thomas Wallace; one sasine to be sufficient: - To be held of the Crown:- Rendering therefor the usual services and dues; with right of redemption to the said Eupham and her heirs.

In 1680 William Wallace of Craigie was retoured, or returned, heir of the lands.

The lands of Wallaceton, at the foot of the Glenmuir, were anciently owned by a family of the name Wallace, believed to be a branch of the Wallaces of Craigie. Wallaceton farm was named by them. The earliest known owner was William Wallace, who died in January 1616. He had taken part as a juror in the trial of Thomas Jardine of Birnock in 1609, charged with theft with violence from a house. A few genealogical details are obtained from his will: 'Legacie – at Wallastoun, the xvi day of .... 1616. The qlk day the said Wm. Wallace makis his testament, &c. Item I ordane and appoynt James Wallace, my sone and appeirand air, and Wm. Stewart

SEVENTEENTH CENTURY

3.5 James Wallace of Wallaceton's tombstone *(Dane Love)*

of Raith, my sone-in-law, to be orsearis to all things, &c.' A James Wallace died in 1678, according to an old grave slab in the parish kirkyard. This may have been the above James Wallace, or perhaps his son.

From the arms on the stone, and the initials MB, we can deduce that his wife was a Boyd. No reference to the family is then noted until the eighteenth century.

The lands of Duncanziemere (which included a number of other adjacent farms) were gifted by John Boswell (3rd of Auchinleck) to his second son, John, around the end of the sixteenth century. He was certainly in ownership by 1600 when he was listed with his elder brother in the charge for abiding from the Raid of Dumfries. In 1617 his name appears as a creditor in the will of George Crauford of Auchincross. Around this time Craigston estate was acquired by John Boswell, as he is sometimes styled as 'of Duncanziemere and Craigston.' Still alive in 1623, John was succeeded sometime afterwards by Mungo Boswell, who had made his principal seat Craigston House. His name appears on testaments dated 1645 and 1661.

William Schaw of Glenmuir succeeded George Schaw in that barony. He himself died in 1626 and was succeeded by George, whose charter lists his lands – the twenty pound lands of Glenmure of old extent, containing the four merk lands of Whitestoneburn, two merk lands of Whiteholm and sixteen shilling and eight pence worth of the forty shilling lands of Dornal. In 1656 George was succeeded by his two sisters, Christian and Jane Schaw. Christian Schaw married John Beg of Waltries [Welltrees] and had a son, also John. Jane, or Jean, Schaw was the younger daughter, and married Alexander Williamson in 'Castel Cavill', or Kyle Castle.

The 'teinds parsonage and vicarage of the lands of Glenmuir . . . the lands of Derreoche [Tarrioch] . . . with all the superiorities and feu-duties within the same' were granted by Oliver Cromwell, the Protector, in 1657 to James Campbell of Loudoun. The lands of Glenmuir were in 1663 granted to Sir Robert Murray, alias 'Creightoun of Glenmuire'. The estate then comprised of three-quarters of the forty-shilling lands of Glenmuir, the two merk lands of Parbrock [Penbreck], the forty-shilling lands of Popperhill, the four merk lands of Shawne [Glenmuirshaw], the six merk lands of Darbase [Dalblair] and Constablemark, the four merk lands of Castle-kerrie [Kyle], the 23 shilling 4 penny lands of Dornell, the merklands of Auchintitauch [Auchtitench]. In 1665 these lands passed to William Crichton, Earl of Dumfries. Castle Kyle and Maclellanston had in 1634 belonged to Robert Farquhar of Gilmilnscroft.

In 1601 William Wallace, minister of the church of Fail, was collecting taxes in order to pay the 100,000 merks he was due to pay King James VI, as voted by the estates. From the parish of Auchinleck he was owed money by a number of people, namely William Crawford of Leifnoreis, due 10 merks for the 5 merk lands of Gass and Welltrees; George Douglas of Pennyland, due 10 merks for the 5 merk lands of McLellandston; John Boswell of Duncanziemere, due 10 merks for the 5 merk lands thereof; and George Reid of Craigston, due 10 merks for the 5 merk lands of Stonebriggs. The whole lands made up a 20 merk land of old extent, as part of the patrimony of the abbacy of Fail. The tenants protested that the letters from the minister were general, not addressed to each individual, and claimed that the minister was greedy, claiming 2 merks for every merk-worth of land, which they had offered him. The case went to trial, but the outcome is unknown. However, by 14 December 1602, King James conceded to Joseph Stewart of Wester Polquhairn the lands of Gass and Welltrees, through the forfeiture of William Cunningham of Tourlands, to be held of the king in place of the minister and convent of Fail. In 1631, during the Episcopacy, Walter Whiteford was minister of Fail and he gave a charter to Robert Farquhar of Gilmilnscroft of the 5 merk land of McClellandston in Auchinleck, to be held of the minister in feu.

AGRICULTURE

Agriculture in the seventeenth century was probably practised very much like it had been for centuries beforehand. Land was divided into small holdings, often considerably smaller than 80 acres in the areas with better soil, and larger nearer the hills and moorland to the east end of the parish. Little survives to indicate how rural workers lived and worked at this time, most of it having been swept away and changed during the period of agricultural revolution in the eighteenth century, when steadings were rebuilt and smaller holdings merged to form larger farms.

In the late seventeenth century, when the period of Covenanting struggle had come to an end, a number of farmers decided to rebuild their steadings. Among those known to have had work done on them at the time was Dornal, by the side of the Glenmuir Water. A new house was erected in 1692, the date stone being carved into a skew putt. This house was built with corbie-stepped gables, a rather refined form of building for the time, indicating that the owner could afford to build more refined buildings. This building was demolished in recent years, but the dated skew putt was saved and is now built into the garden wall.

The names of some of the old farms no longer in existence can be found from old maps, such as Joan Blaeu's *Atlas Novus*, published in 1654. This is the first detailed map of the country, and Auchinleck parish is shown with a considerable degree of accuracy.

Lost farms and buildings indicated on the map include the following, starting from the west end of the parish. Kraighead (Craighead) was in the vicinity of Auchinleck estate, Nether Hoom (Netherholm) was the land south-west of Auchinleck Mains, whereas Langholm was shown on the map as Over Hoom. Kaillywhurn is no longer known, but may have been abbreviated to Whirr. Drumylyn was somewhere along the Barony Road and Sneds in the Cottertax area, near to the foot of the Auchinleck Burn. The excavation of coal in the early seventeenth century is indicated by 'Colpots', around Birnieknowe, and Keths, or

Keiths, appears to be somewhere along the Rigg Road. The site of the present Lugar was occupied by Over, Middle and Nether Kraikstoun, or Craigston. Somerdamsyd is lost, perhaps around Braehead of Craigston, as is Macklellastoun (MacLellandston), which must have been near Carbello.

The sites of many of these farms and cottages are long gone, or else indicated by the odd large tree in the corner of a field. At the east end of the parish, prior to open cast mining, some of the steadings were identified on the ground and an archaeological excavation took place to find out a bit more of their history.

One of the known buildings was excavated in 2012 by Headland Archaeology Ltd, prior to Duncanziemere open cast being dug. Back o' Hill farmstead appears on General Roy's map, but had disappeared by the time the Ordnance Survey produced their maps in the mid-nineteenth century. It was located to the south-east of Hillhead farm, or around half a mile north of Laigh Glenmuir farm itself. During the excavations three buildings were identified – a stone-built building with a cobbled floor, a possible raised barn, supported on timber beams, and a byre. The last-named was probably built of turf on top of a stone base, for little evidence of stone walling was found, though in the floor of the byre drainage channels were excavated, indicating that slurry and other waste was drained from the building. The buildings may have dated from the first half of the eighteenth century, when some improvements were starting, although the building methods used here appear to be those of the previous centuries. Glass from bottles and pottery found on site were dated to the late seventeenth century, and Back o' Hill was certainly occupied around 1730. It appears to have been occupied until around 1790-1800. This was the period of major agricultural reform in the country, and thus the farmstead was probably abandoned at that time, merging with Hillhead farm.

CHURCHES

Rev George Walker was ordained to Auchinleck in 1617. He was the son of John Walker, baillie in Newmilns, and had graduated Master of Arts at Glasgow University in 1607. However, his ministry lasted just three years, for he died in June 1621 at the age of 34. He had a fairly considerable library and a contemporary account notes that 'his hail buiks were estimat at £53 6s 8d.' From his will we find that he left 'the XXs [20 shilling] lands of Kirkland pertaining me, heritable with the pertinents during her lyff,' to his widow, Martha Granger, who died in 1640. His library was left to his nephew, James Walker, 'in case he be ane scollar.' James was also left money to put him through college: 'My broder's sone xl lb [£40] zeirli for the three zeirs beginning Martinmas after my death. How sone he passes to ane college xl lb zeirlie to help entertain him theirat during four zeirs, quhilk is the ordinar term of passing his cours. Also I leif to the said James my haill buiks, in cais he pass his cours at the college as said is.'

The grave of Walker is found built into the old parish church, placed there in 1865 when its lettering was renewed. The slab bears a crest and monogram with the inscription: 'Hunc tumulum conjunx posuit dilecta marito quemque viro posuit destinat hora sibi. This stone was erected in 1621 in memory of the Rev George Walker, who was pastor of the parish. Repaired by Old Mortality in his day.' The Latin lines translate as 'A beloved wife has erected this monument to her husband, and what she has thus dedicated to her husband an hour destines for herself.' 'Old Mortality', mentioned on the stone, was the name given to the stonemason, Robert Paterson, by Sir Walter Scott. Paterson left home to travel Scotland restoring or erecting memorials to the Covenanters. He died in 1801 at the age of 86 and is buried at Bankend of Caerlaverock kirkyard in Dumfriesshire.

Rev John Schaw was presented to the parish in 1631 and like Rev George Walker was a graduate of Glasgow, qualifying in 1617. He was the son of Alexander Schaw in Clauchphymett, and was married to Margaret Douglas, by whom he had a son, William, apprenticed to James Durie, merchant in Edinburgh, on 27 November 1650. In 1632 he gifted 20 merks [£13 6s 8d Scots] to that city to help build a new library. Little else is known about his ministry. He died on 28 March 1649 and was buried in the kirkyard. His gravestone was renovated in 1865 and is found in the old kirk wall. Along with an epitaph, it reads: 'In memory of the Rev John Shaw who was minister of this parish. He died anno domine 1649'.

The population of the parish continued to climb slowly in the seventeenth century. By 1640 the church could not hold all the worshippers at the same time, so the laird, David Boswell, 5th of Auchinleck, made arrangements for the building to be enlarged. It was at this time the building achieved its present size, excluding the mausoleum, though it was probably thatched then. Mason's marks, perhaps from this period, can still be seen carved onto the cope stones. A small belfry was erected at the top of the eastern gable, above the entrance door, and within this was hung the new bell, gifted by the laird. It was cast in Edinburgh in 1641 by James Monteith, a noted bell-founder of the time, whose bells survive at Coylton (1647), and Alloway (1657). The bell for Auchinleck is inscribed: *IACOBUS MONTEETH ME FECIT, EDINBURGH, ANNO DOM. 1641*. Above and below this is a patterned band round the bell, with an anchor beneath. It is 17¾ inches in diameter. The bell remained in its belfry until 1970, when work began on creating the Boswell Museum; it is now located within Auchinleck House.

Attached to the church wall were 'the jougs', or an iron neck-ring, which was used by the kirk session as an act of punishment for the parishioners. Should anyone be caught breaking the Sabbath, by picking berries, fornicating, causing a public nuisance, or some other crime, then they were sentenced to be placed in the jougs for a period of time. Those law-abiding parishioners attending Sunday services could then see the lawbreakers at their place of shame. The jougs remained hanging on the church wall long after they had become disused, but were removed in the nineteenth century. The stone to which they had been affixed remained visible thereafter.

In 1643 the General Assembly issued an act stipulating that no-one 'of whatever quality' should be allowed burial within the churches. Previously heritors and others could be buried beneath the church floor, even although it was condemned at the Reformation. To comply with the act, yet retaining the right of burial in the crypt beneath the church at Auchinleck, David Boswell had the entry from the church closed off and a new external entrance built to the north.

Two years elapsed from Rev John Schaw's death before Rev Andrew Dalrymple MA was ordained on 22 January 1651, although he had been called in 1650. He, too, was a graduate of Glasgow University. In 1662 Rev Dalrymple was one of hundreds of ministers who left their charges for failing to subscribe to an Act of Parliament of 11 June and Decreet (or court judgement) of Privy Council of 1 October which required all ministers to swear an oath of allegiance to the king, recognising him as head of the church. He was removed from his charge that year, but became an 'indulged' minister at Sorn from 2 September 1669. There, in 1669, he was fined half of his stipend for failing to observe 29 May as the anniversary of the Restoration of Charles II. On 8 April 1669 he was accused of holding conventicles. When Dalrymple died his body was brought back to Auchinleck for burial. An old stone bearing a shield was raised over his grave by Elizabeth Rose. The epitaph is in Latin but has been translated as:

> Here lies a true follower of genuine piety, a favourer of honesty, an honour to religion, a distinguished pastor of Christ, 'who fed the flock' by his example, and also by his words, which flowed like honey; of a peaceful disposition, second to none in integrity; the tomb holds his members, his mind flies beyond the stars.

Rev Alexander Ramsay MA became the new minister sometime soon after. He was a student of St Salvator's College and St Andrews University, graduating in 1665. He was appointed to Greyfriars Kirk in Edinburgh in 1669 but during his term there his manse was broken into by a mob of rioters. It is thought that they disliked the minister for some reason, though it is not known why. The rioters were tried by the Privy Council in 1671. Ramsay seems to have spent very little time at Auchinleck, for we find him appointed to the High Kirk of Edinburgh (St Giles') in 1672 and back to Greyfriars in 1674. He was translated to the Old Kirk of Edinburgh in 1681. There he was suspended in 1686 for expressing fears of popery. His charge was removed from him in 1689 for his Jacobite adherences (he had prayed for King James and the bishops instead of William and Mary). He died in 1702.

COVENANTING STRUGGLE

The seventeenth century saw many years of religious struggle, following Charles I's claim of superiority over the kirk in Scotland. He tried to impose Episcopacy on the Scots, which was seen by the staunch Presbyterians as little less acceptable than Roman Catholicism. The National Covenant was signed in 1638, and a few locals may have participated in the Battle of Mauchline Moor, in 1647, when the extremists defeated those who wished to negotiate with the king.

Things settled down during the years of the Protectorate (1651-1660), but when the crown was restored and Charles II was put on the throne the troubles became worse. He reintroduced Episcopacy and those ministers who would not conform to the change were 'outed' from their charges. Thus in 1662 Rev Andrew Dalrymple was removed from his manse and church and replaced with a 'curate'. He had been cited by Major Cockburn, an officer of the guards, to appear at Ayr. Cockburn seems to have exceeded his instructions, for some of those called were turned out within 24 hours. Andrew Dalrymple was removed from Auchinleck and placed at Dalgain (Sorn).

Andrew Richmond, a Covenanter from Auchinleck parish, was captured after the Battle of Bothwell Bridge in 1679 and held prisoner in Edinburgh. He was placed on board the Crown of London which was taking captive Covenanters to America when it was shipwrecked off the coast of the Orkney islands on 10 December. Richmond was one of 209 drowned in the wreck. A monument at Deerness on the Orkney mainland commemorates the incident.

In 1680 another curate was installed, Rev John Watson (a Master of Arts graduate of Glasgow, where he qualified on 14 July 1670), who remained until the Restoration in 1689. The parishioners were so against Watson's admission that it took the protection of three troops of dragoons to ensure his safety. Having been forced onto the people, he was never respected in his office.

A party of soldiers, many from Perthshire and Caithness, known as the 'Highland Host' was quartered in the district in 1678 to search out non-attenders of the curate's church. Parishioners were expected to attend at least once in three weeks. Rewards were available to those who told the soldiers of people who failed to attend, and the curate regularly supplied a list to them. This was part of the authorities' attempts at quelling the feared rise of the Covenanters in south-west Scotland. These ill-trained troops were quartered on many suspected Covenanters in the area. They were wont to steal and rob items of furniture and domestic goods from their hosts. Much of this was taken back to the Highlands. The damage done to the cause of the authorities was considerable, and the soldiers were withdrawn. From then on, Highlanders were ill-regarded in the south, the memory of their actions lingering long in the local memory. An account of the losses sustained in many parishes across the area was compiled, it being reckoned that £137,499 6s 0d

Scots worth of damage was done in the county of Ayr. The losses in the parishes of Ochiltree and Auchinleck were linked:

> The parishes of Ochiltree and Auchinleck sustained of loss, by quartering two hundred and forty of Perth's foot, from February 5th to February 24th, nineteen days, besides officers, £1,368. By quartering eighty Perthshire gentlemen, allowing but one servant to each, and reckoning both at 24s each day, from February 5th to February 25th, is £1,920. By quartering sixty foot from February 25th to March 5th, eight days, is £144. Exacted of money and plunder by these former, £1,170 14s 4d. Plundered in money and goods by soldiers in passing through, or by those quartered in adjacent places, £432 6s 8d. By quartering two hundred and forty Caithness men one night, £72. Exacted by them of money £68 6s 8d. Three horses taken by Strathmore's men, for recovering of which was expended, £36. Which, besides baggage horses and other horses ridden down by them, extends to £5,211 7s 8d.

In 1678 James Reid, as heritor of the parish, had to sign a bond stating that 'neither they, their wives, bairns, tenants, cottars, and servants. . . . shall go to field conventicles, or harbour or commune with rebels.'

The most significant event concerning the Covenanters to happen in the parish of Auchinleck was the Battle of Airds Moss, which took place on 22 July 1680. A party of government troops, probably on a sortie from the garrison at Sorn Castle, travelled from Cumnock along the road towards Muirkirk, intending to turn round at Tarrioch and return to Sorn. As they journeyed beyond Boghead they spotted a group of Covenanters out on the moor, resting after having eaten. When the Covenanters saw the troops coming towards them their leader, David Hackston of Rathillet in Fife, told them that they would require to stand up and fight, which all were willing to do. Forming up on the moor, Hackston and 23 men were mounted on horseback, with 40 footmen in front. On the morning of the battle Rev Richard Cameron had prophesised his death. He spent the previous night at Meadowhead farm, near to Sorn, home of William Mitchell. Following washing his face and hands he said, 'this is their last washing; I have need to make them clean, for there are many to see them.'

The government troops advanced from the north-east, their estimated strength being 112 men in total, many of which were mounted. They were led by Andrew Bruce of Earlshall, a noted persecutor. Prior to the attack, Cameron said a prayer, asking the Lord to 'spare the green and take the ripe.' At about four o'clock in the afternoon Bruce sent about twenty of his foot dragoons to attack, whereupon Hackston retaliated by sending some of his. Next, both horse platoons charged, the

Covenanters firing the first shots, killing and wounding a number of the enemy. Hackston charged through the government ranks, being pursued by a couple of dragoons. At length his horse became bogged down in the moss and he had to continue on foot. He fell into combat with one David Ramsay, both using small swords. Three dragoons on horse-back attacked Hackston, leaving him wounded, to be taken prisoner later.

Following Hackston's charge, the battle was still even, but the Covenanters on foot were inexperienced and failed to follow the horses quickly enough, staying behind and firing from a distance. James Gray, although he was to die, was regarded by the king's troops as 'the one that mauled them most.' The battle was short, the greater number of dragoons overpowering the Covenanters. Nine were killed, five taken prisoner, the rest managed to make an escape with various wounds, no doubt assisted by the dark clouds and thunderstorm which erupted over the moor. The government forces lost 28 men.

3.6 Cameron's Stone, Airds Moss *(Dane Love)*

The corpses of the Covenanters were buried where they fell – Rev Richard Cameron and his brother Michael, Captain John Fowler, James Gray, John Gemmel, John Hamilton, Robert Dick, Thomas Watson, and Robert Paterson. Richard Cameron's head and hands were severed from his body, as were those of John Fowler, in error for Michael Cameron. These were taken to Edinburgh in order to claim their reward. Bruce was given £500 for his victory; Sir John Cochrane of Ochiltree got ten thousand merks for having informed of the Covenanters' whereabouts.

Of the five men arrested, two were to die soon after of the wounds they had received – William Manuel of Shotts, and John Vallance of Auchinleck, who died in Edinburgh tolbooth. Of the three remaining prisoners, David Hackston was hanged, drawn and quartered on 30 July, his corpse displayed in various towns as a warning to other Covenanters. Archibald Allison of Evandale and John Malcolm of Dalry were both hanged in Edinburgh's Grassmarket on 13 August. James Skene, Andrew Stuart and John Potter were captured later and hanged in Edinburgh on 1 December.

In 1680 a Covenanter was shot at Bello Path whose name has not survived. The deed was the work of Captain John Crichton, born in Donegal in 1648, a distant relation of the Crichtons of Leifnoreis Castle, long-since demolished and replaced by Dumfries House. He had received a commission to join the king's troops in Scotland in 1674 and had fought with them at Airds Moss, where he suffered severe wounds. Captain Crichton was at Leifnoreis Castle when General Drummond, the newly-made Commander-in-Chief of the government troops, sent for him in haste to attend him in Edinburgh. As Crichton passed through Cumnock a friend told him that David Steel and a party of Covenanters were awaiting him at Bello Path. Having just one dragoon and one drummer with him, Crichton ordered the drummer to gallop to the pass and there beat out a dragoon march whilst he and the dragoon made their way by a back route. The Covenanters, assuming from the drumbeat that a strong party of soldiers was approaching, made their escape to Airds Moss. However, as they ran off one was shot, probably by Crichton himself. In the *Memoirs of Captain John Crichton*, he wrote, 'either I or the dragoon (I forget which) shot one of the rebels dead, as he crossed us to get into the moss.'

In 1682 the Earl of Dumfries, heritor of the parish of Old Cumnock, and acting for Auchinleck parish also, required everyone to appear before him, and fined all those who had children baptised by anyone other than the parish incumbents the sum of fifty pounds Scots, arresting and poinding their cattle and goods until the fee was paid. Rev Robert Wodrow, in the *History of the Sufferings of the Church of Scotland*, noted:

> My information bears that Andrew Pathen [Peden], in the parish of Auchinleck, was forced to pay his fifty pounds because he kept his child unbaptised six weeks, though afterwards carried it to the incumbent. Another in the same parish, Henry Stopton, was fined sixty pounds because he refused to tell who baptised his child.

In 1683 William Boswell of Knockroon had, out of curiosity, stopped his horse in order to watch a company of men who were being drawn up in order to march to Bothwell Bridge, scene later of a battle. Having been spotted by someone, he was reported to the dragoons. Their leader, Major Andrew White, came to his house and ordered him to take the test, and also to pay a fine of £1,000 Scots in order to preserve his lands from forfeiture.

The famous 'Prophet of the Covenant', Alexander Peden, minister of the Gospel at New Luce until 1662 when he was ejected, has a number of associations with Auchinleck, particularly at his death. He was born at Auchencloigh in the parish of Sorn, ordained as a minister in 1659, ejected 1662, arrested 1673 and imprisoned on the Bass Rock until 1678 when he was banished to America. However the ship taking him docked at London where he was set free. He spent about five years in Ireland before returning to his native country, but required to sleep rough and in hiding, for fear of imprisonment and certain death. Near the end of his life, being ill from the rough conditions he suffered, he returned to Ayrshire, where his brother Hugh Peden tenanted the farm of Tenshillingside on Auchinleck estate. Tenshillingside was located on the north side of the Dippol Burn, south of the Long

Avenue, hence in the parish of Mauchline. The Prophet spent most of his last days hiding in a cave by the side of the Lugar Water, below Auchinbay, on the Ochiltree side of the river. This was fortunate, for his brother's house was repeatedly searched by soldiers from the garrison at Sorn Castle.

Two days before his death, Peden sensed the end was near and came to the farmhouse. His sister-in-law warned him that the enemy may come at any time, but Peden replied that he had not long to live. Within three hours the soldiers arrived again and searched the house, barn and cave, but were unable to find his hiding place. He died on 26 January 1686. His friends took the body and buried it in the parish kirkyard by night. After 40 days, when Lieutenant Murray and the soldiers found out where Peden was buried, they went to the churchyard and disinterred the body. Despite the protestations of David Boswell, they took it the two miles to Cumnock where they proposed to string it up on the gallows. However, Lady Dumfries intervened, and her husband told Murray, leader of the dragoons, that 'the gibbet was erected for malefactors and murderers, and not for such men as Peden'. The soldiers dug a hole at the gallows foot and buried Peden there 'out of contempt', according to the gravestone. Previously three other Covenanters, Thomas Richard, David Dun and Simon Paterson, had been buried at the same spot.

At the time of Peden's disinterment, the soldiers burst open the coffin and threw his funeral shroud over an adjacent bush. The wind blew this further, landing it on an old plane tree by the kirkyard dike, and it is said the branch on which the shroud hung never bore leaves again. The tree blew down in a storm sometime in the nineteenth century.

Another skirmish took place between Government soldiers and the local Covenanters in Auchinleck parish. Rev David Houston, an Irish-based minister who had preached at a number of conventicles in Scotland, had returned across the North Channel. Houston was born near Paisley in 1633 and travelled to Ulster around 1660. He is known to have preached to the Route Presbytery in north Antrim. He appears to have been a fiery preacher, often finding himself in trouble with the church authorities in Ireland. On 27 February 1672 he was suspended by the Irish presbytery. It is thought that he returned to Scotland between 1675-79 and was actively involved in the Battle of Bothwell Bridge. He survived, and continued to preach at conventicles in both Ireland and Scotland.

Houston was wanted by the Scots parliament for his Covenanting adherences He was arrested in Ireland and held prisoner in Dublin in January 1688 prior to transportation to Edinburgh. The Covenanters feared that he would be hanged in the capital, so made arrangements to ambush the official party as it took him there. The first plan did not materialise, however, for the soldiers did not arrive at the expected time. The second plan was more successful. Having crossed from Ireland and made their way up through Ayrshire, the soldiers, with Houston, halted for the night at an inn in Cumnock known as the Blue Tower, formerly situated in Tower

Street, hence the street-name. Word leaked that Houston was being held there, so the local Covenanters made arrangements for his rescue. Early in the morning they hid at Bello Path, the narrow defile in the rocks at the east end of Lugar, and awaited the government soldiers. When the dragoons arrived, the Covenanters opened fire, killing several soldiers and 'desperately wounding' others, according to a proclamation of 22 June 1688. Rev David Houston, mounted on a horse with his feet tied beneath its underbelly, was unable to escape, and when his horse bolted he turned off the saddle, his head hitting the roadway below, resulting in concussion. According to Michael Shields' *Faithful Contendings*, he was thereafter discovered to be 'short in his naturals.'

3.7 Memorial marking Covenanter skirmish at Bello Path *(Dane Love)*

Rev David Houston managed to escape to Ireland where he lived for a time in Newtownards. He was present at the Siege of Derry. From 1692 until 1696 Houston lived at Armoy in Antrim. He died in 1696 and was interred at Connor in Antrim. A bishop wrote to the Lord Lieutenant of Ireland in 1694, describing Houston as a 'clergyman that preached up the Solemn League and Covenant, accusing the people of Scotland for not sticking to their League, and having a congregation of 500 resolute fellows that adhere to him.'

The only Covenanter to suffer at Bello Path was John MacGeachan, farmer in Meikle Auchingibbert, parish of Old Cumnock. He was wounded by a soldier's bullet, but managed to crawl towards home, reaching the row of three houses called Stonepark. According to legend, the occupants of the cottages refused to help him, for fear of reprisals, so MacGeachan is said to have placed a curse on their grounds, so that they would grow no crops again. At length he was found by members of his family, but they could not take him to the farmhouse, for fear of a search. Instead they placed him in a turf-built sheep cot where he lay for three weeks, tended by his family, until he died. He was buried at the same spot, where a memorial stone was erected in 1728, probably by Robert Paterson, the 'Old Mortality' of Sir Walter Scott. A larger memorial was raised over the grave in 1836.

Immediately following the incident at Bello Path, the government troops began searching the district for Covenanters who had appeared there. According to tradition they arrived at Barglachan farm where they found a young boy herding the cattle. The soldiers asked him if he knew of any Covenanters hiding in the area, but the boy refused to speak. The soldiers threatened him with torture, but still the boy refused to say anything, so they left him where he was and continued their searches elsewhere. Whether the boy was hiding something is unknown, but tradition states that a Covenanter hid in the barn on the farm at least once, for it is said that there was a Covenanter's mark carved on a stone there, no longer visible.

Rev David Houston held conventicles at a number of locations in the southwest. At one of these, held near Polbaith, Kilmarnock, on 16 January 1687, a number of Covenanters from the Auchinleck, Sorn and Ochiltree areas were captured by the dragoons and sent to prison. One of these was Hugh Gibson, tenant in Darnconner farm, who may have had his child baptised at the conventicle. The soldiers made their way to his house and seized him there. Apparently he had a number of illegal arms, including a gun and gunpowder. He also had in his possession a number of books which were regarded as being seditious, and he was caught trying to dispose of them when the soldiers arrived. He was taken to Ayr for trial, which took place before Captain Douglas on 21 January 1687. The charge read:

> Heuge Gibson in Dargoner, Watersyde's tenant in the parish of Auchenfleck, baptised tuo children with the indulged minister of the Sorn; refuises to tell where his youngest child was baptised. There was a gune and halfe a pund of pounder found in his house; he sayes the gune was his goodfathers; his wyfe gott pairt of the pouder from the dragounes for rubbing his cattell; these rebelliouse books were found betuixt his house and his cottars throune out of ane window.

The case appears to have been un-proven, and we next find him appearing before the Earl of Linlithgow and Foulis of Colinton in Edinburgh courthouse. There the charge laid before him was that:

Hewgh Gibsone in the paroch of Auchinleck, in Watersyde's land, depones he wes not at any of these conventicles, and never wes in any armes against the King; lives regularlie, and swears he will never be in armes against him; owns his authoritie and prayes heartily for him, his long life and prosperous government; and depones he cannot write.

Gibson appears to have been set free thereafter.

With the Glorious Revolution in late 1689, and the replacement of King Charles with William and Mary, Presbyterianism was again recognised as the established religion of Scotland. The curates, who had held their office from the king, were quickly removed from their charges, often by 'rabbling', or forcibly removed. Rev John Watson was pushed from the church into the burial ground by 90 armed men, his gown torn from him, and discharged to preach there anymore. At his death, which occurred between 27 March 1696 and 6 November 1697, his books were valued at £40 Scots.

A minister, Rev John Campbell, served in the church for a short time from 1687 until 1688. He had graduated Master of Arts at Glasgow in 1661 and was ordained on 4 February, 1679. He was allowed to preach under the Toleration Act, but he died in November 1688, aged about 47. He was married, and a daughter married Adam Stillie of Changue.

CHAPTER FOUR

PLANNED VILLAGE & RURAL ADVANCEMENT (1689-1840)

PLANNED VILLAGE

During the eighteenth and nineteenth centuries (from about 1735 to 1850), landowners throughout Scotland established new 'planned villages' on their estates, sometimes replacing old villages, in other cases (like Catrine) creating new villages in what had been rural areas. Two main factors led to the founding of planned villages, the first that the population of the country was rising, the second that agricultural practices were changing, resulting in fewer labourers being required on the land. These men were rehoused in the new settlements, where new trades such as weaving, fishing and spinning were established.

Auchinleck falls into the first of the above categories, for the village replaced the old kirk town, which would have been a fairly irregular huddle of cottages round the church. It may be that the old name of the village, Keithstoun, was lost at this time, the church being the parish church of Auchinleck, but being located in the village of Keithstoun. When the new planned village was laid out it was perhaps then given the name Auchinleck and Keithstoun dropped. This would also explain the old tradition that half the village was in the Burgh of Keithstoun, whilst half was not. The old burgh would have occupied ground round the church and Boswell crossroads, whereas the planned village, because of its linear nature, extended north across the little Cottertax Burn, known locally as the Midge Burn, which marked the boundary, to the bend of Upper Main Street. The Cottertax Burn formerly crossed the road at the former Clydesdale Bank, the depression there surviving from that time.

The formation of the planned village of Auchinleck dates to around 1756, a period of considerable new building in the parish, when Alexander Boswell, Lord Auchinleck, restored the church, added the Boswell vault, built the present Auchinleck House, and erected a new parish manse. The layout he adopted for the village was typical of planned villages of the period, a long main street with a short transverse street forming a Roman cross. Lord Auchinleck would have had experience of planned villages, having visited a number on his journeys, and several of his fellow lords in Edinburgh had, or were to, create villages of their own.

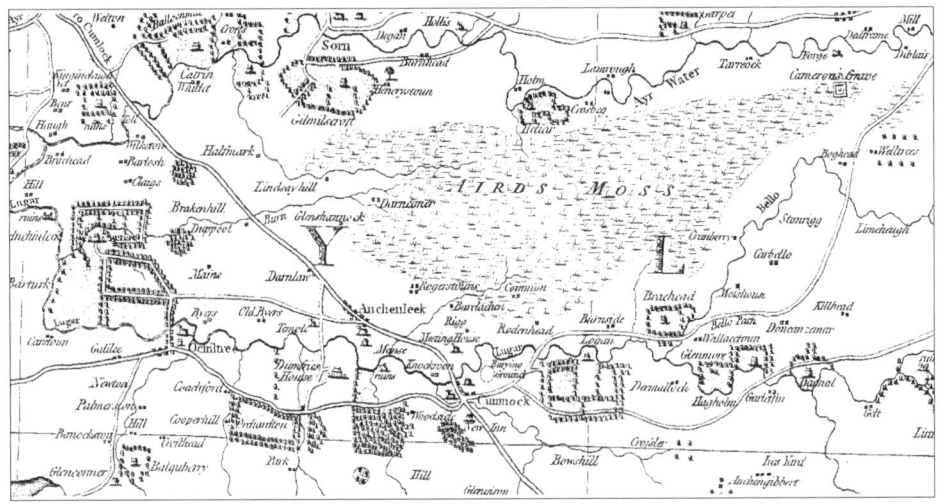
4.1 Auchinleck Parish from Armstrong's Map of Ayrshire (1775)

At Auchinleck, the Main Street was formed 800 yards long, on mainly virgin ground, the original main road probably travelling from around Bridgend Mill past the old church to Merlinhill and then direct to Darnlaw. At a point 167 yards from the south-eastern end the transept arm of the cross was formed (Churchhill and Coal Road), this being 285 yards long in total. Feus were laid out along both sides of the Main Street, about twenty yards wide at the street, going back 40 yards to the foot of the gardens. Only the north side of Churchhill was laid in feus, Coal Road on both, though the southern side extended further.

Lord Auchinleck encouraged all sorts of tradesmen and labourers to settle in his new village, promoting weaving, shoemaking, carpentry and other trades. Not all feus were filled at the onset, some took many years to lease, for by 1860 there were still a few vacant sites in Boswell's plan. The Boswell Arms feu was not filled until Martinmas 1766, when Lord Auchinleck sold a 999 year lease to John Kay, shoemaker. He built part of the present building then, though the distinctive corner turret was not added until 1902.

The house at the corner of Main Street with Churchhill was originally erected in 1765 when a 999-year lease was granted. Similarly, a 999-year lease was issued on a property in Main Street in 1770, latterly becoming a slaughterhouse and flesher's home.

From the Session Records of the parish we find a reference to Lord Auchinleck's feu-granting:

> Oct 26, 1756. The minister produced an extract which he took from one of the feus or long leases, granted by Lord Auchinleck to the people who are building houses on the public roadside to Mauchline,

and we are informed that the other tacks now granted are in the same terms: 'And it is provided notwithstanding, power is granted to the said David Maul, the tenant, to assign or subsett, yet it shall not be in his power, or in the power of his foresaids, to bring in any person to live upon the premises, except by the previous consent of the said Alexander Boswell (Lord Auchinleck), his heirs, or the kirk session of Auchinleck. Likewise, if any person so brought in shall thereafter turn out a bad neighbour or vicious person, he (said David and his foresaids), on the same being declared by the kirk session aforesaid forty days before Whitsunday, is hereby bound to remove him or her at the first Whitsunday thereafter; and also he and said foresaids shall be bound and obliged to free and relieve the parish of Auchinleck of the burden of maintaining any person or persons to whom they shall subset the foresaid subjects, or any part thereof, the which relief is hereby declared to be a burden upon this present right. '

These stipulations were agreed to on pain of 'irritating' the lease, both parties having to agree to them under a penalty of ten pounds.

A few properties were older than the planned village, but were to be incorporated within it. Dunbar Cottage, in Mauchline Road, was erected in 1725 and was held on a 999-year lease. In 1921 it was partially thatched and partially slated.

In 1781 Lord Auchinleck changed the terms of the feus granted from that year onward. Previously, feus had been granted for 99 years, but under the new situation, feus were being granted for 999 years. James Boswell carried out some discussions with prospective feuars and leaseholders in the village in October 1778. The leases could only be for 99 years, but from 8 March 1781, Lord Auchinleck and James Boswell extended the lease period to 999 years. In 1778 a new cottage was erected in Kirkland Brae, at that time known as Church Street, by Andrew Morton, for which James Boswell allocated timber.

Health in the village and parish varied as various illnesses came and went. Smallpox caused a number of deaths in the eighteenth century, according to the burial records of the kirk, in 1782 at least thirteen children died of smallpox alone.

From 1753-54 the old parish church received its final alterations, when Lord Auchinleck had the nave re-roofed and a new mausoleum erected alongside. Previously the Boswell vault below the church floor (carved into the solid rock) had been reached by stairs from the church itself, but with the construction of the new mausoleum this means of access was closed off. The mausoleum was a particularly grand, yet robust, Scots classical building, with rusticated quoins, vaulted roof, and the Boswell arms carved in the north wall. Its architect is unknown, but was most probably the work of the same person who designed

Auchinleck House. Behind the large oak door one enters a room in which stairs descend to the old vault. Behind stone-slabs are chambers in which lie the corpses of the Boswells, without coffins, their initials written on the slabs. In the upper room is a small section with coffins of later Boswells, and various tablets commemorate the family.

In 1792, just before his death, Rev John Dun contributed a chapter to Sir John Sinclair's *Statistical Account of Scotland*. He noted that the parish and village population had been on the decline since at least 1755, the inhabitants leaving to find work either at the Muirkirk Iron and Coal Tar Works, or, to a greater extent, to the newly-established cotton works at Catrine, which offered good wages and where work was plentiful. The parish population in 1791 was 775, of which 380 resided in the village, a parish decrease of 112 since 1755. In 1801 the first Census was taken across the country; the population in Auchinleck parish was found to be 1,214.

In the village the largest occupation was in weaving, of which there were fifteen weavers, and also a stocking-weaver. There were eight shoemakers, six masons, five shopkeepers, four smiths, three millers, two coopers, two hawkers, one baker, one officer of the excise, and one fiddler. From tombstone inscriptions we can get names for some of these people, like the exciseman, William Gill (1726-1793), William Smith, miller in Bridgend Mill, and James Wilson, blacksmith, (1752-1832).

4.2 Bridgend Mill *(Author's Collection)*

Wages were noted as being £7 for a male servant per annum in 1792 (an increase of £3 since 1752), £5 for a female servant (risen from £1 13s 4d). Labourers earned one shilling (up four-pence), masons 2 shillings and sixpence per week (up from one shilling). As for commodities, eggs had risen from one penny for thirteen to four-pence a dozen; mutton from two pence to four and a half pence per pound; hens from four-pence to one shilling a piece. Beef cost five-pence per pound, veal four and a halfpence and lamb three-pence.

Around 1825 unemployment was rife in the village, with weavers on the verge of starvation. A special meeting of the heritors was held to try to work out a method of dealing with the problem. They ascertained that the average weaver's wage at the time was five shillings per week. It was decided to raise a subscription among those who could afford it, which realised £130. This was added to £80 that was already in the bank and it was agreed to purchase yarn. This was given to every weaver described as a 'decent man' to keep him busy, and he was paid a fair wage for the task. The cloth produced was kept in a central loft and was sold the following year when times had improved.

Around 1826 a new gravedigger was appointed in Auchinleck, being paid £1 per annum, with an additional payment of £1 if he managed to prevent unruly children from breaking the glass windows of the church.

A few incidents that occurred in the parish have been recorded, for example, in January 1803 a resident of the parish surnamed Peden was found dead on the road from Kilmarnock to Eaglesham.

According to the *New Statistical Account*, written in 1837, there were 329 families in the parish, 98 of which were chiefly employed in agriculture, plus 122 in various trades or manufacturing work. Around 29 burials took place each year, thirteen marriages and around 36 births. There had been twelve illegitimate births over the previous three years.

LANDOWNERS
The seventh Boswell of Auchinleck, James, was an eminent lawyer and member of the Faculty of Advocates. In 1733 he acted as one of the two arbiters in the case between the Burgh of Ayr and Sir John Kennedy of Culzean over who had the rights of fishing on the lower River Doon. Boswell studied at Leyden in Holland, at that time a noted university for students of law. He was reported by his son to have a 'melancholic turn', but was never troubled with this during session time, being devoted to his work. At the vacation he had so few hobbies that he suffered from depression. He was married on 26 March 1704 to Lady Elizabeth Bruce, daughter of Alexander, 2nd Earl of Kincardine, by whom he had two sons and a daughter - Alexander, John and Veronica. Alexander succeeded; John was a doctor, graduating from Edinburgh University, in which city he became President of the Royal College of Surgeons; Veronica married David Montgomerie of Lainshaw. James Boswell,

7th of Auchinleck, revived some of the family fortunes, and repurchased most of the lands which his predecessors had sold, as well as some new lands. He died on 21 April 1749.

ALEXANDER BOSWELL - LORD AUCHINLECK (VIII)

Alexander Boswell succeeded to the estate of Auchinleck in 1749, becoming the eighth Boswell laird. He was born on 1 April 1706 and in his youth was described as a 'sound scholar'. He was also regarded as a 'respectable and useful country gentleman,' and was educated for the bar at Leyden University in Holland, where he graduated on 29 December 1727. He was admitted a member of the Faculty of Advocates exactly two years later.

Alexander Boswell married Euphemia Erskine, daughter of Lieutenant-Colonel John Erskine of Alva, grandson of the Earl of Mar, but she died on 11 January 1766. Two silver communion cups were gifted to the parish church at this time, in Lady Boswell's memory.

4.3 Auchinleck House in 2015 *(Dane Love)*

Alexander and Euphemia Boswell had three sons – James, the diarist, John Boswell, who served as an officer in the army, and David Boswell, who was a merchant in Valencia, Spain, for ten years. An elder daughter, Euphemia, died in 1740, and a fourth son died at birth in 1754.

Whilst in Spain, David Boswell adopted the name Thomas Boswell, the Spaniards regarding David as a Jewish name. David Boswell returned to Britain and was employed in the Navy Office, being for twenty years head of the Prize department. He was able to purchase the estate of Crawley Grange, in Buckinghamshire, and established a Boswell family there. David Boswell was married to Anne Catherine Green, daughter of Colonel Green, who was killed at the Battle of Minden, and sister of Sir Charles Green, Baronet. They had one son, Thomas Alexander Boswell of Crawley Grange.

In 1748 Boswell was appointed sheriff-depute of Wigtownshire, a position he resigned in 1750. Up until his appointment the sheriffdom was a hereditary position, held by the Agnews of Lochnaw. That year he represented the Burgh of Ayr in the General Assembly and in 1754 had the right of burgess of the town conferred on him.

In 1732 Alexander was admitted a burgess of Prestwick, 'for good services done and to be done.' His estate at the time brought in around £1,000 per annum, and in addition to this he earned around £900 as a judge. Although he lived in comfort, his income was not huge by landowner standards.

In 1744 he presented the Advocates Library in Edinburgh with a fourteenth century illuminated manuscript. He appears to have acquired this around 1740, possibly saving it from being thrown out by a professor at the University of Aberdeen. The manuscript, which is one of the most important illuminated documents of its type, written in London around 1340, became known as the Auchinleck Manuscript, and is now possessed by the National Library of Scotland.

Following the resignation of David Erskine, Lord Dun, his position as a lord of session was filled by Boswell, taking his seat on 15 February 1754, with the title Lord Auchinleck. On 22 July 1755 he was appointed a Senator of the College of Justiciary and Lord Justiciary, in place of Hew Dalrymple, Lord Drummore. This second position he resigned in 1780 when his health began to fail, but he retained his ordinary lordship of session until his death.

Lord Auchinleck was married a second time, on the same day as the wedding of his eldest son, James, 25 November 1769. He married his full cousin, Elizabeth, daughter of John Boswell of Balmuto. In 1782 Lord Auchinleck purchased a new house in Edinburgh's New Town, which he left to his second wife in life-rent, much to the displeasure of James.

Boswell spent most of his time in Edinburgh, dealing with the matters of court. However, he was able to use his wages to good effect back at Auchinleck, for he was responsible for making the most significant improvements to the property. Samuel Johnson was to write that, although Lord Auchinleck was 'not wholly at leisure for domestick business or pleasure, has yet found time to make improvements in his patrimony. He has built a fine house of hewn stone, very stately, and durable, and has advanced the value of his lands with great tenderness to his tenants.'

He built up a magnificent library at his home, comprising many old and rare volumes which 'conferred on the Auchinleck library a fame that few other private collections have acquired'. He wrote a book of *Observations on the Election Law of Scotland*, not published until 1825.

It is recorded that Lord Auchinleck and his heir, James, did not see eye-to-eye on many occasions. Sir Walter Scott makes a number of references to the situation in his writings, which also give a flavour of his character:

> Old Lord Auchinleck was an able lawyer, a good scholar, after the manner of Scotland, and highly valued his own advantages as a man of good estate and ancient family; and, moreover, he was a strict Presbyterian and Whig of the old Scottish cast. This did not prevent his being a terribly proud aristocrat; and great was the contempt he entertained and expressed for his son James, for the nature of his friendship, and the character of the personages of whom he was engoue one after another. 'There's nae hope for Jamie, mon,' he said to a friend. 'Jamies is gane clean gyte. What do you think, mon? He's done wi' Paoli – he's off wi' the land-louping scoundrel of a Corsican; and whose tail do you think he has pinned himself to now, mon.' Here the old Judge summoned up a sneer of most sovereign contempt. 'A dominie, mon – an auld dominie! He keeped a schule , and caud it an academy.' Probably if this had been reported to Johnson, he would have felt it most galling, for he never much liked to think of that period of his life; it would have aggravated his dislike of Lord Auchinleck's Whiggery and Presbyterianism.
>
> It may be surmised how far Lord Auchinleck, such as he is here described, was likely to suit a high Tory and Episcopalian like Johnson. As they approached Auchinleck, Boswell conjured Johnson by all the ties of regard, and in requital of the services he had rendered him upon his tour, that he would spare two subjects in tenderness to his father's prejudices; the first related to Sir John Pringle, President of the Royal Society, about whom there was then some dispute current; the second concerned the general question of Whig and Tory. Sir John Pringle, as Boswell says, escaped, but the controversy between Tory and Covenanter raged with great fury, and ended in Johnson's pressing upon the old Judge the question, what good Cromwell, of whom he had said something derogatory, had ever done to his country? – when, after being much tortured, Lord Auchinleck at last spoke out, 'God! Doctor, he gart kings ken that they had a lith in their neck' – he taught kings they had a joint in their necks. Jamie then set to mediating between his father and the philosopher, and availing himself of the Judge's sense of hospitality, which was punctilious, reduced the debate to more order.

Lord Auchinleck died at his house in Edinburgh on Friday 30 August 1782. The minister at Auchinleck recorded the death in the local records:

> August 31st: Died at Edinburgh of a complaint in the bladder and kidneys, Alexander Boswell Esq., Lord Auchinleck, one of the Senators in the College of Justice in the seventy seventh year of his age. Was with great reputation for the space of twenty seven years, an advocate, and afterwards for the space of twenty eight years one of the Lords of Session, and for [no numbers] years a Lord of Justiciary.

Lord Auchinleck's funeral was probably one of the largest seen in the parish, the corpse brought back from the capital for burial in the mausoleum which he had previously erected. Two days of funeral teas were supplied to well-wishers. The funeral cost almost £300. The parish schoolmaster, William Halbert, wrote an *Essay towards a Character of Lord Auchinleck* at his death, which contains the lines:

> Employed with indefatigable pains,
> In every numerous and important scenes,
> And as his fame for justice was well known,
> His clemency no less conspicuous shone:
> Reliever of the needful and opprest,
> The generous benefactor of distrest,
> Ready to hear and rectify a wrong,
> To re-establish harmony among
> Contending friends, or such as disagreed,
> And of his interposing aid had need;
> Successfully he laboured much and long,
> As healer of the breaches us among.
> And still from jarring order brought about,
> Carefull searching unknown causes out.
> A name of veneration and respect,
> Of honour and esteem - Lord Auchinleck.
>
> For every Sovereign virtue much renowned,
> Of Judgement steady, and in wisdom sound.
> Reliever of the needful and oppressed,
> The gen'rous benefactor of distrest.
> And ready still with sympathizing grace,
> To wipe the tear from every mourning face.
> The honest councillor as all will own,
> And most indulgent landlord ever known,

> And let the undissembled voice of fame,
> To distant ages celebrate his name:
> A name of veneration and respect,
> Of honour and esteem – Lord Auchinleck.

With the estate proving to be reasonably profitable, and Alexander Boswell holding a position in the College of Justice as Lord Auchinleck, it was decided that a new house be built to replace the old tower house, or Place of Auchinleck. Exact dates for the building cannot be given, but it was certainly erected sometime between 1750 and 1760, perhaps around 1754 when Alexander Boswell was created Lord Auchinleck. Likewise the architect is not known, but James MacAulay, in *The Classical Country House in Scotland*, attributes it to John and Robert Adam, who had just started work at Dumfries House for Lord Dumfries. John Adam had been a business associate of a relative of Lord Auchinleck's. In 1753 it is known from Lord Auchinleck's diaries that he met Lord Bute at Leifnorris Castle 'where politicks and House building made the subject of conversation at a plentiful dinner.' A few tantalising glimpses into the construction of the house have come to light, such as the discharge wages slip of 1 November 1760 to Edinburgh square-wright, John Johnston. Some think that he may have designed the building.

Other expenses throughout the period 1755-1760 indicate the most likely time of construction, with payments being made for nails, lime, steel, lead and timber. The peak in expenses occurs from 1758-60, and the first window tax had to be paid for the house in 1760, there being 31 windows liable. At the end of May 1762 the bill for Easdale slates was settled by Lord Auchinleck with James Bowie, slater in Ayr, for 18,000 slates at £1 9s 0d per thousand.

he flanking pavilions and wings were not added for another decade or so. James Boswell was in Europe at the time, and Lord Auchinleck tried to get him interested in their design. In 1765 he wrote to James asking his thoughts. The wings were completed in 1773-4, the different stone indicative of a different period of building. In August 1775 James refers to the towers as being 'new whitened', perhaps an attempt at toning down the red sandstone to make it blend more with the pale sandstone of the house.

Auchinleck House was not as grand as Lord Dumfries's new home. It consists of a single rectangular block about 95 feet by 38 feet, whereas Dumfries House's centre block measures 95 feet by 66 feet and has two sizeable wings also. More decorative than Dumfries, Auchinleck rises to three storeys, a grand staircase leading to the principal rooms on the first floor. The central three bays at the front, four at the rear, stand proud, the front adorned with Corinthian pilasters, arched and triangular pediments over the door and windows. The main pediment is decorated with carvings in stone, including trumpets, maces, foliage and scrolls, on the entablature an inscription from Horace's *Epistle to Bullatium*, Epistle IX, 29-30:

> Quod petis, hic est;
> Est Ulubris, animus si te non deficit aequus.

This was translated as 'What thou seekest is here, even at Ulubrae (or Auchinleck) if contentment do not fail thee.' At eaves level is a balustrade, with urns at the principal corners.

Internally the house was every bit as grand, with a long library on the second floor, four windows looking down to the old castle. Five bedrooms occupy the same floor, the principal bedroom located on the first floor, along with the Dining Room and Morning Room. The service rooms were on the ground floor. The house had one of the first indoor sanitation systems in the country. According to A. Allardyce, in *Scotland and Scotsmen in the Eighteenth Century*, the house was built 'so slowly and prudently that [Lord Auchinleck] hardly felt the expense.' It is thought to have cost him the equivalent of one year's wages. The roof was slated in 1758, the slates being delivered from Ayr, and the building was probably completed internally in 1759. Adjoining the house are walls hiding the service court, linking the main block to two pavilions, adorned with towers and urns. Two similar pavilions exist at the rear.

JAMES BOSWELL (IX)

The most famous son of the parish was James Boswell, born on 29 October 1740 at Edinburgh, son of Alexander, Lord Auchinleck. It is likely that his place of birth was Blair's Land, in Parliament Close. He was educated at various places, for a time by John Dun, later to be the parish minister, from 1746 to 1749 at James Mundell's School in Edinburgh, and from 1753 at Edinburgh University. He spent time studying civil law, as was his father's wish, but he personally wanted to follow a military career. James was troubled with illness and melancholia all of his life, and spent a number of months recuperating at the spa town of Moffat. On 14 August 1759 Boswell was admitted as a freemason in the Canongate Kilwinning Lodge in Edinburgh. Later the same year Boswell enrolled at Glasgow University, and it was also the year of publication of his first book, *A View of the Edinburgh Theatre*. His earliest known published work was a poem entitled October, published in *The Scots' Magazine* in August

4.4 James Boswell (Author's Collection)

1758. His interest in literature began to grow, as did his involvement with actresses and prostitutes. His father often quarrelled with him, not least when James determined to become a Roman Catholic priest. In March 1760 he ran away to London where he converted to Roman Catholicism. Lord Eglinton, a family friend, however, persuaded him to become a libertine and he returned to the Presbyterian faith. He also tried to join the Guards in London in 1762, but failed to receive a commission.

Returning to Auchinleck in June, Boswell resumed his studies and passed out in Civil Law from Edinburgh in July 1762. His first journal, *Harvest Jaunt*, was issued in the autumn of 1762, the first of many journals and diaries for which he is known to this day.

In November 1762 Boswell returned to London, this time with his father's permission. He revelled in the life of the city, associating with literary and thespian types, and resorting to prostitutes for more earthly pleasures. He became friendly with the Duke of York and with the father of Percy Shelley.

Boswell longed to meet Doctor Samuel Johnson, and did so firstly on 16 May 1763 at the bookshop of Tom Davies in Russell Street. Johnson took a liking to the burly Scot, inviting him to his house and discussing various books. Boswell continued to write his journals, encouraged by Johnson, and wrote down virtually everything Johnson said in conversation. For this Boswell seems to have had a particularly good retentive memory.

From August 1763 to June 1764 Boswell studied civil law at Uttrecht in Holland, mainly to appease his father who had threatened to disinherit him following his antics in London. From June 1764 until December he went on tour through Germany and Switzerland. In December Boswell visited Jean-Jacques Rousseau and Francois-Marie Arouet de Voltaire in Switzerland, managing to gate-crash the celebrated writers. His father then granted permission for Boswell to extend his tour to include Italy, followed by Corsica and France. Rousseau gave him a letter of introduction to General Pasquale Paoli, hero and governor of Corsica. An *Account of Corsica: the Journal of a Tour to that Island; and Memoirs of Pascal Paoli* was written and published on 18 February 1768, Boswell selling the rights for one hundred guineas. The book was a considerable success, being translated into several languages. On his return to Scotland he spent some time in London, basking in the glory his book had brought him.

Boswell returned to Britain in 1766 and was admitted as an advocate . It was during this time that he published *Dorando, a Spanish Tale*, in 1767. Written anonymously, it was based on a topical case of the time, which was still *sub judice*. In 1773 he was elected to membership of Johnson's literary club. From 1777-83 he contributed a series of monthly articles to the *London Magazine*, under the pseudonym 'The Hypochondriack'.

4.5 James Boswell *(Author's Collection)*

James Boswell married his cousin, Margaret Montgomerie of Lainshaw, on 25 November 1769, after a three month engagement. He failed to settle down, returning alone to London to cultivate Johnson's friendship. Throughout his life he dallied with numerous prostitutes and mistresses. The list is quite extensive, from common whores to Rousseau's mistress, Therese Le Vasseur.

Although James and Margaret's marriage was sometimes difficult, due to Boswell's philandering, they had five surviving children. These were Alexander (born 9 October 1775), who succeeded him to the estate of Auchinleck, James (born 15 September 1778), Elizabeth (born 1780), Euphemia (born 20 May 1774) and Veronica (born 15 March 1773). A sixth child, David (born 15 November 1776), died in March 1777.

Doctor Johnson was eventually persuaded to come to Scotland where he and Boswell made their tour to the Hebrides in 1773. Johnson wrote his account of the travels in *A Journey to the Western Isles of Scotland*, published in 1775. This tour took Boswell and Johnson from Edinburgh up the east coast of Scotland and across country to Inverness, from where they travelled westwards to the islands of Skye, Mull, Coll and thence back to the mainland. They journeyed south through Dumbarton and to Auchinleck, where they stopped for a few days.

Doctor Samuel Johnson, the famous English author and dictionary-compiler, visited Auchinleck House from Tuesday, 2 November, to Monday, 8 November, 1773, on his and Boswell's return journey from their highland tour. Boswell feared the outcome of the meeting of his father with Johnson, the former a Whig and Presbyterian, the latter a Tory and Episcopalian, but no great disagreement arose, both men managing to converse intelligently by avoiding three subjects, 'Whiggism, Presbyterianism and Sir John Pringle.' Pringle was both a friend of Boswell and his father, and had helped to settle the many differences between father and son. It being November, it not unexpectedly rained all the first day, so Johnson passed the time in Lord Auchinleck's library. The weather on Wednesday was just as bad, but the day was passed in the library and with visits from local lairds. On Thursday Boswell and Johnson clambered among the ruins of the old Place of Auchinleck and ancient castle. Boswell told Johnson that he would erect a monument here to him if he survived him, only to be told by the doctor that he hoped to see his grandchildren! Rev John Dun dined at Auchinleck that night, and on Friday Boswell and Johnson dined at Dun's manse.

The feared 'collision' between Johnson and Lord Auchinleck took place on Saturday, when they hotly debated Whiggism, Presbyterianism, Toryism and Episcopacy. Lord Auchinleck nick-named Johnson 'Ursa Major', or the Great Bear, and is said to have dismissed him on one occasion by calling him an 'Auld Dominie that kept a schule and ca'd it an Academy.' On Sunday both Boswell and his father went to church, but Johnson could not be persuaded to join them. The next day they parted, when Boswell and Johnson left for Edinburgh. In his *A Journey to the Western Isles*, Doctor Johnson wrote warmly of Auchinleck, but noted that it was 'incommoded by very frequent rain'. Nevertheless, he praised the laird's work in planting trees and advancing 'the value of his lands with great tenderness to his tenants.' However, he 'was less delighted with the elegance of the modern mansion, than with the sullen dignity of the old castle.'

Boswell's account of the journey, *Journal of a Tour to the Hebrides*, was published in 1786, after Johnson's death, the first print-run of 1,500 selling out within a fortnight.

In the same year as the *Journal* was published, Boswell became a Barrister-at-Law of the Inner Temple, London. From 1788-90 he held the position of Recorder of Carlisle.

Lord Auchinleck died in 1782 whereupon James Boswell became the 9th Laird. Though absent for much of the time, he was seen as a reasonable, if not good, landowner, who wished the best for his tenants. The estate brought in £1,600 per year, but unfortunately his business acumen was not of the best and he was forced to sell off parts of his inheritance. In 1788 he sold Templand Wood for £650 to repay a debt. Prior to his death, Lord Auchinleck had bailed James out on more than one occasion, settling a debt of £1,000 in 1775. In 1780 Boswell complained that he couldn't support his family on his father's allowance of £300 per year, and was frightened to tell his father that he owed his in-laws over £700. However, in 1785 he bought the farm of Willockshill in Mauchline parish, adjoining the estate to the north.

Doctor Johnson died on 13 December 1784, creating a void in Boswell's life. However, for over six years he filled the gap with Johnsonia, collecting information for a biography of the lexicographer. This was to be Boswell's greatest work, and *Life of Johnson* was described by Thomas, 1st Lord MacAulay, as the best biography ever written, and by Thomas Carlyle as 'Beyond any other product of the eighteenth century.' Published in two volumes on 16 May 1791, by 22 August later that year the Life had sold 1,200 out of a print run of 1,700. His fame grew, much to Boswell's relief, for in 1785 Hester Piozzi had published *Anecdotes of the Late Samuel Johnson* and Sir John Hawkins' *Life of Samuel Johnson* appeared in 1787. The biography is still in print today and is regarded as a masterpiece.

At the time of publication Boswell was again in debt. He had bought Knockroon estate in October 1790 from John Boswell for £2,500, but still owed £1,000 on it, as well as sums of £300 to Edward Dilly, £200 to William Temple and £100 to John Wilkes, friends of his. He had thought of selling the rights of the Life for 'a cool thousand,' but had been persuaded against it. This was fortunate, for the first edition alone earned him £1,550. Estate profits at the time were £900 per annum.

Boswell's bouts of melancholia, his drinking, and his trips to London continued but in 1793, following a mugging whilst in a state of intoxication, he resolved to be a sober man. Whilst in London in the spring of 1795 he took ill at the Literary Club and had to return to his London house, in Great Portland Street. There he died on 19 May, at the age of 54. His corpse was brought back to Scotland and interred in the family vault at Auchinleck.

That Boswell thought kindly of his tenants is shown through his writings. On succeeding to the estate he spent some time visiting all the farms leased from him, making himself acquainted with the farmers and their problems. An example was John Colville, a retired servant on the estate, who was placed by Boswell 'in a good house' at Tenshillingside, in his 89th year. 'He was lying in bed and conversed very distinctly, and told me it was the best house he had ever been in.' Boswell's will, dated 28 May 1785, is noted for its references to ensure the kind treatment of the tenancy.

Margaret Boswell had died on 4 June 1789, following a short illness. Boswell was in London when she died, and on returning to Auchinleck was comforted to find that nineteen carriages followed the hearse from the house to the kirk.

In 1771 James Boswell brought the Corsican leader General Pasquale Paoli to Scotland and took him on a tour of the country. For two nights, 6 and 7 September, they stayed at Auchinleck House, Boswell noting in a letter to David Garrick, 'You may figure the joy of my worthy father and me at seeing the Corsican Hero in our romantick groves.' However, Sir Walter Scott claimed that Lord Auchinleck was less enamoured of Paoli than Boswell implied, and that he regarded him as little more than 'a land-loupin' scoundrel of a Corsican.' With Paoli was Count Tadeusz Burzynski (died 1773), Polish envoy to the Netherlands and Great Britain, perhaps the first link with the parish and Poland.

Robert Boswell, son of Dr John Boswell (Lord Auchinleck's brother) was born on 30 January 1746 and married Sibella Sandeman on 1 June 1769. He joined the 'Glassite' church, being chosen by them to be a teaching elder in Edinburgh. In the city he was a Writer to Signet from 1773, Lyon Depute from 1770 , and interim Lord Lyon King of Arms from 1795-96. He wrote a number of psalms, published in 1784. Whilst delivering a sermon at the Glassite church in London's Barbican he was seized with illness and died instantly on 1 April 1804. He left a large family of over ten, the eldest son, William (1779-1841) of Crawley Grange (Newport Pagnell), marrying Elizabeth Boswell, daughter of Boswell the diarist. From the second son, Alexander (1781-1850), descends the chiefly line of Boswell of Auchinleck, but long since resident distant from the parish.

SIR ALEXANDER BOSWELL, 1st BARONET (X)

On the death of the great diarist his eldest son, Alexander Boswell, succeeded as 10th Boswell of Auchinleck. He had been born in Auchinleck House on 9 October 1775 and was educated at Westminster School followed by Oxford University. There he did not do so well as his younger brother, James.

Alexander was a tough and chivalrous lad, traits that remained with him all of his life. A story is told of a time he was walking home from Cumnock when he spotted two tall boys annoying a female tinker. She appealed to Alexander for help. He went up to the larger of the two lads and asked what honour he would have by molesting a shoeless beggar, who had given him no harm? The lad replied, 'What hae ye to dae wi't?' Within seconds the lad was on his back, pleading for mercy, and the second lad had ran off, lest he receive the same treatment.

Like his father, Alexander was interested in literary pursuits, though was more a poet than a diarist. His first published works appeared in 1803, entitled *Songs, Chiefly in the Scottish Dialect*, which included 'Jenny's Bawbee', 'Auld Guideman', 'Ye're a Drucken Carle', 'Jenny Dang the Weaver', and 'Taste Life's Glad Moments'. In the same year 'The Spirit of Tintoc' appeared, followed by 'Epistle to the Edinburgh Reviewers'. In 1809 he contributed five songs to George Thomson's collection of Welsh airs. In 1810, 'Edinburgh, or the Ancient Royalty' appeared, under the pseudonym 'Simon Gray'. 'Clan Alpin's Vow' was published in 1811, 'Sir Albyn' in 1812. He contributed seven songs to George Thomson's collection of Irish airs, 'Paddy O'Rafferty' becoming well-known, and in 1816 he wrote 'Skeldon Haughs, or the Sow is flitted', published by 'A & J Boswell'.

On his succession to the estates, Alexander Boswell carried out the obligatory grand tour of Europe, which young lairds and heirs were wont to do at that time. He was no absentee landowner, indeed he appears to have taken a keen interest on farming and improvements to the lands. He supported his tenants in ploughing matches and showed a keen interest in new developments in machinery and methods.

He was still a bachelor on succession, marrying Griselle or Grace Cumming on 26 November 1799. She was the fifth daughter of Thomas Cumming, a banker in Edinburgh, and representative of the ancient family of Erenside. They were to have four children, James, who succeeded as 11th Boswell laird of Auchinleck, Theresa, who was to marry Sir William Francis Eliott, of Stobs and Wells, Baronet, Grace Jane, who died at a young age, and Margaret Emily, who was married to General Vassall.

Alexander's influence grew across Ayrshire, and soon he was serving as one of the Road Trustees, a Commissioner of Supply, and Colonel in the Ayrshire Yeomanry. He kept a small pack of hounds on the estate, and would ride out with them in search of vermin. He was a keen curler and a member of the masonic lodge.

At Auchinleck in 1815 Alexander established a printing press in a thatched cottage, republishing some of the old Scots classics. The cottage, named Barnsdale, was erected in 1790 by the side of the Dippol Burn. One of Alexander Boswell's poems is entitled 'On Erecting a Printing Press at Barnsdale Poultry Yard':

> Sires of the typographic skill
> Who sav'd us from the sluggish quill,
> And gave the faculty to mind,
> To body hitherto confi'nd,
> And more – its offspring never die,
> But live, increase, and multiply.
> Great Fust and Guttenberg renown'd!
> If thy proud spirits hover round
> Frown not that in this lowly shade
> We profit by thy wond'rous aid.

In a letter addressed to Dr Dibdon, dates 5 May 1819, Alexander relates the background to the business:

> Having resolved to reprint a facsimile of a black-letter tract in my possession, which was considered to be unique, vizt., *The Disputation between John Knox and the Abbot of Crossraguell*, for this purpose I constrained to purchase two small founts of black-letter and to have punches cut out for eighteen or twenty double letters and contractions. I was then enlisted and articled into the service, and, being infected with the type-fever, the fits have periodically returned. In the year 1815, having viewed a portable press, invented by Mr John Ruthven, an ingenious printer in Edinburgh, I purchased one, and commenced compositor. At this period my brother, having it in contemplation to present 'Barnfield' to the Roxburghe Club, and not aware of the poverty and insignificance of my establishment, expressed a wish that this tract should be issued from the Auchinleck Press. I determined to gratify him, and the portable press being too small for general

purposes, I exchanged it for one of Ruthven's full-sized ones; and having increased my stock to eight small founts (Roman and Italic), with the necessary appurtenances, I placed the whole in a cottage, built originally for another purpose, very pleasantly situated on the bank of a rivulet, although concealed by the surrounding wood, not a quarter of a mile from my house.'

The Auchinleck Press produced around 40 known publications, varying from treatises, chap ballads, leaflets and accounts of history. Employed in the press on a part-time basis was James Sutherland, and when Alexander was absent, Patrick Simpson, the schoolmaster, corrected the proofs. Boswell is known to have enjoyed the full process, however, for it is recorded that in 1817, whilst he dined with Sir Walter Scott in Edinburgh, he presented the bard with a thin quarto volume which he stated had been 'written, printed, and bound by himself', according to Joseph Train. This book was *The Sow is Flitted*.

In 1816 Alexander was elected MP for Ayrshire. He contributed twelve songs to George Thomson's, *Select Collection of Original Scottish Airs* in 1817, of which 'Goodnight and Joy be wi' ye a', 'Jenny's Bawbee', and 'Jenny Dang the Weaver', became very popular. He was elected MP for Plympton in Devon in 1818, holding it until 1821 when he applied for the Chiltern Hundreds.

4.6 Boswell Arms *(Dane Love)*

Sir Alexander and Sir Walter Scott were firm friends, the former often dining with Scott at Abbotsford or in Edinburgh, as on 10 February 1822. Sir Walter's biographer, John Gibson Lockhart, wrote that Sir Alexander 'had all his father Bozzy's cleverness, good humour, and joviality, without one touch of his meaner qualities, - wrote *Jenny dang the Weaver*, and some other popular songs, which he sang capitally – and was moreover a thorough bibliomaniac.'

In 1818 Alexander Boswell was responsible for instigating the erection of a monument to Burns at Alloway. The erection of a memorial mausoleum in Dumfries two years earlier was the catalyst that set Ayrshire folk into action. He had also attended one of the first major Burns Dinners to have taken place, held in Edinburgh in May 1816. In attendance were 'Christopher North', Sir Walter Scott and George Thomson, some of the most revered literary figures in the country at that time. Boswell was there, acting as chairman of the dinner, reciting verses in praise of the bard. According to the *Caledonian Mercury*, the occasion included numerous toasts proposed by Boswell, delivered 'with much felicity and fancy and with that judicious brevity which so well fitted such a numerous auditory; and we never witnessed a happier flow of social and animated feeling, which was frequently kindled into enthusiasm, and the warmest admiration of the Poet in consequence of the well-seasoned wit and humour of the Chairman [Boswell], reciprocated with the utmost ingenuity by Mr Walter Scott and intermixed with many of Burns's inimitable songs.'

Sir Alexander advertised a public meeting to be held in Ayr Court House but only two people turned up, himself and Rev Hamilton Paul, a noted promoter of the Burns Supper. Nevertheless, the meeting continued, proposals made and seconded, and at the end a vote of thanks made to the chairman, Boswell, by the secretary, Paul. The minutes of the meeting were written up, and then published, with copies circulated throughout the country. This generated publicity in the press, the minute being recorded in the *Ayr Advertiser* of 31 March 1814. A committee was also appointed, of eminent gentlemen of the county, whom Boswell tracked down and received their permission. From this funds began to accumulate, £3,300 being subscribed within two years. The records of the Burns Monument Trustees note the debt owed to Boswell:

> Where so many exalted characters have contributed to this gratifying work, and where each man, from the prince to the peasant, has cast his stone to the cairn, it may perhaps be wrong to distinguish one more than another. But the enthusiasm, perseverance, liberality, and personal attention of Mr. Boswell of Auchinleck have been so marked and so excessive, and his nature evidently was so congenial to the task, that he falls unquestionably to be characterised as its first, best, and most steadfast friend.

The foundation stone was laid by Boswell on 25 January 1820, as Deputy Grand Master of the Mother Lodge of Kilwinning. Numerous other masonic lodges from across the county were in attendance and there was a large audience. The architect was Thomas Hamilton. Work on the monument continued for three years, the memorial being officially opened on 4 July 1823, however, by that time Boswell was dead and he missed the opening of his creation.

In 1819 Alexander Boswell purchased the House of Ochiltree, an old tower house, which became the dower house after his death.

From 1820 to 1821 feelings ran high in Britain over the right to vote and though parliament was reformed in 1821 the radical risings were soon seen as a threat to the stability of the country. Riots took place in various cities and armed bands gathered in various communities. This spread to Ayrshire, and locally meetings were held in Mauchline. Boswell was the colonel in charge of the Ayrshire Yeomanry, the largest militia force in Scotland, consisting of three full regiments. As Tory MP he vowed that he would 'ride in Radical blood up to his bridle reins.'

Boswell wrote and circulated an address 'To the Deluded Operatives', which concludes with the following paragraphs:

> With the unprincipled and degraded instigators to rebellion we know how to deal, and the outraged laws of their country shall sweep them away. But to the unhappy victims of their diabolical machicolations forbearance and forgiveness ought to be extended. They have done much evil, and although they themselves must be the greatest sufferers, they have atonement to make for their country, and let them make it. Let them return to their duty and allegiance, and give up for punishment those who have misled and betrayed them, and learn the salutary lesson, that their existence depends on the maintenance of public tranquillity.
>
> Much has been done to alleviate by the sympathy of those who, under Providence, have inherited wealth, or who have acquired it by honest industry. Ingratitude has too often been the requital. If, however, there is a prompt return to duty, we trust that the influence of our blessed religion will operate on all, and that while on one hand there is submission to the laws and contrition for the past, on the other there may be no lack of forgiveness, brotherly love, and charity.
> In name of the Magistrates at Mauchline,
> Alexander Boswell, J.P.

On 23 April 1820 seven yeomen under him and some special constables arrested about thirty radicals at Mauchline and seized some arms. A letter of Boswell's from this period survives:

> Auchinleck.
> The commanding officer having received a sudden order to call out the corps under his command, however much he regrets the inconvenient time, he relies on the spirit of all individuals, and that every man will turn out in this emergency to put down those who render property and everything valuable to men insecure; all that can be wished is, that by one well-directed effort, we may be spared further annoyance. The first and third troops will assemble tomorrow at twelve noon o'clock in Ayr, in marching order, with necessaries. The second troop, in like order at the same hour, in Mauchline. The fourth troop, at the same hour in like order, at Kilmarnock.
> Alex. Boswell, Lt-Colonel Commandant.

Boswell was active with the Ayrshire Yeomanry in Renfrewshire, where it was expected that a group of rebels were to march on Glasgow. He took part in the campaign to quell the rising, and his men were so grateful of his leadership that he was later presented with a gold snuff box.

On 19 July 1821, the anniversary of George IV's coronation, Boswell wrote and sung 'Long Live George the Fourth' at Ayr, latterly published in Edinburgh. This was no doubt as a result of a letter received a few days earlier in which he was notified of his honouring by a baronetcy. The letter read:

> Whitehall, July 13 1821
>
> My Dear Sir
> I have great pleasure in acquainting you that His Majesty has signified his gracious intention of conferring upon you, forthwith, the dignity of a Baronet of the United Kingdom. This distinguished mark of royal favour is to be attributed, not merely to the just view which has been taken by His Majesty of those fair pretentions which arise from your station in life, your property, and character; but also, in a high degree, to those principles of loyalty, and of attachment to the constitution of your country which you have invariably manifested; and to the important services which, at periods and under circumstances the most critical, you have rendered in that part of the kingdom in which you reside.

These considerations make it peculiarly gratifying to me to be the channel of this communication; and I need not assure you that the satisfaction which I feel on this occasion is heightened by the sincere regard with which I have the honour to be,
My Dear Sir,
Your faithful and obedient servant,
Sidmouth.

In August he was officially created a baronet. To celebrate the event many of the villagers of Auchinleck marched behind a fife and drum along the Barony Road to Auchinleck House. Unfortunately Sir Alexander was not aware this honour was coming his way and was out shooting grouse. On the following day he paid for two hogsheads of ale at the Boswell Arms from which anyone who wished could freely drink his health. Firstly Sir Alexander and young James drank a toast to the good health of all their friends in the village.

It was during the political excitement of the 1820s that Boswell brought about his own death. He contributed a number of articles to a magazine called *The Beacon* which gave great offence to the Whigs. Because of the upset it caused the committee responsible for publication ceased production in August 1821. However, the *Glasgow Sentinel* was started in October that year and in the first issue appeared 'The New Whig Song' from the pen of Boswell. It was an attack on James Stuart, Younger of Dunearn, who prosecuted the publishers to find out who had been responsible for the verses. To his surprise it was his half-friend, Sir Alexander, at the time in London to attend his brother James' funeral. On his return to Edinburgh, on Saturday 23 March 1822, a letter was handed to Boswell as he stood down from his coach. It was written by the Earl of Rosslyn, asking for an interview. This took place on the Monday morning. Rosslyn had a challenge from Stuart, and demanded to know if Boswell had written the verses. He refused to say – it is said that there were a number of men who had written for the *Sentinel* and that they had all agreed to refuse to reveal the authors. The matter was then passed on to the Hon. John Douglas (afterwards Marquis of Queensberry), who arranged that the pair should meet within a fortnight. Things changed quickly, and the Sheriff bound both parties to keep the peace within the city and county of Edinburgh. John Douglas thought it would be best if both parties met somewhere else, and so they headed for Fife. He was accompanied by his second, as well as Dr George Wood. As he made his way to Auchtertool, Sir Alexander informed his companions that he bore no ill-will towards Stuart, and thus would fire into the air. On 26 March 1822 they fought a duel at Balbarton farm, near Balmuto Castle, seat of his distant cousin, Lord Balmuto. Boswell's collarbone was shattered. Two pieces of bone were removed by Dr Wood, as well as Mr Liston, the surgeon who came with Stuart. Neither could find the ball. He was taken to Balmuto Castle and was attended within hours by Dr

Thomson, professor of military surgery. When asked how he felt, Sir Alexander replied, 'I feel exactly what I am – a man with a living head and a dead body mysteriously joined together.' As the ball had passed through the clavicle and touched the spine, Boswell was left paralysed from the neck down. He hung on until half past three on the following day, breathing his last by the side of his wife and daughter. His son, James, did not reach his deathbed until half an hour after he had passed away.

4.7 Boswell family burial vaults, Auchinleck *(Dane Love)*

For many years thereafter, a B and an S were carved into the ground, marking where the duellists stood. Sir Alexander's good friend, Sir Walter Scott, was to use the duel in his novel, *St Ronan's Well*, John Gibson Lockhart noting that 'several circumstances of [Boswell's] death are exactly reproduced in the duel scene' within the book.

Sir Alexander's corpse was returned to Auchinleck and buried in the family vault. Initially it had been planned to have a very private funeral, but the family were soon persuaded to have a more public event. Just after midday on 10 April a religious service was held on the lawn in front of Auchinelck House, led by Rev James Boyd of Auchinleck and Rev John Lindsay of Ochiltree. The funeral cortege was considerable, comprising, in order:

The First regiment of the Ayrshire Yeomanry, under the command of Captain William Campbell of Fairfield.
The tenantry and gentlemen of the district (approximately 500).
The undertaker and his assistants.
The hearse, drawn by six horses.
Sir Alexander's groom and other servants.
Young James Boswell, with Lord Glenlee, Lord Balmuto and Sir James Montgomery Cunninghame.
Lord Glasgow, the Lord Lieutenant of Ayrshire, Hon. John Douglas, and General Leslie.
Twenty to thirty carriages, carrying the principal friends of the Boswells, and the chief gentry of the county.

The party made their way along the Barony Road to the kirkyard, where Sir Alexander was laid to rest in the newly-prepared vault. It is reckoned that there were around 10,000 spectators lining the route and in the kirkyard.

A number of locals were inspired to write verses on the occasion, including 'Lines on the Funeral' by John Goldie, editor of the Ayr Courier. Sir Walter Scott is also supposed to have written verses in Boswell's honour:

> 'Oh! Where have you been, my gallant Knight,
>   So far from the West Countrie?'
> 'I have been to weep o'er a brother's bier
>   Who was right dear to me!'

Descriptions of his character vary, but most agree that Sir Alexander was a 'high spirited, clever, and amiable gentleman and, like his father, of a frank and social disposition' (Rt Hon John Wilson Croker), though Henry, Lord Cockburn, stated that 'in general he was boisterous and overbearing, and addicted to coarse personal ridicule.'

At the time of Sir Alexander's death his heir, James, was still a minor, aged 15, and so continued to live at Auchinleck House with his mother. When he was married in 1830 his mother moved to Ochiltree House where she died in 1864. It was noted that Lady Boswell 'spent the remainder of her days in strict retirement', and following Sir Alexander's death she kept the windows in her room closed for many years.

JAMES BOSWELL JR.

James Boswell, younger brother of Sir Alexander and second son of the diarist, was born on Tuesday 15 September 1778. He was educated at Soho Square followed by Westminster School. He decided to follow a career in law, entering Brasenose

College, Oxford, in 1797 and graduating as a Bachelor of Arts in 1801, and Master of Arts in 1806. He was called to the bar of the Inner Temple on 24 May 1805 and was appointed commissioner of bankrupts. He was elected a Fellow of Brazenose College upon the Vinerian foundation.

James was a noted literary editor and was to become the literary executor of Edward Malone, producing the final copies of his 21 volume edition of Shakespeare, *Variorum Shakespeare*. Boswell added many of his own notes to the work. He was also to write *Memoirs of Malone* and an *Essay on the Metre and Phraseology of Shakespeare*. He also contributed to the third edition of his father's Life of Johnson and edited the sixth edition, his contributions being identified by the initials 'J.B.O.' He also contributed articles to the *Gentleman's Magazine*.

James was a member of the Roxburghe Club, and presented it with a facsimile of the poems of Richard Barnfield in 1816 and *A Roxburghe Garland* in 1817.

Boswell was friendly with many of the literati of the period. Among these was Robert Southey, with whom he made an evening ascent of Skiddaw in the Lake District on 21 August 1815. They planned to set a bonfire to commemorate the victory at Waterloo. With them were Lord Sunderlin (with whom James resided), William and Dorothy Wordsworth, and others. Tar barrels were taken to the mountain top and lit, causing a large bonfire to spread its light. As the flames subsided they roasted steaks on it, but the party accidentally spilled the kettle of boiling water that was proposed for the punch. The party sang *God Save the King* and other songs whilst standing in a circle around the fire, 'which fairly put out the moon.'

James wrote a few poems himself, perhaps the most noted being 'Larghan Clanbrassil':

> Larghan Clanbrassil, how sweet is thy sound,
> To my tender remembrance! As Love's sacred ground;
> For there Margaret Caroline first charmed my sight,
> And filled my young heart with a fluttering delight.

James died at the Middle Temple in London on 24 February 1822, aged 42. Scott's biographer, Lockhart, described him as 'a man of considerable learning and admirable social qualities.' However, he was in a financially embarrassed condition. He never married.

In 1825 James Boswell's library was broken up and placed on the market. Within the documents sold was a small manuscript which was his father's Scots Dictionary, achieving sixteen shillings. This became lost for many years until it was rediscovered in the Bodleian Library in Oxford in 2011. It extends to 39 pages and includes the definitions of about 800 Scots words.

A few additions to Auchinleck estate were made during the time of the baronets. In 1830 the North Drive bridge was erected over the Dippol Burn.

4.8 The Boswell Mausoleum (Dane Love)

OTHER LANDOWNERS

The estates of Duncanziemere and Craigston passed to David Boswell, 3rd of Craigston, who was born in 1660. He was one of the Commissioners of Supply for Ayrshire, for his name is listed in the sederunt from 1712 until 1727. This position was similar to a county councillor, who took over the work in 1889 when county councils were formed. David probably held office until 1728, in which year he died. From his gravestone (formerly located in Auchinleck kirkyard) we find additional information on both him and the extent of his estates: 'Here lieth the corps of the deceased David Boswell, Laird of Craigston, Pathhead, Dickstone, Braehead, Burnside, and Bellow Mill, who departed this life upon the 30th day of November in the year of God 1728, aged 68, leaving behind him Jean Hunter his spouse, 3 sons and 5 daughters.' These sons were David, who succeeded, Charles and John, the last-named marrying Margaret Fergusson of Knockroon. David Boswell, 4th of Craigston, seems to have hit financial trouble for he sold off most of the lands. Duncanziemere went to Alexander Millikan (1721-1781), a Commissioner of Supply in 1750, Craigston to James Boswell, 7th of Auchinleck. Charles Boswell, his brother, emigrated to Jamaica. Duncanziemere was sold on Millikan's death to

John Reid whose wife, Mary White, died of fever at the age of 60 in 1875.

Elizabeth Boswell-Fergusson, 4th of Knockroon, was born in 1690 and married John Fergusson. They had but one child, Margaret Fergusson, who married her third cousin once removed, John Boswell, second son of David Boswell, 3rd of Craigston. As well as succeeding to Knockroon, Margaret obtained the farm of Underwood in right of her father. This she later sold to the Earl of Dumfries. John Boswell and Margaret Fergusson had six children, John, 6th of Knockroon, and five daughters, Elizabeth, Jean, Margaret, Agnes and Anne. Margaret Fergusson died in 1787.

John, 6th laird, was born in 1741 but, in 1772, on the failure of the Douglas Heron & Co. Bank of Ayr, he was forced to sell Knockroon. It was bought by James Boswell, 9th of Auchinleck in 1790. John subsequently became a tax collector in Ayr and one of the trustees of the Ayr Turnpike Roads. He served as a trustee from 1771 until 1782. Boswell married Christina (1740-1807), daughter of a Hamilton of Everton, and had five children, Hamilton, who married Jane Douglas of Garrallan; Margaret, who married Capt. Charles Dalrymple; Christian, married Alexander Walker WS; Jacobina, married Captain William Hamilton of Dowan; and Charlotte. John Boswell died on 25 May 1805 and was buried in Ayr's old kirkyard.

Waterside was still the possession of the Cochrane family at the turn of the eighteenth century. John Cochrane, the Covenanter, died around 1734 and was succeeded by his son, also John. He was married in 1733 to Elizabeth Cairns, and had a son, William, born 12 February 1738. John's brother, James, was an advocate, mentioned in the parish records for 1765. He had a son, William, who also became an advocate, succeeding his father as judge-advocate of Scotland in 1757. A third brother, D. Cochrane, is mentioned in the session records of 1758, having left £10 5s towards the appointment of a schoolmaster. Around the middle of the eighteenth century the Cochranes sold the estate, it being acquired by the Earl of Dumfries.

Wallaceton was still owned by the Wallaces, a William thereof being baptised in the kirk in 1732; on 17 July 1733 Janet Wallace was baptised. James Wallace of Wallaceton had a daughter, Effie, baptised in 1737, a son, John, in 1738 and a daughter, Jean, in 1740. John succeeded James, implying that William must have died previously. John Wallace studied medicine, qualifying as a doctor. He was succeeded by William Wallace, who married Margaret Cochrane, by whom he had two sons, John and Hugh, and four daughters, Anna, Jean, Margaret and Janet. Hugh succeeded, and though the name of his wife is unknown, the births of three children were recorded – Janet, born 1807, William 1815, and Agnes 1817. Wallaceton was sold around 1850 and the family dispersed. One son remained in the parish as a surgeon.

The old barony of Glenmuir was by now broken up. The Schaw family became extinct in the male line, and by 1711 Glenmuir was the property of William Dalrymple. He acted as a Commissioner of Supply from then until 1727. The

Mitchell family acquired it, and certainly were owners in 1775. Alexander Mitchell was the proprietor in the late 1770s. His mother was a Boswell, sister of John Boswell of Knockroon. The Mitchells sold out to Hugh Logan of that Ilk, the noted humourist (1739-1802). He ran into financial difficulties in 1773, having to sell off most of his property, including Logan House, and moved to Wellwood. Glenmuir was then bought by David Limond of Dalblair. Dornal and Whiteholm were broken from the parent lands and sold to John Begg, a Commissioner of Supply in 1740 and a member of Auchinleck kirk session in 1752. The lands then passed to Hugh Mitchell of Dornal, mentioned in the parish records of 1756. The Dornal was subsequently owned by Alexander Aird of Crossflat in 1840.

Dalblair was probably the replacement for Kyle Castle, the old lodge standing to the west of Dalblair farm. In 1654 it was owned by the Crichtons of Castlemains. James Gibb is noted as the owner from at least 1733 until he sold it in 1767. Gibb owned a soapworks in Ayr and built Dalblair House in that town, naming it from his Auchinleck property. James Boswell, the diarist, purchased Dalblair from Gibb, but did not retain it for very long, despite revelling in the title 'Dalblair' and walking over his property to the summit of Wardlaw Hill on 4 May 1767. Quintin MacAdam of Craigengillan was owner in 1792, Messrs Hunter & Company of Ayr in 1796. In 1800 it passed to David Limond. Limond was born in Ayr, where his father was the town clerk from 1783 to 1817, dying in 1819 'at an advanced age.' He went to India where he built up a reasonable fortune. On his return to Scotland he bought a number of properties in Ayrshire. He acquired Dalblair House in Ayr's Alloway Street, and from which Dalblair Road got its name. He served as a councillor for Ayr Burgh, becoming provost in 1820 for two years, again in 1824, and from 1834 to 1841.

Lesser landowners in the parish included John Boyd, owner of Cronberry in 1715, latterly the property of Charles Howatson of Glenbuck (1833-1918). At the Rigg the Samson family acquired the lands from the Cochranes, who were owners in 1756. On George Samson of Rigg's death, James Templeton of Ayr acquired it. Templeton was a carpet manufacturer in Ayr.

Darnconner was owned by the Lennoxes, James in 1760, and John in 1780. It then passed into the hands of the Alexanders of Ballochmyle, who remained owners until the twentieth century, along with Common farm. The parish had a total of thirteen landowners in 1791, of which five were residents. They collected a total of £3,800 Scots (£316 13s 4d Sterling) in rent annually.

CHURCHES

The patronage of the church was divided in 1698 between James Reid and Viscount Stair, but in 1700 the teinds and patronage were purchased by David Boswell, 6th of Auchinleck. The first parish minister to be presented to the church after the revolution did not arrive for three years (until 1692) when Rev John Lawrie MA (or

Laurie) was translated from Penpont Parish Church in Dumfriesshire. He had graduated with a Master of Arts degree from Glasgow University on 27 July 1676. He was active in helping to establish the Presbyterian Kirk in Ireland, going to that country to preach at Macosquin, Colerain, where he was ordained. He was called to Penpont before 8 October 1689. He served in the rural parish for three years, before being called to Auchinleck in November 1692 and admitted on 29 December 1692.

A grave slab commemorating some of Rev John Lawrie's family survives in the kirkyard, inscribed: *MARY LAWRIE, BORN MAY 1697. IOHN LAWRIE, YOUNGER, BORN JULY 1698, DIED ULT MAR 17016 [sic] IN SACRIS NIL OBITER*. John Lawrie himself died in June 1710 aged about 54. A number of his family joined the ministry – Rev James Lawrie (sometimes spelled Laurie) was minister at Kirkmichael from 1711 until his death in 1764. Rev James Lawrie's son, Rev Dr George Lawrie (1727-1799) was known to Robert Burns and was responsible for promoting his work in Edinburgh. He served as a minister at Loudoun from 1763. George's son, Rev Dr Archibald Lawrie (1768-1837), was also a friend of the poet and corresponded with him.

Rev John Grant was called to Auchinleck from Kilmuir Wester (or Knockbain, Ross & Cromarty) on 29 May 1712 and was admitted on 7 July. He was the son of Lewis Grant of Whitetree and following training for the ministry was ordained to Knockbain Church on 27 September 1711.

He seems to have been a rather undedicated minister, for on his mother-in-law's death in 1719 he went to her home for the funeral and did not return for seventeen weeks! On another occasion he remained in Edinburgh for a month when attending the General Assembly. Finally, on 28 April 1731, the Presbytery charged him with neglecting his parish, for he had left it in October 1729, supplying a replacement for just one month of the eighteen! Other charges included the fact that he had held communion just three or four times in his nineteen-year ministry, and visited the families of the parish just once in four years. He admitted the charges and resigned on 9 June 1731.

Rev Grant moved to London, where he was to accept the charge of a presbyterian congregation there. His wife, Henrietta Campbell (daughter of Donald Campbell), inherited a considerable sum of money in 1729 on the death of her brother, Colin Campbell, a noted Scots architect and author of *Vitruvius Britannicus*, who is believed to have designed Drumlanrig Castle and numerous other important buildings. Rev John Grant died in January 1732, his wife predeceasing him on 6 June 1731. They left four sons, Colin, Ludovick (who became Adjutant of Chelsea Hospital), John and Donald, and three daughters, Elizabeth, Ann and Jean. A fifth son, Alexander, had predeceased him.

Rev David Cooper was called to Auchinleck on 6 December 1731 and ordained on 26 April 1732, having been presented by Alexander Boswell. He had studied at

Rotterdam in Holland, where the reformed religion was fought for as much as it had been in Scotland, and he was licensed in that city. Like many of the parish ministers he seems to have been quite a literary man, and one of his sermons was published in Edinburgh in 1735; another in Glasgow, 1747. He married Janet Carstairs in May 1723, by whom he had two sons, David and William. She died on 25 March 1770. He died whilst still the parish minister on 9 July 1751. During his ministry, Elizabeth Bruce, wife of James Boswell, 7th of Auchinleck, presented new communion vessels to the church in 1734. These were two silver cups, two pewter tankards and two pewter plates.

a   b   c   d

4.9 Communion Tokens (a-c Parish Church; d Associate Church) *(Author's Collection)*

Around this time communion tokens were in vogue, and a few mid eighteenth century examples from the parish survive. Those used by the parish church tended to be rectangular in shape and bore the name 'AFLEK' in Latin capitals. Surrounding, or else above and below this, was a border of zig-zags, the reverse side plain.

Once Lord Auchinleck had finished restoring the church he turned his attentions to the state of the manse. He found the existing building to be unsuitable for repair and so decided to erect a new manse in 1756. It was to be erected in the glebe, adjoining the wood alongside the Auchinleck Burn. The building was described by Rev John Dun as 'one of the most commodious neat small houses to be met with,' and was two storeys in height. Attached to it was a glebe of six acres on which the minister could grow crops or raise cattle to supplement his stipend, which at the time amounted to £71 13s 4d. This was made up of £50 3s 11½d Sterling in cash plus additional payments in kind, which comprised two chalders of meal, and one chalder of bere (barley). This stipend had been settled in 1649, meaning that there had been no increase for over a century. Not until 1798 or thereabouts did the minister receive an increased stipend. In 1796 the manse was extended and again around 1820. The latter additions comprised of a dining room and drawing room above, with oriel windows, to the south-west of the house. From the dining room one could step out into the manse garden, which afforded views of Dumfries House and which was 'gay with tulips and anemones.'

The vacancy at the manse was filled by Rev John Dun, one of the most remarkable ministers the parish has yet seen. He had been tutor to Boswell the diarist in his youth, before his appointment to the kirk on 9 November 1752. He was a native of Eskdale, in Dumfriesshire, where he was born in 1724, and he was educated at Edinburgh University. He was licensed to preach by the Presbytery of Irvine on 11 September 1750. He had two sermons published in 1766 and 1780, followed by *Sermons in Two Volumes by John Dun VSM*, at Kilmarnock in 1790. This book had a poem entitled 'The Deil's Answer to His Verra Friend, R. Burns', written in response to Burns' 'Address to the Deil'. The first verse reads:

> So zealous Robin stout an' fell –
> True champion for the cause of Hell –
> Thou beats the righteous down pell-mell,
>   Sae firm an' frothy,
> That o' a seat where devils dwell,
>   There's nane mair worthy.

4.10 Old Parish Church *(Dane Love)*

Sales of the *Sermons* were poor, even with Boswell's help, and the latter wrote to his friend Rev William Temple that the minister would end up 'a sad loser' by his book. John Dun was married twice, firstly on 21 November 1757 to Mary Wilson (died 2 June 1765 aged 32) by whom he had two daughters – Elizabeth (born 8 August 1758), and Isabella (born 16 March 1760), who was to marry Rev Alexander Gillies of Kilmaurs. He married for a second time to Deborah Blackstock (1732-13 December 1795), widow of a Mr Williamson, on 28 December 1770, by whom he had a son, named Alexander Boswell Dun (born 3 July 1772). Rev John Dun purchased the farm of Rigg in 1782. He was responsible for much good work in the parish, and was in the process of compiling a contribution to Sir John Sinclair's *Statistical Account of Scotland* when he died on 11 October 1794 after a long illness, hence the Auchinleck entry being rather short.

In the winter of 1782 there was a scare that the farmers would sell their meal distant from the parish in the hope of receiving a greater price for it. This would have meant that meal would be in short supply in the village, so Dun called a meeting of the heritors and farmers of the parish on 2 January 1783 and suggested to them that each keep a percentage of their produce for sale at home, at the market price of 15d per boll (six bushels). James Boswell was accountable for half of the eighty bolls kept for the villagers, and as a measure of goodwill ordered that three bolls of meal be distributed from Bridgend Mill at a reduced price of 14d.

4.11 John Dun's Sermon upon Occasion of the Death of Lady Auchinleck (1766) *(Author's Collection)*

In 1752 Rev John Dun looked into the situation of the session records and register of births, marriages and deaths. Though records existed back to 1693, these were not entire, the session clerk failing to fill them in regularly. From Dun's appointment to the present the session records give an accurate note on the life of the kirk and community. A few of the early entries are of interest:

> December 31, 1752. This day collected, for the poor Protestants in America, at the church, ten pounds and four shillings Scots. Collected, the Sabbath day before this, at the Dornal, two pounds and eight shillings Scots for the same purpose.

From this extract we can note a few things, one of them being that the parish was not failing in its charitable nature, sending assistance to those colonising the new world. The amounts collected were still noted in Scots money, even though by law this became obsolete at the Union of Parliaments in 1707. Scots money was the equivalent of one twelfth of Sterling. In 1753 the kirk session decided to count the poor's funds in what was termed 'English money'. Though the record does not state it directly, it may be assumed that the minister held services at Dornal farm, probably in a barn, for the benefit of the parishioners who resided in the upper part of the parish. How often this took place we know not, nor whether the Dornal was the regular location of the services or whether they were held on different farms.

In 1753 the church became involved in a complicated issue over an acre of land which had been mortified to the poor by John Cochrane of Waterside. John Cochrane the Younger, his son, got his hands on the title deeds and subsequently sold the acre to Alexander Boswell, later Lord Auchinleck. On 23 September 1753, the kirk session resolved to approach Lady Waterside to see if she could intervene and help get the acre returned to the poor's fund. This failed, for the minutes of 20 November 1755 note that, 'Lord Auchinleck agrees to pay an adequate price for the acre mortified by the first John Cochrane of Waterside, and bought by his lordship from the late John Cochrane, his son.' A note entered for 23 September indicates that at that time the poor fund stood at £56 14s 3d. By 1792 this had increased to around £100 and was lent out to those who wished it at an annual percentage rate of between 4 and 5 per cent. From around 1760 to 1790, and perhaps longer, the kirk session did not distribute any of the funds, except by way of a loan, so that should any of the poor inherit money they would be liable to repay the money.

Collections for the poor between 1740 and 1751 averaged out at £6 6s per annum, rising to around £18 per annum between 1771 and 1791. In addition to freewill donations, the session hired out various mort-cloths for use in draping over coffins at funerals for around five shillings, collected dues for marriages and baptisms, and received interest on the capital sum, the whole amounting to £6 per year. Should more money be required for poor relief than was available, Rev John Dun asked for assistance from the heritors of the parish, it being noted in the *Statistical Account* that 'the two principal heritors, the Earl of Dumfries and Mr Boswell of Auchinleck, have never refused the late incumbent money for the relief of the poor when necessary.' By 1837 24 parishioners were regularly receiving money from the poor fund, averaging around thirteen pence each per week, or around £2 16s 4d per annum. The fund paid out around £72 10s in total each year, raised by collections in the church (£19), donations from heritors (£45), renting out seats in the church (£4 10s – the seats in the galleries were rented out to parishioners, giving them the option of certain sittings), interest on a mortification of £100 (£2 10s) and from renting out the mort-cloths (£1 10s). In 1845, on the passing of the Poor Law, the kirk session no longer had any responsibility for looking after the poor, this passing to the Inspector of Poor.

With Rev Dun's failing health, Rev Robert Steven was appointed in 1784 to be his assistant. He is thought to have been the third son of John Steven of Glasgow. He was educated at Glasgow University and was licensed to preach by the Presbytery of Stranraer on 4 December 1784. He served at Auchinleck as an assistant for seven years, but on 12 September 1792 he was ordained as minister at Catrine chapel-of-ease. As a result, he did not become Rev Dun's successor. Rev Steven was subsequently minister of Dalrymple (from 1798) until his death on 25 July 1828. He had married Annabella Earle (died 30 August 1829) on 14 April 1794, but they had no children.

On 26 February 1793 James Boswell wrote to his friend William Temple regarding the appointment of a new minister to succeed John Dun:

> I am within a few hours from setting out for Auchinleck. It is quite right that I should now go down. The choice of a minister to a worthy parish is a matter of very great importance, and I cannot be sure of the real wishes of the people without being present. Only think, Temple, how serious a duty I am about to discharge. I, James Boswell, Esq. – you know what vanity that name includes – I have promised, to come down on purpose, and his honour's goodness is gratefully acknowledged. Besides, I have several matters of consequence of my estate to adjust.

Thus Boswell indicates that he took the wishes of the parishioners into account when presenting a new minister, unlike many parishes where the patron appointed ministers against the congregation's will, leading to the Disruption of 1843 and various earlier secessions.

In March 1793 Boswell appointed Rev John Lindsay, who had just left Edinburgh University, and who proved to be a respected minister. He was licensed by Edinburgh Presbytery on 28 April 1790. His first charge was at Auchinleck, where he was ordained on 29 August 1793. He was translated to Ochiltree on 5 June 1818 and died on 6 July 1832. The memorial stone on the kirk wall notes that he 'was instrumental in gathering many souls into the fold of the Redeemer.' Lindsay had married Janet Blackstock on 28 April 1802. They never had any children, and she died on 16 November 1842.

The successor to Lindsay was Rev James Boyd, born 1785, licensed by the Presbytery of Edinburgh on 28 June 1815 and ordained on 11 February 1818 as chaplain to the Caledonian Asylum, Hatton Garden, London. He was presented to Auchinleck in November 1818 and admitted on 6 May 1819. There survives an:

Account of the Dinner and Drink at Auchinleck Village on the Admission of the Reverend James Boyd to be minister of the Parish, 7 May 1819.

Dinner for 46 @ 2/6	£5	15	-
1 Bottle of Brandy		7	-
1 do. Rum		5	3
8 Bottles best Whisky tody	2	6	8
2½ Dozen Porter & Ale		15	-
2½ Dozen of Wine @ 52d	6	10	-
Corn & hay for 2 horses		3	-
Dinner & drink for Coachman		2	6
Allowed Mrs Dalrymple for House &c	1	5	-
The Cook		10	6
2 Waiters @ 7/6		15	-
	£18	14	11

His son, Andrew (who wrote with the pseudonym 'AKHB') was born in the manse in 1825, of whom more in Chapter 5. On 18 April 1833 James Boyd was translated to Ochiltree, and subsequently to the Tron Kirk, Glasgow, on 18 April 1844. He was granted a Divinity Doctorate and served as a minister for a total of 48 years. He died on 27 March 1865 and was buried in Glasgow's Necropolis.

With the rise in population, the old parish church could no longer accommodate all the worshippers on many occasions, with only 400 seats within it. Indeed, at times the next minister, Rev James Chrystal, held services in the kirkyard, particularly at communion, when a tented structure was erected in which he could stand. In 1832 the presbytery informed the parish heritors, of which there were eleven, that a new building was required. Considerable wrangling took place for four years thereafter, between the kirk session, presbytery, heritors and patron. However by 1836 it was agreed that a new church be built, on a new site north east of the old kirk. The estimated cost was to be £750, and the presbytery set 1 October 1837 as the deadline for completion. They appointed a sub-committee to supervise the work, with Rev Chrystal a member. The deadline came and went, however, in September 1837 the building was just 'so far advanced as to be roofed in.' The building was constructed from freestone, obtained from a quarry across Kirkland Brae, known from then on as the Church Quarry, the entrance to which is now occupied by Quarryknowe Cottage. The quarry was the property of the Boswells, who did not charge for the stone. The architect/designer is believed to have been James Jamieson, a Catrine wright, who used a traditional Scots design, with a gallery in each arm of the T-plan, two of which were reached by external stairways. No other examples of work by Jamieson are known. Prior to his plan being adopted, designs for a new building were prepared by two well-known architects, James

Ingram in 1831 and William Kay in 1835. It may have been that Johnstone adapted these and was more probably the master of works. When the new church was finally completed is not exactly known, though it is believed to be in October 1838. Other accounts place it as late as 1844. The new bell for the tower was not added until 1858 when one of 30⅛ inches diameter was placed in the frame. It bears the inscription: *JOHN C. WILSON, FOUNDER, GLASGOW, AD 1858, No. 616, AUCHINLECK CHURCH.*

OTHER CHURCHES

Following the Revolution in 1689, when Presbyterianism was again recognised, some of the more extreme Covenanters did not return to the parish church but instead formed themselves into a praying society. They met at Wallaceton farm, the farmer no doubt being an active member who willingly allowed the society to use either a barn or a large room in the farmhouse. They had no recognised minister, but it is known that Rev John Hepburn of Urr (Stewartry of Kirkcudbright) visited on occasion. On 13 April 1738, five years following the Secession and the establishment of the Associate Presbytery, the Wallaceton congregation declared their adherence to that group. To mark the event the Revs Nairn and Mair preached at a special service at Wallaceton. However, Secession ministers were still few in number and the Wallaceton society had to rely on sermons from its own members when a visiting preacher was unable to attend. On 22 April 1738 the ministers, Messrs. Nairn and Mair, observed a fast at Kirkconnel, and on the following Sabbath preached at Wallaceton. The congregations at Wallaceton and Kirkconnel appear to have seen themselves as one for a time, appointing elders to serve in both places. However, with the formation of a society meeting place in Sanquhar, the Kirkconnel members gradually joined that group, and the Wallaceton society was left on its own.

In 1740, when Rev David Smyton was ordained to the Secession church in Kilmaurs, he was instructed to preach at Wallaceton four times each year. From the baptismal register of the church at Kilmaurs it is known that Rev Smyton conducted baptisms at Wallaceton when he visited. No doubt his quarterly services were eagerly anticipated by the congregation, and the amount of church business conducted would result in a lengthy day. William MacGavin, author of The Protestant, wrote in his works that his father and mother often rode on the same horse twenty miles each way just to hear Rev Smyton preach.

The Wallaceton Preaching Society was advised by its presbytery to seek a minister of their own, should their numbers increase. This did take place, and in 1756 a Secession Church was built at the Rigg, the site chosen since the congregation comprised members from both Auchinleck and Old Cumnock parishes. The ground on which the church stood was bought from John Boswell of Knockroon on 2 June 1764. The plot on which the manse stood was bought on 26

June 1766 from William Cochrane. The congregation had divided into Burghers (who went on to found a church in Cumnock's Tanyard Lane) and Anti-Burghers, who remained at Rigg. This division had been a national one, taking place in 1747, over the legal standing of the taking the oath of burgess.

The church at the Rigg went without a minister until 30 November 1763, when Rev Robert Smith from Mid Calder was ordained, the first minister the congregation had since its establishment 74 years previously. A few communion tokens survive bearing his initials 'Mr R S' and date '1765'; with the words 'Auchinleck Associate Cong.' These are single-sided, square, with a circular pattern. In 1778 Smith published a leaflet against the Burghers, entitled *Self-inconsistency Exemplified*. He also published a treatise on *Original Sin*.

Sometime between 1775 and 1780 a new box-kirk was erected in Auchinleck, with manse adjacent. The old manse at Rigg was abandoned, but was restored in 1826; in 1875 the thatched roof was removed and a second storey added, probably using stone from the old church. At the same time the two adjoining houses were erected. Membership of the church stood at 20 in 1791, and 35 Burgher Seceders lived in the parish, but they had to worship at the Anti-Burgher Church in Cumnock (later known as the West Church).

In 1803, due to Rev Smith's age, the congregation proposed appointing his son, Alexander Smith, to be his colleague. However, Alexander died on 20 September that year. Rev Robert Smith resigned his post on 31 January 1809 due to age and infirmity, the congregation awarding him a pension of £26 per annum. He retired to Kilwinning, where he died on 12 June 1817 at the age of 83 at the home of his son, Rev Robert Smith (1769-1835), minister at Kilwinning. William MacGavin described Smith thus: '[He] was a man of feeble and deformed body, such as I suppose Alexander Pope to have been, but of a most acute and vigorous mind; and his congregation became distinguished all the country round for the extent of their religious knowledge, correct acquaintance with their principles, and the ability with which they maintain them.' During Smith's ministry, in 1787, the Auchinleck congregation joined those in Kilmaurs, Colmonell, Kilwinning 1st, Ayr 1st, Newmilns and Kilmarnock (Clerks' Lane), in forming the Presbytery of Kilmarnock of the Secession Church.

The Anti-Burgher Secession Church in Auchinleck called a new minister to serve them in 1811, Rev Robert Crauford of Craigmailen being ordained on the 29 October that year. He was the subject of considerable scandal within the church. The first case occurred soon after his arrival, in May 1812. The Kilmarnock Presbytery brought a charge of immorality against him to the Synod, and a full investigation took place. He was acquitted by the Provincial Synod of Glasgow, but a year later he protested against a sentence of suspension which the Kilmarnock Presbytery had pronounced. He was called before a committee where he 'acknowledged imprudences and under-went rebuke.' Seemingly milder charges of the same type had taken place throughout the year. Robert Crawford asked to be dismissed from his charge and this was done on 13 May 1813, six elders of his church having asked for his dismissal also. Crawford later took an Oath of Purgation and his name was added to the probationer list. He was inducted to the South Street Church in Elgin in 1817, remaining as minister until his death in 1828. At Elgin he gained considerable respect from his congregation. In 1811 the Auchinleck congregation had 201 members, from as far afield as Mauchline, Ochiltree, New Cumnock and Muirkirk. By 1827 the roll had fallen to 114.

The church at Auchinleck searched for a new minister, calling Andrew Scott and Andrew Isaac at times, but both accepted different charges. On 3 April 1816 Rev Peter MacDerment (or MacDermid) from Ayr was appointed, the call being made by 52 male members and 22 adherents at Auchinleck. They offered him a stipend of £100 and a manse adjacent to the church.

In 1820 the Anti-Burghers and the Burghers re-joined to form the United Associate Secession Church. Peter MacDerment, however, was against the union and with his co-presbyter, Rev George Stevenson, took part in the formation of the Society of Protestors on 29 May 1821. His followers at Auchinleck were not all of the same opinion as he and a number of elders and members wrote to the United Presbytery for some advice 'in their present trying circumstances.' Despite some meetings between the parties to try to solve the differences, no compromise could be made, so those who disagreed with MacDerment left to join the Secession Church in Cumnock, a Burgher congregation prior to the union. Peter MacDerment died on 26 September 1833 in his fifty-third year and seventeenth year of ministry and was buried in the parish kirkyard. His parishioners erected a memorial over his grave to their 'much esteemed pastor.'

According to the *New Statistical Account* the Original Secession Church in Auchinleck had 86 members plus 14 from other parishes in 1837. They offered £70 plus a manse to prospective ministers but were not able to fill the charge for four years after MacDerment's death, until on 8 November 1837 when Rev George Roger MA was ordained.

EDUCATION

One of the aims of John Knox at the Reformation was to establish a school in every parish of the kingdom. This forward-looking idea proved difficult to carry out for many years, however, and in 1616 the Privy Council issued an act which stated that, 'In everie parroche of this kingdome, whair convenient means be had for interteyning a scoole, that a scoole sal be establishet and a fitt persone appointit to teach the same.' This act was ratified by Charles I in 1633, but still was not fully implemented and in 1638 the General Assembly strove to establish schools. However, on 18 May 1642, according to the Presbytery of Ayr records, there were still seven Ayrshire parishes (of which Auchinleck was one) in which schools had yet to be founded. The reasons given for Auchinleck were that there were no means of funding a dominie's wages nor was there a location conveniently placed for a schoolhouse, '... thair culd not be ane convenient place for a schoole, in respect of the great distance of the parochiners from the kirk, bot that honest men keiped thair bairnes at shoole at home besyde themselves. And that thair wes no setled maintenance for a schoolmaster, and thairfor the Moderator in name of the Presbiterie desyred the said Mr Johne [Shaw] to tak paines for provyding of competent mantenance for a schoolmaster.' A teacher was appointed, for in January 1615 mention is made of 'Adame Watson, late schoolemaster at Achinleck.'

Charles I issued another act in 1646 which stated that there should be a 'school founded and a scholemaster appointed in everie paroche (not already provyded)' and another appeared in 1696 when William II issued an 'Act for Settling Schools' in every parish where there was still none. Getting a teacher still seems to have been a problem, for on 31 January 1721 it is noted that, 'The paroches of ... Achinleck ... have no setlement for a schoolmaster at all ... and they appoint Ministers ... to lay it befor their heretors in order to their more easie going into the s[ai]d setlement without a legall pursuit.'

A few teachers seem to have taught for a short time at Auchinleck, probably in the church, such as James Dryden, 'schoolmr at Achinleck,' who signed the Confession of Faith on 6 April 1727. In 1735 the

THE

PRACTICAL FIGURER;

OR, AN

IMPROVED SYSTEM

OF

ARITHMETIC

CONTAINING,

A large Exemplification of the several Rules in common Arithmetic, with the Doctrine of Vulgar and Decimal Fractions; abounding with numerous Examples, useful, subtle, and entertaining, for gaining the Attention and improving the Genius of Youth.

Many new and concise Methods for finding the Price of Goods Interest of Money, &c, with one Rule entirely New, called Irregular Progression, never before heard of in Arithmetic.

A large practical System of Algebra, containing a great variety of new and entertaining Problems, with a direct Method of solving Cubic Equations, by an easy and simple Operation.

By WILLIAM HALBERT,
SCHOOLMASTER AT AUCHINLECK.

Omne tulit punctum, qui miscuit utile dulci.   HOR.

PAISLEY:

PRINTED BY JOHN NEILSON.

MDCCLXXXIX.

4.12 William Halbert's The Practical Figurer (1789)
(Author's Collection)

Presbytery took instruments against the heritors of those parishes which had no school provision, nor a salary for a schoolmaster. Auchinleck was one of the twelve parishes listed.

The situation remained thus until 1764 when the heritors decided to appoint a teacher. From the Session Records we read: 'Nov 4 1764. Alex Mitchell of Halglenmuir; James Lennox of Darnconner; John Boswell for his grandmother, Mrs Fergusson of Knockroon; Lord Auchinleck; and Alan Whiteford of Ballochmyle, met and agreed to assess one hundred pounds Scots for a year for a schoolmaster – ten shillings sterling to give to one man to teach up the parish, and as much to teach down.' The teacher appointed to Auchinleck was William Halbert, who proved to be a rather educated man. He wrote *The Practical Figurer, or an Improved System of Arithmetic*, a very ingenious treatise, published in 1789, and a number of verses, some of which were published. Halbert was also the session clerk in the church, responsible for recording marriages and deaths. However, James Boswell visited him in September 1780 and noted that the registers 'had been much neglected in our parish record… I put him on a regular plan, which he promised to follow; I being to pay three-pence for each death provided he missed none. He is paid by legal right from baptisms and marriages.'

In 1762 £5 Sterling had been left by Dr Cochrane, son of Cochrane of Waterside, 'for the encouragement of a schoolmaster at Kirk of Auchinleck, now (with interest) valued at £10 15s.' This was used to buy a piece of ground suitable for building 'a school-house upon, a yard or park for the schoolmaster, and a court or place for the scholars to play in.' The site of this school was at the top end of the village, roughly at 217 Main Street. The two other parish schools were to be located near or at Burnhouse (on Barony Road) and Duncanziemere. The teachers at these schools were to be chosen annually. They were to charge 1s 6d per quarter for teaching English alone, 2 shillings for writing, or English and writing, or half a crown for English, writing and arithmetic. 'But when parents are poor that then the session shall have a power of modifying the wages for their children, restricting the number whose wages are to be thus modified to eight in the winter quarter and two in every other quarter of the year in the school at the kirk and to four in the quarter in each of the other two schools.' Halbert died sometime around the end of the eighteenth century.

Another teacher was noted for being an excellent educator, but attendance at his school fell due to his intemperate habits. Alcohol was something that even the pupils were introduced to, being given a glass of weak toddy on New Year's Day.

There does not seem to have been a replacement appointed after Halbert, for there was no school at the time of the *Statistical Account* (1792). In 1821 the Commissioners of Supply for the county were forced into appointing a schoolmaster for the parish. The commissioners were empowered by the 1696 act to appoint a schoolmaster where the heritors failed to do this, and to charge the cost to them. This situation occurred just twice in Ayrshire, firstly at Auchinleck and again in 1851 at Kilmarnock. In 1793 there is reference to school at Weilside run by William Scott.

By the time the *New Statistical Account* was written in 1837, a school and schoolhouse had been established 'close by' the village, both of which were reported to be in 'tolerable order'. The school had been erected in 1803 and the schoolmaster was paid the maximum salary, that is £34 4s 4½d, but there were no Latin scholars. Nevertheless, hardly any individuals in the parish could not write. A private school was also run in the village, which attracted numerous pupils. Three miles west of the village a third school operated (no doubt at Burnhouse), and though there was no similar school building for the pupils of the eastern end of the parish, a teacher was employed by the farmers and other residents there.

INDUSTRY
During the first half of the eighteenth century an important stage in the development of the parish from rural to industrial took place with the establishment of an iron works at Tarrioch, also spelled Terreoch, on the banks of the River Ayr. Located near to Muirkirk, but within Auchinleck parish, these works were built by the Earl of Cathcart, probably around 1730, two years before succeeding, though one account puts the date as early as 1705. The ironworks stood on what is now known as Old Foundry Holm, on the opposite bank of the river from Townhead of Greenock farm. Here the remains of the lade, dam and race can still be made out on the ground, the buildings little more than piles of stone. The Tarrioch foundry converted pig iron into malleable iron, water power driving the bellows and

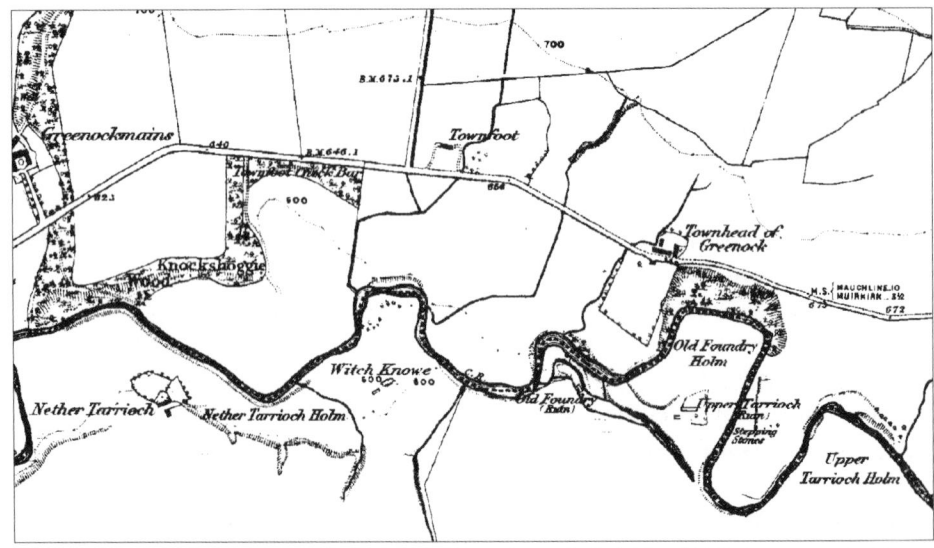

4.13 Tarrioch as shown on Ordnance Survey Six Inch Map of 1860

hammers. Heat was provided by burning wood and peat, though the former became scarce and the latter was not obtained readily enough nor given sufficient time to dry. It was this problem with fuel which led to the closure of the works.

Most of the workforce employed at Tarrioch were Englishmen, and their houses were situated on the north side of the Sorn to Muirkirk road, between Townhead and Townfoot. An unusual circumstance regarding the supply of pig-iron to the forge was the fact that, even though the haematite ore was quarried on the slopes of Blackside, below Pennelburn Linn, in the parish of Sorn, and had an iron content of up to 80%, it had to be taken on pack-horse to Ayr and then shipped to Bunawe, near Taynuilt in Argyll, where it was smelted by the Lorn Furnace Company. From there the pig-iron was carried back to Tarrioch, along with salt from Ayr. This inconvenience and additional expense no doubt was another reason for the foundry's closure.

According to John Smith, in *Prehistoric Man in Ayrshire*, the foundry was known as the 'Spade Works', implying that spades and shovels formed the greater part of its output. The two Tarriochs, Upper and Nether, subsequently became the property of the Duke of Portland. The farms were abandoned, the land being attached to Nether Wellwood.

At Wallaceton a quarry existed for a black stone which proved to be fireproof and was in great demand for building ovens. It was worked in the latter half of the eighteenth century, as was a quarry for mill stones on the banks of the Lugar, until around 1840. A lead mine existed at Bell's Park, but this was abandoned early in the eighteenth century, if it ever worked. Two mineral springs were used for medicinal purposes, one at Cub's Craig, on the Glenmuir, the other at Welltrees farm. Both had petrifying qualities, one a chalybeate (containing iron) the other purgative (used to clean the intestines). A number of sandstone quarries were then in production, the stone used for building purposes.

Though the *Statistical Account* of the parish, written in 1792, states that coal had been 'wrought from time immemorial' on the estate of Auchinleck, this was done on an extremely small scale, indeed, the writer goes on to indicate that it is only worked 'wherever any demand prevails.' Similarly, in Old Cumnock parish, in 1804, coal was 'wrought only on the surface by digging holes and drawing water till the quantity wanted was obtained.' In Muirkirk, only one collier was employed in the parish, for a period of one month in the year, to pick coal with hand tools, and this seems to have satisfied demand prior to the establishment of the ironworks in 1786. Most households in the district burned peat or turves on the fire, and the parish of Auchinleck was well supplied with both. However, it is known that 'wheel and cylinder pumps' were installed at Birnieknowe coalworks in 1767 and at Gasswater a 'water machine for drying the coalwork' was installed in 1769. In 1788 John Murdoch, father of the gas-engineer, installed a 'small fire engine' or steam-operated pump, at Birnieknowe for the Boswells.

The limeworks at Gasswater were established in the early nineteenth century, converting limestone into lime. A number of bell pits were sunk to supply coal for the works. On Friday 21 October 1831 two men died in a coal pit near to the Gasswater Limeworks. The men were brothers of the name Baird, sons of a local farmer. They had gone to the mouth of the pit that was being sunk at the time, and which had reached five fathoms (30 feet) in depth. One of the lads persuaded the other to lower him to the bottom, but when he got there he fell down, asphyxiated by the gas. The brother on the surface raised the alarm, and a man surnamed Murdoch came to his aid. He was lowered down the pit, but also collapsed due to the gas. A second helper, David Macleod went down the pit, and he, too, collapsed. James Davidson then made an attempt at a rescue, but as he neared the bottom he felt the gas and called out to be hauled back up. He tried again, but had to be hauled back up by a rope that he had tied around his body. A fire was lit and lowered into the pit, but the smoke caused difficulty in seeing. However, it caused one of the asphyxiated men to moan. Those on the surface turned the windlass and discovered David MacLeod hanging onto it by one hand. He managed to recover sufficiently to be able to walk back to Auchinleck at night. The two men who were left in the pit died, the man named Baird and that named Murdoch, the latter leaving a wife and young family.

4.14 Glenmuir Limeworks in 1990 *(Dane Love)*

The first real demand for coal came with the establishment of the limeworks, at that time still only supplying lime for agricultural purposes. The first collieries were established adjacent to the limeworks or, more correctly, limeworks were established close to coal and lime deposits. Thus small coal pits were sunk on the hill of Benalt, south of High Dalblair, and at Hawk Hill, north of High Glenmuir. Some outcrops in the Lugar and Cronberry area were worked, miners receiving wages of around ten-pence per day. These pits were established by Lord Auchinleck who, like Lord Dumfries, had looked into his estate's potential from minerals. Indeed, for some time he 'exported' coal to Cumnock, but in 1784 it was reported that Lord Dumfries sold more coal in 'the village of Cumnock as for some time Lord Auchinleck's coal did not go regularly.' A few small pits became more permanent and in the 1830s the first two steam engines arrived in the parish, used for pumping water from the shafts.

According to the *New Statistical Account* new developments were being made on the Auchinleck estate, and also on land belonging to William Maxwell Alexander of Ballochmyle (that is Darnconner and Common). The seams worked varied from three to four feet thick, around 50 fathoms below the surface. Each pit employed between 20-24 men and annually produced about 8,456 tons in total, sold by the pits from five shillings to five shillings and sixpence per ton, or around £2,100 per annum. The big leap in coal output had still to arrive, when the railways were built and the ironworks established at Lugar.

Death in these small pits was all too common, and a number of incidents are recorded in old documents and gravestones. For example, Janet Merry, the twelve-year-old daughter of James Merry, was killed 'by the machine at Birnieknow coalwork' on 23 September 1786. On 22 March the following year, William Merry, son to John Merry in Birnieknowe, was killed when he fell into a coal pit, at the age of fourteen. Robert Merry in Birnieknowe died 'somewhat suddenly' on 5 December 1788, aged 80 years.

As with a few other local Ayrshire villages, notably Cumnock and Mauchline, Auchinleck was an important centre of box-making. Small wooden snuff boxes were made by a number of individuals in the village, and it was in Auchinleck that the secret of the Laurencekirk hinge was discovered. These hinges were extremely difficult to make, and no-one outside Laurencekirk in Kincardineshire knew how it was done. However, it is said that on one occasion a Frenchman was visiting Sir Alexander Boswell at Auchinleck House when he discovered that his snuff mull was empty. He sent it to the village to be refilled, but unfortunately it was broken in the process. The only person in the village able to sort it was John Crawford. According to an early account of the incident in the *Scots Times*, after the mull was repaired, Crawford 'sought it as a model to make another for Sir Alexander; and in this he succeeded so well that others were ordered, and so on till the manufacture of these boxes had become his sole employment.' Other accounts state that the mull was sent to a Mr Wyllie in the village for repair. Wyllie was trained as a blacksmith, but was so good at his work, and capable of such intricate detail, that he branched into watchmaking and gunsmithery. Working with him was one William Crawford. The snuff-box sent to be mended so confused them that it took a while to work out what to do. Some solder applied had run into the hinge making it useless, and should heat be used to re-melt it would result in damaging the box. At length William Crawford managed to make a tool with which to cut out the solder in a most ingenious way. The snuff-box was mended and returned to its owner, and Wyllie and Crawford started to produce boxes of their own, keeping the hinge secret for twelve years.

The partners had a disagreement around 1810, whereupon Crawford moved to Cumnock to set up in business for himself. He employed a watchmaker from Douglas to make a copy of the special tool, but the watchmaker suspected what the tool was for, and soon divulged its secret. Many other box-makers began business, resulting in the cost of the boxes plummeting from five pounds to just eighteen pence each. The box-makers in the district diversified to keep up sales, and instead of just snuff-boxes made containers suitable for needles, hat-pins, calling cards and stamps. Made from wood of the sycamore or plane tree, the boxes were highly polished and varnished, some using transfers, others with original paintwork. A small machine was used to print on a tartan check, at one time very common. In 1837 there were 64 people in the parish employed in box-making, producing about 656 per week, most of which were exported to London. Their average weekly wage then was thirteen shillings and sixpence. Names of box-makers in Auchinleck include William Johnston (1813-1892) and George Murdoch. The trade diminished in the second half of the nineteenth century, Johnston and Murdoch probably being among the last men employed in the trade. Helen Steven, in her *History of Auchinleck*, noted in 1898 that 'there is still a little box-making in Auchinleck.'

Auchinleck, with its origins in semi-modern times as a planned village, was a typical community in which the weaving trade was carried out. By 1792, when the *Statistical Account* was written, there were fifteen weavers, plus one stocking-weaver. This rose to around sixty or seventy, according to the *New Statistical Account* (1837), but by 1898 there were no weavers in the parish. When trade was at its peak, those who wove light silks could earn from ten to twelve shillings a week, those weaving coarser cloths from seven shillings and sixpence to eight shillings. Light silks and muslins were the most common fabrics made, the webs mainly supplied from Glasgow by agents who took them back to the city markets.

Many women in the parish added to the family income by muslin-flowering. Cloth was sent to them by agents of Glasgow fabric houses. The women used a fine needle to form flowers, ferns, leaves and Paisley swirls on the muslin, a most tedious task, but with considerable practice the women became very adept at it. Indeed, the work produced in Ayrshire was of a better quality than that manufactured elsewhere, and a higher market price was paid for it. It has since become known as 'Ayrshire Needlework,' having been first devised by a Mrs Jamieson, wife of an Ayr cotton agent. Women of all ages in the parish worked at it, not only villagers but farmer's daughters also. They could earn from five to eight shillings a week, more if they worked at it longer. Flowering went out of fashion early in the second half of the century, removing a good source of income. This came about mainly due to the American Civil War (1861-65) which prevented raw cotton being imported to this country, and latterly by the invention of machinery which could sew similar styles at a reduced price.

COMMERCE

In 1837 J. Pigot & Co. compiled their *National Commercial Directory of Scotland*, which gave a reasonable account of every community in the country. Auchinleck, 'a respectable village' according to the directory, was listed along with Cumnock. Listed in the directory associated with Auchinleck were: Andrew Gibson, John Millroy, James Murdoch, agents to manufacturers; John Templeton, baker; James MacKerrow, blacksmith; David Hamilton and John Wilson, boot makers; William Morton, carpenter and cartwright; Daniel Eadie, George Templeton, grocers and spirit dealers; Andrew Morton, mason; Daniel Eadie, John Findlay, John Gibson, James MacGregor, James MacKie and David Murdoch, snuff-box makers; Alexander Gregg, surgeon; Walter Wilson, tailor; Robert Murdoch, horse dealer; and James Wyllie, gunsmith.

The post office in the village was located within the Auchinleck Arms Inn in 1837, Janet Dalrymple being the post-mistress. General letters arrived every morning at nine o' clock and were despatched at five o'clock in the evening. The post from London arrived at half past four in the afternoon and were despatched in the evening at half past seven.

From the 'Map of Post Roads in Scotland', dated 1813, we find that Auchinleck was served by a foot-runner who travelled daily with the mail from Cumnock to Mauchline, and thence to Kilmarnock and Glasgow. The post was collected once a day, six days a week. By 1838 the 'Map of the Circulation of Letters in Scotland' indicated that though Auchinleck was still served by a foot-runner, from Mauchline the post was taken by gig to Muirkirk, Kilmarnock or Ayr as required.

In 1791, when the *New Statistical Account* was compiled, six inns existed in Auchinleck village, one of which was at the Old Mill, or Bridgend Mill. The 'loupin' on' stone which existed there was removed in 1927. According to Pigot there were four inns in the village in 1837. These were the Auchinleck Arms (proprietrix Janet Dalrymple), William MacKerrow's inn, the Black Bull Inn (Robert Morton, proprietor), and George Templeton's inn.

AGRICULTURE

In 1778 Andrew Wight compiled two volumes on the *Present State of Husbandry in Scotland*, in which he made reference to the condition of agriculture in Auchinleck parish, as well as the planting of trees being carried out by Lord Auchinleck:

As I advanced toward Cumnock, I passed through a farm of Lord Auchinleck's estate, mostly a thin moorish ground. I cast my eye upon a very good crop of oats after fallow and lime. The ridges were raised so high as to leave the furrows bare of soil, and without a single stalk of corn. I do not pretend to condemn this method in a wet climate. High ridges preserve dry four-fifth of the surface; and better abandon the remaining fifth, than that the whole should be wet. But I did find speculative improvers, and now and then a practical farmer, doubting whether very narrow ridges, well gathered up, and carefully water furrowes, would answer better. I am confirmed, by long experience, that no ridge should be narrower than 15 feet.

Lord Auchinleck is a most assiduous planter, and equally careful of his trees, though indeed in that wet climate, they require little else but to be fenced from the cattle. His closures are extensive, and his own farm is mostly in grass. Upon his broad walks lined with trees and consequently well sheltered, hay is commonly taken. But the culture of corn, a most laborious operation in a wet climate, and clay soil, is generally left to tenants; nor, in such circumstances, can success be expected but by a lose and punctual attendance. His Lordship, therefore, in my opinion, judges rightly in confining himself to the propagation of trees, which require not close attendance. His office as judge in the two sovereign courts of session and justiciary, occupies at least two thirds of his time; and every time he returns home he has the satisfaction to find his plantations in a prosperous state, and every tree growing more and more beautiful.

In 1793 Colonel William Fullarton of that Ilk compiled a *General View of the Agriculture of the County of Ayr*, in which he refers to the improvements being made across the county at the time. Although Auchinleck is not specifically mentioned, from the appearance of the land soon after this period, it can be safely assumed that the parish, at least the better agriculturally western end, underwent such improvements. This included planting of woodlands and hedges, draining soil and liming.

Fullarton's *General View* also noted that the parish had thirteen proprietors owning property in the parish. He states that there were 72 farmers, 220 horses, 1,000 cows and 12,000 sheep. The greatest part of the parish was arable, with a clay soil, and large tracts of heath.

In September 1837 Rev James Chrystal contributed the entry on Auchinleck parish to the *New Statistical Account of Scotland*. At that time there were eleven landowners in the parish, Sir James Boswell owning two thirds of it, followed by the

2nd Marquis of Bute and Limond of Dalblair. 5,040 acres of the parish were cultivated, 370 acres under wood, and there were 13,590 acres of rough moorland. He noted that several hundred acres of moss had recently been reclaimed. Arable land was leased at 17 shillings per acre, grazing at £3 per cow or five shillings per sheep. Most leases were issued for nine years, but some were for 14 or 19 years, hence a reluctance by the tenants to spend money draining. The annual gross produce of the parish was: grain £4,800; potatoes, turnips, etc., £600; ryegrass and hay, £1,820; dairy produce £4,100; produce of sheep, £1,650; wood, £75.

TRANSPORT

The first proper roads in Ayrshire were not constructed until the middle decades of the eighteenth century. The earliest known road in the county was perhaps constructed in the 1730s, when the 4th Earl of Loudoun laid one out across his estate. By 1768, the roads constructed were still of a very poor condition, and Alexander Montgomerie of Coilsfield noted that 'the great roads leading through [Ayrshire are] next to impassable for six months in the year.'

One of the earliest detailed maps of Auchinleck parish was that drawn around 1750 by General William Roy. At a scale of about one inch to one mile, Roy's Military Survey was drawn up following the Battle of Culloden to assist the British Army should any future uprisings take place. At this time there were few roads in the parish, and those travelling from farm to farm or to church would journey across country by whichever route they wished, there being few fences or hedges. Roads in the parish existed from the ford at Stepends (Cumnock) across the Lugar Water (bridged in 1753) by way of 'Affleck Kirk' and the tiniest of clachans, to the ford across the Dippol Burn at Fordmouth. From the kirk a road passed through the enclosed policies of Waterside, with a branch north to Pennyland, and beyond Waterside House to the Lugar Water just below Pennyfadzeoch Mill and perhaps a ford. Another short stretch of roadway existed in the policies of the Place of Auchinleck, from the castle to Auchinleck Mains. Another length of roadway went from Cumnock to Muirkirk, passing through the parish from the ford at Holmhead farm, through the Bello 'Pass' to beyond Boghead.

In 1767 the Ayrshire Road Act was passed, allowing trustees to create turnpike roads across the county and to charge a toll for passing along them. The act provided for the construction and improvement of many miles of roadway, as well as associated bridges and other civil engineering works. The 1767 Act resulted in the formation of two roadways through Auchinleck parish. The principal one was that from Mauchline to Cumnock, with a secondary route from Auchinleck to Sorn. There were no other routes in the parish taken over by the trustees at this time. A toll bar was set up at the junction of these roads, the site of the toll-cottage now occupied by Liddell's offices. The toll-house at Rigg, midway between Cumnock and Auchinleck, survives, typical of the gatekeeper's cottages of the period.

It was not until 1772 that permission was granted for the erection of toll-bars on the Auchinleck to Sorn road. On the Sorn road the next check-bar was at Mossfoot (near South Logan).

A second act of 1774 brought the roads between Cumnock and Muirkirk, through Lugar, and from Cumnock to Crawfordjohn, via Laigh Glenmuir, Dornal and Glenmuirshaw, into the care of the turnpike trust. The road through Lugar had a toll-bar at Logan Braehead (hence Logan Toll), a toll-bar at Wallaceton road-end, and another at Smallburn, near Muirkirk. In 1784 there is reference to John Murdoch of Bello Mill being involved in 'reparations about Craikston Bridge and on the Publick road'. The turnpike road via the Glenmuir to Crawfordjohn, though officially established, was never popular, and much of its route cannot be made out on the ground today.

4.15 Rigg Toll Cottage *(Dane Love)*

Road politics caused some difficulty throughout the period of turnpike roadways. In 1786 James Boswell sent a request through his cousin, Bruce Campbell, to the Kilmarnock to Cumnock road committee that a new funds collector should be appointed for Auchinleck parish. According to the request the present collector, William Halbert, the local schoolmaster, had been negligent in his duties. The committee agreed, and appointed John Boswell Senior of Cumnock in his place. He was to receive a salary of 5% of the funds collected. The funds collected were to be paid to James Boswell, who would be responsible for keeping the road from the Dippol Bridge to Cumnock in good repair. By June 1787 the committee was still having some difficulty with Halbert, and Claud Alexander of

Ballochmyle, convener of the road committee, reported that Halbert 'acknowledges to have been very negligent in his Accounts and that he keept his money in an open drawer without Lock or Key. His Memory seems to be very much impaired, and a very improper man for such an office.' At the same time it was found that Boswell owed some money to the committee and as a consequence:

> A new account is making out of Mr Boswell's debt on the roads in the above parish. In which he is to admit to his debit some money charged in the former account delivered and to give the trustees credit for the statute money of the farmers in his own possession.

Travel at this time was made by horse and cart, should the person afford to keep one. In 1791 the parish had a total of 80 carts and around 200 horses, used also in agriculture. The roads were typical of those in the rest of the county – unfenced in many places, full of holes, bridgeless and often impassable in winter.

As mentioned, some of the estate grounds were being enclosed, fences erected and shelter belts planted. The most extensive policies were located around Waterside House, from the Balance Holm eastward to Knockroon. Auchinleck Old House was also surrounded by enclosed pastures, the policies spreading north into Mauchline parish. Woodlands existed at Templand and eastward by Craigston to the Bello Path. Lesser woods and enclosures were to be found at Wallaceton, Duncanziemere, Stonebriggs, Boghead, Cronberryshield, Dornal and around the Dalblair area.

In the third quarter of the eighteenth century, Lord Auchinleck made a number of improvements to the estate and road network. New drives were made within the policies of Auchinleck New House, notably that by Langlands, the road from the Mains to Gibston, and the north drive, which went straight on at the Dippol Bridge and followed a dogleg within the woods.

Lord Auchinleck's biggest roadbuilding project was the Barony Road, a three mile long, almost straight, avenue from the policies to the parish church. The full length of it was lined with beech and oak trees, the initials of which spelled BO of Boswell. Lord Auchinleck nick-named the road the 'Via-Sacra' (the sacred road) and according to his son it had been made 'at great expense'.

The Boswells and their neighbours, the Dumfries's, had a quarrel over the roads in the parish to the west of Auchinleck. Lord Auchinleck was in the process of enclosing fields in this area, and Lord Dumfries was planning a new road from near Darnlaw to the John Adam-designed Avenue Bridge. This is the oldest known structure designed by John Adam. On 11 February 1760 John Adam furnished a plan for 'a Temple and walls adjoining' which was erected at Pennylands, an ornate Gothic structure with two houses. The houses at the Temple were occupied as late as 1933, when they were abandoned due to mining subsidence.

To this gateway Lord Dumfries constructed a new roadway, but once through it the problems began. Lady Dumfries was under the impression that Lord Auchinleck had granted permission for the roadway to be built, and wrote to him on 26 August 1773 to ask for confirmation:

> My Lord,
> As your Lordship was so polite as grant a request of mine to have a road (through some fields you have lately enclosed) from the Gateway built by the late Lord Dumfries to the turnpike road between Kilmarnock & Cumnock – the season being now advanced it is necessary to have it ascertained so as your promise was given to me I beg you will name what day I shall attend your Lordship to see it lin'd & I will bring one or two of my Lord's servants to do it.
> With Lord Dumfries & Lady Penelope's compts to your Lords Lady Auchinleck and Miss Boswell.
> I am your Lordships most humble servant.

Lord Auchinleck replied stating:

> I have thought maturely upon that road, and as when the late Earl of Dumfreis [sic] was alive, I made out my inclosures on the plan they now are and inclosed a Road for his Lords use which he was well pleased with and have at immoderate charge made a road for my own use to the Church of Auchinleck which indeed gives me great satisfaction & to an old fellow like me is a mistress. Your Ladys and My Lord Dumfreis I hope will excuse me when I say that after long deliberation I cannot submitt to have my Plan altered. But this much I am willing to agree to, that there shall be a road to communicate from the Gateway to the Earls present road if so be the Earl chooses it and fences it properly. . .

Thus the roadway was made: on passing through from the Dumfries House side the road took a sharp right, to join the Runnels Road. The dispute rumbled on for some years, for in 1778 James Boswell makes reference to it in his journal. There he wrote:

> The Earl of Dumfries was [at Treesbank House]. He was exceedingly attentive to me and pressed me much to give him a day at his house this week. But I told him I was afraid it would not be in my power. I was upon my guard, as I knew that he and his Countess flattered themselves that they would get from me that road through our estate

which my father had refused, and which in truth I was still more positive for refusing. While my father was not on visiting terms with the Earl I thought it not decent for me to visit him; and it was my resolution that if ever his Lordship and I should be neighbours, a stipulation never to mention the road should be a preliminary of our intercourse.

In 1780 Boswell still held out – 'I was a little awkward, not having seen the Countess for years, and the families not being upon visiting terms on account of a misunderstanding about a road from Lord Dumfries's gateway. I was resolved they never should have it.'

In November 1782 James Boswell laid out the new road from Auchinleck towards Sorn. This left the Barony Road at Merlinhill and travelled in straight line sections towards South Logan.

Transport from village to village in those days could be made by coach. In 1819 two different services passed through the village, 'The Independent' from Glasgow, or 'Robert Burns' from Carlisle. Coach travel could be quite eventful in those days, for as well as taking four hours to travel from Auchinleck to Glasgow, the coach on at least one occasion became stuck in the snow just one mile from the village, and on another overturned on the Main Street, near Manse Avenue. In later years 'The Independent' travelled from Cumnock to Ayr twice weekly, the Cumnock to Kilmarnock run operated by the 'Lass of Ballochmyle' and the 'Marquis of Bute.'

4.16 The Temple, Dumfries House Estate (Author's Collection)

LEISURE

There was little time for leisure activities in the nineteenth century, but the sport of curling began to grow in popularity. Reference is made to competitions between different parishes, some of the games being of some consequence. For example, in January 1820 Auchinleck parish played against Sorn parish on the Whirr Loch, on Auchinleck estate. The game was played 81-a-side, and for refreshments 'baiks [biscuits] and whisky' was supplied. This may have been when Auchinleck Curling Club was first formed, as it is known to have been founded in 1820. It appears to have closed some years later.

SONS AND DAUGHTERS

One of the most notable sons of the parish was the inventor William Murdoch. He was born at Bello Mill on 21 August 1754, the second son of John Murdoch (1725-1806) and Ann Bruce (died 1800), whom he married on 4 December 1747. She was the sister of James Bruce, land agent on Auchinleck estate. Some folk, however, claim that William Murdoch was born at Bridgend Mill, Auchinleck, where his father had been the miller prior to his removal to Bello Mill. John Murdoch served with the Woolwich Company of the Trains of Artillery from January 1744. He served in Holland and perhaps at Culloden.

John Murdoch was a notable inventor in his own right. The family claim descent from Flemish engineers, and John Murdoch is credited with having invented the first cast iron-toothed pinion gear wheel in 1760, for use at Bello Mill. The first example of this was cast at the newly-constructed Carron Iron Works, near Falkirk, Stirlingshire, by Dr John Roebuck. This first-made pinion was later preserved for historical exhibition. Soon, cast-iron gear wheels became the norm across the world, being a considerable boon to the industrial revolution, but Murdoch did not receive any reward for his part in creating them.

4.17 Bello Mill in 1954 *(Author's Collection)*

From around 1759 to 1767 William Murdoch received an education at the school in Cumnock and followed it with training as a millwright. Around 1770 he and his father built a form of cycle, in which the feet turned the wheels by means of connecting rods. This vehicle was used to travel from Lugar to Cumnock and predated Kirkpatrick MacMillan's bicycle by some 70 years. In 1817 Hugh Campbell made reference to 'Murdoch's Horse' in some verses:

> Murdoch, the world should know thy scientific fame...
> Sprung from a curious deep designing sire
> Who rode a horse no mortal e'er could tire.

Murdoch began experimenting with gas from coal to form light around 1777, his first trials traditionally taking place in the cave below the mill-house, overlooking the weir. Some say that it was he who cut the cave out of the rock, creating a small fireplace within with a flue leading into the kitchen chimney above.

It was also in the year 1777 that Murdoch began work for the great inventors and engineers, James Watt and Matthew Boulton, at their Soho works in Birmingham. He got the job when he dropped his top hat during the interview. From the sound it made as it hit the floor Boulton began to ask questions regarding it. It was revealed that Murdoch had turned his hat from wood on an oval lathe of his own manufacture. He was employed on a rate of fifteen shillings per week.

Murdoch moved to Redruth in Cornwall in 1779 where he was employed to look after Boulton & Watt's many pumping engines in the mines. In 1792 he managed to make a retort which converted coal to gas which he piped from his yard to the house to light it up. The first public demonstration of gas lighting was made in 1802 when Murdoch lit up the Soho factory, and by the following year the factory was regularly lit in this way. Soon other factories used Murdoch's methods to light them, and he was in considerable demand for advice. He became the manager of the Soho factory in 1803, remaining until retiring in 1830. He had married Ann Paynter of Redruth in 1785 and had two sons, William and John. Ann died soon after John's birth at the early age of 24. Murdoch himself died on 15 November 1839 at his home of Sycamore Hill, near the Soho factory. He was buried at Handsworth, alongside Boulton and Watt.

Murdoch is mainly remembered for his gas-lighting invention, but he was responsible for other discoveries also. He invented a small locomotive in 1786; a revised version which could travel freely along the ground frightened the vicar of Redruth. He made a number of improvements to the steam engine, including the 'Sun and Planet' motion. Patents included a method of driving a machine which bores cylinders, the bell-crank engine, stone pipes, a steam gun, 'iron cement' and a special form of paint for ships' hulls.

4.18 Murdoch's Cave and Bello Mill *(Author's Collection)*

William Murdoch was the tenant of Commondyke farm in the early nineteenth century. He was a relative of Murdoch of Bello Mill. He left Commondyke and moved to Glasgow, where he set up as a millwright and engineer. His business, Murdoch & Cross, built engines for various steamers, including the 'Port Glasgow' in 1819. He married a woman named Aitken, a relative of Thomas Carlyle's mother. He died in 1833.

From 1818 to 1822 a son of the parish achieved national fame with the publication of his essays entitled *The Protestant*, later issued in a four volume series which passed through several editions. The author was William MacGavin, third son of James MacGavin and May MacMillan, born on 12 August 1773 at Darnlaw farm, where his father was a tenant of Lord Auchinleck. At the age of seven he spent a short time at the village school, the only formal education he ever received. In 1783 he moved with his family to Paisley where he was apprenticed to a weaver, working as a draw-boy for one shilling per week. He tried his hand at weaving silk, but found his interests drawn to the world of literature. In 1790 he worked with John Neilson, printer and bookseller in Paisley, where his knowledge of the English language was greatly improved. He served his apprenticeship with Neilson, and as a result came into contact with a number of literary figures, including Alexander Wilson, poet and ornithologist. Paisley weavers were at the time great proponents of reform, and MacGavin sided with them.

From 1793, having left Neilson's employ, he spent some time teaching in his elder brother's school, where he taught English, arithmetic and mathematics. He was also able to teach the pupils geography, astronomy and some areas of natural history. MacGavin was soon to become the sole master, but he gave up the school in 1798. For a short period he established a thread-making business in Paisley, but he was unable to compete with the larger firms, and this was closed down.

In January 1799 he became a bookkeeper and clerk to David Lamb, an American cotton merchant based in Glasgow. Simultaneously, MacGavin acted as tutor to Lamb's two sons. When Lamb returned to his native America in 1803, MacGavin became manager of the business, and on Lamb's death in 1813 became a partner with Lamb's son. The business was transformed into a West India business in Glasgow, known as MacGavin and Lamb. The business operated for a number of years, was never greatly profitable, and eventually it was closed down in 1822. In that year he took over the agency of the British Linen Company's bank in Glasgow, remaining manager until his death.

In 1805 MacGavin married Isabella Campbell, a lady from the West Indies and a former pupil of his school at Paisley. They were never to have any children.

MacGavin was brought up in the Presbyterian church, as a member of the Anti-Burgher denomination. Around the year 1800 he assisted Rev James Ramsay (d. 1824) in founding an Independent Congregational Church which met in the Trades' hall in Glasgow, followed by the Anderson's Institution hall. MacGavin preached on a number of occasions and in April 1804 was ordained as Ramsay's co-pastor. During this time he contributed articles to the Glasgow Chronicle on the main points of controversy between the Presbyterian and Roman Catholic religions.

In 1808 MacGavin joined the Tabernacle Congregational Church in Jamaica Street, followed by the Nile Street Congregational Church in Glasgow, both under the ministry of Rev Dr Greville Ewing (1767-1841), and was soon appointed as a deacon. He turned down offers from the minister to preach in the church, due to work commitments, but he would undertake to fill vacant pulpits in surrounding villages on occasion. He wrote numerous tracts and stories of a religious nature from 1818-1822. When issued in book form, *The Protestant* quickly passed through seven editions in its first ten years. Apparently, one of the most eminent bishops of the Church of England offered to give him holy orders, based on his works. MacGavin also supported a number of Glasgow benevolent and religious societies and became a popular speaker at their meetings.

However, a reference in *The Protestant* regarding the erection of a Roman Catholic chapel in Glasgow led to an action for libel against him in April 1821. He was fined £100 plus expenses, which brought the total to in excess of £1,200. Such was MacGavin's following that a public subscription to pay this raised £800. MacGavin paid the remaining £400 by himself, but his publisher came forward and reimbursed him, such had the popularity of the books been.

Other works published include a sermon, *True Riches*, a refutation of Robert Owen's principles, and an edition of John Knox's *History of the Reformation*. He wrote a number of books for the young and an edition of John Howie's *Scots Worthies*, a notable biography of the Covenanters, published in 1827. A number of smaller pamphlets were also issued, including *Church Establishments Considered*, in a *Series of Letters to a Covenanter*.

MacGavin died on 23 August 1832 of apoplexy and was buried in the crypt of Glasgow's Wellington Street Chapel. In Glasgow's Fir Park, later to become the Necropolis, a large monument was erected in his honour, second only to John Knox in order there, which he had been instrumental in erecting. The monument stands 35 feet tall, with a four-winged pedestal and statue of MacGavin surmounting it, sculpted by Robert Forrest. Designed by John Bryce, the memorial includes the inscription:

> To the memory of William MacGavin, merchant Glasgow, author of the 'Protestant,' &c &c, who died on the XXIII August MDCCCXXXII aged fifty-nine years, this monument has been erected by his fellow citizens, MDCCCXXXIV.

Two further volumes of MacGavin's works were published posthumously in 1834 and he was commemorated in his own parish on the obelisk erected in memory of the notables of Auchinleck. The relevant inscription reads:

> Sacred to the memory of William MacGavin, author of 'The Protestant.'
> He was born at Dernlaw in this parish in 1773.
> Died at Glasgow, 23rd August 1832, aged 59 years.
> Princes and lords are but the breath of kings,
> An honest man's the noblest work of God.

In 1792 there died in the village one Matthew Tait who must have been a notable character. According to his tombstone, which was re-erected in 1864, he 'was born in the reign of Charles II. He served as a private soldier at the taking of Gibraltar in 1704 and died at Auchinleck village 19 March 1792 aged 123 years.' Two carved heads adorn the stone. Tait lived in the village's Main Street, in a white-washed and thatched cottage. There was formerly a plaque on the cottage commemorating him, but the building was demolished to make way for Dacre Terrace (218 Main Street) which was erected in 1897.

Also in the kirkyard, but from a slightly later period, is the stone to A. Baird Gregg, noted for its epitaph, which has been copied on both sides of the stone. Gregg was the local doctor and was noted for his habit of putting patient care before his own wants. He was appointed Medical Officer for the parish around 1830 on a half-yearly salary of £3. He died on 7 January 1848 aged 53. Now partially illegible, the epitaph reads:

> Here lies the dust of A. Baird Gregg
> Wha was a skilly Doctor,
> His labours he did freely gie,
> It wasna gowd he wrocht for;
> A fee he seldom ever sought,
> And ne'er frae a puir body,
> Was weel content gif he gat food,
> And whiles a gless o' toddy;
> As long's he dwelt among us here,
> Baith rich and puir did bless him,
> And noo that he's been ta'en awa',
> At weel-a-wat we'll miss him.

BURNS AND AUCHINLECK

Scotland's poet, Robert Burns, even though he resided in the neighbouring parish of Mauchline for a number of years, and would often pass through the village on his way from Mossgiel to Dumfries and back, seems to have had little to do with the parish. However, a tradition long maintained in the district was that John Murdoch, Burns' teacher at Alloway and Ayr Grammar schools, was a son of the village and that his father David Murdoch was Session Clerk of the parish kirk.

A couple of lines in Burns' 'The Vision', written around 1785, make reference to Auchinleck House in a suppressed stanza:

> Nearby arose a mansion fine,
> The seat of many a muse divine.

In a footnote Burns explained that this mansion was Auchinleck, and he mentioned it as a compliment to James Boswell, a fellow literary figure whom he hoped to meet, but the two great sons of Ayrshire were never to share each other's company. Another line in the same poem, 'An aged Judge, I saw him rove, Dispensing good,' is said to refer to Alexander, Lord Auchinleck.

A letter by the poet to Bruce Campbell of Mayfield and Milrig (Galston) written from Mauchline on 13 November 1788, records the poet's wishes:

> Sir,
> I inclose you, for Mr Boswell, the Ballad ['The Fete Champetre'] you mentioned; and as I hate sending waste paper, or mutilating a sheet, I have filled it up with one or two of my fugitive pieces that occurred. –

Should they procure me the honour of being introduced to Mr Boswell, I shall think they have great merit. – There are few pleasures my late will 'o' wisp character has given me, equal to that of having seen many of the extraordinary men, the Heroes of Wit & Literature in my Country; & as I had the honor of drawing my first breath almost in the same Parish with Mr Boswell, my Pride plumes itself on the connection. – To crouch in the train of mere, stupid Wealth & Greatness, except where the commercial interests of wordly Prudence find their account in it, I hold to be Prostitution in anyone that is not born a Slave, but to have been acquainted with such a man as Mr Boswell, I would hand down to my Posterity as one of the honors of their Ancestor:-
I am, Sir, your most obedient & very humble servant,
Robert Burns.

'The Fete Champetre' refers to Boswell also, in the last two lines of the first verse:

> Or him wha led o'er Scotland a',
> The meikle Ursa-Major?

This refers to Boswell as the person who took the great bear, that is Johnson, on a tour of Scotland. He is mentioned by name in 'The Author's Earnest Cry and Prayer', a poem written to the Scots Members of Parliament. Boswell's long-windedness is implied in the line: 'Or gab like Boswell'.

Probably the person from Auchinleck most associated with Burns was Rev John Dun, parish minister. Following the publication of the 'Address to the Deil', Dun wrote a reply entitled 'The Deil's Answer to his verra friend, R. Burns', in a volume of his sermons which were published in 1790, by the same printer as Burns' first volume, John Wilson of Kilmarnock. Dun, whilst travelling in the Borders, fell from his horse at Watcarrick, near Eskdalemuir, landing in the River White Esk. Burns heard of the incident, and penned his satirical verses, 'Ye Calvinists o' Auchinleck':

> Ye Calvinists o' Auchinleck,
> In mournin weeds yourselves bedeck,
> An' shew how much ye did respect
>   Your great divine,
> Wha fell, poor soul, and broke his neck,
>   On Esk langsyne.

Had he been deaf, blind, dumb or lame,
Like many a priest that I could name,
Wha's merits nae encomiums claim,
    You might indeed
Let dark oblivion blast his fame,
    Since now he's dead.

But sure an aye ye a' can say
He took good tent for mony a day,
That name 'mang Whigs might do it astray
    To yon hill head;
He was a nonesuch in his way,
    But oh! he's dead.

His hame-spun zeal an' catechizin',
His lecturin' an sermonisin'!
Set mony an auld wife's heart ableezin;
    But now I dread
In spite o' fate they'll a' fa' freezin',
    Since now he's dead.

When frae his horse his carcase fell,
His soul went - but I darena tell -
Ye cannot fail to guess yoursel';
    For fifty head,
Can swear his Reverence wrote frae Hell,
    Since he was dead.

In the eighteenth century John Templeton achieved some degree of fame as an opera singer in London. He was born in Riccarton parish, near Kilmarnock, in 1802, but he claimed that he was a descendant of the Templetons of Hapland, a farm located just off the Barony Road. He was noted as a fine choir boy in his youth. He went to join his elder brother in Edinburgh. He was a concert-singer and teacher there, also being a precentor in a secession church under the ministry of Rev John Brown. John Templeton decided upon a career as a singer and set off for London. He appeared in a few operatic performances but was catapulted to fame when he had to stand in and take the part of Don Ottavio in Mozart's Don Giovanni, then being performed in Covent Garden.

    In 1833 Maria Malibran, the diva of her day, famed across the whole of Europe, selected Templeton to be her tenor in *La Sonnambula*. He was thereafter known as 'Malibran's Ten'. Malibran died in a riding accident in 1836, just before they were due to set off on a tour of England, Ireland and Scotland. Templeton therefore set off on a successful solo career, performing at Drury Lane and Covent Garden on the same night on many occasions. In 1843 he started a journey around the country lecturing and singing songs of the period. In a subsequent tour he performed in many of the principal American cities. This lasted for ten years, after which he retired. His final concert took place in New York, which was the largest ever audience to turn up for a single performer thus far. He retired at the age of fifty to his house, Tempe Villa, near the River Thames at Hampton in Middlesex. He died in 1886.

CHAPTER FIVE

INDUSTRIAL GROWTH
(1840-1901)

VILLAGE LIFE

The second half of the nineteenth century was Auchinleck's 'boom-time'. The railway arrived, ironworks were established at Lugar, and coal and ironstone pits were sunk to supply the raw materials. More employees were required than could be found locally, resulting in a considerable influx of workers from surrounding parishes, as well as numerous labourers arriving from Ireland. Where the population of the parish had risen slowly from 775 in 1791 to 1,659 in 1841, by 1851 it had almost doubled to 3,697; to 4,213 by 1861 and 6,174 by 1871. The rate of increase began to tail off, peaking at 6,681 in 1881, dropping to 6,202 in 1891, before rising again to 6,605 in 1901.

The first full census of the population of the country took place in 1841; however, the records for Auchinleck parish were lost in 1910 when a ship carrying them and other records back to Scotland from England was lost at sea. The village in 1865 had 727 houses, considerably more than Cumnock's 425 houses in 1871. According to the 1851 Census the 'Village of Templetown' was separate from Auchinleck.

The increase in population did not greatly affect the size of Auchinleck itself, for most of the incomers were housed in miners' rows erected in the central part of the parish, at Darnconner, Commondyke, Lugar, Cronberry and Gasswater.

At Auchinleck advances were being made in sanitation and the supply of water to the village. The two wells in the village that had served the community for years were no longer suitable. One of these was located at the top end of the village, where Market Road and Main Street meet. The other was located near to the parish church, and was known as the Kirkland Well. In 1883 the lower well in the village was closed off by the Medical Officer of Health as the water was unsuitable for human consumption and a likely source of epidemic diseases. In 1880 and 1885 the Auchinleck Parochial Board applied to the council in Cumnock to extend the water main from the town (supplied from Borland reservoir) on to Auchinleck. However, on both occasions the Cumnock board had to turn the request down, having problems supplying its own inhabitants.

Instead, a separate water supply was piped into the village from a different location in Old Cumnock parish. John and James Park were the two principal instigators in this project, which saw the piping of water from Avisyard Hill into the village. Their father, James Park, had been killed in the Common Colliery in the 1800s. New water valves were located along the Main Street, the cast iron heads being manufactured by Glenfield & Kennedy of Kilmarnock. These were located in front of the Toll Cottage in Mauchline Road, in front of Albion cottage, near Brownlee Place, at the foot of Station Road, at Beechwood Square, outside the present Masonic Lodge, at the corner of Main Street with Coal Road, opposite Orchard Place, in front of the Town Hall, and in front of the east gate into the parish church grounds. A further three were located in Mauchline Road, including Templeton Place.

Dr James Lawrence was appointed as surgeon to Lugar Ironworks in 1849 and in 1851 became Parochial Doctor to Auchinleck and Old Cumnock parishes. He was born in Kirriemuir, Angus, in 1829 and was educated at Aberdeen University. He was succeeded by Dr John Gilmour Kerr MB CM JP (1867-1906), who lived at Stepends House, Cumnock. In 1865 a Mr MacGregor was the village's Inspector of Poor. Robert Hutchinson was the village surgeon in 1856.

In 1895 a small portion of Auchinleck parish was removed and attached to that of Old Cumnock. The piece of land comprised of the Holm, 'Boo'd Scotland' and Stepends, which was located just over the Lugar Bridge from Cumnock and on which a number of houses had already been built, including the United Presbyterian Manse and Lochnorris, James Keir Hardie's home. He had been a member of Auchinleck School Board from 1885-1887. The Congregational Church had stood in the parish from 1883. This loss of land was not unnaturally contested by the Auchinleckites. In 1898 Holmhead Hospital was opened, on ground owned by the Marquis of Bute, but within Auchinleck parish.

A number of police constables had residence in the village, each serving in the police station for a few years before moving on to other towns. Constables included Charles Gallacher, Beechwood Square, in 1858; John Watson 1858/1864; John Craddoch 1866; James Pitt 1871/73; Robert Reid 1875; Alexander Findlay 1880; William Orr 1885; David Kirkwood 1887; John MacKie 1896 and James Miller Kellie 1898. Police stations were from 1858 run by the Commissioners of Supply.

The tolls on the roads were abolished in 1878 to be replaced by a levy on the rates. At Auchinleck Toll the toll keeper in 1851 was James Gibbs; in 1858 William Freeland. At Rigg Toll David Gibb was toll keeper and snuff-box manufacturer in 1851; by 1861 Agnes Auld ran this toll.

The latter part of Queen Victoria's reign was one of considerable fortune in the parish. The population was still rising, and much new building was undertaken to house the many families coming to the area in search of work. In Main Street a number of traditional thatched cottages were demolished and replaced with new double-storey buildings. In some cases larger houses or tenements were erected, with three or more floors. At this time there was a fashion in the village for erecting blocks of houses or terraces and giving them a distinctive name, something which even a neighbour like Cumnock did not tend to do. It was perhaps due to the village's long Main Street which for many years was divided into 'Upper' Main Street and 'Lower' Main Street by the railway bridge. The lack of street numbers also influenced this practice.

Some of the older blocks of houses were Campbell Place, Easton Place, Dalziel House, and Jamieson Place. They were joined by Dacre Terrace in 1897, Horse-Shoe Corner in 1898, Searle Terrace around 1900, and Shiloh Terrace in 1905. Campbell Place is a two-storey block with a shop and houses, located at the corner of Sorn Road and Mauchline Road. Easton Place was a three-storey tenement block, the lower floor occupied by four shops. Over these were 22 flats. Dalziel House was located to the north end of Easton Place, where the health centre is. Jamieson Place was located between the Boswell Arms and Orchard Place.

The proposals for a town hall in Auchinleck first occurred in the latter half of the nineteenth century. A committee, associated with the Debating Society and the Mutual Improvement Society, was formed to organise fundraising activities. In July 1890 they purchased the old Lady Boswell's School for Girls from Lady Boswell's Trustees, and commissioned Robert S. Ingram to draw up plans for a new hall. These were accepted and work began, Mr Richmond of Cumnock being the mason, James Dalziel of Auchinleck the joiner, Mr MacKinnon of Cumnock the slater, and Mr Elder of Kilmarnock the plasterer. A grand bazaar was organised in August 1890 which raised £760, sufficient to bring the funds over target.

The plans incorporated part of the old schoolhouse as retiring rooms and caretaker's house, the new hall having a Dutch-style appearance. It could seat 350 people, was lit by gas, had cost £1,500 to build and was officially opened on 24 August 1891. Rev Dr Chrystal said a prayer, John Henderson, the schoolmaster, gave a short account of the construction, and Julia Mounsey of Auchinleck House declared the building open. She was afterwards presented with the golden key which she had used. An amateur concert followed, with music by

5.1 Town Hall, Auchinleck *(Author's Collection)*

a quadrille band under Mr Williamson of Ayr. The first main use of the hall was Auchinleck Flower Show, held on 19 August. The hall had been built to commemorate Queen Victoria's Golden Jubilee in 1887 and was thereafter operated by the Auchinleck Public Hall Trust.

At the north-western end of the village was the small community of Templeton, originally comprising of a row of three thatched houses of that name, as well as a second row of five thatched houses named Greenockmains Lodge. Between the two was a well, from which drinking water was drawn. Sometime in the 1890s a block of seven houses was constructed between these two rows, named Templeton Place. There were three wash-houses located to the rear for the use of the occupants.

LUGAR

The village which had been established at Lugar grew rapidly following the erection of the ironworks. In 1840 there were no inhabitants other than a few families who lived on the farms which formerly occupied the glen. The first houses for the workers were erected at Craigstonholm Row, built by William Gibson of Auchinleck. By the 1861 Census the village population was 753. Ten years later it had risen to 1,374, the maximum attained. For the next thirty years the population remained fairly static, being 1,353 in 1881, 1,288 in 1891 and 1,286 in 1901.

One of the most economical means of house-building was the rows, where many homes could be built without the need of expensive gables. By 1860 there were seven rows of houses erected in Lugar - Craigstonholm Row (27 houses), Store Row (7 houses), Back Row (15 houses), Dellowholm Rows (24 houses in two rows) and the Peesweep Rows (23 houses in two rows). At Commondyke in 1860 there existed the High Row of 24 houses, the Long Row, later called the Store Row when the Company Store opened there (23 houses plus store), Dyke Row, later called the Chapel Row (6 houses), Birnieknowe Row, adjacent to the farm, with six houses, and the Commondyke Row, known as Kilpatrick's Row, also of six houses. At the foot of Common Loch was the Common Row, later called the Stable Row, from its proximity to the stables where the pit ponies were kept, which had 8 houses. At Darnconner there were 34 houses, formed into the High and Low squares. At Mosshouse Pit, near Cronberry, there were about 24 houses formed into Mosshouse Square, and two rows at Carbello contained another 24. Four rows existed at Gasswater in 1860 - Brick Row (24 houses), Stone Row (14 houses), Baxter's Row (3 houses) and School Row (4 houses), and at the Gasswater Limeworks were another dozen, divided into two rows (the Stone and Stable Rows).

In 1892 William Weir of Kildonan (who resided at Adamton House, Monkton), a senior partner in Bairds, gifted the Lugar Institute to the citizens of the village. The building, erected with white freestone, stood two storeys high at one part (the hall-keeper's house below) and was designed by R. S. Ingram. It was opened on 20 April 1892. Within it was a large hall which could seat 350, a library of 582 books located in oak bookshelves, each volume bound in leather, a billiards room with two tables, and a games room, which contained chess, draughts, backgammon and similar board games. The reading room had the national papers and a selection of magazines. In the institute the Lugar Literary Society was held, the president being Robert Angus. There was also a skittle alley and two boards on which summer-ice (a form of curling) could be played. Helen Steven, in her short history of the parish, noted that 'the hall boasts a piano - a much appreciated adjunct.' However, far more unusual was the fact that within the building was an indoor heated swimming pool! This measured 50 feet long, 24 feet wide and up to 6 feet deep. It was lined with white glazed bricks and was heated using water released from the ironworks. As well as diving boards, other water appliances were available. In addition to swimming instruction, galas were often held. A separate private bath was available, the user paying an additional fee for its use. Villagers who wished to avail themselves of the facilities of the Weir Institute could join for an annual subscription of half-a-crown.

5.2 Lugar *(Author's Collection)*

In 1898 around 2,000 men were employed by Baird either at the ironworks or in the mines which supplied it. The managing partner of the works, Robert Angus, lived in Craigston House, which had been rebuilt by Baird. The works foremen were housed in the new cottages created at Craigston Square on the site of the old ironworks. By 1900 additional workers' rows had been erected in the village - a new and lengthy Back (or Brick) Row of 77 houses, and a Crescent (formerly Peesweep Crescent) of 29 houses, located opposite the Peesweep Row. At this time workers paid seven shillings per month for the rent of their homes. Baird's operated a company store in the village, located where the houses of Craigston Holm now stand, run on co-operative lines, but not associated with the national co-op movement. Here the villagers could buy bread, there being an excellent bakery, meat, vegetables and other provisions, as well as all forms of hardware and clothing. As with the co-op, the Lugar store paid out an annual dividend, the total of this being around £5,000 in 1900. As early as 1872 there was a lodge of the Loyal Orangemen of Scotland established at Lugar.

5.3 Weir Institute, Lugar *(Author's Collection)*

Around 1860 a timber bridge was erected across the Lugar Water from the Spout to Hollowsholm farm (or Hollis Holm, as it was sometimes spelled). This bridge caused some consternation in the area, for the woman at the farm tried to charge a halfpence to cross it. A joiner involved in the construction is said to have felt that this wasn't right, he cut some of the supports and the bridge was washed away in a spate. For many years thereafter only a plank bridge existed, with adjoining ford. Around 1865 a woman drowned when she was crossing this. The planks were icy and she slipped and fell into the river.

Other drowning accidents occurred in the village – on 8 November 1868 brothers Thomas and Daniel Muncie were drowned together. The former was thirteen years old, the latter ten years old. On 10 January 1898 James Murray was drowned at the age of 9 years.

CRONBERRY & GASSWATER

The formation of a village at Cronberry dates back to 1862 when William Baird and Company erected seven rows of houses running perpendicular to the Bello Water. The seventh row, known as the Store Row, was the most superior, being built of stone and roofed with slates. The other rows were of brick, three of them roofed with felt, hence their nickname, the 'Tarry Rows.' A branch of Lugar Co-op was established at the foot of Row No. 7 and a small school behind railings at the top end of the same row, the schoolmaster's house attached. In a house in Store Row was the Post Office. Matthew Alexander was a confectioner in the village. The population of Cronberry in 1871 was 997. This fell quite considerably over the next ten years to 799, and again to 632 by 1891. The number of residents increased again to 664 in 1901.

At Gasswater a sizeable population continued to grow as new rows were erected. In 1851 the Census lists some of the houses which existed at that time: Red Row of sixteen houses; High Row; Roadend Row; High Gilhaugh; Low Gilhaugh; Stables; Railway Row of four houses; Plantation Row of ten houses; Brick Row of 24 houses; Quarry Row of nineteen houses; and Store Row.

A resident at Cronberry farm for a short time was George Douglas Brown (1869-1902), the notable Scots novelist. Born in Ochiltree, he was the illegitimate son of a farmer in that parish. He worked at Cronberry for a short time, but was to be educated at Glasgow University then Oxford University. He wrote a number of articles, followed by the very successful *House with the Green Shutters*, published in 1900, and regarded as the novel which killed the Scottish 'kailyard' novels tone dead.

5.4 Gasswater *(Author's Collection)*

DARNCONNER

At Darnconner Baird extended the community by erecting new rows to either side of the two existing squares. North-west of the High Square two rows (the Railway Rows) of 24 single-apartment houses were built parallel to each other. Next to the Low Square, in which the Co-op operated by Baird was located, were the new Store Row of six houses and a School Row also of six houses. The school was located due north of Darnconner farm and had five rooms. William Tweedie was headmaster for a time, along with five teachers, some of them pupil teachers. Tweedie married Margaret Paterson in 1885 but she died soon after (on 13 August 1886) aged 28.

Darnconner Store was the principal shop in the immediate district, the store at Birnieknowe being smaller. In 1861 the storekeeper was John Provan. Adjoining it was a bakery, the butcher's meat being brought by horse-drawn van from the main Baird store at Lugar. Baird's employees were expected to buy all their requisites in the company store, indeed they often bought items on tick, to be paid for from their next wage. At Darnconner an office next to the store opened for a couple of hours each Wednesday to allow employees to draw out a little of their wages if required. The village had a police station in one of the rows, to which constables seem to have been appointed for a short period. These include George Smith (1878), John Innes (1881), James Mowat (1885) and G. R. Mair (1887).

5.5 Commondyke *(Author's Collection)*

By 1900 the new Common Row (or Commonloch Row) was built at Darnconner, the original Common Row of six houses becoming known then as the Stable Row. The Common Row was built alongside the old tracks which were laid to the Common Coalworks of the early nineteenth century, facing across the road to the Common Loch. To reduce the cost of erecting houses, the row was built continuous, with a total of 96 houses forming a dog-leg. Built of stone, some of the materials were brought from old houses which Bairds owned at Dalry.

Behind the Common Row was the much shorter Walker's Row of twelve houses, located perpendicular to the roadway into Darnconner farm. This row was owned by the William Walker Coal Company, hence its name. Also owned by Walker's were the Ballochmyle Rows, two rows of 24 houses each, on both sides of the road between Common and Glenshamrock farms. These probably date to around 1876 when the Ballochmyle Pit was sunk. Outwith the parish was the Burnside Row, of twelve houses, better known as 'The Poverty', which was also owned by Walker.

RAILWAYS

The railway age reached Auchinleck in 1848 when the Glasgow, Paisley, Kilmarnock and Ayr Railway Company built the line from Kilmarnock through the village to Muirkirk. Eight miles of track were constructed through the parish, the numerous cutting and sidings formed by squads of navvies from Ireland, many of whom lodged in Beechwood Square. The largest civil engineering structure on this line was the triple-arched viaduct at Cronberry crossing the Bello Water. In Auchinleck a number of dwelling-houses had to be demolished to allow the railway bridge to be built across the Main Street. A new Station Road was formed from the bridge to the railway station, a double-platformed through station with a double-storey office and station-master's house. The station-master was Joseph Irvin (1825-1905) from 1858 to 1896. He also served as precentor in the church from 1861 to 1895. At the top end of the Main Street a Railway Inn was established.

Commondyke Station was created adjacent to the miners' rows, access to the platforms being from the new road bridge over the railway. This station was opened on 9 August 1848.

About the same time Lugar Station was built, half a mile from the houses, at Witch Knowe, above the Mill Pond. To reach the station the villagers had to climb the Peesweep Brae then cross the moor past the Craigston Ironstone Pits. The stationmaster in 1893 was John Dinning.

When the Cronberry Rows were built around 1863 a new station was established on the line. It was situated on the opposite side of the Bello Water from the rows, reached by a new footbridge. Adjacent to it were built four station cottages for railway workers. Lugar also had five Station Cottages and another four were situated at Carbello Crossing. The first engine to traverse the Auchinleck to Muirkirk line was the 'Orion' (number31), which passed along the rails to great cheers from the crowds on 17 July 1848.

Though the railway offered a passenger service, it was built mainly to service the two ironworks, at Muirkirk and Lugar. The finished product from these works could thus be more readily transported to their markets. Also the raw materials could be brought more easily to the works, and soon numerous branch lines were laid across the moors of Airds Moss to take coal or ironstone to Lugar. By studying the Six Inch Ordnance Map of 1860 we find branches had already been laid from the main line to Barglachan Coal Pit, the two Dickston Ironstone Pits, the three Craigston Ironstone Pits, the Common Maid Pits (for coal and ironstone), the Glenlogan Ironstone Pits, the Gasswater Limeworks, Dalfad Coal Pit, Mosshouse and Braehead Ironstone Pits and Welltrees Coal Pit.

In 1850 a branch railway was built south from Auchinleck Station to Cumnock, to be continued southwards to join the line north from Dumfries. The divide at Auchinleck was called the Muirkirk Junction, where between the lines an engine shed was built. The line south to Cumnock required an even greater amount of construction, large embankments created at Orchard farm and Templand Mains. At the latter farm, partly within Old Cumnock parish, a tall viaduct had to be constructed across the Lugar Water. The height from the bed of the river to the rails is 145 feet 9 inches, making it one of the highest railway bridges in Britain. The viaduct has thirteen arches, nine of which have a span of 50 feet and five of 30 feet. As with the Muirkirk line, hundreds of Irish labourers were employed to do the work, the engineer being John Miller of Grainger & Miller of Edinburgh, who thought the Bank Viaduct more attractive than his other notable bridge – the Howford Viaduct. This viaduct, known variously as the Bank or Templand viaduct, was opened on 20 May 1850. By 28 October that year the line had reached Closeburn, allowing trains to travel from Glasgow to Dumfries and beyond. On the same day the G. P. K. & A. railway company amalgamated with the Glasgow, Dumfries & Carlisle railway company to form the Glasgow and South Western Railway.

The final section of mainline railway to pass through the parish was the Cumnock Branch of the renamed Glasgow and South Western Railway, of which a mile was located between Cronberry Junction and the Glenmuir Viaduct. This line was opened in 1872 (on 11 June for goods, 1 July for passengers). The seven-arched viaduct was designed by the engineer William Johnstone. Auchinleck parish thus had 10½ miles of mainline track within its bounds, and many mineral lines which came and went as pits were established and closed. One of the earliest fatal accidents on the local railways occurred on 31 January 1856 when William Yulle, aged 38, was accidentally killed on the Darnconner branch line, near to the Glenlogan Ironworks.

LAND OWNERSHIP AND AGRICULTURE
Land ownership in the latter half of the nineteenth century was still under the control of the local estates. In 1850, when James Paterson compiled his *History of Ayrshire*, he noted that the parish was owned by just eleven or so proprietors, namely Sir James Boswell, the Marquis of Bute, John Robertson, Alexander Aird, David Limond, James Templeton, Charles Howatson, William Brown, John Harvey, William Alexander of Ballochmyle and the Duke of Portland. In 1873 Lady Jessie-Jane Boswell owned a total of 11,977 acres (not all in the parish) which had a gross annual value of £8,256 plus £3,633 for mineral rights. Charles Howatson of Dornal (who resided at Daldorch House, near Catrine) owned 1,888 acres, with a gross annual value of £738. The only other landowner belonging to the parish was Robert Maider, who owned one acre in Auchinleck, grossing £18.

Auchinleck estate, just after the time of Lord Auchinleck's death, brought James Boswell an income of £1,600. By the time of his own death in 1795 this had risen to over £3,000, mainly through the excellent management of Andrew Gibb, employed by Boswell as factor and overseer. Gibb held this position for fifty years, until his death on 2 March 1837 at the age of 71. His eldest son, also Andrew (1798-1874) lived at Bridgend Mill, the two younger sons, James and John, were both employed in the East India Company.

5.6 Boswell coat of arms from Burial Aisle *(Dane Love)*

On the death of Sir Alexander Boswell his son succeeded as Sir James Boswell, 2nd Baronet of Auchinleck, though he was only fifteen years old, having been born in December 1806. As he aged he took his father's likeness, being described as tall, handsome and fine-looking. He was married in 1830 to Jessie-Jane, daughter of Sir James Montgomery Cuninghame, 6th Baronet of Corsehill. They had two daughters, Julia, who married George Mounsey of Kingfield in 1867, and Emily, who married the 5th Lord Talbot de Malahide on 26 June 1873. On the occasion of the girls' birthdays, Sir James placed a barrel of ale at Auchinleck cross, under the charge of the gamekeeper or some other estate worker, from which anyone who wished could drink to their health. At night there was a bonfire and partying. Sir James was a keen curler, being a member of Auchinleck Curling Club. He was also the commanding officer of the Ayrshire Yeomanry, and following the yeomanry's part in keeping the peace during a coal-miner's strike in Irvine in 1842 he was awarded the Freedom of the Burgh of Irvine. He acted as Depute Lord Lieutenant of Ayrshire until his death on 4 November 1857. Lady Jessie Boswell died in 1884.

Lady Boswell held a number of balls at Auchinleck House, one of the last being in 1860, the programmes of which were printed on silk. Dancing was to 'Lady James Boswell's Silver Band, under the direction of Mr Agnew, bandmaster, Queen's Own

R. R. G. Y. C.' Noted for her philanthropy, Lady Boswell contributed to numerous charities. She was also responsible for having the wall and railings erected around the churchyard, and during her lifetime paid for the upkeep of the grounds within, keeping them 'like a garden.'

5.7 Dumfries House Gardens Cottage *(Author's Collection)*

George Mounsey died at Auchinleck House on Wednesday 19 October 1904 at the age of 86 years. Mounsey was essentially a Carlisle man, being a solicitor in that town. He served his apprenticeship in the office of Messrs Mounsey, entering in 1837. A year later his elder brother, James, was appointed the first clerk to the Carlisle Board of Guardians. Sometime after that George Mounsey was appointed joint clerk, and in 1850, on his brother's resignation, he became the sole occupant. He led this position for 35 years. In 1850 he was appointed Superintendent Registrar for Carlisle, remaining in office until death. He was also clerk to the Income Tax Commissioners for Cumberland. He served as Mayor of Carlisle from 1856-7. Mounsey was a regular supporter of local charities, contributing funds to Silloth Convalescent Institution, in addition to other causes.

The Marquis of Bute owned land in the parish, on the southern side of the Barony Road, around Knockroon and Broomfield on the Cumnock road, and the grouse moors at Dalblair, Kyle and Glenmuirshaw. The grouse moors were often let, the tenant getting the occupation of the shooting lodge at Dalblair, described in Valuation Rolls of the period as a 'mansion house'. In 1875 the shooting tenant was Archibald Buchanan (d. 1890), who lived at Barskimming House, Stair parish, one of the proprietors of the Catrine Cotton Works.

By 1838 the small estate of Duncanziemere, Nether Carbello, Hillhead and Wallaceton was owned by John Robertson WS. By 1875 Alexander Hamilton Robertson CA was the proprietor. He resided at 79 St Vincent Street, Glasgow.

At the same period, the Cronberry and Lugar area was owned by James Baird of Cambusdoon (Ayr), one of the proprietors of William Baird & Co., owner of Lugar Ironworks. The estate of 1,040 acres had been placed on the market in 1844 by the Howatson family. At the time it incorporated Cronberry farm, the tileworks and a grouse moor. The lands of Common and Darnconner were owned by the Alexander family of Ballochmyle estate.

Dornal estate was purchased by Charles Howatson (1832-1918) in 1865. He added a few other properties to it soon after, and acquired Glenbuck Estate in 1872.

CHURCHES

The patron of the parish, Sir James Boswell, had presented Rev James Chrystal on 25 April 1833 and he was subsequently ordained on 19 September 1833. The second son of Dr William Chrystal DD, rector of Glasgow Grammar School, he was born on 16 January 1807 and had studied at Glasgow University. He graduated as a Master of Arts in 1825 and was licensed by the Presbytery of Glasgow on 7 October 1829. At his ordination the service was held in the kirkyard, with tents and platforms, due to the smallness of the church. The principal heritors, Sir James, the Marquis of Bute, John Boswell of Garrallan, Charles Howatson of Cronberry, and others, were present, the weather being favourable, but it was one of the first instances when a bigger church was suggested.

The stipend in 1837 was £44 13s 10d in money, plus 109 bolls of meal and 25 bolls, 3 firlots and 31/5 lippies of bear in kind. In 1844 the manse was extended, the work being designed by the local wright, James Jamieson.

Chrystal was a devoted minister, acting as Presbytery Clerk for 13 years, awarded a Divinity Doctorate from Glasgow University on 18 January 1861, and a Literary Doctorate from St Andrews in 1893. On 22 May 1879 Dr Chrystal was appointed the Moderator of the General Assembly, serving for the following year. During that time he had published his Assembly Address – *The Doctrine and Position of the Church of Scotland*.

In 1853 Lady Boswell of Auchinleck presented a baptismal vessel to the church. Rev Chrystal was married on 1 October 1834 to Sophia Playfair, daughter of Patrick Playfair of Dalmarnock, a West India merchant. She died on 21 July 1890. Together they had six sons and two daughters. These were William (born 30 July 1835-died 12 April 1845), Patrick, who emigrated to Bombay, India (born 28 June 1838-died 17 June 1895), Rev James Robert (born 6 October 1839-died 1914), who became the minister of Cults (1864-1879) then Coltness (from 1879-1885); Andrew (born 19 January 1841-died 16 February 1885), who became a merchant in Montreal, Canada; David (born 17 September 1843-died 16 February 1857), John Smith (born

12 October 1845), Jane Playfair (born 12 February 1837-died 29 November 1884), and Sophia Ann (born 3 June 1847-died 12 November 1907), who married Rev Dr Pearson MacAdam Muir DD (1846-1924), minister of Glasgow Cathedral from 1896 until 1915. Patrick and John Chrystal were partners in P. Chrystal & Co. which traded in Bombay, Karwar and the Southern Maratha Country.

In 1890, when Dr Chrystal was 84 years old, an assistant minister, Rev James Hill, was appointed to help with the duties of the parish and Darnconner kirks, succeeding him in November 1893. The minister's salary was then £162. As he grew older, he became 'the father of the Church of Scotland'. Dr Chrystal died on 6 February 1901, at the age of 94. Around 1840 he had planted an avenue of plane trees between the church and manse. By 1872 the glebe had been extended to nine acres, valued at £32 (Gross Annual Value).

5.8 Parish Church *(Dane Love)*

In 1894 the parish church was extended and repaired, the external stairways being enclosed, the seating re-arranged, a new heating system installed and a Gothic tower added. This tower was erected to commemorate the diamond jubilee of Rev Dr James Chrystal's ministry, which occurred in 1893. These alterations did not really increase the seating capacity of the church, and as more was required a second chancel was erected in 1897 on the south side of the church, completing the cruciform shape. Within this an organ was installed, the first organist being a Miss Rae from Partick, who was a very popular player. The organ was inaugurated in October 1897.

A three-light window was installed in memory of Lady Jessie Boswell, widow of Sir James, 2nd Baronet, who died in 1884. The funds were raised by public subscription, and R. S. Ingram was commissioned to design the memorial. He based the scene on the painting called 'Charity' by Sir Joshua Reynolds and the glass work was executed by Messrs Stephen Adam and Son, of Glasgow. It includes the Boswell arms, the family motto, and texts, 'Charity suffereth long and is kind'; 'It is more blessed to give than to receive'; and 'Other foundation can no man lay than that is laid, which is Jesus Christ'. Pictured on it is the figure of a woman, 'Charity', with a child in her arms and two others at her feet. On completion of the additions and alterations, the church was reopened by the Very Rev Dr A. K. H. Boyd in August 1897.

5.9 Auchinleck Manse *(Author's Collection)*

LUGAR PARISH CHURCH

In 1866, once the old ironworks at Lugar were cleared away, Messrs Baird converted an old building into a church in which their workers could worship. The building had formerly been an engine house, and the slot in the wall where the beam passed through was long visible. The church was opened in October 1867 to serve the village's 1,000 inhabitants. Known as a proprietary church, the building was later gifted to the Church of Scotland, along with a small adjoining manse. The church, though lacking typical ecclesiastical architecture, is a pleasing edifice, the interior lit by long narrow windows. A small belfry adorns one end. Internally the church has a gallery, the total seating being for 500, with a platform at the opposite end, the organ to one side. The roof is open, with dark oak beams, but the interior is 'cheerful and bright'. Lugar was created a Quoad Sacra parish, the Court of Teinds of the Church of Scotland establishing it on 8 March 1867.

The first minister was Rev Simon Somerville Stobbs, appointed in 1867. He was transferred from Swallow Street Church in London. He remained at Lugar until 1876, when he emigrated to St Matthew's Church, Montreal, Canada. He was latterly minister at Elder Street Mission Church in Edinburgh, and died in 1911.

5.10 Lugar Parish Church *(Dane Love)*

Rev Stobbs was followed by Rev John Skeoch Clelland, who was licensed by the Presbytery of Glasgow on 6 December 1871. He is thought to have been the son of Rev James Clelland, minister of the Scots Church in Bolton, and Mary Skeoch, daughter of John Skeoch of Corsehillmill. He was ordained to Cobden Street Chapel in Glasgow's Townhead in 1873. He was inducted to Lugar Church in 1876. He remained at Lugar until 1881.

The vacancy in the pulpit was filed by Rev Walter Milne BD. Milne was born in Dundee in 1853. He was educated at St Andrews University, graduating Master of Arts in 1874 and Bachelor of Divinity in 1877. At St Andrews he had the distinction of being the best classical scholar of his year, especially in Greek. He was licensed by the Presbytery of Dundee on 3 October 1877. He was ordained at Lugar on 30 June 1881 where he remained until 1905.

DARNCONNER PARISH CHURCH

A mission station of the parish church had been established at Darnconner in 1874, but the 'more airy than comfortable' corrugated-iron shed in which the villagers worshipped was blown over in a storm. On 14 March 1897 a new Gothic church with adjoining manse was erected with funds provided by Robert Angus of Craigston. Built of red Ballochmyle sandstone externally, internally it was finished in white Kilwinning freestone. It comprised a nave, small transepts and chancel, the latter floored with small tiles. The architect of the kirk was R. S. Ingram and it was built to accommodate 300 worshippers at a cost of £3,000. The opening service was conducted jointly by the Revs Chrystal and Hill.

The church at Darnconner had a number of ministers over a short time, amongst these being Rev Benjamin Brown (nephew of Rev Dr Chrystal), Rev A. D. Scott MA, and Rev James Higgins.

5.11 Darnconner Parish Church *(Author's Collection)*

Rev James Higgins was born on 14 November 1871 at Milngavie in Dunbartonshire, the son of Frances Higgins and his wife, Agnes Mathie. He received his education at Milngavie, followed by the High School of Glasgow and the University of Glasgow. He was licensed by the Presbytery of Dunbarton in 1896. His first position was at Darnconner. He was ordained as minister at Rendall, Orkney, in 1910. In 1919 he was translated to Orphir, also Orkney, and in 1926 moved on again to Amulree in Perthshire. He was married to the infant mistress at Darnconner School, Grace Johnston Girvan, on 21 April 1910. They had four children, Janet Davidson (b. 4 April 1911), Agnes Mathie (b. 22 April 1913), Francis Higgins (b. 16 April 1914) and William Girvan (b. 4 March 1916, died 1995).

ORIGINAL SECESSION CHURCH

The Secession Church in Auchinleck refused to accept the union of Anti-Burgher and Burgher congregations and thus remained out, becoming an Original Secession congregation. Shortly after the death of Rev George Roger on 4 April 1870, at the age of 59, the church in Auchinleck called Rev Professor James Spence DD. An Orcadian by birth, he was a Professor of Hebrew and Literature and, later, a Professor of Greek and Literature, in the Original Secession Divinity College. In 1877 he was appointed Professor of Systematic Theology in the Synod of the United Original Seceders at Glasgow University. Membership of the church in Auchinleck dropped, 'for want of denominational feeders', there being only 28 members in 1884. Rev Spence, however, kept the church going for fifty years in all, retiring when it closed on Sunday 5 February 1922. In 1921 he was awarded a Doctorate of Divinity by the University of St Andrews. He died at Norrieston Manse, Perthshire, on 27 November 1927 aged 82 and was buried in Auchinleck. He had been married twice, his first wife, Helen Morton dying in 1875. His son, Rev John A. Spence, became minister, successively, of Fisherton Parish Church, Dunure, and Norrieston Parish Church, Perthshire.

The supporters of the union formed the United Presbyterian Church, and there appears to have been a congregation in Auchinleck for a time. The first minister was Rev Matthew MacGill from Mauchline, who was ordained on 25 May 1832. He was deposed from his office on 24 May 1864. The church may have closed thereafter, but in 1892 there were proposals to establish a new United Presbyterian Church in Auchinleck, but these came to naught.

OUR LADY OF LOURDES AND ST PATRICK'S R. C. CHURCH

Catholicism, which had been made illegal at the Reformation in 1560, was legalised once more in 1833 when the Catholic Emancipation Act was passed. At that time there were only two Roman Catholics in the parish, a 'pig-man', or seller of coarse cloth, and his sister. Soon, at least by 1840, priests began to make visits to the parish, to preach to a growing number of Catholics who had settled in the area, many from Ireland. Around 1850 a separate mission was established which covered Cumnock and Auchinleck districts, the first priest being Father William MacCabe. He lived at Caponacre near Cumnock and held services in a small hall opposite the Dumfries Arms Hotel. The next priest, Thomas Wallace, held services variously in the Black Bull Hall, a hall in Ayr Road, and latterly in a small chapel adjoining his house in Barrhill Road (all Cumnock). In 1855 Rev John O'Dwyer became priest, and he set about raising funds in order to build a proper chapel. He collected donations from all his parishioners, as well as £50 from the Eglinton Iron Company, and obtained a site near Commondyke for the church from Lady Boswell. She allowed him the use of a nearby quarry and sandpit and with volunteer labour he supervised the erection of a church and presbytery.

The church building was a simple, but dignified, gothic building, with porch to the north and an apse to the south, opened in 1867. Father O'Dwyer died in 1873 and for the next year Rev John MacGinnis took charge. He was succeeded by Rev Patrick Wright in 1874. Father Wright was responsible for establishing St Patrick's School at Birnieknowe, opened on 15 August 1878 behind the presbytery. Lord Bute had donated a considerable sum to aid its erection, and it soon had 150 pupils in attendance. Father Wright was the school manager, Miss Somerville the principal teacher, with the Misses MacGuinness and Jordan as pupil teachers. Father Wright died in 1881 and was followed by Rev John O'Neil (d. 1922), who remained until 1883. In the same year the new chapel of St John was erected in Cumnock by Lord Bute, the Catholics of that town transferring from Birnieknowe to St John's. Father O'Neil conducted the first service at St John's before that church was taken in charge by Rev Daniel Collins. From 1882-83 Rev Henry Stuart Laverty served as assistant priest at Birnieknowe.

In 1883 Rev Patrick Murphy took over at Birnieknowe. Born and educated in Ireland, he was ordained there in 1880. He was lent by the Irish church to the Galloway diocese, serving in Girvan from 1880-82, followed by Dalbeattie for a year. He persuaded four Sisters of St Joseph of Cluny to join him from Girvan to operate the school. On 21 August 1882 Lady Boswell had sold a strip of ground adjoining the chapel to the Marquis of Bute upon which he erected a convent, opened on 1 March 1885. The first recorded confirmations to take place at Birnieknowe occurred on 10 August 1885 when Bishop John MacLauchlan confirmed 120 males and 97 females.

5.12 Our Lady & St Patrick's Chapel, Birnieknowe *(Author's Collection)*

In 1888 the Catholic community in the district was stunned when Sister Laurienne Cusack was killed by a train on the branch line which served Commondyke No. 1 pit. Sister Laurienne had been the principal of the school but had to resign her duties in the spring of 1888 due to the contraction of an infection which affected her hearing. She went to Girvan to convalesce and on returning to Birnieknowe her position as headmistress was taken over by Sister Columba. Sister Laurienne was given the task of looking after the sick and needy in their homes. She undertook this task with vigour, but on 7 August 1888 she was knocked down by a railway waggon as she was crossing the railway, making her way to the High Row. She was killed almost instantly. Within two hours hundreds of people, including non-Catholics, were at the convent to offer their services to the Sisters, or were praying in the chapel. Over one hundred offered to guard the corpse through the night. Father Murphy, who had been at Rothesay, returned as soon as he heard the news, to conduct the service prior to her burial at Girvan. Commondyke Station had to be closed when the corpse was taken away, for too many people were trying to get onto the platform. Eight priests attended the funeral service.

Father Murphy wrote to the Mother General at Girvan:

> The sad death of dear Sister Laurienne is a calamity for all of us in this parish. Oh! what a holy sister she was! Her sanctity was above the ordinary and I knew her soul sufficiently well to vouch for that. You and your congregation have suffered a heavy loss through her death, but it will be a consolation for all to know that she was a faithful, religious person right to the end and that she gave her life in an actual accomplishment of her duty - striving to procure the salvation of souls.
>
> I have never witnessed such a display of grief at the loss of anyone. The entire parish, men, women and children, came to pay their last tribute to her. It was heartbreaking to see so many men in tears! Such sympathy has helped to lighten the cross that God has sent to us.
>
> May God bless you and may He give us Sisters to continue our good work here and may He preserve the peace and happiness which reigned here in our little Convent.
>
> Very respectfully and Sincerely in Jesus Christ,
> [signed] P. Murphy.

Father Murphy's wish did not come to be, however, for in a short time Sister Columba Fogarty became seriously ill and had to return to Girvan. The remaining sisters' health began to show signs of failing, so they withdrew their services from Birnieknowe and returned to Girvan on 31 July 1889. About this time a memorial, of the Celtic wheel-cross type, was erected in memory of the sister killed by the train. It bears the inscription:

AT A DISTANCE OF EIGHT FEET IN FRONT OF THIS SPOT
THE REVD SISTER LAURIENNE WAS ACCIDENTALLY KILLED ON THE
7TH DAY OF AUGUST 1888.
'BEHOLD,' MY BELOVED SAITH UNTO ME, 'RISE UP, MAKE HASTE,
MY LOVE, MY DOVE, MY FAIR ONE, AND COME AWAY.'

In 1889 Rev Patrick Murphy returned to Ireland, where he continued to serve in the church. He died there on 28 January 1924.

In 1889 Rev Michael P. Hickey became priest at St Patrick's. He was born in Ireland and educated there. He was ordained at Waterford in 1884 but served in the Diocese of Galloway, at first in St Andrew's Church, Dumfries, from 1884-85, followed by St Joseph's in Kilmarnock (1885-86) and Wigtown (1886-89). Father Hickey invited sisters from the Franciscan Abbey of St Marys, Mill Hill, London, to take over the school and convent. They came for only three years, finding the rural atmosphere too different to the city life. Secular teachers were again used. Father Hickey left Birnieknowe in 1893, returning to Ireland, where he died on 19 November 1916.

In 1893 Father O'Neil returned to Birnieknowe and persuaded sisters of the Order of the Cross and Passion to take charge. They

5.13 Rev Sister Laurienne's Cross *(Dane Love)*

were to remain for 72 years. Around this time the church building was altered, a new porch built, a gallery added and the roof raised and supported by new oak beams. Members of the church established the Birnieknowe Brass Band, using second-hand instruments, but they were later able to buy new ones at a cost of £250 due to their fundraising efforts. Their fame began to spread, and soon the 'Birnie Band' was officially recognised as a 'First Class' band.

OTHER DENOMINATIONS

The Christian Brethren were founded in Auchinleck around 1875 or 1876. Known as the 'Plymouth Brethren' nationally, from their having been founded at Plymouth in 1830 by John Nelson Darby, this organisation commemorates the Lord's Supper every Sunday but rejects all other ecclesiastical tenets. In the 1870s there was a surge in membership throughout the mining communities in Ayrshire, and Auchinleck, with Dalmellington and Galston, was one of the first three Ayrshire villages in which a group was formed. The founder members were James Finnie and George Houston, who with their families met regularly in the Finnie home in Coal Road. They went out into the community to preach the Word of the Lord and soon had other members.

The Auchinleck Brethren had a sizeable increase in numbers and so a larger meeting place had to be found. 'Tailor Stewart's' shop at the corner of Churchhill and Main Street was used initially. Shortly premises were found in an old house in Beechwood Square in which a dividing wall was removed to create a larger hall. However, this soon proved to be too small, and on completion of the Town Hall the Brethren hired it for meetings. This proved to be unsatisfactory as they could not use the hall for all of their meetings and so they moved into a hall attached to the Railway Hotel, known as Milligan's Hall from the proprietrix. Here the 100 members could be accommodated.

A large population at Lugar resulted in the formation of a brethren assembly around 1875. This group continued to worship in their meeting place until around 1893.

Another assembly of Brethren met in a hall formed from a former cottage at Ballochmyle Row. Located in Number 57, this assembly was founded in 1891.

The Christian Union in Ayrshire was founded around 1880 and soon there were branches in Lugar (existed 1900) and Auchinleck. The Auchinleck branch met originally in a building at Templeton Place.

EDUCATION

The school in Auchinleck was located originally at 217 Main Street (recently the site of George Muir's betting shop, but now converted into a house) but was moved lower down the Main Street, opposite the Railway Hotel. David MacRae Kennedy was teacher at the school, and also acted as the session clerk. A noted citizen of the village, he died on 25 January 1883 aged 72. Elsewhere in the parish schools were kept at Burnhouse, serving the west end of the parish, and another at Duncanziemere, covering the east end of the parish. With the arrival of the coal and iron industry new schools were established at Cronberry, Lugar and Darnconner by the Eglinton Iron Company, all between 1859 and 1869, Darnconner certainly by 1861. A school existed at Gasswater for a time, John Cooper being teacher there in 1859.

Lady Jessie-Jane Boswell established a school for girls at the Townfoot sometime in the latter half of the nineteenth century. One of the teachers was Fanny Spence, second wife of the Secession minister. Lady Boswell continued to operate the school until December 1889, when the pupils were transferred to the parish school. The last teacher at Lady Boswell's school, Miss Telfer, was taken on at Auchinleck School.

The Education (Scotland) Act of 1872 brought about the formation of school boards in every parish, responsible for educating children between the ages of five and thirteen. In 1873 these youths had by law to attend school and in the same year Auchinleck Parish School Board was constituted. The first meeting took place on 13 February, when it was proposed to hold an election of board members, David MacCrae Kennedy appointed as returning officer. The election was held on 14 March and the first school board had five members - Charles Howatson of Dornal, Rev James Spence, Robert Dalgleish of Templand, David Crichton in Auchinleck, and Dr James Chrystal, the latter appointed chairman. The parish school was run by John Ballantyne who was retained as school-master, being paid £70 a year. One of the board's first improvements to the school was the erection in 1873 of a dividing glass partition in the main school-room. They approached Lady Boswell and the Eglinton Iron Company regarding their respective schools, but both proprietors refused to transfer them to the board's control. At the time the Eglinton Iron Company were planning to extend Darnconner School.

Accommodation at Auchinleck school was rather cramped, so in November 1873 the board commissioned R. S. Ingram to provide plans for an extension capable of holding 120 pupils. In 1874 school fees for pupils at the board's school were infants 10d, Standards I and II one shilling, Standards III to VI 1s 2d per month. Those being taught languages paid an extra 2d per month. In 1876 the number of pupils in the parish schools were 346 at Lugar, 187 at Cronberry, 450 at Darnconner, 173 at Mr Ballantyne's Auchinleck School, 117 at Mr Duncan's Auchinleck School, 22 at Glenmuir, and 3 pupils at Auchtitench, the school-master there being paid £1 per year for his work. In 1861 the teacher at Auchtitench was Robert Harkness.

In June 1878 the school board conducted a census of the parish to plan for future accommodation. The figures were as follows:

Total Inhabitants	Children 5 - 13	
1,480	257	Auchinleck Village
1,489	341	Lugar & Rosebank
929	204	Cronberry
308	67	Gasswater
554	134	Darnconner
619	144	Common Lochside
509	106	Ballochmyle
332	73	Commondyke
813	135	Country District
193	22	Barony District
7,226	1,483	TOTAL
99	17	Increase since June 1877

In 1880 fifteen children were taught at Glenmuirshaw by Mr Donaldson, to whom the board paid a wage of £8 per annum. Pupils in this upper part of the Glenmuir proved to be something of a problem to the board over the years, because of the distance to their nearest school. In 1882 the Glenmuirshaw School was closed, and in 1889 a school was established at High Dalblair. In 1890 a Threeshire District association was formed by the parishes of Auchinleck, Kirkconnel and Crawfordjohn to organise the schooling of pupils living in the Threeshire Hills. This association proved to be troublesome, for there were many disagreements over who should pay how much.

In 1881 the School Board arranged to enlarge the village school again, and Robert S. Ingram was appointed to draw up plans. This extension was completed in 1882. At the same time ground to the rear of the school was purchased from the Boswells. John Ballantyne retired as the school-master in 1882. He died on 12 May 1902 aged 70. His replacement was John Henderson, appointed in January 1883. Henderson was born in Sanquhar and became headmaster at Ormiston School, near Edinburgh, prior to accepting the job at Auchinleck. He was married to Jessie MacGill (1856-1934). Further extensions at Auchinleck were erected in 1894 (again designed by Ingram) and whilst the alterations were underway the pupils were educated in the Town Hall. At this time an extra storey was added to the old school. In 1891 the parish had school accommodation for 1,538 pupils, the average attendance being 1,087. The schools received grants totalling £968 13s 6d. Auchinleck School had an average attendance of 240 pupils, a further 52 attending evening classes. Grants for this school amounted to £221 plus £26 10s for evening classes.

A school building was erected at Lugar in 1859 by William Baird & Company at which the children of the ironworkers could be taught, thus avoiding the journey to Auchinleck. It was built at the top of the Peesweep Brae (sometimes known thereafter as the School Brae) on what had once been a small field attached to Craigston House. The building was described as being far in advance of its time, yet it just had one large classroom. In 1889-90 a new wing was added to increase accommodation. In 1894 the roll was 302, the headmaster being William Hume. Each August the attendance dropped due to 'boys being engaged at the shootings.' On 20 December 1895 the head wrote in the Log Book that there was 'Good spirit in school over new books.' The Inspectors' Report for 1896 notes that 'Military Drill forms a pleasing part of the curriculum.' The roll had fallen to 279 by 1897, taught by seven teachers. This rose to 300 in August 1898, 289 in 1899. The Drawing Report of December 1899 noted that 'Finish is lacking in many drawings, but better pencils should improve this.'

The school at Darnconner was erected in 1853 by the Eglinton Iron Company who deducted a monthly fee from its employees in order to pay the school-master an annual salary of £50. It had been erected at the instigation of Rev Dr Chrystal. Over the years it was added to, but by the end of the century was deemed as an unsuitable building. On 5 January 1875 William Tweedie was appointed headmaster, previously being assistant teacher at Lugar. He was paid a salary of £150.

A similar tale can be told of the first school at Cronberry, erected by the coalmasters. John Sharp (1850-1926) was headmaster at Cronberry School for a time. He was the son of William Sharp, weaver in Auchinleck's Churchhill. He trained and became a pupil-teacher with John Ballantyne, schoolmaster at Auchinleck. He was appointed headmaster at Cronberry before moving to become headmaster at Dalmellington. He retired around 1906 and died in 1926. He was buried in Auchinleck. In 1875 James Hyslop was appointed as headmaster. He was married to Margaret B. Crossan.

On 1 November 1887 Darnconner, Lugar and Cronberry schools were transferred to the School Board who took over their running. At Darnconner the teacher was William Tweedie who continued until after the Great War. In 1899 he moved into the new schoolmaster's house which the board erected next to the school.

In 1873 the School Board consulted with Old Cumnock Parish Board over the possibility of erecting a jointly funded school at or near Guelt farm to serve the children of the Glenmuir. This was turned down by the Cumnock board and so in December that year the Auchinleck board commissioned R. S. Ingram to draw up plans for a 100 pupil school to be erected in the area. It was reckoned at the time that there were 70 children living in the area and that new iron mines would result in an increase in population. Ground extending to just over one acre was acquired from Major Burnet at Laigh Glenmuir farm and work commenced on the new school. Costing £542 8s 8d, the board received a grant of £114 16s 3d from the Scotch Education Department. Opened on 1 May 1876, the first teacher at Glenmuir School was a Miss Spreull who moved from Leswalt in Wigtownshire. There was an attendance of 22 pupils. Later teachers in the nineteenth century included Miss Smith and Miss Bone. The building was also used for Sunday services by the local residents.

INDUSTRY

During the nineteenth century the industrial landscape around Auchinleck changed considerably. From 1825 to 1865 trade in weaving plummeted by 80%, and a similar drop was experienced in snuff-box manufacture. Coal, which had been dug on a small scale for centuries, was starting to develop on a larger scale.

Mining became an even greater means of employment in the parish in the nineteenth century. In 1842 an Act of Parliament prohibited the employment of women and girls in collieries, and of boys less than ten years. Mines became larger but remained in the shallower seam areas east of Auchinleck and north of Lugar. Old Coal Pits are shown on the first six inch map of 1860 at Roadinghead, Dykes, Dickston, Commondyke, Birnieknowe, Common, Darnconner, Dalfad, Hawk Hill and even on the slopes of Benalt, east of Dalblair. These mines were small businesses, employing up to half-a-dozen people, and selling the coal locally for use in domestic fires or else in the lime-smelting industry. Around 1850 the Common coalworks (two mines) were opened, the coal seams from three to four feet thick. The pits were thirty fathoms deep, producing 8,456 tons of coal each year, sold at 5s 6d a ton at the pithead.

When Lugar ironworks was first established in 1848 a few small ironstone mines were sunk, those in operation in the second half of the nineteenth century including the pits at Roadinghead, Craigston, Cronberry Moor and Wallaceton. By the time the new ironworks were built much larger ironstone pits were in production, employing larger numbers and often connected by mineral railways to the Auchinleck-Muirkirk line. These larger ironstone pits included the Holm Pit (south of Roadinghead, by the side of Lugar Water), Dickston Pits (two), Craigston Pits (three), Darnconner Pit, Braehead Pit, Mosshouse Pits (two) and Rosebank (Lugar). They were joined by Dykes Pit, Lugar Ironworks Pit and another Common Pit in 1876, by which time the lesser mines were closed. Lugar was closed by 1894, the Common continuing with different shafts until 1925. All these mines were operated by William Baird and Company, the Common and Lugar pits managed by Richard Sneddon in 1861 (resident at Common Cottage), followed by William Gray (around 1900). Dykes was managed by C. Jamieson but it was closed in 1894. In 1878 there were around eighty steam engines in the parish used mainly for pumping water and hauling hutches from the pit bottom.

The first proper coal mines were being created in the early nineteenth century. Around 1820 Mr Edgar took the lease of the Gilmilnscroft coal works, which lay on the boundary of Sorn parish with Auchinleck. Around 1840 blackband ironstone was dug there by the New Cumnock Iron Company, and two small shafts were sunk at an outcrop. A railway line was laid to a depot at the Sorn/Auchinleck parish boundary, constructed by Mr MacNaughton. The ironstone was drawn by horses along a wagonway, before being emptied into carts and taken to Auchinleck station. The ironstone was transported by rail to New Cumnock, where it was smelted at the Bank furnaces. These mines did not last long due to a reducing quality of ironstone and the cost of transportation.

Around 1850 Messrs William Dixon & Co. took on the lease and employed James Watchman to sink test bores, but these were not pursued. Watchman, however, acquired the lease around 1856 and opened the first new pit, closely followed by a second. These were established before the railway reached the district. He sold approximately 100 tons of coal per day in the winter, but virtually none in the summer. In the early 1870s he sold the mines to Gilmour, Wood & Anderson, iron and coalmasters from Cumberland. They erected a new rail link to Auchinleck and sank another two mines. Around 1890 the works were sold to the Gauchalland Coal Company of Galston. This firm also purchased the Ballochmyle pits of William Walker & Co., some of which were located in Sorn parish. The coalmaster, James Watchman, had one son and six daughters. He owned some property within Auchinleck, including cottages and shops.

The first developments at Lugar Ironworks were made sometime around 1845 when John Wilson, father and son, of the Dundyvan Ironworks, Coatbridge, joined with James and Colin Dunlop of the Clyde Ironworks to begin working the local ironstone and establish the works at Lugar. Wilson had previously taken over the Muirkirk Ironworks in 1843. A 99-year lease of 37·1 acres was obtained from Sir James Boswell on Whitsunday 1845. The four furnaces were built by William Nelson of Glasgow. By 1846 the original iron furnaces had been erected at Craigston, where previously there had been nothing but a small country house and farm. A new Craigston House was erected at the same time as a dwelling for the manager.

The blast engine at Lugar was manufactured by Messrs Murdoch & Aitken, the former a cousin of William Murdoch of Bello Mill. The rights to the minerals were obtained from Auchinleck estate from Martinmas 1848, three tacks of 27 years each. Small mineral railways transported coal and ironstone from the pits to the smelt mill. These furnaces were located on Craigstonholm, the site now occupied by the church and Craigston Square. Two of the four furnaces were put into commission immediately. In addition to the ironworks, associated industries were established, such as the ammonia, creosote, pitch and briquette works. Alexander Hamilton Mann was accidentally killed at the works on 1 January 1850 aged 45.

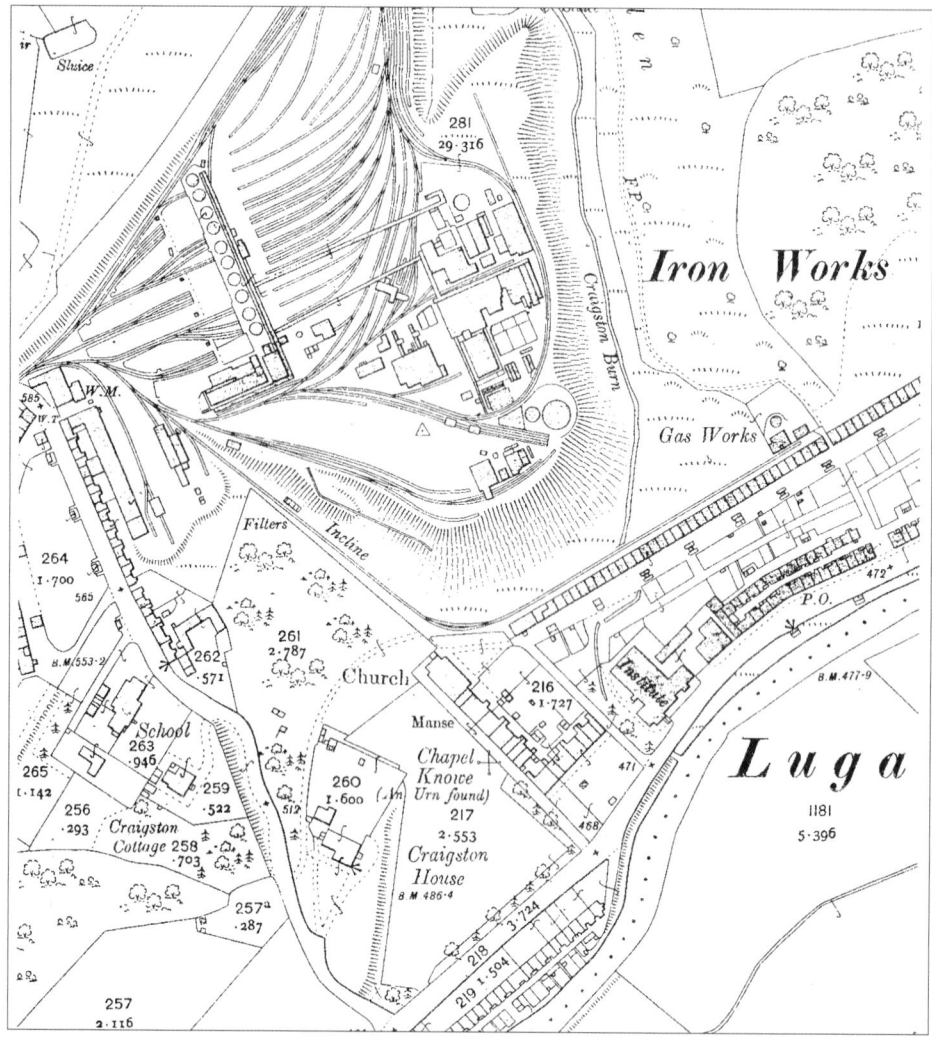

5.14 Lugar Ironworks on O.S. Map of 1911 *(Author's Collection)*

The iron trade took a turn for the worse in the years to follow and in May 1856 Wilson sold his interests at Muirkirk and Lugar to the Bairds of Gartsherrie. James Stevenson WS bought the works on Baird's behalf, the £61,100 price including the ironworks, mines and miners' houses. The major holding company was William Baird & Company, the name used in Lanarkshire, but in Ayrshire all Baird's works went under the name Eglinton Iron Company. This name was used up until around 1892 when all works were embraced in the single name, William Baird & Co. Ltd. The works came to a standstill in 1857, and remained dormant until 1863-64. Some of the mines remained active even although the ironworks was closed, such as Gasswater (closed 1861), Birnieknowe (closed 1865) and Lugar (closed 1880).

Robert Angus came to manage the Ayrshire works in 1860, living at Craigston House. He was the son of an engineer at Gartsherrie Ironworks in Lanarkshire. He trained as a civil engineer and worked with William Baird. He was promoted to become above ground manager at Dalry before moving to Lugar. He was influential in the opening of many mines, as well as developing ironstone mines in Spain. Active in the affairs of Lugar, he served on the school board from 1873 until 1911, and for 25 years was chairman of Auchinleck School Board. He served as a Justice of the Peace and Depute Lieutenant. Among the public works he was influential in establishing were the Weir Institute at Lugar, Darnconner Church, Lugar war memorial, and Auchinleck Public Hall. His wife, Jean Young Angus, died on 17 March 1919 at the age of 82. Robert Angus remained at Craigston until around 1899. He died at Ladykirk House on 14 April 1923, aged 88. He was survived by Robert L. Angus and six daughters.

William Baird decided to move the location of the ironworks from the holm to the top of the hill and work seems to have started around 1864. The new site proved to be more suitable for the furnaces, there being more room for expansion, and also the waggons no longer had to make their way up or down the steep tracks to the valley bottom. Two of the five new furnaces were operational by December 1865. Business boomed. In 1871 the Blair Ironworks were closed and some of the plant was transferred to Lugar. Two new furnaces were then brought into operation. The fifth furnace was commissioned in 1880, making Lugar the most modern Ayrshire plant of the time.

In 1869 James Smith was appointed manager of the Lugar Works, a position he retained for many years. He was born in 1820, the son of a miner in Clarkston, near Airdrie. He married Elizabeth Drysdale, daughter of a seedsman. Their eldest son, John Smith, became a noted archaeologist and geologist, of whom more later. James Smith had been manager of the ironworks at Dalry from 1852 until his move to Lugar. James Smith lived at Craigston Cottage, Lugar, and on his death was buried in Cumnock cemetery.

To supply the need of the works new pits were sunk, Barglachan, Berryhill No. 1 (coal 1876-1881), Blackston, Braehead, Carbello, Common (coal and ironstone 1850-1925), Commondyke (ironstone 1878-1881), Cronberry (coal and ironstone), Craigston (ironstone 1878-1881), Dykes (coal and ironstone 1876-1888), Highhouse (coal 1894-1983), Mosshouse (ironstone 1873-1877) and Templand (ironstone 1873-1878). It will be noted that all the ironstone pits closed in 1881, those continuing after that date producing coal only. Ironstone was then imported from Spain, where Baird owned iron-ore mines in the north and south of that country. In 1871 Baird advertised in the Irish newspapers for workers, being at that time in short supply in Scotland. Thus the parish population continued to climb, and the Roman Catholic element increased considerably.

The Common coal works had many different mines and pits, extracting both coal and ironstone. They were sunk by William Baird & Co. to supply raw materials to Lugar Ironworks. In 1896 the Common mines had two managers, William Gray and James Smith, and seven pits were still working. These had an under-manager each – W. MacLelland (No. 6 pit), John Merry (No. 10 pit), Edward Shirkie (No. 11 pit), Richard Hall (No. 12 pit), James Lorimer (No. 14 pit), J. Morton (no. 15 pit) and Thomas MacBlane (No. 16 pit). Across all of the Common pits there were 696 miners in 1896, plus 120 surface workers.

Accidents in the Common Coal Works, as the mines were often known, were fairly common. An example occurred on 25 June 1850, when John Nimmo, a boy of twelve years of age employed to dig coal, was seriously injured by a fall of coal from the roof of the mine. He was lying in the pit when a large block of stone fell from above, breaking one of his legs and seriously bruising the other. He suffered for a few days before he died. He was buried in Catrine.

Some of the Common pits worked ironstone, such as No. 14 pit, located far out on Airds Moss, halfway between Common and Templandshaw farms. On 22 February 1883 George Moon, a miner aged 61, was killed when a block of stone fell on him, cracking open his skull and killing him instantly. He had worked at the Common pits since they had opened forty years before.

The Barglachan Colliery extended over Barglachan and Birnieknowe farms. The first pits were sunk in the 1850s, and these appear to be small workings, often suffering from flooding. Once one pit was worked out another was brought on stream. In 1857 a fatal accident occurred at Barglachan Colliery. The Inspector of Mines Report of that year makes reference to it:

> At the time this accident-occurred, various rumours were current about it of a mysterious nature. A partial combination was stated to exist among the enginemen of the district, and it was understood that the engineman (the deceased) was not a member of it. According to the evidence of parties, the engineman had left his work on the afternoon of Saturday (28th November, 1857) and with some acquaintances had afterwards been indulging at a public house till a late hour, after which he went with two of them to 'draw' some men who were engaged on a night shift, but the person in charge of the works had visited them during the engineman's absence and drawn the men out of the pit. When the engineman and his two associates reached the pit, one of them accustomed to underground work was lowered, to see if the men had finished their shift and were ready to be taken up. Whether the engineman had been getting uneasy about the return of his acquaintance, or had been listening at the pitmouth for his return, no one can say; he was found the following morning in the

sump of the pit, and his acquaintance who had been lowered to enquire after the men on the night shift, though in the pit all night, knew nothing of it. A singular part of the case was, one of the deceased's boots was found in a hutch 9 feet along the level road from the bottom of the pit. This, coupled with other circumstances, and that one of the two who were with the deceased couldn't give any information of where he had been, or anything connected with the mysterious affair, caused a considerable amount of speculation, and a strong feeling existed that there had been foul play in some way or another.

I took a good deal of trouble, along with the Procurator Fiscal, in investigating this case, and I felt satisfied that the deceased fell down the shaft accidentally while in a state of intoxication, and that his companion who was last seen with him in the engine-house had not been sober enough to remember anything of it.

Death was a regular occurrence in the pits, and numerous men were killed by accident. Of these only a few can be mentioned – On 7 February 1857 John Vickers was drowned in Craigston No. 19 pit at Lugar.

A new mine was sunk at Carbello in 1873 by William Baird & Co. to mine both coal and ironstone. Extraction of the latter ceased in 1881, but coal continued to be dug until the end of the century. In 1896 the mine was managed by James Smith, the underground manager being John Weir. There were 102 miners working below ground at the mine, plus a further 15 on the surface.

At the same time as Carbello was sunk, Blackston Ironstone Pit was sunk nearer to Auchinleck. The pit only operated for eight years before it was closed. On 21 May 1879 William Baird of Lugar was killed by a stone fall at the pit.

In Braehead No. 6 pit a fourteen-year-old boy surnamed Barbour was killed on 6 April 1883 when he fell down the shaft. He was still alive at the bottom, and the men were able to lift him to the engine-house, but he died soon after.

A new coal and ironstone pit at Braehead was sunk in 1888 by Baird. In 1896 the manager was William Gray and the under-manager was R. MacIntyre. At that time the pit employed 80 men below ground plus a further ten above. It was closed in 1897.

A larger Barglachan Colliery was sunk in 1889 by William Baird & Co., located to the north-west of Barglachan farm. By 1896 the mine was managed by William Gray, as were other Baird mines, the under-managers employed at the pit being J. Biggans (No. 1 Pit) and George Weir (No. 2 Pit). At the time there were 125 men employed underground, with 17 working on the surface.

The Craigston pits were located around Lugar Ironworks and were used to mine ironstone and coal. The pits were fairly small, and as one became worked out a further one was sunk. On 11 April 1849 James Mackay was killed at Craigston No. 12 pit. He was ascending the shaft in a cage which came up with such a speed that he was thrown from it at the surface and was killed when he fell. The counterbalance cage had not been properly connected to the gears, which slipped. The case went to the Ayr Circuit Court, where Robert Reid was charged with having removed the 'shuts' or trapdoor over the shaft, causing the other cage to descend. The Lord Justice Clerk stated that the charge was not proven, and advised the miners to take greater caution in the future.

Alexander Blain, aged 23, was killed in Craigston No. 19 pit on 24 November 1853. James Gillespie and James Scott were both killed in Caigston No. 19 pit in February 1857.

Some of the accidents were not due to safety failures or poor conditions. In a number of cases miners under the influence of alcohol caused their own deaths. One example was Redman Kellan, who worked at Braehead Pit, near Lugar. On 2 January 1864 he went to the pithead to collect his tools. As he wandered around the pitmouth he stumbled and fell to the bottom of the shaft, a depth of around 480 feet. He was found dead at the bottom. He left behind a widow and two children.

At the Craigston - Roadinghead pit three men suffered death in a single incident on 15 April 1865. James MacIntosh, William Carnochan and Peter Folley were ascending in the cage from the pit bottom when the cage caught on the sides of the pit and tipped the men out. They fell around 120 feet to the bottom of the shaft, dying instantly. MacIntosh left behind a wife and three children; the other two men were unmarried.

Cronberry No. 1 coal and ironstone pit was sunk in 1864 by William Baird & Co. This was located about half a mile north of the village. Production of ironstone ceased in 1881, but coal continued to be mined until the pit was closed in 1893. Five other pits with the name Cronberry were sunk from the 1860s onwards, closing from 1876 until 1886.

In the Mosshouse pit, which was sunk near to Cronberry, John Cameron lost his life on Saturday 17 December 1859. He was placing a hutch onto the cage when he slipped on the frosty ground. He plummeted 360 feet down the shaft, his body being severely mangled by the fall.

The works at Lugar used a mixture of clayband, blackband and Spanish ores to make pig-iron, along with white lime and coal for smelting. A certain weight of each was loaded into the furnace by wagon where the ore was smelted and the slag removed. When ready, the molten iron was poured into large sand moulds, arranged in rows, and allowed to set. When this occurred sand was thrown over the top and men, wearing shoes with wood and iron soles, walked over the bars, breaking them apart with heavy hammers.

For many years the gases produced in the smelting process were allowed to escape into the atmosphere, but in 1882 work began on a gas treatment plant at the east end of the works, being operational by September 1883. Here the gas was cooled and washed, producing ammonium sulphate, potash, tar, creosote and pitch. The first two were used in fertilisers for agricultural purposes, the ammonia selling for around £22 per ton, though as more ironworks began producing it the price dropped to around £9 per ton in 1898. The creosote, as well as being used in timber preservation, was burned in 'Lucigen' lamps, invented around 1880, three of which were used to illuminate the works in 1898. The pitch was used in the works also, being mixed with finely ground coal and compressed into Eglinton briquettes, much loved in domestic fires. A further by-product recovery plant was erected in the mid-1890s. The manager of the ammonia works for many years was William Lindsay (1850-1921).

The original Common Ironstone mine employed up to 716 men. A new Braehead Ironstone Pit was established in 1894, managed by William Gray and employing 103 men, but it closed just four years later. At the Common farm the Maid Pits, which exploited both coal and ironstone, worked from around 1850 to 1905. Ironstone was also mined just north of Auchinleck parish, at Glenlogan, and transported to Lugar by rail past Darnconner. Coal mines in operation in 1860 included the Barglachan Pit (No. 30), north-east of the farm, Stepends Pit, at Holmhead, near Cumnock, the Common Coalworks (near Darnconner) and Dalfad Pit.

In 1894 William Baird & Co. began work in constructing the new Highhouse Pit. This was located just west of Auchinleck, the first coal pit to mine the deeper seams in this area. The site chosen for the pit was Merlinhill farm, which was demolished, and six fields were taken over for the surface buildings and spoil heap. The winding engine was manufactured in 1896 by Grant, Ritchie and Company Limited of Kilmarnock, the first coal raised later that year. This engine was a single-cylinder double-acting beam engine with a bore of 18 inches and stroke of 3 feet 6 inches. Developing around 65 horse power, the engine raised coal from the pit bottom to the surface in fifteen minutes, producing about 150 tons per day. This engine was noted in the parish for its distinctive sound which could be heard throughout the village. The pump was known as 'Auld Ben' from its first operator, disabled miner Ben Anderson. The colliery's first manager was James Smith, with T. S. MacCulloch as underground manager. In 1896 the pit employed 110 miners, plus 16 surface workers.

It wasn't long before the new pit saw its first fatalities. Perhaps the first was John Richmond, who lived in Auchinleck, who was killed when stone fell from the roof of the pit on 5 November 1900. His brother, George Richmond, was injured by the same fall, but survived.

Bairds was not the only company to operate mines in the parish. Gilmour, Wood and Anderson of Auchinleck had a couple of small mines, notably the Gilmilnscroft Pits. Six of these existed, mostly located on Gilmilnscroft estate in the parish of Sorn, the last shaft (No 6) sunk in 1909. At one point Gilmilnscroft pit employed 408 men, 343 of which worked below ground. The manager was William Hastie JP (1843-1925), who retired in 1906 after being manager for thirty years. The company was latterly known as the Gauchalland Coal Company (from Gauchalland near Galston), but still owned by the same group. Adam Wood was head of the business by 1900, residing at Portland Villa, Troon. Bairds latterly took over the company.

William Walker and Company, of Auchinleck, operated the Ballochmyle collieries, located straddling Auchinleck and Sorn parishes. The name Ballochmyle came from Ballochmyle House, near Mauchline, owned by the Alexanders, on whose estate the pits were located (Roundshaw and Darnconner farms). In 1875 Ballochmyle Pit was managed by Robert Whiteside, and at that time had 210 men working below ground, plus 33 above. Ballochmyle pits operated until 1899, the manager being Adam Hunter. There were 42 men working on the surface, 220 below. Seven different shafts were sunk at various locations. To house the employees and their families, the company built the Burnside Row (latterly nicknamed 'The Poverty'), Ballochmyle Rows and Walker's Row (sometimes known as Stable Row).

William Walker's daughter married into the Hood family, which took on ownership of the pits. The Hoods lived in Cumnock Square, in the house at the corner with Hamilton Place. The business expanded into the Edinburgh area, and when the local pits were closed, many of the employees moved to the Lothians for work. William Walker Hood became a millionaire through his ownership of coal-mines. He died in 1923.

The Cronberry brickworks were opened at the same time as Lugar Ironworks, the first lessee being Mr MacDougall. The works became more involved in making drainage tiles, using clay quarried on site to make rectangular section clay pipes for field draining. These works actually preceded the formation of the village itself and were owned by William Baird. For many years the tile manufacturer was Alexander Duncan (1819-1902). He was born in Ochiltree parish, and originally worked at Ochiltree Tileworks. He later took over the tileworks at Failford, and then moved to Shawneuk Tileworks at Catrine. He moved to the tileworks that existed at Auchinleck, before moving to Cronberry. The works at Cronberry were taken over by his son, John Syme Duncan (1852-1925), who enlarged them. The son also took over the Ochiltree tileworks in 1906, where he continued until his death.

Sometime between 1860 and 1910 the Lugar Brickworks were erected. Located north of Lugar station, the works used spoil from the mines to produce bricks.

Following the erection of the new ironworks at Lugar, Bairds required to build houses for the vast number of employees which came to work both there and in the pits which supplied coal and ironstone. Many of these workers were Irish, some of them having left home due to the potato famine of the 1840's, others men who moved to mining following the completion of the railway south to Dumfries in

1850. In 1848, James Baird noted that two-thirds of his miners (ironstone) were Irish, as were one quarter of the colliers (coalminers). It was at this time the parish population soared, from around 1,700 in 1841 to 3,700 in 1851.

With the opening of the ironworks at Lugar the demand for lime grew again, being required as a flux in the smeltmill. A new limeworks was established near Dalfad, known as the Gasswater Limeworks, quarrying the same band of rock that had been worked due south at the Glenmuir Limeworks. Indeed, the High Glenmuir and Laigh Glenmuir limestone quarries continued to produce stone, even though the kilns there were disused. The Gasswater Branch of the Muirkirk railway was laid into the works, leaving the main line at Carbello and describing a large radius across Dalfad Moss almost as far as Snipe Hill. Two rows of workers' cottages were erected, on opposite sides of the road, one higher up than the other. Two sets of kilns were positioned just south of the upper row, the railway located behind them.

As with the rest of Scotland, following the Union of Parliaments, Auchinleck parish found a new degree of prosperity never before realised. The benefit of spreading lime on the fields both as a fertiliser and as an antidote to acidic soils was soon discovered, and from the late eighteenth century limeworks were established in the parish. By 1837 the parish's limeworks produced almost £900 worth of lime per annum. The *Statistical Account* states that it was used as manure on all the farms. It was common for farmers to rise up at one or two o'clock in the morning in order to be first at the kilns. This was so that the shells they got were cold, for later in the day the shells could be so hot as to set their carts on fire. Three limeworks existed at the turn of the century, at High Glenmuir, High Dalblair and Penbreck.

At Penbreck the limestone was mined, whereas at Laigh and High Glenmuir it was quarried. Limestone was also quarried at Boghead, Tarrioch, Springhill and Dornal, from where it was transported by horse and cart to the kilns. In later years some farms had their own smaller kilns -these formerly existed at Common and Barglachan. The latter was mentioned in the Diary of Henry Richmond (1823-1824), and existed until about 1975.

The High Glenmuir kilns were the largest producers in the parish, and the good quality masonry indicates a prosperous business. Owned by the Boswells, the Glenmuir lime works had two sets of kilns, one of which was double-draw, the other having a single-draw arch but with two pairs of draw holes. This may indicate that it had been an oval kiln. In 1837 these kilns produced about 50,000 bushels (5,000 cart-loads) of lime per annum, mainly used for agricultural purposes. In the mid-century the proprietor was a Mr Richmond. In the 1850s the lessee was a Mr Kirkland.

At High Dalblair the kiln was owned by David Limond of Dalblair and produced 20,000 bushels each year. At both works the limestone was layered with coal in the kiln and set alight. The lime produced was spread on the fields, about twenty carts per acre on good ground, up to thirty loads per acre on ground being reclaimed. Where quarried, the limestone was found in beds from six to fourteen feet deep. Some of the lime was used for building purposes, to create a mortar, and it was also in demand as a flux in the iron-smelting industry to a lesser degree.

The kilns at Glenmuir and Dalblair closed in the middle of the nineteenth century, when better and cheaper fertilisers became available, and the newer Gasswater limeworks became established, making lime for Lugar ironworks. Limestone may have been worked here earlier, for Armstrong's map of 1775 notes 'Limehough' at this point. The first examples of labourers' rows were formed for workers at the limeworks. At High Glenmuir, apart from Quarryhouse and Glenmuir cottages, there was also a row of four houses for quarrymen.

5.15 High Dalbair lime kiln *(Dane Love)*

In 1857 the Auchinleck Gas Light Company Limited was formed, and on ground acquired adjacent to Bridgend Mill a gasworks was erected. An advertisement was placed in the *Ardrossan & Saltcoats Herald* of 16 May 1857 inviting contractors to build the works. In its first year the works had pipes supplying town or coal gas to sixty households in the lower half of the village. In 1874 the gas manager was James Telfer. Coal was burned in large furnaces in order to heat other loads of coal to around 1,000°C, causing it to give off coal-gas.

One of the busiest of businesses in the parish was Wilson's sawmill, located in Market Place, next to the railway. The mill was founded by Adam Wilson (born 1823 in Minishant) who had leased a sawmill at Sorn in 1856 and another at The Haugh, Mauchline. Around 1860 he moved to Raggithill, Tarbolton. These sawmills proved to be too small to supply the growing demand for pit props, timber for iron moulds, and general agricultural wood, so in 1876 he bought the old sawmill at Auchinleck, where he set up a new large mill adjacent to the railway – the yard having its own branch for unloading tree trunks and loading sawn timber. Steam-driven saws were used to convert timber which found a market outwith the parish - at Catrine cottonworks, McCartney's works in Cumnock and Mauchline boxworks. Timber was at first obtained from the Auchinleck and Dumfries estates, but the supply failed to keep up with the demand for Wilson's products and so temporary sawmills were located in various woods. A second sawmill was established at Troon harbour in 1888, to deal with timber brought in from Argyll and beyond by boat. A third mill was leased at Dailly in 1893, but Auchinleck remained the company's headquarters. Adam Wilson died at Mauchline in 1898, the company surviving to be run by his sons.

The quarries at Auchinleck were leased in the late nineteenth century by Smith & MacMillan. William Smith (1849-1924), son of George Smith, was in partnership with Robert MacMillan. As well as quarrying, the firm was responsible for various building contracts, including mason work on the Town Hall, Baird Institute and Lochnorris, all Cumnock. William Smith moved to Glasgow around 1890 and retired in 1911, moving to Cowdenbeath.

COMMERCE

As the Victorian era dawned in 1837, the number of shops and commercial premises in Auchinleck began to grow. By 1850 there were now eight shopkeepers, a baker, two shoemakers, a monumental sculptor and a blacksmith. From old Valuation Rolls, for example 1875, we find the following businesses in existence in the Main Street. Andrew Hamilton (shoemaker); Andrew Morton (baker); David Gibson (watchmaker); David Giffen (grocery); Robert Stewart (tailor); Andrew Hyslop (wright); and John Girvan (grocery). In 1878 Robert Greenshields was a draper based in Coal Road, at that time often known as Lugar Street.

The first plan to establish a Co-operative Society in Auchinleck was mooted in 1889 but it met with little success. There had been two earlier co-op ventures in the village, but both collapsed after a time. A public meeting was held in the Railway Inn hall on 19 December 1889 with the intention of establishing a new co-op venture, and though the attendance was small, talks from James Deans of Kilmarnock and Robert O'May of Paisley resulted in 25 of those present wishing to form a society. A committee was formed, comprising William Wilson (chairman), James D. Gibson (secretary), James Smith, William MacConnell, Matthew Wallace, Patrick Haining, David Stevenson and James Reid. These men went round the village looking for members, 107 of which signed up, buying 179 shares at ten shillings each. The committee reckoned this was insufficient numbers with which to proceed and so asked the co-ops of Mauchline and Catrine in turn to open a branch. Both rejected the request on the grounds that Auchinleck was too distant from either village. The committee therefore went ahead themselves and founded the Auchinleck Co-operative Society Limited.

Within ten years the society's turnover was equal to the combined turnover of both Mauchline and Catrine. At a general meeting of shareholders held on 5 February 1890, William Wilson was appointed president, Thomas Gracie as secretary, and James MacIntyre as treasurer. They obtained a lease of a cottage in Main Street for five years at £13 per annum which was converted into a shop, the committee members doing the alterations following their day's shift in the mines. Stocked with goods from the Scottish Co-operative Wholesale Society, of which the Auchinleck branch joined at the outset, the shop opened for business on 25 June 1890 with James Haugh as salesman. The first quarter's sales were greater than expected, at £930 19s 5½d, giving the 110 members a dividend of 2s 3d per pound.

The shop was soon found to be too small, so the adjoining kitchen was leased at £7 per annum. By the end of the year membership stood at 190, the sales £1,677 19s 9d, with a dividend of 2s 8d per pound. A boot-repairing department was added in 1891 and in 1892 the society purchased its premises for £506, now converted to an ironmongery store and head office. A new bakery was opened in January 1894 with R. Matthews coming from Ardrossan to act as foreman. However, by 1894 a miners' strike almost brought the society to its knees. A drapery and shoe shop was opened in 1895 along with the formation of a Penny Savings Bank. The founding president, William Wilson, of Larchville, Mauchline Road, retired on 24 January 1896, and was succeeded by James Smith. Thomas Steele became managing secretary in 1898. A branch shop in Ochiltree was opened in 1899 and a third shop was opened at Ballochmyle Rows in 1900. By 1900 a powder store belonging to the society had been established at Darnlaw. This sold gunpowder, used by the miners to blast the coal free underground, and which they were responsible for buying themselves.

Auchinleck Post Office was located in the bakery adjoining the Commercial Inn. At Lugar the post office was operated by William Murdoch from 1872, assisted by his daughter, Marion Murdoch. His son, Sergeant Hugh Murdoch was killed in action during the First World War. The post office at Darnconner was run by Mrs Annie Rae from 1897.

In 1850 there were six public houses - the Railway Inn, Market Inn, Eagle Inn, Commercial Inn (latterly Cross Keys), Boswell Arms Inn and the White Heart Inn, located near the bottom end of the village. This last-named inn closed by 1890.

The Railway Inn was operated by Janet Milligan for a number of years, she having moved to the village from Dumfriesshire in the 1870s to take over the inn. Her daughter, Mary Milligan took over nearer the end of the century.

At the Market Inn Alexander MacLeod took over as mine host in 1883. He died in 1897 and his wife (d. 1915) continued to run the inn for a time before handing the business over to their son, David Macleod.

5.16 Clydesdale and North of Scotland Bank *(Author's Collection)*

The Eagle Inn had James Park as the landlord in the late nineteenth century. When he died the inn continued under the proprietorship of Mrs J. S. Park. Margaret Goldie took over just before the end of the nineteenth century.

The Commercial Inn was run by John Fleming (1843-1893). He was followed by James Hope, who ran it until his death on 16 November 1901, aged 52.

The Boswell Arms was run by Thomas Adams.

AGRICULTURE

The principal industry in the parish changed from agriculture to mining and smelting in the second half of the nineteenth century. A number of smaller farms were abandoned, their steadings becoming ruinous and their lands attached to other farms to create larger units. Farms abandoned prior to 1860 include Woodside (located west of Hapland), Dippolburn (to the north-west of Darnlaw), Craigston, Pathhead and Burnside (all occupied by Lugar Ironworks, etc.), Cubs Mill (south of Wallaceton), Cronberryshield (east of Templandshaw), Welltrees (west of Boghead), Bogside (north of Boghead), Blackhillhead (north of Langholm), Dykehead (near Stevenston), Roddinhead (north of Thirdpart), Headburn (near Townhead), Mounthooly (south of Knaigshill), Dyke, Airdhillock, Muirhouse, Hillhead (all in Auchinleck vicinity), Bonnyton (west of Roadinghead) and Upper Tarrioch (by the

River Ayr). By 1900 a further series of farms had been abandoned, including Broomhouse (west of Langholm), Whin and Mosside (west of Knowe), Gibston, Loganston and Weilside (west of Stevenston), Hapland (west of Glenside), Orchard and Woolmill (south of Fore Rogerton), Wee Rigg (south of Blackston), Woodend (at Boo'd Scotland, Holmhead), Blackcroft (south of Sunnyside), Cubs (west of Laigh Glenmuir), Shawfield (north-east of Dalblair), High Shaw (north-east of Glenmuirshaw), Broom (west of Boghead) and Nether Tarrioch (by the River Ayr). Some of these steadings survived as cottages for a time, but most are now ruinous or else non-existent.

During the time when Sir James Boswell owned the estate (up to 1857) great improvements were made to the farmsteads. The old thatched cottages, with clay floors, adjoining directly on to the byres, were demolished and replaced with more substantial stone and slate-built houses, with wooden floors and attic bedrooms, many of which survive in a slightly modified form to this day.

In the lower half of the parish dairying remained the most popular form of agriculture. Most farmers converted their milk into butter and cheese to sell at the market, whereas a few sent it to the Glasgow markets by rail.

In 1860 there were three mills operating in the parish, Mill of Auchinleck (or Mill Affleck), Bridgend Mill and Bello Mill, but by the turn of the century only Bello Mill still produced meal. The older mill at Bello Mill appears to have been built parallel with the river, but it went on fire and was rebuilt at right angles to the river. This allowed the building to be erected against the banking, thus the top floor, where the grain came in, was at ground level. The mill originally had three pairs of stones – one for shelling, one for finishing oatmeal, and a third for provender. These stones were powered by a breast wheel producing around ten horsepower.

Mill Affleck became a farm, whereas Bridgend was converted into a smithy. At Bridgend, sometime before 1860, the main road was realigned between the mill buildings and the mill dam, in order to remove the sharp left-hand bend which the road took on the south side of the Auchinleck Burn.

Bello Mill was aptly tenanted by David Millar, who died in 1900 aged 68. His eldest daughter Catherine married Thomas Laird, whose descendants still own it. The actual mill building dates from the eighteenth century, though it probably replaced an older building. Formerly thatched, the mill was reroofed with corrugated iron and remained thus until it was de-roofed around 1980. The dam across the Lugar was washed away in a flood, but by then the mill was operated by diesel engine. Formerly the six-spoke low-breasted water-wheel (around ten feet in diameter and three feet across) operated a single pair of stones. Connecting belts drove an oats bruiser. The mill was still operational into the early 1970s, but by then just served the farms owned by the Lairds.

The growing of crops still proved to be unprofitable but some farmers did grow turnips for feeding cattle and the odd field of potatoes. Corn and barley was grown only where the soil was sufficiently rich, but the crop obtained was far poorer than that which grew nearer the Ayrshire coast.

The Lamb Fair continued to attract many farmers and shepherds to Auchinleck on the last Tuesday of August each year. It was still held at Market Place (or Market Road, or Square, as it was sometimes known) and pens for livestock were a permanent feature. As the century progressed the fair began to decline, the first notable drop being in the sale of cheeses. In 1890 lamb crosses sold for between 20 shillings and 23 shillings, wedders from 9 shillings to 13 shillings, Cheviots 16 shillings and blackface ewe lambs from £10 to £20 per clad score. Almost nothing was done in cheese sales that year, and the number of lambs was not great. A second annual fair was held on the last Thursday of March, mainly for trade in grit ewes and hoggs.

For leisure, farmers enjoyed the annual ploughing competition held by the farmers of 'Glenmuir and Bello Waters.' In 1890 it was held at Broomfield farm, near Cumnock.

5.17 Mauchline Road, with Toll Cottage to left *(Author's Collection)*

LEISURE

The few idle hours enjoyed by villagers were spent participating in sport. In winter curling was the most popular hobby and Auchinleck boasted a Curling Club. The first curling pond was formed at Holmhead, near to Cumnock, the site of which is now occupied by numbers 6 and 8 Holmhead Road. This pond measured around 150 feet by 25 feet, the water fed into it by a small stream. It was created some time prior to 1856. Nearer the village the Marquis of Bute allowed the construction of a large pond for curling to the west of the market stance. Called Merlin Loch, this stretch of water measured around 500 feet by 250 feet, thus allowing more than one game to take place. To prevent the pond from draining it was lined with clay and at its southern end a set of sluices constructed which could restrict or release the water. The club was re-established on 30 December 1861 at Merlin Loch. Early presidents of the club included James Park of the Eagle Inn, followed by Hugh Alexander of Fore Rogerton, who was appointed as president in 1896.

A large curling pond was created near to Dickston farm, off the Rigg Road, sometime between 1897 and 1911. This pond had a low embankment forming a dam on its western edge, and in total measured around 300 feet by 150 feet.

A specially dug-out curling rink was formed in the field to the east of Craigston House at Lugar, between it and Craigston Square. This rink measured around 150 feet in length by 50 feet wide.

The village weavers were noted curlers, and it is recorded that when the loch was frozen they tended to spend more time there than working at the loom. A tale was told of one wife who placed a curling stone on the morning breakfast table as a warning to her husband that unless he earned some money the stone was all they would have to eat!

In the 1860s the Auchinleck Games were popular. There was a growing support for the annual competitions, a bit like Highland Games, in different communities, and Auchinleck was no different. In addition to various athletic events, the August games at Auchinleck also included quoiting.

In the second half of the nineteenth century there were numerous organisations to which the villagers could belong. In 1859 Auchinleck boasted a brass band and the Thistle Flute Band. There was also a branch of the Young Men's Christian Association which had premises in Main Street. Auchinleck Angling Association was founded in 1883. The Auchinleck Quoiting Club was a very active one, and they had a pitch in a field across the railway from Park Road. The Auchinleck Horticultural Society held an annual show of produce in the Town Hall in August of each year.

In the latter half of the nineteenth century the sport of football became very popular throughout Scotland, the oldest team being founded in 1867 (Queens Park Football Club) which did not accept the standard rules until 1870. Teams sprung up all over the country, virtually every village containing at least one, even tiny settlements such as Commondyke managing to operate in Juvenile games as Commondyke Celtic for a time. The oldest team in Auchinleck was known as the Auchinleck Primrose XI, playing at Juvenile level, but it became defunct in 1901. Auchinleck Boswell played from around 1881 to 1890 at Glenshamrock Holm, sporting black and white strips, and using the Eagle Inn for changing. Locally these teams played against each other, hoping to win the Auchinleck Juvenile Cup, presented by football fans in the village.

At Lugar, in 1878, Lugar Boswell Thistle was founded, playing at first on a field behind the Brick Row, then at Thomarston farm, changing in the farmhouse, and wearing scarlet jerseys, white shorts with black stripes, and black and white socks. The team played in a number of different formations in the first year, but in 1879, during a game with Mauchline, they introduced the well-known 5-3-2-1 line-up, the first team to do so.

Lugar changed grounds in 1882, moving to Rosebank within the village, the field being created by the team members themselves on the site of the former Rosebank Mine. Villagers helped to flatten the bing, clear the rubbish, and transport soil to the new field. Robert Angus of Craigston House assisted with funds to finish the field, build a club-house and fence the ground. In 1881 Lugar beat Annbank 5-1 at Rugby Park, Kilmarnock, to take the Ayrshire Senior Cup. Two years later they again made the final, but were beaten 3-2 by Kilmarnock Athletic. The game was played at Rugby Park in front of 5,000 spectators. Lugar's team comprised of Gillespie, Lundie, Kerr, MacLaren, Rankin, Lafferty, MacCulloch, Goldie, MacGinn, Thomson and MacGhee. A more notable win from this period was when Lugar beat Glasgow Rangers 2-0 at Rosebank.

Other football teams from this period playing at Junior level were Darnconner Britannia, existing from around 1888 to 1900. Their field was known as Pablin Ground, their colours red, white and blue. Common Thistle was founded around 1898.

At the beginning of the nineteenth century abstinence from alcohol became a popular cause throughout Scotland and organisations promoting the good life were formed. The International Organisation of Rechabites established its first 'tent' in Ayrshire at Largs in 1841, extending to other communities thereafter. The William Murdoch Tent, No. 1,958, was opened at Auchinleck on 23 December 1889, followed by a juvenile tent. Membership in 1913 stood at 154 state members, 197 ordinary members, 13 members' wives or widows, 2 honorary members, and 127 juveniles.

A tent was formed at Darnconner in 1896, named the Hope of Darnconner Tent, No. 2,648; joined by the Star of Darnconner Juvenile Tent in 1897. Membership stood at 76 state members, 107 ordinary members, 3 members' wives and 69 juveniles in 1913. The Lugar branch, the William Robertson Tent, No. 1,695, opened in 1897, the branch for juveniles, named after Richard Cameron, the year following. William Robertson was formerly the cashier to Bairds. Membership in 1913 included 61 state members, 72 ordinary members, 6 wives, 11 honorary and 37 juvenile members. In 1906 two juvenile members from Lugar represented the Ayrshire district in the first year of the Order Temperance Knowledge Competition, winners in their age group being David M. Young and Jeanie Macdonald. A tent was opened at Cronberry on 19 January 1900, named Airds Moss Tent, No. 2,920, the Juvenile Tent (named Bello Water) in the same year. In 1913 membership stood at 82 state members, 64 ordinary, 7 wives and 151 juveniles.

SONS AND DAUGHTERS

Robert Samson Ingram, architect of the town hall and many other buildings in the parish, lived for a time in Auchinleck, in a cottage on Barony Road. He was born in 1840, the son of James Ingram, himself a noted architect, who had his practice in Kilmarnock. James was born in Catrine and was responsible for numerous buildings in Ayrshire, notably the Town House in Irvine, the Corn Exchange (now the Palace Theatre) in Kilmarnock, and St Marnock's Church in the same town. More locally he designed New Cumnock Parish Church, Catrine West Church (now a house), and Glaisnock House.

Robert Ingram entered his father's office where he served his apprenticeship, followed by a time in London where he extended his experience. He returned to Scotland where he became a partner in his father's practice, remaining the sole partner when his father died in 1870. He continued to work alone until 1906 when he was joined by D. M. Brown. Ingram later moved to Mauchline where he lived at The Grove. He died there on 6 October 1915 and was buried in Kilmarnock's High Kirkyard. He was survived by his wife, Frances Hay Torrance, leaving £357 14s 6d in his will.

Ingram designed numerous schools, churches, institutes, houses and monuments throughout the west of Scotland. He had contracts with a number of school boards, the Roman Catholic education committees, and with William Baird & Company, the latter giving him commissions for public buildings within mining communities owned by the company. Among Ingram's more notable works are the Grange Church (Kilmarnock), Barrhill Parish Church, Hurlford Parish Church, Gartsherrie Parish Church, Glenbuck Parish Church, Cumnock Town Hall, Baird Institute (Cumnock), A. M. Brown Institute (Catrine) , Dick Institute (Kilmarnock), Kilmarnock Academy, the old Public School in Cumnock, Burns Monument (Kilmarnock) and the Peden Monument (Cumnock).

John Smith, a noted Ayrshire antiquarian, lived in Lugar for a time. Smith was born on 14 September 1846 at Clarkston, Airdrie, the eldest son of James Smith and Elizabeth Drysdale. They were married the year previously. In 1847 James Smith and his young family moved to Dalry in Ayrshire to supervise the sinking of new pit shafts in the district. James became an important man locally, being coal and ironstone mining manager, and he lived in a fair-sized house called Kirkland. John was taught in three local schools at Dalry, followed by Irvine Academy. He then went to Glasgow where he was apprenticed as a mining engineer. Whilst there he joined many of the academic societies, furthering his knowledge in botany, archaeology and geology.

Smith's first job was to be under manager at Lugar pits, a position he took up around 1868. He remained for around two and a half years, before being promoted to manager of the Eglinton Ironworks at Kilwinning. Whilst at Lugar he started to investigate local archaeological sites, and it is said that it was during this time that he conceived the idea of writing his noted book, *Prehistoric Man in Ayrshire*, which was published in 1895. Smith retired from the ironworks in 1890, after which he spent all of his time researching. He produced over seventy articles and booklets, as well as columns in the *Ardrossan and Saltcoats Herald*.

John Smith died on 30 November 1930. He was buried in Cumnock cemetery, alongside his parents. A memoir, *The Biography of John Smith, Ayrshire Geologist and Naturalist* was published just two months after his death. The author, A. Boyd, had been working on the book for some time prior to Smith's death.

Born in Auchinleck Manse on 3 November 1825, the son of Rev Dr James Boyd, was another notable literary son of the parish. Andrew Kennedy Hutchison Boyd was educated locally at first, then in Ayr, followed by study at King's College and the Middle Temple in London, with plans to be a barrister. However, once he had nearly completed his course, he changed his mind and, following study at Glasgow University, graduated as Bachelor of Arts in 1846, and was licensed to preach in 1850.

Boyd's first charge was of Newton-on-Ayr parish church where he remained for three years. In 1854 he was translated to Kirkpatrick Irongray (near Dumfries) and remained there until 1859. During his term at Irongray, Boyd began contributing articles to

5.18 Rev Alexander Kennedy Hutchison Boyd *(Author's Collection)*

Fraser's Magazine, his *The Recreations of a Country Parson* being avidly read throughout the country. These articles, signed 'AKHB', were collected into book form in 1859, subsequently passing through numerous editions. A second series was published in 1861 and a third in 1878.

Boyd took up the charge of St Bernard's Church, in Edinburgh, the university there subsequently awarding him an honorary Doctorate of Divinity in 1864. In the same year he published *The Autumn Holidays of a Country Parson*. In 1865 he accepted the first charge of St Andrews, at Holy Trinity Church, seemingly a life-long ambition, for he wrote, 'Never once, for one moment, have I wished to go elsewhere.' He was associated with the town for the remainder of his life. Many visitors to the university town made a point of attending the church in order to hear him preach. In the late 1800s there was some disturbance in St Andrews when the first Roman Catholic place of worship was erected, resulting in some demonstrations. However, Rev Boyd accepted the new Priest, Father George Angus, as a friend.

Boyd became well-known throughout the country and beyond for his religious strength, and his numerous articles became widely read in America. He acted as convener of a committee which was formed to compile a new hymn book for the Church of Scotland, published in 1870. In April 1889 St Andrews University awarded him an honorary Doctorate of Laws, and the following year he was appointed Moderator of the General Assembly of the Church of Scotland. Boyd was friendly with many distinguished people of the period, including Archbishop Whately, Charles Kingsley, James Anthony Froude and Bishop Thorold of Winchester. In 1895 Rev Boyd took ill, his wife of forty years, Margaret Kirk, nursing him back to health, but she died soon afterwards.

Dr Boyd remarried in 1897, to Janet Meldrum. His ill-health returned in the winter of 1898-99 and he travelled south to Bournemouth in search of better weather and improved health. His strength seems to have returned, for he began writing sermons and essays again, but on 1 March 1899 he mistook a bottle of carbolic lotion for his medicine and died of acid poisoning. His body was interred in the cathedral-yard of St Andrews. Within Holy Trinity Church in the town is a memorial font in his honour. Boyd's second wife, Janet Meldrum, died at St Andrews in July 1917.

Andrew Boyd wrote over thirty books, mainly works of personal reminiscence, which were noted for their display of shrewd observations, lively anecdotes and candid comments. Among the better known volumes were *Lessons of Middle Age* (1868), *Twenty-Five Years of St Andrews* (1892), *St Andrews and Elsewhere* (1894), *Last Years of St Andrews* (1896), *Landscapes, Churches and Moralities* (1874), and *Occasional and Immemorial Days. Our Little Life* appeared in two series (1882 and 1884). According to the *Dictionary of National Biography*, Boyd was 'probably better known than any other Scottish clergyman of his day.' A small volume of collected writings was published in 1914 under the title *A. K. H. B.*, edited by his fourth son, Charles Boyd.

In 1865 a local mason, John Murdoch, spent some considerable time renewing old tombstones in the kirkyard, erecting new memorials to sons of the parish. Among the stones renewed were those of Rev John Shaw, Rev George Walker and Matthew Tait. New memorials erected by him were the obelisk of freestone standing near the gate adjacent to the mausoleum in memory of a selection of parish notables and the tablet in the west wall of the old kirk, in memory of the ministers of the kirk from 1669. The obelisk commemorates William Murdoch, William MacGavin, Alexander Peden and the nine martyrs killed on Airds Moss. Previous to 1874

5.19 Auchinleck Notables' Monument *(Dane Love)*

Murdoch had built the Lord Clyde Well at the village's Townfoot. He had fought with Lord Clyde in Crimea and named the well in his memory. His home, Alma Cottage, was also named from his war experience. In that year Murdoch was given a lunch in his honour, at which he was presented with a purse containing a number of sovereigns.

Matthew MacTurk (1813- 1899) was the Auchinleck correspondent to the Ayr Observer and earlier to the *Kilmarnock Journal*. He was the son of William MacTurk (1770-1839), tacksman of Gasswater Works. Matthew was a building contractor, and had worked on the first railway through Auchinleck to Lugar. He established a quarry or open cast there, but found it to be unsuccessful, losing a considerable amount in that venture. He also acted as a school board officer.

Nineteenth century characters included John Williamson, weaver in the village. As with most weavers he had time to think on politics as he sat working at the loom. He loved to quote the papers, telling people what 'My Lord this' or 'My Lord that' had said in parliament, so much so that he was eventually nicknamed 'My Lord, and not unnaturally his wife was known as 'The Duchess'.

CHAPTER SIX

WARS AND DEPRESSION (1901-45)

VILLAGE LIFE
The Edwardian period was one of much new building in the village. The parish population, according to the Census of 1901, was 6,605. This rose to 7,424 in the 1911 Census, and in 1921 to 7,178. The population of the village in 1901 was 2,828, rising to 3,616 in 1911.

Many of the old thatched cottages were demolished or reroofed and a considerable number of new buildings were erected. The built up area extended into Mauchline Road, or Templeton, from Campbell Place westwards to Templeton Place. Owners of land or old buildings developed their plots, and often named the new buildings 'terraces' or 'places', rather than part of Main Street. Searle Terrace, with eight houses, was erected around 1900 by John Wightman and his wife Annie Morris. His father, also John Wightman, was born in Muirkirk in 1824 and was employed as an underground mine manager, living at No. 18 Darnconner Squares. Adjoining Searle Terrace Shiloh Terrace was erected by the same person in 1905, his initials carved on the corner turret.

Brownlee Place, Cowan Place, Jamieson Place, Smithfield Place and Peden Place were all erected in the Main Street, Greenside Place in Coal Road. John Dalziel erected a block of houses and three shops in 1903, into which the post office moved in 1930 from 105 Main Street (next to the Commercial Inn). John Dalziel was the son of James Dalziel, who moved to Auchinleck from Dumfriesshire. James Dalziel set up his own joiner's business in Auchinleck in 1876, dying in 1895. John was born in Auchinleck and set up in business as a draper, joining his father to start the joinery in 1876. In 1895 he took over the business. He served as the Registrar in the village for 43 years, from 1884-1927. He joined the School Board in 1892 and became Clerk to the School Board in 1917. He was appointed as a Justice of the Peace in 1910. In 1887 he was involved in creating the Auchinleck Special Water District. He served for three years as a Liberal councillor on the County Council. He died in 1927 aged 69. The joinery business was transferred to his son, James.

Opposite the new Dalziel House a new cottage was also erected in 1903 for Matthew Hamilton. George Brown erected new shops and flats in Main Street in

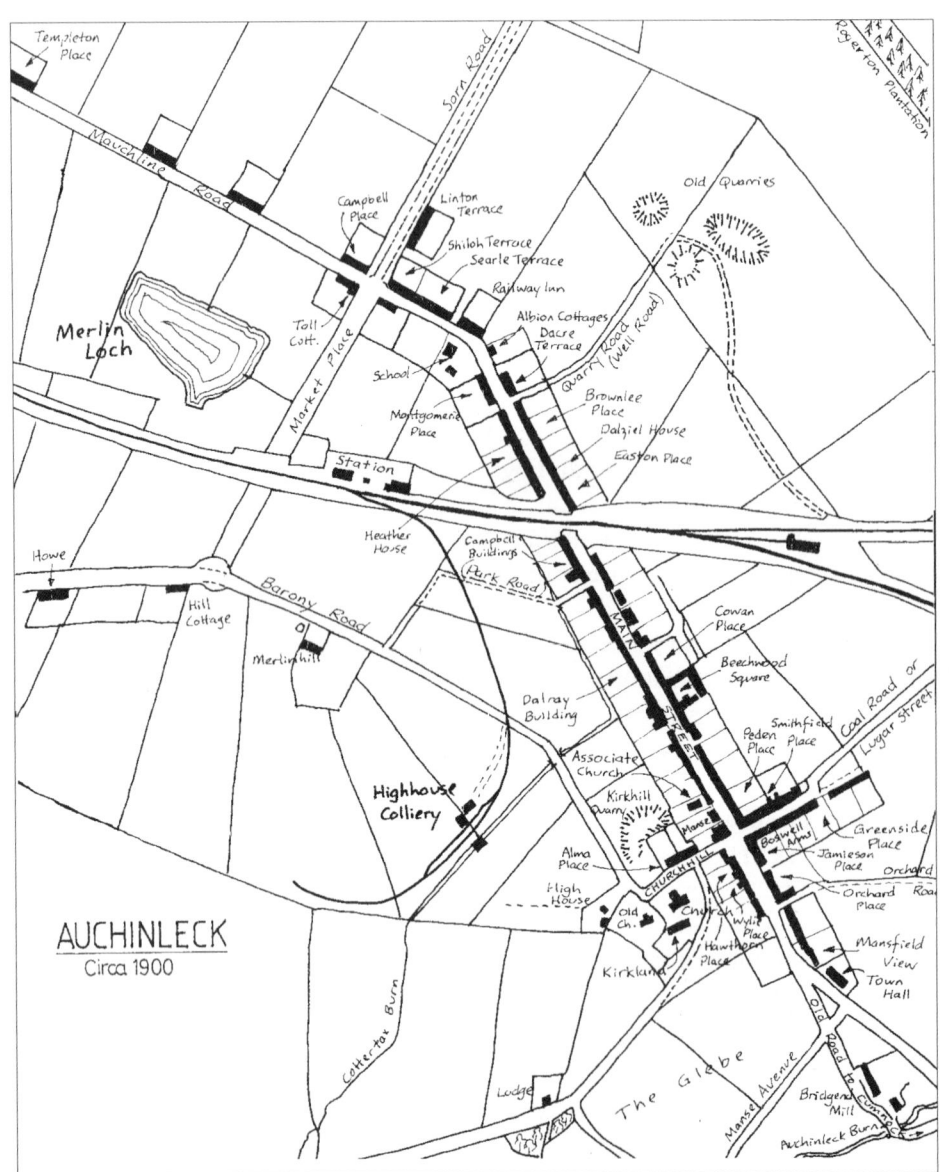

6.1 Auchinleck around 1900 *(Dane Love)*

1905 on a site where the previous house had burned down. William MacCulloch erected a new tenement building next to the railway bridge in 1906, the mason work by James Reid & Son of Mauchline, the joiner work by Findlay & Son of Mauchline. This new block had two spacious double shops and seven flats. The architect was James Davidson of Cumnock.

Further down Main Street, opposite Orchard Place, Thomas Murdoch built himself a new cottage in 1906, replacing an older thatched cottage. His grandfather was a cousin of William Murdoch, inventor of gas-lighting. Murdoch was a joiner, his workshop being located in an old cottage next door which retained its thatched roof, and which had the distinction of being the last building in Auchinleck to have it. Murdoch had been involved in carrying out joiner work at Glaisnock and Logan houses.

Campbell Buildings were erected in Mauchline Road, at the junction of Sorn Road. In 1929 the buildings, which were occupied by a shop and a long-established fish restaurant, as well as seven houses, were placed on the market.

In May 1918 the tenants left a thatched cottage located in Main Street, near Coal Road corner, which was reckoned to be at least 100 years old. On the day after the tenants removed the cottage collapsed. Not all thatched cottages were being done away with, however, for in October 1919 four houses in Coal Road were offered for sale, three of which were still thatched, indeed, had only recently been re-thatched.

A terrace of four houses (37-43 Mauchline Road) was erected in 1904, also by Wightman, known locally as the 'Holy Cottages' from their occupation by the McCombes and others active in the Christian Brethren. In 1903 double cottages were erected in Mauchline Road by David Campbell, mason, for Mr MacMurtrie, from Darnconner, and Mr King. A new cottage was erected in 1905 for Mr Kelly.

Detached and terraced cottages began to be erected in Sorn Road - 'Lilybank' in 1902; another for James Thomson, teacher, in 1903; two double cottages in 1905 for Mr Steele of Manchester; two cottages in 1906 for David Scott, engineer, designed and built by Provost Richmond of Cumnock in Ballochmyle stone, one cottage of 1906 for Mr Greenshields, and Linton Terrace of eight houses for John Dalziel. In 1924 R. MacIntyre built his cottage in Sorn Road.

In 1913-14 three rows of miners' houses (144 in number) were erected at Dalsalloch by William Baird. These houses were designed by Allan Stevenson, architect. The builders were Miller & Renwick of Bothwell. Findlay of Mauchline did the joinery work, Ballantine of Ayr the slating, William Lapraik of Ayr the foundations and Kerr of Maybole the plastering.

After the First World War there was a realisation that housing stock across the country was in very poor in many cases. Grant funding was available to councils for the erection of new houses for rent. In 1922 Ayr County Council commenced the new housing scheme in Auchinleck. Three blocks of four houses were erected in

Sorn Road in 1924, ready for occupation in December. In 1925 Ayr County Council approved the erection of sixty new houses in the village, at an average cost of £394 each. The houses were to be built in new streets that were created parallel and at right angles to Sorn Road, subsequently named Lambfair Gardens and School Road. In 1925 Ayr County Council also decided to build two steel frame houses at a cost of £375 each. In 1928 there were 28 three-apartment flatted houses erected.

There were a total of 424 houses erected by Ayr County Council at this time, most of them of the flatted variety, blocks of four houses, two on the first floor. These were built in Arran Drive (86 houses), Sorn Road (20), Hillside Crescent (26), Stoner Crescent (42), Old Avenue (38), Lambfair Gardens (40), Heathfield Road (52), School Road (20), Well Road (18), Beechwood Avenue (37), Boswell Crescent (32), Coal Road (7) and Main Street (4), the latter replacing the demolished Beechwood, or 'Pole', Square, from the number of inhabitants of that nationality dwelling there. Accessed through a vault from Main Street, the square was built around on all four sides, apart from a gap on the southern side. By 1925 it was owned by the trustees of the late Robert Barclay Waugh, and at that time there were 33 houses in the square in occupation. In 1932 38 houses were erected by the county council in Auchinleck at a cost of £12,718 3s 8½d. At the time of war breaking out in 1939 the houses in Stoner Crescent and Hillside Crescent were still under construction.

Stoner Crescent was named after Villiers Stanley Stoner JP, who lived in the village's Heathfield Road. He was born at Ballingcollig, County Cork, Ireland, in 1896, son of the artist Frank Stoner. He was educated at Auchinleck Public School and Cumnock Academy, and served with the Royal Navy during the Great War, taking part in the Battle of Jutland on HMS *Tiger*. In 1919 he married Jeanie Black. He was elected to the Parish Council in 1925 and retained his seat until 1929 when the new Ayr County Council was set up. He was thereafter elected to the county council, representing Auchinleck.

With the increase in the quantity of houses in the village, in November 1925 it was decided for the first time that buildings should be numbered. Similarly, in 1926 there were a few suggestions put forward for names for the streets that were being developed. The roadway from Sorn Road to Quarry Road was proposed as Boswell Street (it became School Road). Lambfair Gardens' original proposal was Angus Street or Wilson Street. Another suggestion was Cook Street after a mining stalwart, or Murdoch Street after William Murdoch.

Transport and roads were improved in the new century. Within Auchinleck, Ayr County Council laid tarmacadam on some of the pavements in the Main Street for the first time in August 1911. The arrival of the motorised automobile required that roads be smoother than they were before, and as the number of these increased, roads were altered and improved to ease traffic flow. Lower Main Street, from Knockroon Brae to Station Road, was coated in tarmacadam in 1923. In 1924 upper

Main Street and Mauchline Road were covered with tarmacadam for the first time. In 1927 ownership of Market Place was transferred to Ayr County Council from Auchinleck Estate. Although it had already been partially upgraded, in August 1929 much of Main Street was improved by the removal of the camber, with new kerbs installed and old gas-lamps removed. The street was then re-metalled. To replace the gas lamps electric lights were introduced, there being 32 60 watt lamps and three 200 watt lamps being lit by electricity for the first time on 6 September 1929.

In 1923 there were plans to realign the road from Cumnock to Lugar to alleviate the difficult brae and corner at Holmhead farm. One of the possible solutions was to make a new road from Holmhead in a straight line to a new bridge across the Lugar Water at Craigstonholm Row. These plans did not materialise.

6.2 Highhouse Rows *(Author's Collection)*

From 1890 to 1940 the village population trebled from 1,489 to 4,837 as the rows at Highhouse and Dalsalloch were built, and new council houses were erected east of Sorn Road. The new houses required improvements to the sewerage system, and in 1909 new filter beds were constructed. When these were being dug an old sundial bearing the date 1763 was discovered. Sewage plants were erected at Darnlaw and the Howe in 1927. The sewerage system was improved with the laying of a twelve inch pipe along Main Street, leading to a new sewer tank and filters. The scheme was designed by Allan Stevenson and constructed in 1926.

Domestic waste was dealt with very locally – Ayr County Council leased the former Willie's Well Quarry, which had closed by the First World War, from Auchinleck Estate and used it for a refuse coup.

The telephone arrived in Auchinleck in 1903 when the exchange was opened in Cumnock, and soon a few well-to-do proprietors had it installed. Amongst the early subscribers were James Girvan, fruiterer and confectioner in Main Street, with telephone number Cumnock 51.

Parish Councils existed to run local communities, and a number of locals distinguished themselves by serving on them for many years. Among these were James Kilpatrick JP, chairman in 1911. He had worked for over thirty years for William Baird, the first 24 of these at Muirkirk. In 1908 he came to be chief of the office at Lugar Works, replacing William Robertson. A native of Stevenston, he had previously served on Muirkirk Parish Council.

In 1912 Ayr County Council purchased a small portion of land at Barglachan farm from Lord Talbot de Malahide and there built a water distribution tank. This was used to supply the village with a new supply of water, replacing the old water pumps which had been located at various points along the Main Street and which were subsequently removed.

Tradesmen in the village operating for themselves were fewer, though some existed. John Dalziel, Archibald Riddall and Thomas Murdoch had joinery shops, and Adam Wilson & Sons were proprietors of the steam saw mill in Market Place. Hugh Boyle operated the smithy; in 1928 it (Market Place Smithy) was operated by J. Watson. John Lapraik was on hand to mend those thatched roofs which still existed. The last house in Auchinleck to have its thatch replaced was Murdoch Lawrie's (29 Main Street). In Orchard Road John Davies of Kilmarnock owned the aerated water factory. Further down the brae, Joseph Smith was a farmer and grain dealer at Bridgend Mill. Willie's Well Quarry was still in operation, leased by William Kerr, builder, of Ochiltree. The Churchhill Quarry was by now closed.

At the railway station Andrew Findlay was stationmaster until 1916, followed by Archibald Wilkie (1867-1925) until 1925, then James M. Robertson (around 1928) then John MacCulloch. On 23 October 1909 the stone bridge carrying the railway across Main Street was demolished and it was replaced with an iron girder one. On 30 October 1926 there was a train crash at Templeton Bridge during the night.

In 1901 it was recorded that 67 criminal offences had taken place in Auchinleck. In February 1914 the new police station in Auchinleck was opened, located at 226-228 Main Street in what had been Albion Cottages. New cells were erected to the rear of the building, one cottage retained as a police house, and the reporter for the *Ayr Advertiser* of the time wrote that the two policemen stationed there were 'now on the lookout for anyone requiring their hospitality!' One of the first major crimes they had to investigate was the breaking and entering of the Eagle Inn whilst the owner, Mrs Dunn, was away. £31 in cash was stolen. George Harrison was the policeman in 1901, Constable James Morrison was the local policeman until 1926, followed by Constable Cruikshank and James Harrison in 1925.

The fortunes of the Auchinleck Gas Light Company continued to grow, and many more houses were connected to the supply. In 1900 Mr Young restored the

Auchinleck Gas Works. He was a relation of William Murdoch. The manager, John Devine, died on 14 December 1903 at the age of 64, to be replaced by Hugh Devine, known as 'Gassy' Devine. In 1910 the gas main reached Upper Main Street for the first time, allowing households there to connect to the system, over forty years after those in the bottom half of the village. The increase in demand for gas meant that a third gasometer had to be erected at the gasworks in March 1915. With a capacity of 33,500 cubic feet, this was more than double the combined volume of the other two tanks.

On 26 July 1913 the North British Association of Gas Managers unveiled a bronze plaque at Bello Mill in memory of William Murdoch. With a bas-relief of the inventor's head, the plaque includes the inscription:

> THE BIRTH PLACE OF WILLIAM MURDOCH,
> INVENTOR OF LIGHTING BY GAS, 1754-1839.
> 'THAT INCOMPARABLE MECHANIC' NASMYTH. ERECTED BY THE
> NORTH BRITISH ASSOCIATION OF GAS MANAGERS, 1913.

The plaque was sculpted by Henry S. Gamley ARSA, and it was unveiled by G. R. Hislop, gas engineer, of Paisley. Following the unveiling, luncheon was served in the institute. Previously, on 13 September 1912, a bust of Murdoch was presented to Lugar Institute by Duncan B. Murdoch of Hawaii. It was presented on his behalf by his brother, R. Barclay Murdoch, of Johnstone.

6.3 William Murdoch's plaque, Bello Mill *(Dane Love)*

> **North British Association of Gas Managers.**
>
> UNVEILING OF MEMORIAL BRONZE PANEL
> (The work of H. S. Gamley, A.R.S.A.)
> AT THE BIRTHPLACE OF WILLIAM MURDOCH,
> INVENTOR OF LIGHTING BY GAS. :: :: ::
>
> THE COUNCIL INVITE
>
> ......To.. *July 1913*
>
> to be present at BELLO MILL, LUGAR, on SATURDAY, 26th curt., at 1.15 p.m., when the ceremony of unveiling will be performed by G. R. HISLOP, Esq., Gas Engineer, Paisley.
>
> On the invitation of Robert Angus, Esq. (of Messrs William Baird & Co.), Ladykirk, the company will be entertained to Luncheon in the Lugar Institute, at 2 p.m., when Mr Hislop will deliver an Appreciation of Murdoch and his Works.
>
> *Reply to J. W. Napier, Gas Works, Alloa, before Monday, 21st curt.*
>
> TRAIN SERVICE.—Lugar is situated one mile from Lugar Station and two miles from Old Cumnock (G. and S. W. Railway). Leave Dumfries 10.35 a.m., arrive Old Cumnock 12.5 p.m.; leave Glasgow (St. Enoch) 9.30 or 11.15 a.m., and Kilmarnock 10.10 a.m. and 12.2 p.m., arrive Lugar 10.53 a.m. and 12.43 p.m. Train leaves Old Cumnock 5.41 p.m., arrive Dumfries 7.5 p.m.; leave Lugar 4.8 p.m., arrive Glasgow 5.31 p.m.

6.4 Invitation to unveiling of Murdoch plaque *(Author's Collection)*

William Wilson (1850-1918) ran the sawmill of Adam Wilson & Sons, the business continuing to expand. As well as supplying sawn timber to the pits and ironworks, farms and other businesses, Wilsons began making a few timber products of its own - long-carts, timber wagons, potato-seed boxes, gates and fence-posts. William Wilson was born in Mauchline, but moved to Auchinleck in 1876 to manage the Auchinleck sawmill. He lived at Larchville, Mauchline Road, an eminently suitable name for a woodman's home. Married to Annie, daughter of William Ramsay, Ballochmyle Smithy, they had six daughters. He died on 17 June 1918 having taken ill on the bowling green where a game had been organised as part of Red Cross Week, he being chairman of the committee. His obituary noted that he was a member of the School Board, Parish Council, Kyle Union Poorhouse, County Road Board, Licensing Board, chairman of Auchinleck Gas Light Company, director of the Picture House, elder in the church, member of the Freemason's Lodge, Silver Band, Red Cross, and Bowling Club. 'It is certain that no man, who has passed away from our village in recent years, in truth for many years, will be so much missed.... Under his direct supervision no fewer than twelve sawmills are working throughout Scotland, from as far north as Oban and scattered throughout Ayrshire, Argyllshire, Dumfries and other southern counties.'

The Lamb Fair did not long survive the new century, the final one taking place on the last Tuesday of August 1902, and at that one no lambs were on sale! Helen Steven, writing in 1898, noted that though it was a great event in the village, with farmers crowding to it from far and near, trade had fallen off somewhat and had become 'an excuse for a day's merry-making in the village'. For a number of years, on the day of the Lamb Fair, the shows came to the village as usual, but in 1911 they failed to turn up, and 'not a single cloot [was] in evidence', according to the Cumnock Chronicle. When the new houses were erected off School Road in 1925 the street was named Lambfair Gardens in commemoration of the market.

A few tragedies brought the village together in grief. A fire on Wednesday 8 August 1917 destroyed seven houses in the row at Templeton Place. All of these houses had thatched roofs apart from one. On Christmas Day 1916, two young boys from Auchinleck were drowned in an old quarry at Churchhill behind the Peden Kirk. These were Patrick Byrne, aged 7 years and 8 months, and William Carle, aged 7 and a half years. William's brother, Robert Carle, had been killed at Highhouse Pit a fortnight earlier, on 10 December 1916. He was 12 years and eight months old. The two boys had stood on the ice over the quarry pool, but fell in when it broke. Help was sent for, and local fruiterer, Robert Hopkins (1878-1946), swam into the water to try to rescue them. Eventually, all he could do was pull their lifeless bodies from the water.

6.5 Men filling in Churchhill Quarry *(Author's Collection)*

During the miners' strike of 1921 a Polish boy named Joseph Pazik, who lived at Highhouse Rows, was also drowned in the Churchhill Quarry, on 15 June. He was only six years of age. Again, Hopkins pulled the body from the waters. Because of the accident, and with the two lads from a few years earlier still in memory, many of the miners barrowed loads of dirt from the Highhouse Bing with which to fill the hole in. John Judge, president of the Miners' Union, organised the infilling, with three shifts arranged, sixty workers in each eight-hour shift. Eventually old hutches and rails were acquired from the pit, and these were employed in transporting the dirt. The ground was later made into a putting green and tennis courts. After the quarry was filled in, the men then moved their attentions to Willie's Quarry, which was located 100 yards behind the shirt factory, to the left of Well Road, and it too was infilled. Well Road was also known as Quarry Road at one time, and also as Willie's Well Road, before Well Road became the accepted name.

Major events attracting the attentions of the residents included the burning down of the Toll Garage, which took place in December 1925. Run by Joseph Shearer, a new brick-built garage was being erected and was awaiting a roof when the walls were blown down in a storm in March 1926. On 17 September 1926 a girl of twelve years, Helen Smith, was killed by wagons on a railway siding at Highhouse.

The politics of the country at the turn of the century was dominated by the women's suffrage movement, and in Auchinleck meetings were held to promote this. On 11 May 1911 the notable activist Frances Parker spoke to a large audience in the public hall. Auchinleck Nursing Association was formed on 6 September 1911.

In the autumn of 1913 James Brown of Annbank, latterly MP for South Ayrshire, representative of the Ayrshire Miners' Union, toured the county with Thomas MacKerrell and compiled a report on the conditions of housing within the miners' rows. The parish of Auchinleck was naturally included in this survey, which found that living standards were generally poor.

At Highhouse Rows, where the occupants long regarded themselves as independent of Auchinleck, Brown found two rows of houses, 49 and 48 houses respectively, all owned by William Baird and Company, and rented at 2s 1d per week for a two apartment dwelling, 3s 6d for three. Baird had erected the 96 new houses at Highhouse in 1905 to accommodate workers at Highhouse Pit.

Every four houses shared a wash-house and a water closet, distant from the home by eighteen feet. Despite having a 'clean appearance', with paved pathways, the rows had open syvers, or drains, containing stagnant water, and the outlet from the closets, which was supposed to be flushed regularly, produced a bad smell. The residents told the visitors that in summer the flies were 'something awful'. The Highhouse Rows had been built facing south, so that the residents could not stand at their front doors and watch Lord Talbot's family journey to church.

LUGAR

The years of the new century before the Great War were Lugar's high point. The village had a larger population than Auchinleck, with 3,776 residents in 1901 and 3,808 in the 1911 Census. The ironworks were still operating full blast and the village prospered. From 1891 to 1908 it had risen from 1,300 to around 1,850. The manager, and part owner, of the ironworks, Robert Angus (died 1923), and his son, Robert L. Angus, lived at Craigston House. (The elder son, James Angus, died at

Ochiltree House on 17 December 1908 aged 38; his son, Robert Edward Angus was killed in action in France, 1916. Both are buried in the old kirkyard.) The Angus family later moved to Ladykirk House, near Monkton, where the descendants lived until the late twentieth century.

Lesser managers lived in the twelve houses at Craigston Square, the ordinary workers in the many other rows. Even the village constable, Alexander Geikie, had his home and police station in one of Bellow Mill Row's 24 houses. Other rows occupied at the turn of the century were Craigstonholm Row (27 houses), Store Row (7 houses), Front Row (7 houses), Burnside Holm Row (12 houses), Back Store Row (15 houses), Peesweep Row (23 houses), Brick Row (77 houses) and the Crescent (29 houses). The houses were not numbered regularly, for example, 1 to 7 Store Row, but as a number, followed by Lugar, and so addresses like No. 116, Peesweep Row, Lugar, were used.

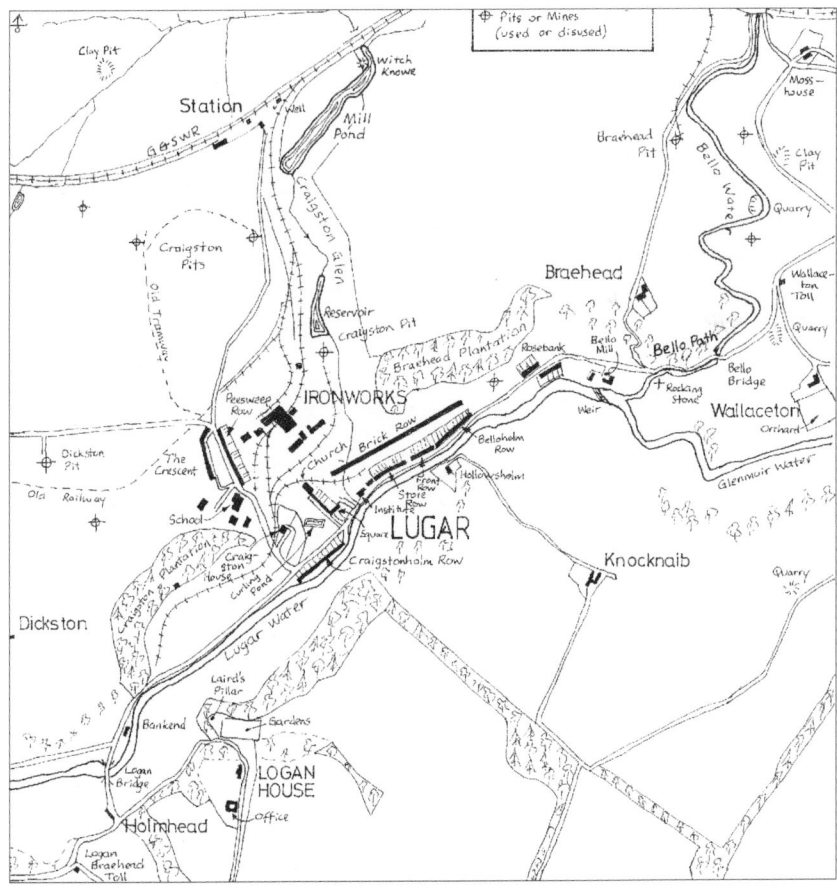

6.6 Lugar around 1900 *(Dane Love)*

Improvements to the sanitary conditions in the village were made in 1923 when a sewer main was laid through the village to the new treatment works at Dixtonholm, Hugh Hastie of Barglachan being the contractor.

Businessmen in the village included James Muir, draper; James Scott, shoemaker; James Morris, clothier; John Reid, draper, most of whom worked in the Ironworks co-operative. The smithy was empty in 1900. The furnace manager at the ironworks up to 1904 was Alexander Reid. Thomas Gilmour died in 1906, having been pattern-maker in Lugar works for over 34 years. The Lugar Ironworks Co-operative Society continued to thrive, with Mr Clark as store manager. At the Ironworks Store the managers from around 1900 were Messrs Goldie, John Clark,

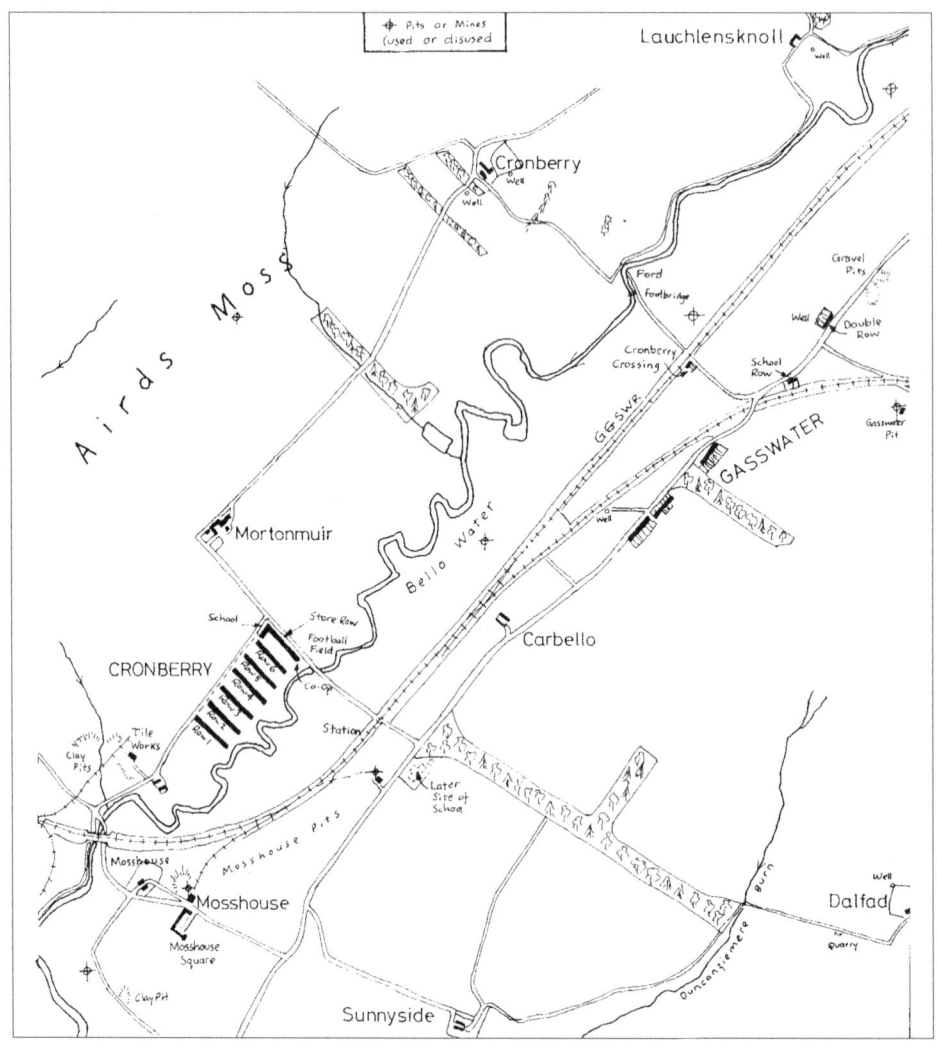

6.7 Cronberry (*Author's Collection*)

William Rankin, Elios Yates, Adam Simpson and Matt Houston. The butchery did a roaring trade, and the cattle were grazed in the field behind Park Terrace prior to killing.

Horse-drawn vans (later motorised) took produce to various other rows in the district. At Lugar Station Alexander MacIvor was station-master until his death in 1914 at the age of 50. A later stationmaster was J. Johnston.

Lugar comprised mainly of workmen's rows, 267 houses in total, owned by Bairds. A few private houses existed at Rosebank. New, better quality homes were erected in the Store Park, creating Park Terrace, six blocks of four houses, laid out to either side of the bowling green. The foundations were laid in April 1924 and the first houses were ready for occupation in April 1925. It was at this time sanitation was first introduced to the village at Park Terrace, and later the ten cottages in Craigston Square had bathrooms installed.

The first electric street lighting was installed in the village in 1928 after a long campaign by the locals.

In the village the police station was served by various constables, including Alex. Geikie (c.1900), Constable Thomson (1920-1924); Constable Gardiner (until 1928); and Constable John Dickson (from 1928 into the 1930s).

In 1928 a new bridge was constructed across the Lugar Water, leading to Hollowsholm farm. This was almost complete in June 1928. It had three brick piers and a footway of cement tied together with iron rails and metal cross bars. The Lugar Water continued to cause some problems to the villagers. On 23 April 1912 John Kerr was drowned at the age of five years and on 25 March 1917 Jan Gathie was drowned at the age of three years.

CRONBERRY

The population of Cronberry in 1901 was 664, living in 145 houses. A considerable number of the residents were of Irish descent. The village was a compact settlement of seven rows, with a branch of Lugar Ironworks Co-op located in the bottom house of Row No. 7, hence its name of the Store Row. Mr Gibson was the manager for a time, followed by John MacDonald. The Tarry Rows were to be closed by 1 May 1915, most of the residents being rehoused in the Dalsalloch Rows in Auchinleck.

When Brown and MacKerrell visited the village of Cronberry they found it to have seven rows, six of brick and one of stone. The total population was still around 600, but there was no wash-house for this number. No windows were able to be opened, and there was only one coal-house, in the superior stone-built Row No. 7. The smell from the open drains was terrible, one tenant told MacKerrell that in summer it cost them a shilling a week for flypapers. Many of the houses were found to be empty, particularly those in rows numbered 4, 5 and 6. Row No. 7, which had thirteen houses, was where the schoolmaster, policeman, and colliery foremen lived.

These houses were leased at £4 4s per annum. The village was owned by Bairds who employed a scavenger, the water obtainable from fourteen wells, two per row.

Baird also owned Cronberry Brickwork, which was at this time operated by John Syme Duncan. These works closed by 1910, but the Duncans continued to reside there, converting the buildings into Brickwork farm, which they ran as a small-holding. John Syme Duncan died at Ochiltree Tileworks on 15 May 1925 aged 73. At Cronberry his son, also John Syme Duncan, took over the Brickwork farm, until his death in 1960 aged 77.

William Crichton was the village constable, followed by Robert Gray and Robert Pyper. The school was located at the opposite end of the Store Row from the co-op, and a football field lay north-east of the row.

A few major incidents from the village's history can be mentioned. On 18 February 1911 William C. Alexander, gamekeeper at a cottage known as The Isle, fell into the Bello Water, which was raging at the time, and he was drowned. Alexander Baxter fell ten feet onto the railway line near Cronberry trying to retrieve his hat. He died in hospital in August 1934.

At Cronberry the 'Tarry Rows' (rows numbered 4, 5 and 6) were gradually emptied of tenants and by 1925 were demolished. This removed 83 houses from the village. William Baird proposed twenty new houses in the village in 1924, the plans for which were passed. Designed by the architects Allan Stevenson & Cassells, the houses were to be built by Findlay of Mauchline. However the county council still had plans for the village and in 1924 erected seven blocks of four houses, named Riverside Terrace. The station was still open, William Walker being stationmaster for a time. There was an incident when a dog was being transported from Auchinleck to Muirkirk in the guard's van. At Cronberry someone opened the door and the dog escaped, running up the line. One of the porters ran after it, yelling, 'Catch that dog - it's a parcel!'

At the Cronberry branch of Lugar Ironworks Co-operative Society John MacDonald was the manager before he moved on to Darnconner. He was replaced by Matthew Begg, with assistants, George Campbell, George Munro, Charles Baillie, Jim Hope, Charles MacKnight, Jean Soden and William Ritchie. The telegraph office in the village was opened on 23 January 1907, the first postmaster, Frederick Aitken, dying in 1909 aged 36. His widow continued, the office located in the 7th Row, followed by John MacKean from 1925, then by Henry Parker. On the opening of the new school across the water the old building was used as a community hall, where social dances and various meetings were held, and services on a Sunday.

The elongated and dispersed community of Gasswater was also owned by Baird. Here were two stone rows and two brick rows, the population in 1913 being 97, living in 34 houses, though a number of houses were empty. Water was obtained from a trough 300 yards distant from one row, or else from a pump 200 yards distant from the other three. The closets had no doors and so were not used by the adult population. The community had begun to decline at the turn of the century. Carbello Pit closed in 1906, and many of the smaller mines were by then abandoned. Houses still occupied were in the Brick, Stone, Baxter's and School rows, the six houses of the Stable Row closed by 1910. By 1920 around half of the other rows had been vacated and by 1930 only the three houses in Baxter's Row were still occupied.

DARNCONNER & COMMONDYKE
Darnconner continued to be an active community in the new century even although most of the local mines were beginning to be closed. The population in 1901 was 457. In 1914 there were 80 houses in the various squares and rows, but no repairs were being carried out on the houses. They were given up by William Baird on 11 November 1914 and ownership returned to Ballochmyle estate. By 1925 Darnconner and Commonloch rows were owned by James Clark of Carskeoch, near Patna. The long Common, or Commonloch, Row had 96 houses, the Stable Row a further six, and Walker's Row had twelve houses. The two Ballochmyle Rows had a total of 48 houses. There were 52 houses at Commondyke.

6.8 Darnconner *(Author's Collection)*

Thomas MacKerrell visited the village as part of the survey into miners' housing in 1914. At Darnconner were 94 houses, 17 each in Low and High Squares, 48 houses in the two Railway Rows, built back to back, and six each in the School and Store rows. The total population was around 400. In the Low (or Laigh) Square there were no washing-houses, but a few boilers stood in the open air. Two doorless closets served the seventeen families who lived there, the open ashpits overflowing with stinking refuse. The condition of some of the coal-houses was such that a few

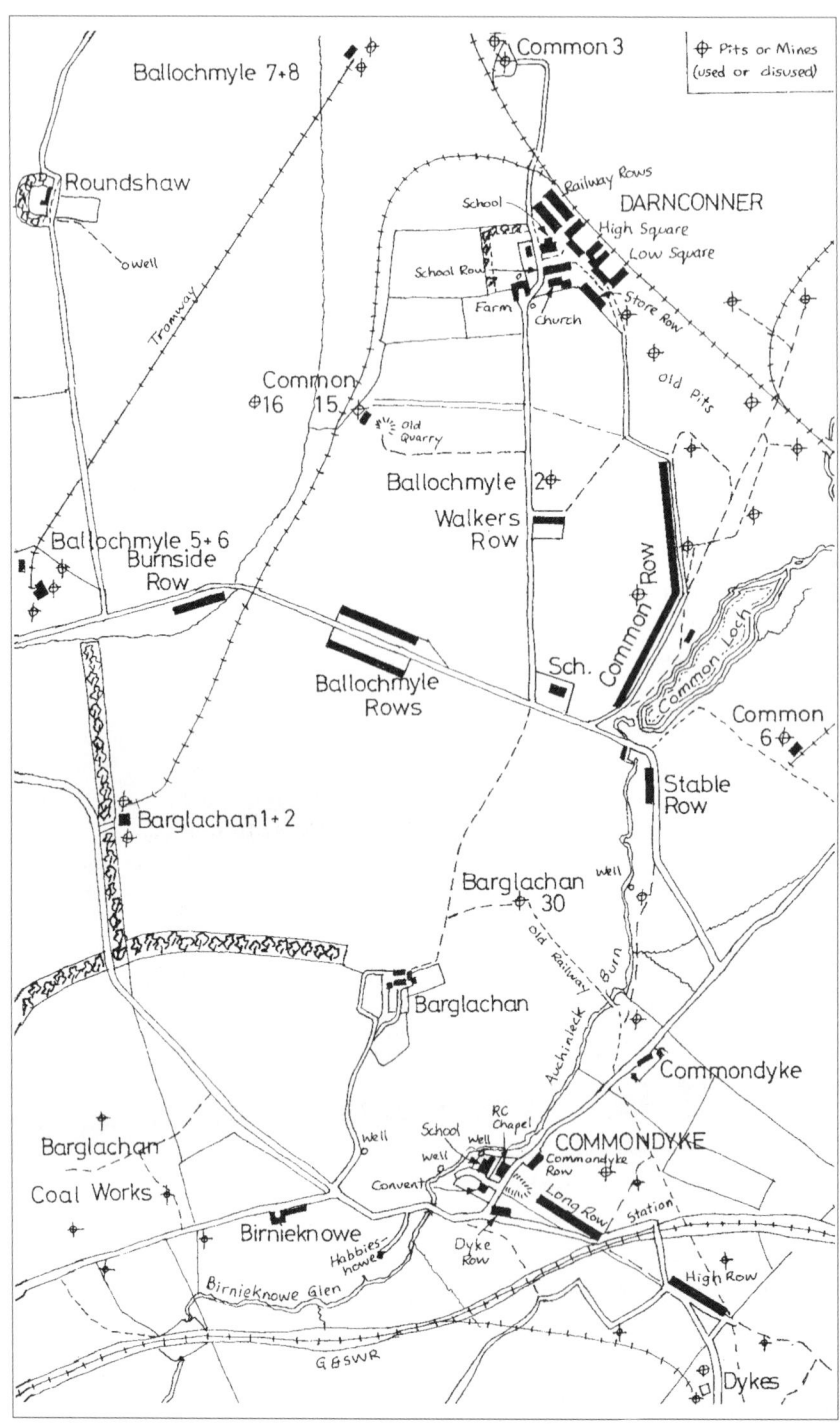

6.9 Darnconner and Commondyke around 1900 *(Dane Love)*

tenants kept their fuel beneath their beds. The High Square had similar conditions, and the 'glaur' was inches deep at the house doorways. The Railway Rows, let at five shillings per month, were very damp, the floors made of broken brick tiles. The closets had no doors, some surrounded by a sea of human excrement. The School and Store rows likewise had poor amenities, the Store Row having no closets and needing to share those in the School Row. The village also had a church and store, the whole owned by William Baird and Company.

In April 1913 fire ripped through the store at Darnconner, destroying the building and stock, and causing some damage to neighbouring properties. John Dempsey managed to photograph the fire-ravaged ruins and sold postcards of the scene soon after. By 1928 the Darnconner Nursing Association existed.

On a roadway from Darnconner heading south, overlooking Common Loch, stood the Common Row, 96 two apartment houses built in a continuous line without a gap. This was done to reduce the cost of their erection. Though the population stood at 506, there was not a single wash-house and only seventeen doorless closets for the whole row. The smell from the closets was described as abominable, the floor being covered in human excrement. The pathway in front of the row was unpaved, and the inspectors could not walk along it without going up to the ankles in dirt. The sewage passed down an open syvor before being discharged into the Auchinleck Burn.

Ballochmyle Rows stood to either side of the road which separates Darnconner and Barglachan farms and, like the Common Row, were owned by Bairds. There were 24 houses in each row, let at two shillings per week, the total population 227. When the Ballochmyle Colliery was closed one of the buildings was converted into a branch of the Auchinleck Co-op to serve this community.

The Stable Row, owned by Sir Claud Alexander of Ballochmyle's trustees, had only six two-apartment houses and one single apartment. There were 37 people living here, the rent £5 per annum. There was a single wooden closet for the six houses, and no ashpits or wash-houses. The sewage ran into a ditch to the nearby burn. This row stood at the southern end of the Common Loch and was originally known as Common Row.

At Darnconner there was still a busy group of Rechabites, and one of Gardeners, and the Darnconner Branch of the Independent Labour Party held an annual social and dance from 1910. The manager at the Ironworks Co-op branch at the time was Robert Thomson. The village constable was James Wilson. Postmen were Andrew Mitchell, who lived at Common Row, and Hugh Mullen. At Commondyke store David Hall was manager for a number of years.

On 5 December 1914 the Housing Committee issued a new report. They found that at Commondyke extensive repairs were being made on Baird's 52 houses. Wood lining was being affixed to cover damp walls, new window sashes, doors and floors were being installed. Outside, the ashpits were being cleared away, and new toilets, coal-houses, wash-houses and small ashpits erected. Though noting the improvements with delight, the committee recommended that water be piped into the washrooms. At Darnconner, however, nothing had been done since their last visit, Baird having given up their eighty houses which reverted to Ballochmyle Estate, on which lands they had been built.

By the end of the First World War the community at Darnconner was in decline. Messrs Baird's tenancy of the houses expired at Martinmas 1920 and the tenants were told to leave by December that year. In 1920 many of the houses in the Squares, Front and Back rows were empty. Only squatters occupied some of the houses, or at least those who failed to leave by the due date were termed squatters. Ownership of the houses returned to Ballochmyle estate, who became liable for the rates. The estate claimed that the houses were uninhabitable, and therefore should not be liable to rates, and that anyone still living there had not been asked for rent and had paid none. At the Lands Valuation Appeal Court in Edinburgh in February 1922, Ballochmyle estate was deemed responsible for the houses.

In 1926 a group of labourers built rough homes for themselves at the former Common Pit Number 10 bing, half a mile from Darnconner itself. These were partially dug into the side of the bing, and rough stone walls were constructed to support the sides as well as the roof of timber and turves. The semi-subterranean community stayed here for a number of years, in 1929 there being nine occupants occupying the dwellings. One of the residents, Michael Mulryan, was murdered by three other men here in that year. Mulryan, who was 57 years of age, was known locally as 'Mad Harry'. Charged for the murder were Hugh MacNaughtan, James Kelly and Joseph Donnelly.

By 1930 the Ballochmyle, Walker's and Stable rows were uninhabitable. Ownership of them had passed to Mrs Christina Gordon of Carskeoch, near Patna, who bought Darnconner and Common farms from Ballochmyle estate. She also owned the Common Row (or Commonloch Row as it was also known) which was abandoned in 1928. In the 1930s a start was made by the county council on rehousing the remaining occupants in new houses at Auchinleck. By 1932 only 27 families remained at Darnconner.

In 1933 many of the tenants from Darnconner and Commondyke went on a rent strike in their new Auchinleck homes, claiming that Ayr County Council were charging them rents in excess of what the Slum Clearance Act allowed. Twenty-one court summonses were issued by the council in December 1933 and at court the tenants were found in the wrong, having agreed to the new rents prior to their moving.

At the end of the Great War John MacDonald was the manager of Darnconner Co-op branch and he remained until the shop closed in 1931. In 1939 both the school and the church were closed, each building becoming stores, the former for the council, the latter for the farmer. In 1940 the Common Row was demolished, the final row at Darnconner to be removed. The school was demolished in 1955, the church in 1979, leaving the manse standing. In 1958 the belfry had been removed and the bell gifted to Catrine Congregational Church. The font was gifted to the Peden Kirk. J. L. MacArthur came to Darnconner at the Second World War with the job of demolishing the church, but found it so attractive that he bought it and the manse and resided there for many years.

WORLD WAR I

The outbreak of war in Europe in 1914 changed the face of the parish considerably. Many of the shelter belts of trees that had been planted were cut down and not replaced when peace resumed. Hundreds of men left their homes to fight abroad, often the first time they had left the county, let alone the country. The first two deaths from Auchinleck parish were Lance Corporal Joseph Black, killed in action on 26 October 1914 and Sergeant David Black, killed on 4 November 1914. Both were in the Seaforth Highlanders. Casualties were numerous, and the parish war memorials list their names - from Auchinleck 62 died, 15 at Lugar, and many others from Darnconner, Cronberry and the other mining communities.

Back in the village life went on - money was tight, and work was hard. To help supply the food required to feed the population the Auchinleck Plots Committee held land in Sorn Road which was used to grow vegetables. The effects of the Great War were felt by the village Co-op, many younger members of staff being called up

6.10 Lugar Armistice Celebrations, 1918 *(Author's Collection)*

for service. The horses and transport vehicles were commandeered for army use, making distribution difficult. The number of members rose, however, and sales stood at around £40,000 per quarter. Thomas Steele retired as managing secretary in 1915, to be replaced by James Morrison in 1916. Many refugees came to Auchinleck, there being an influx of Belgians at the time.

Fundraising events took place on a regular basis in the parish. In War Weapons Week in 1918 funds were raised for two seaplanes, which were later named 'Auchinleck' and 'Lugar'.

Those killed in the Great War were commemorated on the war memorials erected in the villages. In Auchinleck, initial enthusiasm seems to have waned. A public meeting held on 17 June 1919 to consider a memorial proposed either a monument in the kirkyard or else the erection of some cottage homes for soldiers' widows. At a meeting on 24 June the cottage homes proposal was voted in 11/10 but support for this appears to have died. By July 1919 the idea for war memorial cottages was dropped in favour of a monument. In November 1919 a new committee was formed with the intention of erecting a memorial at a cost of £500 and fund-raising commenced.

The war memorial was erected in the kirkyard, between the old church and the parish church. Designed by the architect, James A. Morris of Ayr, it was unveiled on Sunday 24 December 1922 by Colonel John Douglas Boswell of Auchinleck. Constructed of yellow sandstone, the four faces have bronze inserts listing the names and regiments of those who suffered death. The main plaque reads: *To the glory of God and in abiding and affectionate remembrance of the men of Auchinleck and neighbourhood who gave their lives in the Great war 1914-1919. 'They died the noblest death a man can die, fighting for God and right and liberty, and such a death is immortality'*.

On it are 59 names of soldiers who died for their country. These were:

- Private James Aitken, Regimental Number 52288, 1st Battalion Royal Scots Fusiliers, killed at Haveringcourt Wood, France, 18 September 1918, aged 19½. He is commemorated on the Vis-en-artois Memorial in France.
- Private Andrew Armour, No. 6752, 1st/5th Royal Scots Fusiliers, drowned at Dardanelles, 30 June 1915, aged 20. Son of Andrew and Agnes Armour, 68 Highhouse Rows. Commemorated on the Lancashire Landing Cemetery memorial.
- Bandsman Private William Armour, No. 13913, 7th King's Own Scottish Borderers, killed France 9 August 1916 aged 28. Commemorated on the Thiepval memorial.
- Private John Barrie, No. 34960, educated in Cumnock, signed up in

6.11 Auchinleck War Memorial *(Dane Love)*

Auchinleck, 2nd Royal Scots Fusiliers, killed at Arras, France, 23 April 1917, aged 27. Buried at Chensy Road, East Cemetery, Heninel.
- Private William Benham, No. S/17087, 7th Battalion Cameron Highlanders. Died 31 July 1917 and commemorated on the Ypres (Menin Gate) Memorial.
- Piper Private David Hinds Black, No. 479, 1st Battalion Seaforth Highlanders, 4 November 1914. Lived at Highhouse. Commemorated on Le Touret Memorial.
- Lance Corporal Joseph Black, No. 8667, 2nd Battalion Seaforth Highlanders, killed in action 26 October 1914, aged 28. Belonged to Darnconner, husband of Mary Ewing Black, 78 Highhouse Rows. Commemorated on the Ploegsteert Memorial.
- Sapper David Bryce, No. 79576, Royal Engineers 179th Tunnelling Company, killed 4 July 1916 in France, aged 32. Was a coalminer before enlisting in the Seaforth Highlanders but transferred to the Royal Engineers. Buried in Albert Communal Cemetery extension. Son of David and Margaret Bryce, Cronberry, but lived at Highhouse Rows.
- Private Thomas Steele Carey, No. 37907, 136th Company Machine Gun Corps. Killed in Mesopotamia, 2 February 1917, aged 23. Commemorated on Basra Memorial, Iraq. Son of Alice Steele Carey, 7 Radnor Street, Glasgow.
- Private Andrew Bain Carmichael, No. S/4494, 9th Battalion Black Watch (Royal Highlanders). From Dunfermline but recruited in Ayrshire. Died 25 September 1915 and commemorated on the Loos Memorial.
- Private John Cassidy, Labour Corps.
- Corporal William Clark, Royal Scots Fusiliers.
- Private William Clark, Royal Scots, died of wounds in France, 1917. Lived at Glenside from around 1912.
- Private William Cree, Royal Scots Fusiliers.
- Private Andrew Crozier, No. 841413, Quebec Regiment, 24th Battalion Canadian Infantry. Killed at Passchendaele, France, 6 November 1917, aged 24. Commemorated at Tyne Cot Cemetery, Belgium. Born in Auchinleck on 21 July 1893, the son of Andrew and Elizabeth Grace Crozier.
- Private Thomas Gracie Crozier, 18th Battalion, 3rd Reinforcement, Australian Imperial Forces. Died of wounds received at Armentieres, France, 19 July 1917, aged 28.
- Private John R. Dale, No. 20395, 6th/7th Battalion Royal Scots

Fusiliers, killed in action in France, 10 October 1916, aged 32. Listed on Thiepval memorial. Son of Matthew Dale and Margaret Dale, Main Street, Auchinleck. Married to Margaret Dale, Merlin Place, Auchinleck.
- Private William Denim, No. 56287, Royal Scots Fusiliers, killed Gaza, Egypt, 19 April 1917, aged 20. Also in 155th Company Machine Gun Corps. Buried in Gaza War Cemetery. Also commemorated on New Cumnock war memorial.
- Private Wilson Dunlop, No. 5573, Australian Imperial Forces, died of wounds received in France, 11 May 1917, aged 20, and buried in Grevilles British Cemetery. He enlisted on 15 April 1916 in 22nd Battalion. Born in Scotland, he was the son of James and Elizabeth Dunlop, 13 Herbert Street, Footscray, Victoria, Australia.
- Private Alexander Findlay, No. 201809, 1st Battalion Royal Scots Fusiliers, killed in action in France, 27 September 1918 aged 32. Buried in Lowrie Cemetery, Havrincourt, France. Son of Alexander Findlay, Janetta Cottage, Auchinleck.
- Private Alexander Frew, Royal Engineers.
- Sergeant John Garvin, Royal Scots Fusiliers, killed in France, 1 October 1918, aged 23.
- Private James Gibson, No. 48508, Royal Scots Fusiliers, killed 19 April 1917, aged 27. Buried in Gaza War Cemetery.
- Private Robert Corrie Graham, No. 240243, 1st/5th Battalion Royal Scots Fusiliers. Born New Cumnock, educated in Cumnock, signed up in Auchinleck. Killed in France, 1 October 1918, aged 23. Son of Thomas Graham, Railway Cottages, Auchinleck.
- Lance Corporal Robert Thom Harper, No. 53629, 1st Battalion Royal Scots Fusiliers, killed in action at Courcelles, France, 21 August 1918, aged 20. Son of James and Mary Harper, 4 Shiloh Terrace, Auchinleck. Commemorated on Vis-en-artois Memorial.
- Able Seaman James Hastings, Clyde Z/6139, Royal Naval Volunteer Reserve. Died of illness, 21 February 1917.
- Private Adam Howatson, No. 205235, 1st/5th Battalion Royal Scots Fusiliers, was drowned on 30 December 1917 on HMS Aragon. Commemorated on Chatby Memorial, Egypt.
- Private Robert Hyslop, No. 12770, 6th/7th Battalion Royal Scots Fusiliers, killed 15 September 1916. Born in Cumnock, he lived in Auchinleck, and served in machine gun section. He was the son of Robert Hyslop and Annie Miller, Ayr Road, Cumnock. Married Elizabeth Byrne in 1908. Commemorated on Thiepval Memorial.
- Corporal Donald Johnston, Royal Army Medical Corps.

- Private Henry or Harry Jones, No. 17088, 1st Battalion Royal Scots Fusiliers, killed 14 July 1916 aged 42. Commemorated at Thiepval Memorial.
- Gunner James Kelly, No. 312059, 20th Battalion Tank Corps, died in military hospital, Edinburgh Castle, of wounds, 23 December 1918, aged 28. Buried in Auchinleck parish churchyard.
- Private William Hall Kerr, No. 18134, Royal Scots Fusiliers, killed in Battle of Somme, 30 July 1916 aged 22. Buried in Dantzig Alley, British Cemetery, Marmetz, France.
- Private Robert MacCluskie, No. 527293, Royal Scots Fusiliers, and 460th Agricultural Company, Labour Corps. Died 19 November 1918 aged 27. Buried in Auchinleck churchyard.
- Private David Crichton MacCulloch MT, A. S. C., accidentally killed near London whilst on service, 5 September 1915, aged 19.
- Private John MacCulloch, No. 240450, 2nd/5th Royal Scots Fusiliers, died 1 June 1920.
- Private Allan MacFarlane, No. S/4512, 9th Battalion Royal Highlanders - Black Watch. Died 26 September 1915. Son of R. W. MacFarlane, Methven, Perthshire. Buried in Noeux-les-mines Communal Cemetery, France.
- Gunner MacEwan MacIlwraith, No. 192757, Royal Field Artillery, 13th Battery, 17th Bole. Born 19 January 1893, killed 10 August 1917. Lived at Dailly. Buried in Bleuet Farm Cemetery, Belgium.
- Private James MacIlwraith, the brother of the above MacEwan MacIlwraith, 1st Battalion Royal Scots, killed 29 January 1915.
- Private Robert MacLeish, No. 15639, 2nd Battalion Royal Scots Fusiliers, from Darnconner, killed 16 June 1915 at Hooge, aged 23. Buried at Le Touret Memorial Cemetery.
- Signaller Thomas MacMillan, No. S/41651, 1st/4th Gordon Highlanders, killed in France, March 1918, aged 25. Buried at Arras memorial. Son of John and Margaret MacMillan, Hayfield, Auchinleck.
- Private William MacMurdo, No. 52479, Royal Scots Fusiliers, killed in action in France, 20 October 1918, aged 20. A shell caused his death, along with five other men. A native of Commondyke, he was the son of William and Mary P. MacMurdo, latterly of Dalsalloch Rows. He was a keen sportsman, billiard player, and member of Darnconner Tent of Rechabites. He is buried at Vertarn Communal Cemetery Extension.
- Private Thomas MacNairney, 7th Royal Scots Fusiliers, from Dalsalloch, killed in action in France, 27 February 1916 aged 35.

- Private William MacNaught, No. 240650, 6th/7th Battalion Royal Scots Fusiliers. Died 8 May 1917 aged 24. Son of Robert and Agnes MacNaught, Highhouse Rows, but a native of Catrine. He is buried at Duisans British Cemetery, France.
- Lance Corporal Robert Milligan, Service No. 34988, 2nd Battalion Royal Scots Fusiliers, died of wounds received in France 8 April 1918, aged 32. Husband of Grace Milligan, Orchard Place, Auchinleck.
- Corporal James Robert Paton, Service No. 63803, Royal Engineers, killed 21 October 1916 aged 24. Son of Andrew Paton JP. Born in Auchinleck.
- Private William Rae, No. S/20435, 9th Battalion Seaforth Highlanders, killed 17 June 1916, aged 26. Buried at Bronfray Farm Military Cemetery, Bray-sur-somme, France.
- Private Edward Seymour, No. 240252, 1st/5th Battalion Royal Scots Fusiliers. Born in Sorn on 5 May 1897, he was killed in Palestine, 29 November 1917. He was the son of Elizabeth W. Seymour and grandson of Edward Seymour and Elizabeth Wightman. He lived in Searle Terrace.
- Private Frank Skillen, Royal Scots Fusiliers.
- Private Edward Small, No. 5217, 2nd Battalion Royal Scots Fusiliers, killed in action at Neuve Chapelle, 16 May 1915, aged 36. Buried at Le Touret Memorial Cemetery.
- Gunner Hugh Stewart, No. 242985, 13th/87th Brigade, R. F. A., died of wounds received in France, 14 April 1918 aged 32. Buried at Tyne Cot Memorial Cemetery.
- Private James Hill Stewart, No. 6749, 1st/5th Battalion Royal Scots Fusiliers. Born in Auchinleck around 1894, the youngest son of James Stewart and Barbara Peden. They lived at Mansfield View in Auchinleck. He was educated at Cumnock. Died in Egypt, 17 April 1916 and buried at Kantara War Memorial Cemetery.
- Private David Strickland, No. 17456, 7th Royal Scots Fusiliers. He was born in Sorn, the son of Margaret Strickland and the late Daniel Strickland. They latterly lived at Mansefield View, Auchinleck. He enlisted in the R. S. F. at Bramshott in Hampshire. He was killed in action at Flanders in Belgium on 27 February 1916 aged 26. Buried at Loos Memorial Cemetery. He is also commemorated at the Fisher's Tryst, Ballochmyle.
- Private Campbell Tanner, No. 41948, Royal Scots Fusiliers, killed France, 11 April 1917, aged 27. He was born in Cumnock but moved to Auchinleck. He played the cornet in Auchinleck Band and when he signed up he became bugler to Royal Scots Fusiliers. During the war

he was transferred to the 12th Battalion Highland Light Infantry. He is commemorated on Arras Memorial, Pas de Calais, but he has no known grave. He is also commemorated on the war memorial plaque within Cumnock Congregational Church.
- Corporal Norman Tilley, Royal Scots Fusiliers, killed July 1916 aged 38.
- Sergeant John Toole, Royal Scots Fusiliers, killed German East Africa, 1917, aged 33.
- Private Michael Woods, No. 12769, 7th Royal Scots Fusiliers, killed in action at Loos in France, 26 September 1915, aged 19 years. Buried at Loos Memorial Cemetery, France.
- Corporal Abraham Yates, No. 270338, 12th Battalion Royal Scots Fusiliers. Born in Dalmellington on 26 July 1891 to Samuel Yates and Jeanie Ferguson Hyslop, he was killed in action on 19 April 1918. His parents and siblings latterly lived at Market Place, Auchinleck. He was a keen bandsman and worked as a miner.
- Private George Young, No. 8528, 1st/5th Battalion, Royal Scots Fusiliers, died 27 June 1915, aged 60. Husband of Agnes Jane Hall Young, 9 Highhouse Rows.

At Lugar a second war memorial was erected in front of the Institute. It comprises a grey freestone memorial, ten feet tall, with a white marble tablet on which is a bronze panel listing 25 names of those who died. The foundation was laid in December 1920 and the memorial was unveiled and dedicated on Saturday 18 December 1920. In attendance were Rev James Young, Robert Angus and Brigadier General Pollock MacCall. Unlike many other war memorials, the memorial at Lugar also lists those who served in the war but were fortunate enough to return. A total of 145 names were included. Unfortunately, this part of the memorial began to weather, preventing many of the names from being read. When the memorial was relocated to outside Lugar Church, a new granite slab was attached to the front of the memorial, listing the names. In the list are a number of men who were given special medals for their service. Military Medals were awarded to S. Abernethy, William Conn, Thomas B. Ross and John Stewart. David Geekie was awarded the Distinguished Conduct Medal.

Those from Lugar who died were:

- Captain Robert Edward Angus, 64th Squadron Royal Flying Corps and Ayrshire Yeomanry. Son of James Angus JP and Elizabeth Angus of Ochiltree House. They previously lived at Craigston House, Lugar. R. E. Angus lived at Hill House, Leckhampton. Died 20 November

1917 aged 23. He is buried at Arras Flying Services Memorial Cemetery.
- Private Thomas Baillie, No. 203733, 1st/5th Royals Scots Fusiliers, accidentally killed in France, 2 October 1918, aged 28. Buried at Mashieres British Cemetery, Marcoing, France.
- Private Charles Baird, No. S/14291, 1st Battalion Cameron Highlanders, killed France 9 May 1915 aged 23. Son of the late Robert and Sarah Baird. Buried at Le Youret Memorial Cemetery.
- Lance Corporal James Begg, No. 240343, 1st/5th Royal Scots Fusiliers, killed Palestine, 1 December 1917, aged 30. Son of James and Mary Robertson Begg of Lugar. Buried at Ramleh War Cemetery.
- Sergeant William Begg MM, No. S/3977, 9th Seaforth Highlanders, died of wounds received in France, 23 December 1917 aged 27. He was the son of George and Jeanie Begg, New Row, Lugar. He is buried at Tincourt New British Cemetery, France.
- Corporal Andrew Cairney, No. 12287, 6th Battalion Royal Scots Fusiliers. Brother of James Cairney, Barquharrie, Ochiltree. Died 26 September 1915. Commemorated on Loos Memorial.
- Denis Cairney, No. 13035, 7th Battalion Royal Scots Fusiliers, died of wounds 28 October 1915 aged 24. Brother of J. Cairney, Crescent Rows, Lugar. He is buried in Noeux-les-mines Communal Cemetery.
- H. Cairney
- Private James Carson, Cameronians.
- Private Maitland Crowley (on war memorial) or Crolley, No. 8559, 2nd Battalion Cameron Highlanders, killed in France on 23 April 1915, aged 23. Buried at Ypres (Menin Gate) Memorial Cemetery. Also commemorated at New Cumnock.
- Private Alexander Geekie, No. S/16169, B Company, 6th Battalion Cameron Highlanders, killed 6 July 1916 aged 27. He was the son of Alexander and Christine Geekie, Lugar, and is buried at Vermelles British Cemetery.
- Private James Glencorse, No. 41636, 10th/11th Battalion Highland Light Infantry, killed France, 11 April 1917 aged 21. Buried in Orange Trench Cemetery, Monch-le-preux. Son of John Glencorse, 445 Brick Row, Lugar.
- Private Harry Kinnear, No. 16033, 4th Regiment South African Infantry, killed 10 October 1918. Son of Mr H. Kinnear, Johnstone, Renfrewshire, but ex-Lugar. Buried in Bertry Communal Cemetery, France.

- Private Robert Lundie, No. 7235, 1st/5th Battalion Royal Scots Fusiliers, killed in action at Dardanelles, 12 July 1915, aged 42. Buried at Helles Memorial Cemetery.
- Private James Morris, No. 7317, 1st Royal Scots Fusiliers, killed Hooge, Flanders, 16 June 1915, aged 39. He was the son of John and Annie Morris of Craigstonholm, Lugar and the husband of Catherine R. B. Bell Morris, of Dunard Street, North Kelvinside, Glasgow. He previously served in the Sudan (1898) and the South African campaign with the Seaforth Highlanders. Buried at Ypres (Menin Gate) Memorial Cemetery.
- Corporal William Muir, No. 17441, 2nd Battalion Cameron Highlanders, died December 1918, aged 28. Buried in Turin Town Cemetery.
- Colour Sergeant Hugh Murdoch, No. 7282, 5th Battalion Royal Scots Fusiliers, wounded 12 July 1915, died August 1915, aged 47. Buried at Lancashire Landing Cemetery, Turkey. He was the son of William Murdoch, late post-master in Lugar.
- J. Patrick
- Corporal William Patrick, No. 8522, 12th Battalion Highland Light Infantry, killed 3 May 1917. Buried at Etaples Military Cemetery.
- Private James Scott, No. 240471, 1st/5th Royal Scots Fusiliers, died of wounds in Egypt, 5 May 1917, aged 20. Buried at Alexandria (Hadra) War Memorial Cemetery. He was the son of Robert and Jane Scott, 449 Brick Row, Lugar.
- Private John M. Smith, No. 15040, 16th Highland Light Infantry, killed in action, 1 July 1916, aged 43. Buried at Authuille, France.
- Private William Surgeoner, No. S/13494, 7th Battalion Cameron Highlanders. Killed 25 September 1915. Buried at Loos Memorial Cemetery.
- Private Hugh Williamson, No. S/12870, 7th Battalion Cameron Highlanders. Died 25 September 1915 aged 23. Buried at Loos Memorial Cemetery. He was the son of Matthew and Jane Williamson, Lugar.
- Private William Wright, No. S/14294, 1st Battalion Cameron Highlanders, killed in France, 28 September 1915 aged 20. Buried at Ninth Avenue Cemetery, Haisnes, France. Born in Lugar, he was the son of Robert John Wright, latterly of Avon Street, Glasgow.
- Private James Wylie, No. S/14447, 1st Battalion Cameron Highlanders, killed in action in France, 11 October 1915, aged 22. He was the son of John and Janet Wylie, 473 Brick Row, Lugar.

There were also a considerable number of others from the parish, or who were closely connected with it, who were killed in war and who were not listed on the war memorials in either Auchinleck or Lugar. Many of these men lived in the miners' rows elsewhere in the parish:

6.12 Lugar War Memorial *(Dane Love)*

- Private John Bell, No. 34955, 1st Battalion Royal Scots Fusiliers. Died at Langensalza Prisoner of War Camp, Germany, 22 May 1917, aged 37. Born in Auchinleck, enrolled in Catrine. Listed on gravestone in Auchinleck.
- Private James Colquhoun, No. 20782, 6th/7th Battalion Royal Scots Fusiliers, died of wounds in France, 11 October 1916 aged 20. A native of the Common, he is buried at the Dernancourt Communal Cemetery extension in France.
- Private John Crawford, No. 15119, 16th Battalion Highland Light Infantry, died 18 November 1916 aged 22. He was the son of Robert Crawford, 25 Love Street, Paisley. Buried at Waggon Road Cemetery, Beaumont-Hamel.
- Private Patrick Carroll, No. 16236, 1st Battalion Royal Scots Fusiliers, was killed on 19 September 1915. A native of Birnieknowe, he was buried at Brandhoek Military Cemetery, Belgium.

- Gunner John Darroch, No. 110302, 60th Howitzer Battery, Royal Field Artillery, he died in Mesopotamia, 17 July 1917 aged 38. He is buried at Baghdad (North Gate) Cemetery. He was the son of John and Maria Darroch, 175 Common Row, Darnconner.
- Private William Eadie, No. 303376, 1st/8th Battalion Argyll & Sutherland Highlanders, died on 21 March 1918. A native of Darnconner, he is buried at Pozieres Memorial Cemetery in France.
- Sergeant John Fleming, No. 7238, 1st/5th Battalion Royal Scots Fusiliers, died of wounds received at Dardanelles, 3 July 1915. He is buried at Pink Farm Cemetery, Helles. He lived at Burnside Rows, the husband of Janet Hillhouse and the son of John Fleming, Auchinleck.
- Private Robert Foley, No. G/676, 2nd Battalion East Kent Buffs, killed France, 3 May 1915, aged 18. Buried at Ypres (Menin Gate) Cemetery.
- Private Richard Foley, Coldstream Guards, killed in action 1915 aged 17.
- Private Alexander Frew, No. S/3746, 1st Black Watch, killed in France, 26 May 1916 aged 29. Buried at Dud Corner Cemetery, Loos.
- Corporal Samuel Boyce Harper, No. 200047, 5th/6th Battalion Cameronians (Scottish Rifles), killed 20 May 1917 aged 23. Buried at Arras Memorial Cemetery.
- Private Thomas Hewitson, No. 22523, 15th Battalion Highland Light Infantry, killed in action on 29 November 1917. Buried at Passchendaele New British Cemetery.
- 2nd Lieutenant James Hyslop, Royal Engineers. Born in Auchinleck, son of James Hyslop and Margaret Brash Crossan. Father was schoolmaster at Lugar, when they lived at 364, 7th Row. He died of influenza in Ayr County Hospital and had recently been demobbed. He died on 15 February 1919 and is buried in Cumnock New Cemetery.
- Lieutenant James MacCormac Caldwell Johnstone, Royal Army Medical Corps, killed in France on 27 May 1916, aged 32. His parents were Robert Johnstone MBCM and Helen Mitchell MacCormick of Dundee, but he lived in Lugar. He is buried in Ecoivres Military Cemetery, Mont St Elois.
- Private Edward Kennedy, No. 18682, 6th Battalion Royal Dublin Fusiliers, died of wounds in the Dardanelles, 21 August 1915, aged 25. From the Common. Buried at Alexandria (Chatby) Military Cemetery.
- Private William Kilmartin, No. 20124, 6th/7th Battalion Royal Scots Fusiliers, of Common, killed France 11 April 1917 aged 20. Buried at Monchy British Cemetery, Monchy-le-preux. Native of Auchinleck but lived at Prestwick.

- Private John Lockhart, No. 240854, 5th Battalion Royal Scots Fusiliers, killed in France, 26 August 1918 aged 24. Belonged to Common. Buried at Aubigny Communal Cemetery Extension.
- Private James Lundie, No. 4246, 1st Battalion Australian Infantry. Killed in action, 28 July 1916, aged 38. Buried at Puchevillers British Cemetery, France. Son of James and Isabel Lundie, Lugar.
- Private Samuel MacBlane, No. 34961, 2nd Battalion Royal Scots Fusiliers, killed in France, 23 April 1917 aged 31. Born in Kilwinning, but lived at 88 Darnconner. Husband of Janet Fadddes MacBlane. Buried at Bootham Cemetery, Henimel.
- Private Bernard MacCann, No. 240091, 1st/5th Battalion Royals Scots Fusiliers. Killed in action 26 August 1918, aged 28. A native of Lennoxtown, he lived at the Common. Buried at Vis-en-artois Memorial Cemetery.
- Private Thomas MacInernie, Royal Scots Fusiliers.
- Private James MacGregor MacKay, A. S. C., killed in France, 9 April 1917.
- Private Roderick Campbell MacKnight, No. 240303, 1st/4th King's Own Scottish Borderers, died of wounds in France, 2 October 1918, aged 20. Buried at Proville British Cemetery. He was a native of Gasswater, but his family had moved to 10 Nithsdale Cottages, Kirkconnel.
- Signaller John Mair, No. 37552, 18th Battalion Highland Light Infantry, killed in action, France, 25 March 1918, aged 21. Son of James and Mary Mair, 178 Gasswater. Buried at Pozieres Memorial Cemetery.
- Sergeant William Montgomerie, 2nd Argyll & Sutherland Highlanders, killed in action 12 November 1914, aged 36. From Lugar.
- Private John Murray, No. S/2514, 1st Battalion Gordon Highlanders, killed 17 August 1915, aged 25. He was the son of John and Catherine Quinn Murray, Coatbridge, but lived in Auchinleck.
- Private R. Murphy, No. 17456, 250th Protection Company, Royal Defence Corps, died 8 January 1918. Buried in Auchinleck graveyard.
- Private James Neil, No. 12266, 6th Battalion Royal Scots Fusiliers, killed 26 September 1915 at Loos.
- Private William Reid, No. S/12234, 9th Battalion Black Watch (Royal Highlanders), killed in Battle of Arras, 9 April 1917, aged 21. Lived in Ochiltree, but formerly of Cronberry.
- Private William Curragh Rodger, No. 48240, 6th/7th Battalion Royal Scots Fusiliers, died of wounds, 1918 aged 22. Born at Auchtermuchty,

son of Robert Rodger and Agnes Graham. Family lived at 415 Brick Row, Lugar, in 1901. Buried at Grevilliers British Cemetery.
- Private William Steele, No. 240772, 1st/5th Battalion Royal Scots Fusiliers. Lived at Common, killed in Egypt 5 June 1917 aged 25. Buried at Gaza War Cemetery.
- Private H. Vallance, No. 599, 1st Battalion Argyll & Sutherland Highlanders, killed 29 June 1915. Buried in Auchinleck kirkyard.
- Private James Welsh, 1st/5th Royal Scots Fusiliers, killed 30 December 1916 at the Dardanelles, aged 21. Ex-Lugar.
- Private James Ross Wilson, No. 8503, South African Infantry 3rd Regiment, killed France, 25 April 1917 aged 38.

LANDOWNERS – AUCHINLECK ESTATE

At the turn of the century, Auchinleck estate was still the property of Lord Talbot de Malahide. However, during the First World War finance started to become tight, and parts of the property were sold off. In April 1916 some of the contents of the library in Auchinleck House was placed on the market and were sold by Messrs. Sotheby, Wilkinson & Hodge. There were 111 lots from the library, realising £340. The most expensive book sold was a quarto volume, in old monastic bindings comprising oak boards, covered with stamped leather. This book contained some fifteenth century writings by Gregorius Magnus and others and realised £54.

The furnishings and plenishings of the house were sold on 28-29 March 1917. Among the items sold was a grandfather clock which attained £63. The house and estate of 12,000 acres were placed on the market in October 1919 at offers around £185,000, but there were no bids.

For a time the house was leased by Robert MacCrone, who was the manager of the Ballochmyle Creamery, Mauchline. He took on the lease in 1918. He moved out of the house at Whitsunday 1923, but John Douglas Boswell reckoned that he had not maintained the property in a sufficient way during his tenancy and in January 1925 a legal court case took place, Boswell suing for £957 worth of articles removed from the house. MacCrone was by this time living at Dinwiddie, near Hollybush. Robert MacCrone was the father of Guy MacCrone, who gained some fame as an author.

Guy Fulton McCrone was born in 1898 at Birkenhead in England but moved to Glasgow, and was educated at Glasgow Academy. He then studied modern languages at Pembroke College in Cambridge, followed by a course in singing at Vienna. When fund-raising bazaars were being held at Ballochmyle House in aid of the Broomhill and Lanfine Homes in 1922 he organised the concerts in the library. He was one of three founders (with James Bridie and Dr Tom Honeyman) of the Citizen's Theatre in Glasgow in 1943, being its first managing director. He was more noted for his novels, many of which were based on historical Glasgow events and families. These include *Antimacassar City*, *The Philistines* and *The Puritans*, the three novels being collected as a trilogy called *Wax Fruit*, which is still in print. Other novels include *Aunt Bel*, *The Hayburn Family*, *Charlotte and Dr James*, *Red Plush – the Moorhouse Family*, *The Striped Umbrella*, and *An Independent Young Man*. Guy McCrone retired to the Lake District and died at Windermere in May 1977.

JOHN DOUGLAS BOSWELL (XIV)

Auchinleck House and part of the estate were sold to a distant kinsman of Lord Talbot de Malahide, Lieutenant Colonel John Douglas Boswell of Garrallan in Old Cumnock parish. He bought the lands in 1920, comprising Auchinleck House and immediate policies, stables, Burnhouse, Langholm, Mill Affleck, Oldbyres, Highhouse, Merlinhill, Langlands, Blackfauldhead, Auchinleck Mains, West Langlands, Barnsdale, Knowe and Mosside within the parish. The estate of Garrallan was then sold to the Stevenson family, formerly Boswell's tenants at Changue.

John Douglas Boswell was born on 16 February 1867, second son of Patrick Charles Boswell of Garrallan, and great grandson of John Boswell, 6th of Knockroon. His elder brother, Hamilton Boswell (1858-1898), succeeded Patrick in 1892 but died unmarried. He was a scion of the main Auchinleck family, his six times great-grandfather being John Boswell, 3rd of Auchinleck. John was educated at Loretto School, followed by Brasenose College, Oxford, where he graduated with a Bachelor of Arts degree in 1888. He continued studies at Glasgow University, graduating as Bachelor of Laws. He was a military man, being a Lieutenant Colonel in the Territorial Force Reserve, former commanding officer in the Ayrshire Yeomanry, and seeing active service in the Boer War as Captain of the 6th Battalion of the Imperial Yeomanry. He retired from military service in September 1926, retaining his rank, with permission to wear proscribed uniform. The Ayrshire Yeomanry had a shooting range at Langholm, on the Auchinleck side of the river at Ochiltree, between the wars.

John Douglas Boswell was married on 1 August 1907 to Janet Alice, daughter of Robert Angus of Ladykirk, whom he outlived, she dying in October 1930. By her he had three children, John Patrick Douglas Boswell, who succeeded as 15th Laird of Auchinleck when his father died on 5 January 1948, Robert William Douglas Boswell and Jean Campbell Douglas Boswell.

Lord Talbot de Malahide sold off his remaining lands in the parish over the next few years. These were mainly located around Birnieknowe and Rogerton. For example, Barglachan farm, comprising 193 acres, was sold in 1945 to James Templeton, the sitting tenant.

In 1919-20 the Marquis of Bute also sold off some of his property in the parish. However, he still owned much of the land around the Glenmuir Water. The farms

6.13 John Douglas Boswell of Garrallan and Auchinleck
(Author's Collection)

were let to tenants, and the moors were let to sporting tenants. In 1929 this was Brigadier General Wilding and Colonel Watkyn Williams. In 1926 Lord Bute, Lord Column Stuart and others shot over 250 brace of grouse on the Kyle moors.

Charles D. Inglis of Stair House was a keen sportsman, being a member of the Balloch Fishing Club at Loch Bradan and a tenant of the shootings of Dornal and Glenmuir under the Howatsons of Glenbuck until it was sold by them to the Marquis of Bute. Charles Inglis died on 3 February 1929 at the age of 90.

CHURCHES

In the new century Rev James Hill continued his ministry at the parish church. He was born in Dundee on 20 July 1863, son of Alexander and Barbara Hill, and received his education at the West End Academy in that city, followed by St Andrews University. He graduated as a Master of Arts in 1885 and Bachelor of Divinity in 1888. He was licensed by the Presbytery of Dundee in May 1888 and in that year he was appointed assistant minister at Maxwelltown Parish Church (Dumfries) before coming to Auchinleck in 1890, to assist Rev Dr Chrystal at Darnconner Mission Church. He was ordained to the parish church on 23 November 1893. Hill married Agnes Jane MacLellan (1870-1949), daughter of Hugh Blair MacLellan, on 22 April 1903, and they had four sons and a daughter. These were Alexander (born 3 March 1904), Hugh Blair MacLellan (born 20 July 1907), James (born 16 June 1908-died 31 July 1908), and twins, Alison Irene and Eric Alan, (born 15 February 1911). Alison died on 30 May 1972, Eric on 1 November 1986. Hill was a member of the School Board, serving as chairman in 1895. He was a member of the Ayrshire Education Authority in 1919 and served as a county councillor from 1929 to his death, which occurred on 27 September 1940. A memorial window to Hill was erected in the present church and his grave is located in the cemetery.

In August 1901 the old manse was demolished and a new house built on the same site. This was designed by the local architect, Robert Ingram. In December

1921 lands adjoining Auchinleck Glebe were purchased by the trustees of the church from Auchinleck Estate.

Rev James Hill had been active in bringing about the erection of the Barony Church Hall which stood at 116-118 Main Street. The plans were passed in October 1928. In August 1928 a grand bazaar was held in the school to raise funds, the principal patron being Lord Talbot de Malahide. Numerous stalls sold items gifted for sale. At the time, the fund had raised over £1,350, purchasing the site. The first plans were drawn up by William Meikle, architect, Ayr, but these were changed by the time the building was completed.

The hall, which could accommodate 400, was built at a cost of £3,000, and officially opened on Tuesday 18 September 1934. Rev Hill presided, supported by Lord Talbot de Malahide, Rev P. D. Thomson (Moderator of the General Assembly) and Rev Brodie Gilfillan (Moderator of Ayr Presbytery). The hall had been built by subscription, sizeable donations coming from Lord Talbot de Malahide and Robert L. Angus of Ladykirk. Lady Talbot officially declared the hall open, and she was presented with a gift by the architect, W. F. Valentine of Kilmarnock. In 1933 a bronze plaque was unveiled in the church to record one hundred years of ministry by two ministers, Rev James Chrystal and Rev James Hill, who had served from 1833 until 1933.

On the morning of Sunday 3 April 1938 tragedy struck the Barony Church. The beadle, John Robertson, arrived to ring the bell at 9.00 a.m. as usual, but shortly afterwards fire was noticed issuing from the building. He and others rushed into the kirk and managed to save certain papers and important documents, but the fire was so fierce they were prevented from getting other items out of the building. Fire engines rushed to the blaze, but found that they could do nothing to save the building, and just had to dowse the last embers. At one point the beadle disappeared - his body was later found unconscious in the belfry. On being removed from the smoke he recovered. The building was virtually destroyed, the roof collapsed and a number of walls tumbled, leaving just the tower standing.

Services had to be held in the Barony Church Hall for four years thereafter, until the church was restored. Messrs James and J. A. Carrick of Ayr (architects) designed a new building incorporating the surviving tower and ruinous walls. When rebuilt the roof was raised, giving the church a more airy atmosphere, and the Boswell window was restored. The kirk was rededicated on Wednesday 27 May 1942 by Professor J. G. Riddell of Glasgow, Rev Harry Marr of Ayr St Andrews conducting worship, and the new parish minister, Rev David Ross, reading the lessons. The Women's Guild gifted a new pulpit Bible and fall, the Bible Class a vase for the communion table, and the Misses Wilson, of Giffnock, new collection plates and salver to replace those damaged in the fire and which had been originally gifted in memory of their father. An evening social was held in the church hall.

Inside the church new pews had been installed, having been taken from the recently-closed Darnconner Church, the new central aisle meaning that accommodation in the church had been reduced. New lighting had been added and the singing of hymns was improved by the installation of a new two-manual organ. The former rectangular opening into the chancel was altered to the present Gothic arch, more in keeping with the shape of the window behind, but wartime restrictions on timber prevented the main ceiling being restored in wood to match the chancel.

Rev David William Ross BD had been ordained and inducted to Auchinleck on 28 May 1941. He remained in the village for seven years, before being translated to Lochgelly Macainsh Church (Fife) on 22 April 1948.

UNITED FREE CHURCH – PEDEN CHURCH

In April 1922 proposals to establish a new congregation of the United Free Church were made in Auchinleck. A public meeting was held on 2 May 1922 and subsequently the congregation was officially started when 202 signatories signed up to join. The old Associate Church in Auchinleck was sold to the new United Free congregation for £1,000, a figure which included the manse. Membership of the U. F. church began to grow from that point, adherents no longer having to travel to Cumnock to worship. Auchinleck was a Church Extension congregation and had not too long to wait before its first minister, Rev Andrew Higgins MA, arrived. Born in Glasgow, he was educated at the University of Glasgow, graduating in 1920. For three years he studied at the United Free Church College, then for eighteen months assisted Rev B. J. Davidson BD at Springburn North U. F. Church. During the war he served for three years in the Navy as a qualified signaller. He was ordained at Auchinleck church on Friday 27 October 1922. A bachelor, Higgins took up residence in Auchinleck and remained for seven years, before moving to Manse Road Church in Motherwell on 19 February 1930. He later became Moderator of Hamilton Presbytery, retiring in 1964, having served at Motherwell for 33 years. He died there in the early 1980s.

In 1929 the United Free Church nationally re-joined the Church of Scotland, mending the links broken at the Disruption of 1843. Thus Auchinleck got two parish churches within a few hundred yards of each other. It was at this time the two congregations became known as the Barony (original parish church) and Peden (former U. F. church), the latter named in honour of the Covenanter, Alexander Peden.

The Peden Kirk called a new minister, Rev George Robert Fryer, on 25 June 1930, who transferred from Mossvale Church in Paisley. He remained until his demission in 1940. Rev Fryer spent much of his time as a missionary in China. Both he and his wife, a trained nurse, took part in the Boxer Rising. During the General Strike of 1926 he taught a number of miners the art of carpentry and he was also a noted apiarist. Rev George Fryer died on 5 June 1949 at the age of 77 and was buried in Mauchline's Barskimming Road cemetery. He was married to Anne E. Lister, who died on 5 November 1954 aged 85.

LUGAR PARISH CHURCH

Rev Walter Milne continued as minister of Lugar until he resigned on 7 March 1905 due to ill-health. He retired to Dundee, where he died unmarried on 11 March 1916. One of his contemporaries described him as having a 'cheery, genial and social disposition, and was very well liked by many of his parishioners.'

On 8 March 1907 the church was raised to independent status, breaking its link with the parish church. Thus Lugar became a Quoad Sacra parish. Rev Joseph Campbell (born Glasgow, 2 May 1867) was ordained on 7 January 1907. Campbell was the son of Joseph Campbell and Margaret Crockett. He received his education at the Glasgow Highland Society's School, followed by Glasgow University and the Central University, Indiana. He received his Master of Arts degree in August 1915. He had been licensed by the Presbytery of Glasgow in November 1899, serving initially as an assistant minister at Brucefield Church, Larbert and Dunipace. He was appointed to Lugar on 9 March 1905, as assistant minister. He became the first proper minister of the parish on 8 March 1907. Campbell was married on 11 April 1907 to Marion, daughter of George Park M.D., of Kilsyth. He remained at Lugar for seven years, resigning on 16 July 1912. Rev Campbell emigrated to America for a time, but returned to Scotland and began work as assistant minister at Riccarton Parish Church, Kilmarnock. He then accepted a call to Bargrennan Parish Church, Kirkcudbrightshire, where he was inducted on 18 September 1917.

On 19 October 1912 Rev James Morogh Young was appointed. He was born on 6 November 1880 at Dublin, son of James Bristow Young and Matilda Russell. He was educated at St Andrew's School in Dublin, followed by university at Dublin and Glasgow. He received his Bachelor of Arts degree at Dublin in 1902. He was licensed by the Presbytery of Linlithgow in May 1905. At first he served as an assistant minister at the East Church in Stirling, followed by Hillhead in Glasgow. He spent the war years in service, his name included on the war memorial at Lugar as one who returned. He married Jane Hislop (daughter of John Blackburn Hislop FRCSE), widow of John Brown Niven, on 14 July 1915. Rev Young retired on 14 March 1925, and was killed on a railway near Grantown, 23 July 1925.

Young was followed by Rev James Mawer Wallace who was inducted on 17 December 1925. Wallace was born in Edinburgh on 2 January 1891, son of Alexander Wallace and Helen Maxwell Mawer. He was educated at Fossoway Public School (Kinross-shire) and Dollar Academy (Clackmannanshire). He then moved to Canada and studied at Manitoba University, followed by Glasgow University. During the First World War he served in the Canadian 11 Field Ambulance from 1916-18. Wallace served as a missionary in Ontario, Canada, from 1919 until 1923.

He then became an assistant missionary at St Matthew's Church, Blythswood, Glasgow, for one year, before moving to become assistant minister at Dumbarton Parish Church in August 1924. He was licensed by the Presbytery of Dunbarton in May 1925, moving to Lugar soon after. On 3 February 1926 Wallace was married to Ann MacKendrick King, daughter of George MacKendrick King and Jessie Manson Russell. They had two children, Eileen Margaret Wallace (born 19 October 1927) and James Victor Bryden Wallace (born 19 December 1929). In 1928 the church instituted a Women's Guild. Rev Wallace was translated to Thornton Old Parish Church, Fife, on 24 October 1929.

Rev Edward Taylor MA was ordained and inducted on 28 February 1930. He remained at Lugar for five years before being translated to Knoxland Church, Dumbarton, on 25 October 1935.

Rev William Murray Diack followed on 8 April 1936, coming from St Adrian's Church, Pittenweem, and moving on to Craig, 24 November 1943.

DARNCONNER

The new church at Darnconner continued to serve the residents of that mining community and others nearby. The minister for a time was Rev William Eadie, and Rev William Petrie performed baptisms in 1913. Latterly the parish minister visited to perform baptisms, the weekly services being conducted by 'missionaries'. These were James Eaglesham, W. Ross and George Laird. Traditionally, only one wedding was ever to take place in the church. The last baptism performed at Darnconner was of Hendryna Dickson (born 16 September 1937) which took place on 5 June 1938. She lived with her parents at 116 Peesweep Row, Lugar. As the rows in Darnconner were being abandoned and the villagers rehoused in Auchinleck, the church was closed in 1939. It stood until 1979 when it was demolished.

BIRNIEKNOWE

Birnieknowe Chapel and the Roman Catholic community there continued under the guiding light of Rev John O'Neil until 1908, when he became Canon O'Neil, Dean and Provost of the Cathedral Chapter. He died in 1922.

Father O' Neil was replaced at Birnieknowe in 1908 by Rev Joseph Hogan, who transferred from St Sophia's in Galston, where he had been a priest for eight years. A native of Tipperaray, he was educated in Ireland. He began in the ministry in Ayr (1888-89), followed by Girvan (1889-90), Maybole (1890-90), and Galston. In 1911 he was appointed as a canon. The curate, Rev John Murphy, formed a football team entirely of Catholics, and he often played himself. In local competitions they were nicknamed 'The Murphy Boys'. Canon Hogan left for Irvine in 1918, where he served until his death there on 30 April 1936.

Canon Hogan was replaced by Rev Reginald Vignoles. He was born in Ireland and educated there. He joined the Praemonstratensians and was ordained in 1886.

At first he served in Ireland, followed by London and Whithorn. He left the Premonstratensians in 1896 but continued to serve in Galloway as a secular priest. He served at Craigeach and Newton Stewart alternately from 1896-1918, apart from a short spell at Galston.

The Birnie Band, which became well-known throughout Ayrshire, was reformed after the war, but failed to attain the standards it previously held. Sister Reginald ran the choir, and other organisations existing there included the Women's Confraternity, the Children of Mary and the Young Man's Society. During the years of depression, the chapel's condition deteriorated as funds depleted. A garden fete was organised, opened by James Brown MP, restoring the bank balance to a more healthy state. In 1927 the school was extended, with three new classrooms, in order to take pupils from Mauchline, Catrine and Sorn. One of the pupils became a priest, Father Edward Scanlon.

In 1930 Canon Vignoles retired due to ill-health, to be replaced by Rev Martin Doyle. Canon Vignoles took some time out of the church, but returned to Newton Stewart for a year from 1931-32, followed by Castle Douglas from 1932-38. He died there on 17 November 1938.

Martin Doyle was born in Port Glasgow in 1888. He was educated at Blairs College, followed by the Scots College in Rome, from 1906-14. He was ordained there in 1914. During the First World War he served at St Andrews in Dumfries, and then Cumnock from 1918-1920. Six years followed at St Mary's in Irvine, plus a year at Stranraer and three at Newton Stewart, before arriving at Birnieknowe. Father Doyle was instrumental in promoting fund-raising events in order to make right the poor condition of the church and presbytery, renewing the floors, redecorating the buildings, installing electricity and mending the heating. The band was given the honour of leading the recently renewed Pilgrimage at Whithorn in 1931.

Father Doyle was transferred to St John's in Cumnock in 1936, where he remained for a couple of years. He was then transferred to Castle Douglas for six years, and then Stranraer (1944-49). Periods at Dalbeattie and Galston followed, Doyle dying there on 23 May 1956.

At Birnieknowe, Father Doyle was replaced by Rev Joseph Maxwell. Born in Newton Stewart in 1903, he was educated there as well as at Blairs College and the Grand Seminaire, Coutances. He was ordained at Dundee in 1928. Maxwell was lent to Glasgow Archdiocese, and he served at Renton for a year. In 1931-33 he served at Dumfries, followed by Castle Douglas for three years. In 1936 he came to Birnieknowe.

During Father Maxwell's time as priest a parochial hall was erected in Auchinleck in 1940, the plans passed the previous year. The architect was Alexander Dunlop. It was soon commandeered to billet troops in the Second World War and later to act as an annexe to St Patrick's school for pupils evacuated from Glasgow.

At other times it was used for raising funds for War Charities, and similar purposes, so the church had little benefit from it initially.

A number of assistant priests served at Auchinleck in addition to the incumbent. These included Robert Carmont (1903-04, born 1868, died 1937), Michael Carey (1904-06, died 1951), John O'Hanlon (1906-07, born 1878), William J. J. Trainor (1907-08, born 1880, died 1919 following a motorcycle accident), John Murphy (1908-09, born 1883, died 1937), Thomas Joyce (1909-11, born 1873, died 1940), Robert Carmont (1911-15), Frederick Letters (1915-26), and Hugh Mimnagh (1926-28, born 1892, died 1955).

OTHER DENOMINATIONS
At 16 Templeton Place there was a Mission Hall used by Auchinleck Christian Union. This group was increasing in number and in 1927 work began on the erection of a new mission hall in Well Road. The building was designed by James Pollock, architect, Ayr, whose fee was ten guineas. It was constructed of brick, stone and roughcast. The main hall measured 37 feet by 25 feet, having six large windows. It was wood-lined internally to the window sills and could seat 200. An ante-room measured 16½ feet by 12 feet, as well as a kitchen and cloak room, each measuring eight feet square. The Building Fund had commenced on 4 May 1922 with just £2 and funds were raised by holding tea socials, for which the Union became noted, sales of work and jumble sales. The total cost of erection was around £771. The new hall was opened on Saturday 19 May 1928 by James Brown MP, followed by a Christian conference and social evening. The prayers were led by Rev Mark Robson of Cumnock Congregational Church. The hall still had a debt of £200 when it was opened. The Christian Union also held services at the Runnels. In the 1920s there was another hall owned by the Ayrshire Christian Union at Lugar, used for meetings and social events.

The Christian Brethren, too, had increased in number and had built their own premises in Park Road. In the late 1890s a special meeting had been called at which it was determined to erect a hall of their own. Built of brick, the hall has gothic windows and stone quoins. It was first used for a prayer meeting on the day of Queen Victoria's funeral (1 January 1901) but the official opening was not until March 1901. Each family who belonged to the brethren donated two chairs for use in the hall. In the years following, the membership began to drop as many brothers emigrated to America or South Africa, losing the Auchinleck congregation 70 members. John McCombe alone remained to run the group, and he rejuvenated the church. A Gospel campaign was run which attracted new members. James McCann, who was converted from Roman Catholicism, and Andrew Douglas founded the Bible Class which grew to be the second largest in Scotland with 450 children. A Tract Band was founded, which survived for 50 years, and Saturday evening Gospel Tea Meetings were run, attracting folk from all over the village and beyond, members or not. During the 1920s William Turner's Great Gospel Campaign attracted 70 new members.

With the clearance of miners' rows on the moor, the Ballochmyle assembly of Christian Brethren was closed in 1929. Another group of brethren appear to have met in a house at Birnieknowe in the 1920s. Most members transferred to Auchinleck.

6.14 Our Lady & St Patrick's Chapel, Birnieknowe (interior) *(Author's Collection)*

Other locations were used for holding church services. During the 1920s, fortnightly Sunday services were held in Glenmuir School by Rev Hugh MacKinven Agnew MA of Cumnock's West United Free Church, and Rev James Wallace of Lugar Parish Church.

EDUCATION

At the start of the new century the headmaster at Auchinleck school was James Henderson FEIS. The Chairman of the School Board was still Rev James Hill BD. The increasing population meant that the School Board had to yet again consider building an extension to the parish school in Auchinleck. However, in 1903 it was decided to erect a separate building in which the infants would be taught. Robert S. Ingram prepared the plans and when it was found that stone for the outer walls was not obtainable locally, red sandstone was brought from Gatelawbridge Quarries near Thornhill. Cost of construction and contractors were:

Mason Work	George Reid, Catrine	£1,283 4s 9d
Joiner Work	Mr Cook, Catrine	£455 16s 5d
Plumbing & Slating	Hugh Morrison, Cumnock	£391 10s 0d
Plasterwork	Meikle, Catrine	£59 19s 4d

The total cost of construction worked out at £2,611 0s 11d.

In 1903 the board awarded their teachers a rise in wages, James Henderson (Auchinleck), up £15 to £200 per annum, William Tweedie (Darnconner) and

6.15 Public School – building erected in 1903 *(Dane Love)*

6.16 Public School – new building in School Road *(Dane Love)*

William Hume (Lugar) up £10 to £195. There were then four other teachers at Auchinleck, two others at Lugar, four at Darnconner and two at Cronberry. In 1905 238 pupils attended Darnconner, 231 at Lugar and 141 at Cronberry.

Again in 1908 a new laundry and cookery department was added to the school at Auchinleck, designed by Ingram & Brown. These were opened in October 1911. Plans were drawn up again by Ingram in 1914 for a further extension.

The school at Darnconner was leased from Bairds, but by the turn of the century it was deemed unsuitable for educational purposes, and if it was not brought up to standard then Scotch Education department grants would be withheld. Accordingly, in 1904 it was resolved to have a replacement erected, capable of holding 300 pupils. James Hay, architect, of Kilmarnock, drew up plans for a new building, built at the southern end of Common Row, a more central location to cover Darnconner, Common and Commondyke villages. The first sod was cut in the spring of 1905. The mason and plumbing work was carried out by Messrs Melville & MacPherson of Newmilns; the joinery work by Cook of Catrine; H. & T. Morrison of Cumnock did the slating, and M. Taylor of Cumnock the plasterwork. Opened on Monday 15 March 1906 by Robert Angus, the new school had cost £3,934 16s 1d to build. A gold key was gifted to Mrs Angus by Mr Hay and a banquet was held in one of the classrooms. The new school building was erected with terracotta bricks, with dressed stone at the doors, windows and gable tops. The roof comprised green slate. The main entrance was located at the west end of the building, reaching a lobby that ran through the centre of the building. There were seven classrooms, each with 'Boyle's patent air pump ventilators'.

The school board instructed the headmaster at Darnconner that no pupils residing in Sorn parish should be admitted to the new school when it opened in 1906. Prior to the school's erection the board had been in contact with the Sorn parish board to discuss the possibilities of a joint school, but the Sorn board turned this down and refused to offer Auchinleck board any money in respect of its residents educated at Darnconner. When no Sorn pupils were allowed into the new school the board at Sorn quickly contacted the Auchinleck board and agreed to grant some funds to assist in the running of Darnconner School. Most of the Sorn parish pupils resided at Burnside Row, just 1,500 yards from the school. The roll at Darnconner in 1917 was 195.

William Tweedie retired as headmaster in July 1919 after over 50 years of service. Tweedie himself lived until 4 November 1926 when he died aged 74. He was buried in Auchinleck. At Darnconner he was followed by Mr W. Rattray (1919-1926), after which the school was closed.

The School Board granted the use of the parish schools to various groups and individuals for holding concerts, meetings, weddings, etc. In 1905 Ballochmyle Band held concerts and social dances at Darnconner School, and Common Thistle Football Club used it for a supper ball. In 1907 Auchinleck Ramblers' Society (founded in June 1903, the first president being John Henderson), used the village school once a month for lectures in winter. Auchinleck School in April 1906 suffered a minor fire when one of the ventilators was set ablaze by a spark from the chimney. In 1910 the school was extended (by Robert S. Ingram and D. M. Brown), when new manual, cookery and laundry classrooms were erected. Further classroom accommodation was proposed in 1913 and despite getting Ingram to provide plans these were never executed. Instead, in 1914 A. C. Thomson (d. 1925), architect, of Ayr, provided new plans for a separate building, capable of holding 300 pupils, extendable to hold 500. A site on the opposite side of Main Street was acquired, and work commenced on the building. It opened in January 1918, having cost £6,431 9s 6½d to build, and the new access road linking Sorn and Well roads was named School Road. At the time Auchinleck School had 676 pupils. On 27 September 1909 William MacMechan, spirit salesman, Coal Road, assaulted the parish school mistress in Main Street. He claimed that the teacher had wrongly chastised his son. The headmaster, John Henderson, died on 25 July 1914 at the age of 63 and was replaced by James Guthrie.

6.17 Darnconner School, 1906 *(Author's Collection)*

William Hume continued as headmaster at Lugar School until 1910. From the school log book we find that on the 'Glorious Twelfth' of August each year many pupils avoided the school in order to earn money beating the moors. Fourteen were absent in 1903. Three teachers, including Mr Hume, ran the school that year, one teacher in charge of the infants, another, assisted by two pupil teachers, was in charge of Standards ll and lll, the upper school under the headmaster. In April 1903 the large room was subdivided into two rooms. The roll of 310 in 1908 was taught in four classrooms by five teachers. The infants' mistress taught 83 pupils, the middle school of 77 by another teacher, the upper school of 92 pupils by the headmaster and another. A number of pupils travelled to Auchinleck by train for cookery or woodwork on certain days. The school was extended between 1908 and 1910, the plans drawn up by Ingram and Brown.

In 1910 James Guthrie (died 1934) became the headmaster at Lugar and the new subject of crayon-work was introduced. He moved on to Auchinleck on 31 August 1914, being replaced by William McCree. War Savings commenced in 1917 and on 12 March 1918 a half-holiday was awarded because £500 had been brought in by the pupils. Later that year 'war flu' struck, leaving only one teacher, Mrs Agnes Smith, still working, teaching 84 of the 256 roll. The clerk to the school board gave notice that the school should be closed for two weeks. When it reopened only 53% of pupils were fit to return. The School War Savings Association ended on 30 June 1919, Lugar having collected a total of £1,074 4s 10d. The funding grant for the year ending 31 October 1918 was as follows:

Art. 19B1	49 @ 18/-	Under 7	44 2 0
	83 @ 20/-	Between 7 + 10	83 0 0
	79 @ 22/-	Over 10	86 18 0
Art. 19B4	83 @ 1/6	Between 7 + 10	6 4 6
	79 @ 1/9	Over 10	6 18 3
Art. 21	11 @ 50/-		27 10 0
Art. 21(b)	8.88 @ 8/4		3 14 0
			£258 6 9

6.18 Darnconner School – class photograph *(Author's Collection)*

At Glenmuir School a new appointment was Miss Stuart who in 1905 taught 14 pupils. A number of these came from Old Cumnock parish and grants of a few pounds were obtained from the school board there in respect of these pupils. However, with a falling roll it was decided to close the school on 21 July 1916. This seems to have been altered, for a new teacher, Dr Third, served until his retiral around 1926. The school remained closed thereafter. The building was later converted to a private house, but around 2005 it was demolished as part of the Laigh Glenmuir open cast coal mine.

The fall in roll was aided by the creation of a new school at Dalblair, located in the harness room of Dalblair Lodge. Opened on 1 May 1911, Miss Ellen (or Helen, known as Nellie) Campbell was appointed teacher on a salary of 25 shillings per week. Dalblair was a 'side school', that is it was attached to another school. At first its parent school was Glenmuir, but latterly was attached to Cronberry School. In 1929 the school had a roll of 21 pupils, the classroom only capable of holding ten. It measured fifteen feet by fourteen feet, the ceiling seven feet three inches high. Due to the overcrowded nature of the school, it was proposed that the Glenmuir School should reopen.

After the war Miss Campbell continued to teach at Dalblair, moving from the old lodge to a newly-erected school in 1937. In 1931 the school roll was 19. Plans for a new school had been proposed in March 1931 and in November that year were passed. The county architect, William Reid, was responsible for the design, and the building cost £1,280 to erect. To assist pupils travelling to the school from Dornal, Whiteholm and Springhill, a bridge was erected across the Glenmuir Water to Nether Guelt in 1934 by the Ayrshire Education Committee at a cost of £45. In May 1932 the pony and trap which was used by the children resident at Glenmuirshaw to travel to Dalblair School was sold by the county council to Jacob Murray of Dalgig (tenant of Dalblair) for £18.

The children in the upper Glenmuir area went without a teacher for a time, and the Threeshire District scheme collapsed. In the new century the pupils from Auchinleck parish who could not reach the Glenmuir or Dalblair schools attended the school at Fingland, in Kirkconnel parish, to which school board the Auchinleck board granted a fee.

At Cronberry School the headmaster, James Hyslop, died on 25 June 1907 at the age of 56, having served as headmaster for 32 years. He was buried in Cumnock New Cemetery. He was replaced in August that year by James Guthrie, of New Cumnock, who in 1910 was replaced by William McCree on a salary of £160 per annum, plus free house. In 1914 he was succeeded by William MacIntyre (died October 1937) and in 1918 by W. Rattray. The roll in 1917 was 117 pupils.

On 16 May 1919 the new Ayrshire Education Authority took over the running of the county's schools from the parish school boards. At this time the parish had four schools, the headmasters of which were James Guthrie (Auchinleck), William McCree (Lugar), William Tweedie (Darnconner) and W. Rattray (Cronberry).

James Guthrie remained at Auchinleck until December 1932, when he retired to Largs. He was replaced by John Mearns Allan, who had been educated at Aberdeen University, and the Aberdeen Church of Scotland Training College. Prior to arriving at Auchinleck in January 1933 he had been headmaster at Skelmorlie for twelve years. In 1929 the County Council Education Committee assumed responsibility for the schools, continuing to do so until regionalisation. In 1929 they decided to erect a new two-room school, for the educating of special pupils, adjacent to the school in Auchinleck. The cost of construction of this was around £4,000.

At Lugar Public School work got back to normal after the war, though there were still problems with attendance. The woodwork classes at Auchinleck ended in July 1919, resuming in January 1920, 'but boys did not go as they complained of sore feet'. In October 1920 they had to walk back to Lugar due to a strike on the railways.

On 29 October 1919 the school was closed at 12:00 noon as it was Cumnock Fair. Mr Crosbie, of the Band of Hope Union, gave annual lectures on 'Alcohol – its effect upon the body'. On 28 April 1921 it was noted that 'Feeding of children began today. 126 children fed in school today at mid-day. 30th April – Feeding of children in school stopped today. Hereafter children are to be fed from Communal Kitchens. Total number of meals served in school, 388'. The depression and strikes of the time affected attendance. When the officer visited some homes he was given 'lack of food', 'want of clothing', or 'no boots' as excuses for absence. 'Feeding of necessitous school children began on Saturday 29th May [1926]'.

His Majesty's Inspectorate report of 1928 did not give a particularly good write-up: 'The standard reached by the [qualifying] class as a whole falls far short of the average ... the attempt to teach simultaneously two systems of writing should be abandoned ... Senior 3, while still backward in some subjects, particularly in spelling, the pupils have responded to the sound instruction they have received.... Senior 1 did not make a creditable appearance in the main subjects ... [Senior 2] was found to be very weak in Mathematics while poetry was imperfectly memorised and inadequately reported'. In 1931 the headmaster 'issued a warning note to H. Skinner anent clothing of daughters Caroline & Rose'.

The 1933 Inspectorate report showed a slight improvement 'The infant department is in a healthy condition ... the junior division is in important respects unsatisfactory as regards both organisation & work ... Advanced Division, the pupils are inclined to be inattentive & restless: a much stricter control is absolutely necessary if satisfactory work is to be done in this division'. Science lessons were taught to some pupils in Cumnock School, and girls went to Cronberry for laundry lessons. William McCree retired on 27 August 1934, to be followed by George S.

Strachan who remained headmaster until August 1942 when he was replaced by John B. Strachan.

The Inspectorate report of 1937 gives an indication of the building: 'The premises are far from satisfactory. The classrooms vary greatly in size; two of them are very large, four are very small. Most are divided by wood and glass partitions by no means soundproof.... The upper infant classroom and the advanced division classroom are very draughty. In the upper infant classroom the roof leaks and in the adjacent cloak room escaping steam sometimes makes the children's clothes damp.' Later that year, due to a fault in the heating, the temperature of some rooms was just 38 degrees Fahrenheit.

With the outbreak of war the school was closed for a week, and soon air raid drill was practised. In April 1941 the first evacuees arrived at the school, 51 in number, accompanied by two teachers from Gorbals Public School. By 1942 the number of evacuees had fallen to six, with 196 local pupils. School meals began in 1942, and a monthly gas-mask inspection took place. In 1943 it was noted, '100 pairs of rubber shoes, for physical exercises, have been supplied by the authority - none being now available in shops'. With Victory in Europe, the two days' holiday was followed by a service of thanksgiving in the playground. For a short time a school operated at Rosebank.

At Cronberry the Ayrshire Education Authority felt that the old school was insufficiently large and unsuitable for the pupils and with the possibility of further growth in the area decided to erect a new school in 1931. A far superior and larger building, designed by William Reid, Ayr County Council architect, the new school was located outwith the village, by the side of the Muirkirk Road, near to the station. In 1939 the first school sports were held at Mortonmuir Park.

St Patrick's R. C. Primary School, under the sisters of the Cross and Passion, continued to give a good all-round education, and George Loy became a priest and Justice of the Peace in Glasgow, Peter Carroll a Monsignor in Canada. The school building was altered and improved, re-opening in September 1902. Mother Malachy was the headmistress in 1918, assisted by Sisters Patricia, Dominic and Euphrasia.

INDUSTRY – COALMINES

In 1900 William Baird sank a second pit on the farm of Berryhill, called Berryhill No. 2. The shaft was 372 feet deep, but the main seam worked was ell coal (almost four feet thick) located 45 feet below the surface. Some ironstone was also mined. Berryhill No. 3 was sunk the year following, a far deeper pit, with a shaft 1,041 feet deep. As with most of Baird's mines, one manager, in this case Thomas MacCulloch, oversaw more than one pit. There were 167 underground workers at Berryhill No. 2, with nineteen surface workers. At No. 3 there were 32 on the surface, 124 below. Pit No. 2 worked both ironstone and coal until 1914, No. 3 ironstone only from 1908. By 1918 Berryhill No. 1 pit was managed by Robert Bowie, with Hugh Biggans as under-manager. There were 74 miners in the pit at that time, with 11 working on the surface. At Berryhill No. 3 George MacMurdo was the manager, with William MacIlwraith as under-manager. There were 114 men working below ground and 42 on the surface. Both mines were closed in 1925.

At Berryhill No. 2 an explosion struck on 20 October 1909. The pit, which was managed by Robert Bowie, was 61 fathoms (366 feet) deep, the main road in the dook section being 300 fathoms long. Four men, John Anderson (aged 29), Robert Anderson (aged 29), Hugh Ralston or Black (aged 39) and James Currie (aged 32), were killed and two were seriously injured (Robert MacLeish and James Graham). The fatalities were fortunately small, for over 70 men were in the pit at the time, and most escaped with minor burns and bruises. The accident occurred at a spot known as 'The Dook', a portion of the pit which dipped from the bottom of the shaft. Sixteen men were employed at this point. Just after mid-day a loud cracking noise was heard and a portion of the roof began to settle. As men began to prop it up it was discovered that noxious gases were in the area. Whilst the men rushed from the spot an explosion occurred, bringing down a large part of the roof. Robert Anderson was killed in the initial explosion and his brother John 'lost his life in the heroic effort to save his brother,' according to the gravestone that marks where they were buried in the kirkyard.

Currie and Robert Anderson were buried in the fall; Black was overcome by gas and though alive when reached by the rescuers, died within a few minutes. John Anderson was found with terrible burns and it was later discovered that he had escaped the first explosion, only to find that his brother was still below. He had returned to try to help him, but was overcome by the 'afterdamp' and died. Many volunteers arrived at the pit to try to help. Doctors Stuart and Bowie went below, but found it too late to help the four. Robert Bowie and the under-manager, Hugh Biggans, organised the removal of the injured from the pit, which was cleared by 3 o'clock. Currie and Black were both natives of Hurlford, where their wives and families lived, but both were resident in digs in Auchinleck at the time. Black was also known as Hugh Ralston, and was noted as Talbot's first trainer. He was 39 when he died. A large turnout attended the funerals on 23 October, Rev James Hill conducting three services, Father Meagher that of Currie. All were buried in the parish kirkyard.

Other deaths occurring at Berryhill pits included James MacCreadie, killed in No. 2 pit on 13 September 1912, aged 16. In Berryhill No. 3 pit Charles MacAuslan was killed on 21 December 1904. He was 47 years old and was crushed by a fall of stone.

Barglachan, Berryhill and Common collieries were managed by one manager. Mr Wilson left in 1904 to manage a pit at Sanquhar. A presentation was made to him in Auchinleck Lesser Town Hall. Thomas Ritchie followed (until 1909), then

James Miller, who held the post from 1910 until 1916. He was followed by Robert Bowie. The manager lived at Common Cottage.

In 1918 Barglachan No. 2 mine had 89 working below ground, with a further 18 on the surface. In December 1904 James Baillie, of Brick Row, Lugar, was charged under the Mining Regulations Act of failing to put up sufficient supporting timber in the long-wall workings of the Maid Coal seam in Barglachan No. 2 Pit. On 28 December 1910 Alexander Fraser (aged 37) was killed by a fall of stone from the roof. Archie Rankin was killed when a stone fell from the roof on 6 November 1914. He was 27 years old. On 12 March 1924 John Toal (aged 17) was killed by a fall of stone. Accidents at the pit often resulted in serious injury, among these being Andrew Stillie, of Townhead Street, Cumnock (1904) and Adam Davidson (6 December 1915), both of whom were injured by a fall of stone from the roof.

In the same pit there was a serious fire on 7 January 1917. The blaze occurred at the pit-head, destroying the supports of the winding wheel. Previously, on 2 December 1909, explosives at the pit were accidentally lit, injuring John MacCrone and John Bryce. On 7 November 1921 the night-shift stopped work and 150 workers were laid off. They were offered jobs if they wanted at the Barony Colliery. Barglachan Colliery was run down considerably thereafter, being closed in 1924.

In 1906 William Baird & Company began work on a new colliery to the west of Auchinleck on the farm of Oldbyres. Here two shafts were sunk and the Barony Colliery was born. By 1912 both shafts were completed and the first coal came to the surface. A rail siding was laid from the Barony Junction, on Knagshill Moss, alongside a shelter-belt of trees and into the pit complex, located south of Barony Road. A large bing was formed south of the pit, eventually extending to cover most of Balance Holm. The coal was worked by longwall advancing, and transported out by 11 hundredweight capacity tubs on an endless rope, driven by steam winding engines. The first manager was Thomas MacCulloch and 871 men were employed below ground, 203 above. MacCulloch was general manager of Barony, Highhouse, Whitehill and Cronberry Moor pits and died on 16 March 1930 aged 63. From 1916-18 the manager was James Miller, who had moved from Barglachan pit, the under-manager being William Wightman. At that time there were 334 men working below ground, with a further 107 on the surface. Hugh Murray became manager from 1928, at which time a new cottage for him was erected near the Runnels on Barony Road.

There were a number of mining tragedies at the Barony pit over the years. The list of men killed includes the following:

> John Boyd, 1909.
> Jan Baptiste Van der Auwera, 1 April 1916, aged 30. Killed by fall of stone.

Tom Parker, 25 May 1916 aged 26.
John Hazlett, Ochiltree, died 13 June 1919, aged 53, by a fall from the roof.
Francis Korskie, killed 6 November 1925 aged 38. A Pole, living in Beechwood Square.
James MacMurdo, died 1925 aged 44.
Henry Stevenson, Commonloch, 20 April 1927 aged 33, fall of stone in Barony No. 2.
James Blair, 28 June 1927, Mauchline.
Anton Greenshields, 29 November 1927, aged 49. Lithuanian.
Andrew Devlin, 14 October 1930, aged 32.
John Graham, 16 July 1936. Killed by fall of stone from roof.
Robert Wilson (18), killed 4 September 1936 when he was squashed by loaded hutches.
William Roy Colvin (64), 1940, killed by iron pipe.

6.19 Highhouse Colliery *(Author's Collection)*

In March and April 1912 there was a national miners' strike which lasted for five weeks. The cost of living had shot up but pit wages had failed to keep up with it. The miners wanted a minimum national wage, but the pit owners insisted that payment should vary according to production. The strike was not adhered to by the miners at Kirkconnel, so on 21 March the miners from Old and New Cumnock joined those from Auchinleck to take part in picketing there. At the Nith Bridge on the west side of Kirkconnel a large company of policemen were drawn up and a small affray took place. The police were more successful, and a number of arrests ensued.

In 1931 Baird amalgamated with the Dalmellington Iron Company to form Bairds and Dalmellington Ltd and began improvements at many of their works. The pithead baths were opened in 1932. In 1938 a reorganisation scheme was started at Barony, intended to increase output, improve ventilation, and raise the standard of coal produced. New electric winding gear was installed and work commenced on the sinking of a new No. 3 shaft. The outbreak of war brought work to a standstill, but it was resumed when peace returned. In 1940 a miner at Barony earned around £1 13s 1d per week for six shifts with four pence deducted to pay for the pit doctor.

Mining continued to a considerable degree at Highhouse Pit in the new century. In 1918 the manager was James Miller, and Robert Gray was the under manager. He was to become one of the pit's many fatalities, being killed by a fall of stone from the roof on 20 December 1918. He was 27 years of age. At the same time Arthur Scoular (51) was killed by the stone-fall. In 1918 there were 287 men employed in the seams below ground, and a further 67 worked on the surface.

At Highhouse pit a serious fire broke out in the engine-house on Wednesday evening, 22 July 1908, greatly affecting production. Eighty-four men were employed in the pit at the time, of which sixty had to spend the night underground. Luckily the men could be released up the second shaft, but by the time the last men were rescued the cage was so hot that they couldn't touch it. A kettle was lowered with a couple of men in it, and on each return three or four men were brought back up from the pit bottom. It took many hours to rescue all of those trapped below ground. Reports on the surface damage stated that there were six steam engines and some railway plant destroyed, in addition to much of the plant at the top of No. 1 shaft. The first forty miners were rescued up No. 2 shaft, using the standard haulage machinery, but as the fire spread it became impossible to use this.

Prior to the fire the mine employed over 500 men, producing approximately 800-900 tons of coal each day. Production resumed, and in 1910 the pit had 514 miners working in the seams plus 80 surface workers. This figure remained fairly static thereafter. Highhouse produced coal from a particular seam which had so few impurities that when it was burned it produced little ash. This coal was known as 'Highhouse Jewel'. In 1935 the manager was Herbert Lorimer and 500 men worked in the pit. New baths were erected just prior to the Second World War.

Accidents of varying degrees of severity happened on a regular basis in Highhouse pit. David MacClymont was killed by a fall of stone from the roof on 22 March 1911 in Number 2 pit. On 8 August 1935 two men were killed in Highhouse Pit by gas, Stewart Strachan (46) of 12 Riverside Terrace, Cronberry, and Peter MacCartney (34) of 258 Cronberry Rows. Strachan went into an old run, which he had been instructed to brush the previous day, to fetch a heavy hammer, but did not return. After a time MacCartney went to look for him and he too suffered intoxication from fire-damp. Various miners tried to reach the men, George Bryan tying a cable round himself, but he too was overcome and had to be pulled back. Jack Johnstone, underground oversman, found Strachan lying on the ground and he tried to drag his body out but was overcome by the gas. Doctors MacQueen and Campbell of Cumnock and MacClure of Auchinleck were quickly on site, but despite applying artificial respiration for a long time, could not revive the two miners. Johnston was taken to Ayr County Hospital. Over one thousand miners attended the joint funeral. MacCartney, William Guthrie, William Cooper, Johnston, Bryan and Herbert Lorimer (manager) were later rewarded by the Carnegie Hero Fund Trust.

Later the same year another man was killed in the pit. James Latta, 54 Barrhill Road, Cumnock, was working in the slope dook section of Highhouse No. 1 on 11 October. A load of hutches were ready to be hauled out. A miner warned Latta not to ride on them, as the roof was low, but he defied this and journeyed on the fourth hutch. The hutches stopped at one point, and Latta's body was found trapped in the four inch gap between the waggon and the roof. He had started in the pit just two days previously, the same day a farm-hand was killed on Highhouse Bing.

Other deaths in the mine included James Duncan, aged 22, killed 11 December 1902 from a fall of stone. Robert Miller, aged 20, died on 22 June 1906 from a roof collapse. The same cause of death saw the loss of John Fraser on 22 June 1906. Robert Devine was killed in 1907 as a result of an accident. A fall of stone from the roof killed Robert Currie Hazlett on 14 May 1912, aged 16. A similar fate befell Robert MacMillan, killed on 28 March 1917 at the age of 45. Robert Murphy died in January 1918, the result of another fall of stone. John Crawford was killed on 14 January 1918, aged 58 and Robert Gilmour died on 19 March 1919. George Affleck was killed on 17 March 1921 by a fall from the roof. He was aged 22. James Lindsay was killed on 18 November 1924, aged 60. William Carey, aged 41, was killed in February 1929 by fall from the roof. Robert Scott, from Lugar, was killed on 29 August 1935, at the age of 63. Peter MacAloon was killed by a fall from the roof of the pit in 1940, aged 31.

Allan Mair (17), 28 Riverside Terrace, Cronberry, worked at Back Rogerton farm and had been sent to Highhouse bing for ashes with which to mend the farm-road. Later in the day a runaway horse was seen, and on investigation an upturned cart was found at the bing. Mair's jacket was found, so men began digging the ashes away and found the horseman's body. It was suspected that the ashes had been undermined, and heavy rain loosened them, causing them to fall without warning. Mair was buried in the parish kirkyard.

Alexander Orr MacCulloch (67), of 24 Highhouse Rows, was employed in Highhouse pit as a repairer. At quarter past midnight on Christmas day 1935 a three ton block of stone fell from the seven-foot high roof, killing him instantly. He and

Hugh Wallace had been brushing the run. The colliery remained idle all day thereafter.

The Common Pits went into decline and were being gradually closed. Common numbers 16 and 16½ were managed by M. MacCormick in 1915. In 1918 Common Nos. 15, 16 and 16½ were managed by George MacMurdo, with James Lorimer as underground manager. At the time the three pits employed 177 men below ground, plus a further 57 on the ground. The mine at Carbello was closed in 1906. The Common collieries were finally abandoned in 1925 when William Baird & Co. pulled out. At the time No. 16 was still working. As with other pits, there had been a number of fatalities. At Common No. 15 James Steel, aged 17, was killed from fall of stone from the roof in 1904. In Common No. 16 Joseph Richmond was killed in an accident on 19 January 1909 and William MacTurk suffered death in May 1916. At pit Number 16½ David Torrance, of Cronberry, was killed on 4 August 1916 aged 42.

A new mine was sunk at Cronberry Moor in 1922 by William Baird & Co. Ltd. The shaft, which was 45 fathoms in depth, was built of concrete and corrugated iron sheets, instead of timber, as a fire precaution. Hugh Murray was appointed as the first manager in 1923, remaining there for five years. In the pit James Mair, of Gasswater, was killed on 2 February 1924, aged 48, by a fall from the roof. John Fleming was killed on 20 June 1938, aged 43. Employed as a shot-firer, it is thought that a spark from the fire ignited his clothing, causing serious burns. Another fatality was John Kelly, killed when he was trapped between a derailed hutch and the wall of the pit.

6.20 Mines Rescue Station in 1990 *(Dane Love)*

The Lugar Mine, located at the top of the Peesweep Brae, was established in 1942 by Bairds & Dalmellington Ltd. Two drifts were sunk into the hillside, the main mine at a slope of one in five, the return mine being at a slope of one in three.

In 1913 a Mines Rescue Station was erected in the lower part of the Main Street, operated by the Ayrshire Coalowners' Association. The Rescue Station Attendant and Instructor at first was David Hunter, followed by Jonathan Telfer who remained for many years. The station proved to be most effective at times of accident and death in the mines, which was all too frequent. Death in the mines was accepted as part of the risk of the job, but it still sent shockwaves through the district when fatalities occurred. The Mines Rescue Station survived until well after the war when it was moved to the rebuilt Barony Pit.

LUGAR IRONWORKS

In February 1921 Lugar Ironworks were shut down and remained closed for twenty months. The furnaces were not to be rekindled until October 1922. By this time new turbines replaced the old beam blast machinery, making the three furnaces more efficient. The furnaces were closed in February 1925 and 70 men were laid off. The furnaces numbered 1, 3 and 4 were relit in March 1926 but shut down again in May. They were relit again in December 1926.

The Lugar Ironworks did not survive long after the General Strike. It was also proving to be unprofitable to bring the ore from Spain for conversion, the local ironstone having been long worked out. The furnaces were closed down in November 1928 and many of the former employees found new jobs in the coal-mines.

A number of fatalities occurred at the ironworks. On 6 April 1910 Alexander MacDonald was accidentally killed there, at the age of 36 years. He was buried in Auchinleck cemetery.

Though the miners' rows are often remembered with fond recollection, life in them was hard. The miners were tied to their mine managers, and to lose their place of employment would leave them homeless. In 1912 miners all over Scotland went on strike to try to win a minimum national wage for themselves. After six weeks they returned to work. Miners' wages in 1913 were around seven shillings per day. A longer strike took place in 1921, the miners remaining out of work for three months. With no money coming into the house the miners spent their idle hours trying to earn some cash or payment in kind by working on the farms, though the high number of miners meant that only a few found such work. Many men had to resort to poaching in order to feed their families, and in each mining community communal kitchens were set up where wives and children could get a bowl of soup. In Auchinleck the soup kitchen was in the wash-house of the Railway Inn. In Lugar the Works' Unemployed Distress Fund held concerts in the institute. The railway from Lugar Works past Cronberry No. 1 Pit to Lauchensknoll (Laurence Knowe) was laid at this time to employ men laid off at the ironworks.

Many families and individuals left the parish and emigrated to America. A number of miners latterly wished to return to work, but found that the mine-owners were not going to allow them back. Only when they had agreed to accept the owners' new wages and conditions were the pits again opened. The long strike had actually resulted in poorer conditions for the miners.

In May 1926 the miners went on strike again, this time for seven months, the whole country joining in the 'General Strike'. The mine-owners would not give in to the strikers' demands; indeed they brought workers from abroad to keep the pits open and furnaces at Lugar in operation. Baird, importing its iron-ore from Spain, decided to bring a number of Spaniards to Lugar to operate the blast furnaces. Many Irish crossed the North Channel, willing to work as strike-breakers, and earn some much-needed cash for themselves. From Poland came men willing to work in the mines. Thus many of the local families with Spanish, Irish or Polish origin names can trace their arrival in Auchinleck parish to this time. From the records of the period we find Polish surnames like Kalvities, Luskes, Gustis, Nikanoff, Swadzer and Catules living at Ballochmyle Rows, and Spanish names like Gongalez, Lognez, Fernandez, Carballo and Blanco in Lugar. In Auchinleck there were so many Poles living in Beechwood Square (offered for sale in 1925 but demolished in 1933) that it was nicknamed 'Pole Square'. At Highhouse Rows lived the Asbraitis, Burinski, Kuberski, Yancouski and other families. The arrival of these foreigners naturally caused much trouble in the parish and in 1926 one woman in Auchinleck was arrested for throwing stones at them as they went to work.

When the miners agreed to return to work with no increase in pay, most of the Poles and Spaniards returned home, though some remained in the parish, becoming absorbed in the community. Some changed their names to Scots equivalents, other proudly retaining their national surnames.

BARYTES MINES
Mining of a different sort commenced up Glen Gass at the end of the Great War. Four main veins of Barium Sulphate (Barytes) had been noted in the parent sandstone as early as 1870, running in a line from west-north-west to east-south-east on the lower slopes of Wardlaw Hill. Barytes, known also as 'heavy spar', was in demand as a filler in the paint and paper industries, as well as in ceramics and glass-making. It is a dense quartz-like mineral, varying in colour from pure white (high quality) to a light salmon-pink colour. With the advent of war, Britain could not afford to import barytes and so sources at home were exploited.

The Hedworth Barium Company Ltd began development work and mining at their Gasswater Mine in 1917, extracting the mineral both by open cast and by forming an adit level 81 feet below the shaft collar height of 1,054.73 feet above sea level. This mine lasted only until 1921 by which time 7,976 tons of barium sulphate had been removed. A second company, the Wrentnall Baryta Company Ltd, resumed mining operations in 1923, installing new electrical plant for treating barytes. In September 1923 F. Floyd was appointed as manager. In 1924 twelve new four-apartment houses plus one double storey five-apartment house was built at Gasswater for the employees.

Wrentnall excavated in the region of 300,000 tons of barytes during their 24 years of ownership, at which time it was the United Kingdom's largest producer. In 1942 there were 42 men employed in the barytes mines, some of whom were housed in the eight 'Wrentnall Cottages' and one wooden house at Gasswater village. The pit manager lived at Wrentnall House, 10 Barrhill Terrace, Cumnock, and latterly at 31 Auchinleck Road. The house in Barrhill Terrace was erected in 1924 at a cost of around £750. In addition to the Gasswater mine, Wrentnall developed three associated mines, all operated as one unit, the Central, South and Burnside pits, the latter, furthest east, sunk in 1931. It proved to be unproductive, but was redeveloped in May 1956. Wrentnall Baryta continued the work until 1947 when it was taken over by Anglo-Austral Mines Ltd.

At the sawmill, Adam Wilson & Sons became a limited company following the death of William, the shareholders being Adam, John, James, Gilbert and William Wilson, John Ferguson and Alex Mitchell. The company headquarters was moved to the Troon harbour sawmill in August 1919. The main customers for the Auchinleck plant were the various mines and local ironworks. An order from Lugar Ironworks dated 12 June 1925 gives an example of the scale:

Peeled larch	4" - 10' to 18' average length	7,500 pieces
	5" - 10' to 12' average length	13,000
	5" - 8' to 10' average length	45,000
	5" - 18' to 20' average length	7,500
	5" - 20' to 24' average length	11,000
Slabbed crowns	10' x 5" x 2½"	320,000
Sleepers	3'3" x 5" x 2½"	12,500

However things took a downwards turn in 1926 with the General Strike, demand for timber for mines and ironworks dropping to virtually nothing. Wilsons stockpiled for a time, but soon realised that the strike would not be over in a few weeks. They tried to let a work-shop at Auchinleck sawmill but found no takers. At length the sawmill closed in 1928. The firm, however, survives to this day, still trading as Adam Wilson & Sons Ltd. from the sawmill at Troon. The family connection was severed in 2008 when the Wilsons sold the company to Irish-based Glennon Brothers.

The manufacture of soft-drinks in Auchinleck was established by John Davies of Kilmarnock, but the plant was taken over by James Smith by 1910. The factory, at Orchard Road, was known as Smith's Brewery, though it had never made any alcoholic drinks. Early bottles produced at the works had 'J. Smith & Son' moulded on them, the stopper made of ceramic pottery, with rubber seal, held on by a wire. In 1928 Smith's was taken over by the MacMichael brothers, George, James and Robert. They belonged to New Cumnock and had bought over the Currie's Lemonade Company of Patna in 1926. This Patna plant was closed, but the Currie's name was retained at Auchinleck. The MacMichaels built up the business over the years, distributing lemonade throughout the district. Door to door sales commenced, and shops and pits were supplied. When war broke out the lorries were commandeered by the government. The soft-drinks industry was zoned, and Currie's was allocated Cumnock and district. Sugar was rationed, and experiments were made with syrup and other sweeteners.

The Gas Works were still managed by John Devine at the turn of the century. He retired in 1903, after fifteen years' service, and died on 14 December 1903, aged 64. He was replaced by his son, Hugh Devine, who remained for fifteen years, moving on to Lasswade & Bonnybridge Gas Company in 1918. He was replaced by James Beresford, who had previously worked at the gasworks at Ochiltree and Lochgilphead.

The co-operative society established a number of small businesses in the village. On 11 July 1917 a new shirt factory was opened by the Co-op in Auchinleck. Located at the Toll premises, 36 sewing machines were installed, employing 40 people, making shirts for the Scottish Co-operative Wholesale Society, which had its main factory in Paisley. The basic shirt-making process was carried out at Auchinleck, the finishing work being completed at Paisley. By the end of the month 35 girls were employed at the factory, in one week producing 17 dozen shirts. A new factory was built in Well Road, nearly complete in March 1921, and opened on Monday 5 September 1921. It was anticipated that 500 workers would be employed, with room for 800 sewing machines, though when it opened only 192 were in place. The first manager was James Muir, brought from Paisley. Work in the factory was never great, and it was closed down in May 1923 due to a lack of demand for its produce. Over 80 workers were laid off.

In 1924 Messrs Gilmour & Company, hosiery manufacturers from Girvan, opened a small factory located in the hall of the Cross Keys (Commercial Inn). Several machines were installed for the manufacture of women's clothing and children's wear in wool and silk. The company planned to grow to have thirty machines in operation.

At the Kirkbrae Smiddy John Nicol took over from Hugh Boyle on 28 November 1918. At the Townfoot, Thomas Murdoch's joinery was taken over by James D. Judge in 1920.

COMMERCE

Auchinleck Co-operative Society Limited went from strength to strength in the new century. Following the closure of Ballochmyle Colliery in 1900, the former workman's store in Ballochmyle Row was converted into a branch. In 1901 the drapery shop in Main Street was bought for £750. Sales were £6,453 per quarter in 1902, the property and fixtures valued at £4,340. A slaughterhouse was built in 1905 and a new branch opened on the site of the toll cottage opposite Sorn Road in 1915, complete with a hall above. The toll cottage had been demolished in August 1905. The architect of the new shop was W. F. Valentine of Kilmarnock, who went on to design other buildings for the society. At Darnlaw the society's powder magazine, from where the miners bought their shot for blasting coal was later sold to Fleming and Company, Powder Merchants, of Glasgow.

6.21 Auchinleck Co-Operative Society Parade, 1932 *(Author's Collection)*

At the turn of the century there was a good variety of shops in the village, in addition to the Co-op. Andrew Hamilton and William Service were shoemakers, as was T. MacFadzean (1920s). Mary Smith was a shoe merchant. John Wyllie and David Hamilton had bakers' shops, as did D. R. Mitchell for a time at 185 Main Street, selling up to George Keenan in 1926. John Callan, John Auld, Andrew Paton and George MacEwen were fleshers, Callan leasing the Glebe for keeping cattle. Andrew Paton was a JP, eldest son of Baillie Paton JP of Galston. He came to Auchinleck after his marriage in 1872 and set up as a butcher, acquiring premises in Main Street. He was elected to the School Board in 1881, Parochial Board, and was instrumental in getting the path from Auchinleck to Cumnock laid. A staunch supporter of the Congregational Church in Cumnock, he died at Broomhill there in 1928 and was buried in Auchinleck. William Hamilton, James Nairn Gardiner,

John Templeton and John Wagstaff had grocers' shops; Adam Brown a barber's salon. Clothing could be purchased at James Wilson or John MacMillan's draperies, John Brown's hosiery or Robert Stuart's tailor's shop. Birrell & Co., drapers, closed in 1911, as did David Arthur, saddler. The Well Road Garage was operated by William Hamilton (1920s), selling Hercules bicycles.

William Osborne Kay (1849-1924) of Cumnock had a branch of his chemist's business in the village. In 1928 J. Mulholland MPS had a chemist's shop here, as did W. G. Gray MPS, located in the Medical Hall.

6.22 Auchinleck Post Office *(Author's Collection)*

The postmaster was David Crichton (1832-1924), who erected Crichtonlea in Mauchline Road. Crichton was born in Cumnock and in 1847 was apprenticed to Andrew Morton, baker, in Auchinleck Main Street. When Crichton was only nineteen years old, Morton emigrated, leaving him in charge. A few years later he built a bakery in Matthew MacTurk's property, then in 1867 bought John Templeton's bakery, where he remained until 1901. He was the postmaster for 54 years until 1921, latterly assisted by his daughter, Jane, or Jeannie. The business was offered for sale in 1921, when James Dalziel acquired it and was appointed as postmaster.

At Lugar post office the postmaster, William Murdoch, died in 1904. He was succeeded by his daughter, Miss Marion Murdoch, who retired in January 1925. Archibald Rankin then took over, running it until 1939 when David Reid became postmaster.

The post office at Darnconner was run by Mrs Annie Rae, postmistress, until 1911 when she retired. David Brown was postmaster until he died in November 1927.

Business at the Auchinleck Co-operative Society's shops boomed after the Great War, with sales four times the pre-war figures, at £40,000 per quarter. In 1919 there were 1,170 members of the society. Sales fell again in 1921 when the miners came out on strike, only £19,000 worth of sales occurring that year.

After the war a reconstruction programme followed, so that by 1925 matters had improved greatly and new buildings were again proposed. The grocery and bakery department was moved to a new building at 123-125 Main Street, opened on Christmas Eve 1926 by the president, William Kerr, the building of modern Art Deco design faced with dressed pink granite. The architect was again W. F. Valentine of Kilmarnock. A new co-op dairy and tearoom was established in 1926. At this time milk deliveries commenced, proving to be successful from the beginning. In 1929 the former central grocery was re-opened as a hardware and furnishing department. The miners' strike of 1926 affected the society once again, the Coal Department which was opened that April being closed down due to lack of supplies, only reopening in September. On 4 November 1926 a fire raged through the society's garage at the toll, destroying all the motor vans.

In 1927, following five months of negotiations, the Auchinleck Co-op Society took over the Old Cumnock Co-op Society, becoming joint in December. On 20 December 1928 the co-operative opened a new butchery branch in Cumnock. With increased trade the upper flat of the old central branch was changed into an office. The year following saw a peak in the society's sales, £137,000 per annum. A furnishings department was opened that year, but sales diminished during the years of depression, 1930-33.

On 20 January 1934 the new premises in Glaisnock Street, Cumnock, were opened, again the work of W. F. Valentine. At that time the society had a capital of £60,000, averaging at £25 per head of the 2,500 members. It had £5,000 of reserves and sales amounted to around 17s 9d per week per member, with a dividend of £16,000 distributed each year. In October 1936 a laundry was opened in Well Road, the buildings having been erected in 1920 as the Co-op shirt factory. The first laundry manager was John McCreadie. The laundry provided cleaning services for co-operative customers from across Ayrshire, Galloway and into the Borders. During the war the laundry cleaned bedding and uniforms of army personnel based at camps in south-west Scotland.

The Second World War did not overtly affect the Co-op's sales – there was another record year of sales amounting to £172,000 in 1939, but old-time business methods were scrapped. The additional labour required in dealing with the ration books introduced in 1940 added to the work of the staff. However, sales continued to rise, and the society celebrated its jubilee on 29 June 1940. At that time there were 3,081 members, many taking part in the procession of the society's horse and motor transport through the streets. The Scottish Co-operative Wholesale Society's band came to entertain, and tea was served in the Barony Church Hall for guests, department heads, SCWS representatives, delegates from neighbouring societies and members of NUDAW. James Morrison was presented with £100 for having spent fifty years employed in society business; his wife was given a three-stringed pearl necklace.

An unfortunate accident occurred on 23 October 1942. A horse-drawn van belonging to the Co-op was descending Main Street when the horse was frightened, by the sound of a train, as it passed beneath the railway bridge. The driver was thrown to the ground and the horse bolted. At the Co-op's central department the horse tried to take a sharp right into the yard, only to slip and fall and overturn its cart. The horse landed on top of an elderly woman, Mrs David Strachan, aged 76. Bystanders tried to lift the horse, but it required the help of an army van to shift it and the wagon. The woman was taken to hospital but died two days later.

The Clydesdale Bank opened up in new premises in Main Street on Monday 6 June 1917, the previous tenant being Thomas Couperthwaite. The Clydesdale Bank had for many years a branch in Auchinleck, located in Cowan Place, which buildings the bank purchased in November 1925. Between the wars it was joined by a branch of the Royal Bank of Scotland, located at 119 Main Street.

Lesser businesses continued to exist in the villages. Miss Macleod's newsagent and confectionery was sold by her in 1922 to Mrs Allan Reid. At the Cross, Dr Charles Stewart's chemist shop was taken over in 1920 by W. G. Gray. Dr Stewart and Dr W. Simpson dissolved their medical practice on 31 August 1928. John Watson, blacksmith, who opened up in Market Place in 1926.

The mill at Bello Mill continued to operate on a small scale into the twentieth century. The dam was washed away around 1940 and was subsequently rebuilt, but by this time the oatmeal mill had been removed and it was replaced by a hammer mill, solely used for grinding provender.

The inns continued to serve the public. There were five public houses willing to take your money. James Hope had the Commercial Inn and sold spirits in a shop. In 1925 the proprietor was Adam Ogg Brown.

Margaret Goldie owned the Eagle Inn. This was sold in 1910 to Mrs Burnside of Glasgow and by 1924 was owned by Alex Young.

Mary Milligan was licensee at the Railway Inn, or Railway Hotel as it became known, but she sold it in 1906 to James Young of the Castle Inn, New Cumnock. It was later taken over by Robert Dick.

Barbara Richmond ran the Market Inn. David MacLeod was the owner and host in the years after the Great War.

Thomas Adams (of the Black Bull Hotel in Cumnock) owned the Boswell Arms. In 1902 the inn was partially rebuilt, the corner turret and bay windows being added to plans drawn up by Robert Ewan & Sons, architects. William Jamieson Wood Morton was later to be the proprietor – he died in 1915 but the inn remained the property of his trustees for a good number of years thereafter. The pub was then managed by John Ferguson Turnbull (1868-1922), followed by Mrs Brown in the 1920s.

There were at one time six fish and chip shops in the village. One of these was operated by Isia and Argia Antonucci, who came to the village from Farnocchia in Italy around 1930. Their shop, Josephine's, was named after their daughter and was located near the toll. Jeanie Stobo was a tobacconist.

In 1919 Liddell Brothers set up in business as coach hirers. Catherine Liddell had five sons who had served in the war, and on their returned pooled their resources to start the business. They were Archibald, John, David, William and James Liddell. Two daughters were also involved for a time. Liddell Brothers ran local service buses up to the 1930s. In 1931 they moved to new premises in Market Place from the joiner's shop next to the Market Inn. Around 1950 David Liddell left the business and set up on his own at Templeton Place.

6.23 Townhead of Auchinleck farm *(Author's Collection)*

LEISURE

A number of new football teams got themselves organised at the beginning of the twentieth century. In the miners' rows the following was such that both Cronberry and Common could support junior football teams, not only that but teams which did well in competition. In Auchinleck everyone seems to have had some footballing connection. Teams existing in the village included Auchinleck Rangers, playing at junior level, as well as Highhouse Rangers, Auchinleck Garfield, Auchinleck Thistle, Auchinleck Bluebell and Auchinleck Juveniles, all playing juvenile standard. In September 1902 all the local junior teams joined to form the Cumnock and District League, following Ayrshire Junior Football Association rules. Each home club kept their own gate money but paid the opposition's expenses. The ticket money raised at the last home game went to the league to build up its funds. Each team also subscribed five shillings to join. R. Smith of Cronberry Eglinton acted as the first treasurer.

Cronberry Eglinton was founded in 1900 and soon became competent enough to win the Mauchline and District Cup in May 1902, beating Craigbank 3-1. However, during the game an incident involving the referee took place which resulted in much discussion throughout football circles. It had been a very windy day and when Cronberry were awarded a penalty the ball would not remain on the spot. At length the referee decided to hold the ball until it was kicked. Arguments raged for months over whether he should have done so. Another incident for Cronberry involving referees occurred in January 1903 when they travelled to Drongan for a game. The referee failed to turn up, so Cronberry put in a claim for thirteen shillings to cover their railway tickets. The association refunded twelve shillings and struck Mr Auld of Ayr off the roll of referees.

From 1904 until 1914 Cronberry Eglinton were never to be beaten at their home ground of Mortonmuir Park. From 1907 to 1914 was probably the team's best years, for they won numerous trophies. In May 1907 they beat Skares 7-1 to take the Ayr and District Cup, playing at Somerset Park. October 1908 saw them winning the Cumnock and District Cup by beating Glenbuck Cherrypickers 1-0. They held onto the Ayr Cup in November 1908 by beating Skares once again. The Cumnock Cup was won again in May 1909, the same team being beaten in the final 2-1. In 1909 the team won the Ayr and District Cup for the third time in a row.

In 1910 Cronberry won the Ayrshire Consolation Cup, the Mauchline Cup (beating Glenbuck) and the Cumnock Cup (defeating Glenbuck again, five goals to nil). The Ayr and Mauchline trophies fell to Cronberry again in 1911, beating Dunaskin Lads for the former, Muirkirk 4-2 for the latter. Dunaskin again met Cronberry for the final of the Mauchline Cup in 1913, the local team winning 6-2. Cronberry played well in the Scottish Junior Cup during 1914, managing to reach the fifth round, but were beaten 2-1 by Ashfield.

Notable players with Cronberry included Joseph ('Joe') Reid, who was capped for Scotland against England in 1902. He died at Cronberry in 1924. George Halley (29 October 1887-18 December 1941) was born in Cronberry and played as wing half for Bradford Park Avenue from 1911-13, followed by Burnley (1913-22) and Southend United (1922-3). Don Lees (1873-1903) played for Celtic from 1892-3 and Lincoln City 1893-4.

Common Thistle was founded just a few years before the turn of the new century, a close rival to their neighbours, Darnconner Britannia. The club played in a field at Barglachan, known as 'Barglachan Park', with a clubhouse in existence in 1911. In 1900 Common Thistle took the Cumnock and District Cup, Darnconner having won it previously. They won the Mauchline Cup in May 1905, beating the Cherrypickers 1-0. A year later Common took the Ayrshire Consolation Cup following a 1-0 defeat of Kilbirnie Ladeside. The team failed to win any great prizes thereafter, the club folding in 1913 and not being reformed after the war. They had opened a new pavilion on 25 July 1902. The club was officially wound up in January 1918. The pavilion was sold for £6 and even the goalposts were up for offers!

Darnconner Britannia Football Club continued to play until after the First World War. The club folded in 1924 due to a lack of residents in the village to support the team, or as a pool for players. Instead, a joint team with Common was formed.

Auchinleck Rangers was a short-lived team. It was started in 1901 but by September 1902 had folded. There was a campaign to reform the club in 1903 but this came to nought. Playing at junior level, the Rangers took their name to oppose Cumnock Celtic, playing in the Cumnock and District League, but were forced to withdraw due to lack of players and the costs involved. Yet in November 1901 it had been noted that they had the best football pavilion in the district. The field was outwith the village, and at the beginning of season 1902-03 it was reported that they were looking for a new pitch nearer Auchinleck. In the first round of the Ayrshire Cup (August 1902) Rangers went to New Cumnock to play the Afton Lads, but two of their players failed to turn up. They had to scratch the game, but getting two locals went on to play a friendly. The newly-introduced penalty kick was required in the game and it was following one of these that the Rangers were defeated 1-0.

Auchinleck Garfield and Thistle both played at juvenile level in Auchinleck in 1903. Birnieknowe United existed in 1929. Auchinleck Bluebell existed in 1905, also at juvenile standard, its park located off Well Road. The club's pavilion, the 'Bluebell Hut', was the scene of many socials, the site of which is now occupied by the Boswell Centre. None of these teams was as successful as the Highhouse Rangers which based itself at the Highhouse Rows. In March 1910 the Rangers played in the Ayrshire Juvenile Cup final at Beresford Park against Whitletts Celtic. Spectators invaded the Ayr park and the referee abandoned the game with thirty minutes left. The replay took place at Mauchline, Highhouse winning. The club was still in existence in September 1911, but disbanded soon after.

The longest-lasting, and most successful, team in Auchinleck was, and is, the noted Auchinleck Talbot. A number of attempts to reform the Auchinleck Rangers failed, the last being in 1907 when a public meeting was held on Kirkland Green (the field between the kirkyard and later cemetery) but nothing was to come of this.

Two years later, in 1909, the Talbot football club was founded, though at that time was not named as such. The laird, Lord Talbot de Malahide, was approached to see if he could lease the club a piece of ground suitable for a pitch. The ground he gave them was at Beechwood, formerly used on occasion by Auchinleck Prize Silver Band to hold fetes. The rent was to be £5 per annum, but Lord Talbot never collected this, so in his honour the club was named Auchinleck Talbot.

The ground had previously just been a rough field which the club members spent much time improving. When completed, there was no terracing, just a pitch surrounded by a rope on fence posts, a wooden pavilion, and a hawthorn hedge to mark the boundary. The first game on the new ground took place in July 1909 when the 'Old Players' of the village took on 'The Merchants'. The first Talbot game was on 5 August 1909 when they faced Highhouse Rangers in a benefit game for Paddy Wade, the new club winning four nil.

The first Talbot game against another junior team took place on 7 August 1909 when a friendly was played against Kilwinning Rangers Reserve. Though beaten 2-1, Talbot raised £5 at the gate; MacKie scored their first ever official goal. The team members were: Hyslop, Waddell, Smart, Whiteside, Crawford, MacIlwain, Mair, Irvine, Thom, MacKie and Martin. After the game both teams dined in the Boswell Arms, followed by a social hour.

Talbot's first win was to be in September 1909 when they beat Patna Doon Athletic 3-2. In 1911 Glasgow Rangers played at Beechwood, but the game was against Cronberry Eglinton. Rangers had signed two players from Cronberry, for which no transfer fees were payable at that time, so the little team arranged a benefit match against Rangers to raise club funds. The entrance fee was four pence for adults, one penny for children.

In 1922 Talbot beat Cronberry to gain a place in the final of the Cumnock and District Cup. They played Kello Rovers on 1 June at Cumnock's New Station Park, the crowd of fifteen hundred being a record for the time. The final score was Talbot 6, Kello 1, giving the Auchinleck team its first trophy. Four days later they faced the Cherrypickers in the Ayr and District Cup final. Playing at Muirkirk they won by two goals to nil to win another trophy. Their third win was in September 1912 when they beat Rankinston 4-0 at Cumnock to take the Mauchline Cup. This new season saw further success; at Ayr Talbot beat Patna 2-1 to retain the Ayr Cup. At their annual meeting the club was pleased to note a fairly healthy financial position, having made an annual loss of just one penny. This came about by the erection of a new clubhouse at Beechwood, a wooden building erected by a Muirkirk company. The income had been £172 16s 9d, the expenditure £172 16s 10d.

The first instance of the local derby, Cumnock Juniors versus Talbot, took place on 26 May 1914 at Rosebank Park, Lugar. It was the final of the Kilmarnock and District Shield and Nisbet scored the only goal of the game for Talbot. In the years to come the matches against Cumnock were to form some of the club's highlights.

Following the Great War many smaller football teams failed to reform. Even Auchinleck Talbot decided to opt out of the 1918-19 season due to a lack of decent players. They were active the year following, however, and in that season finally adopted black and gold as their main colours. With them they beat Irvine Meadow 3-1 to take the Ayrshire Cup, and in September 1920 beat Craigbank 11-0 in the Scottish Cup, a tournament record. In 1919, in aid of club funds, a Highland Gathering was held at Beechwood. Here one could enjoy the five-a-side football tournament, baby contest and pipe band competitions.

Of other parish teams only Lugar Boswell and Cronberry Eglinton survived the war as juniors, and Auchinleck Juveniles still played at their level. Talbot met Lugar in the 1920-21 final of the Mauchline Cup and beat them 2-0. Around one third of the spectators at that game sneaked in through Braehead Plantation to Rosebank Park, losing a considerable amount of gate money.

In 1921, whilst playing Glenbuck in the final of the Cumnock and District Cup, at Rosebank, the referee disallowed a Talbot equalising goal and the pitch was invaded by spectators. The police helped to restore order, but it was soon invaded again when a second Talbot goal was disallowed. Once again the police had to clear the pitch. When the game resumed for a third time a Cherrypicker knocked the ball from his net using a hand. The crowds bellowed for a penalty but the referee insisted that the game continue. The fans ran onto the field again and the police were required to escort the referee to safety. Following a special meeting in Cumnock, Glenbuck were awarded the trophy, having scored the only allowed goal of the match.

As the 1922-23 season began, the club found themselves in a good financial condition and were able to widen the park and make other improvements. Yet trouble continued amongst the fans, and at a home game that season against Irvine Victoria fans invaded the pitch and beat up the referee and linesmen. The Ayrshire Junior Football Association closed Beechwood for a month. The team, however, managed to beat Ayr Fort 1-0 to take the Coylton Cup. From 1924 to 1926 the club had no significant cup wins and had to wait until 1927 for their next trophy, against Lugar at Beresford Park, Ayr, for the Coylton Cup. Again trouble took place at the final, beginning with two players fighting. Fans ran onto the field to join in but the police managed to restore order and get the game underway again. Following some vicious tackling, a Talbot fan punched a Lugar player and again the police were called. The game was abandoned and postponed until the new season when it was hoped the tempers would have cooled. At the replay at Somerset Park, Ayr, Talbot beat Lugar 3-1. A week later Lugar beat Talbot 3-2 at Connel Park, New Cumnock, to take the Mauchline Cup. This win was to be Lugar's first ever as a junior team.

Support for the Talbot fell and due to the drop in game receipts and the increase in the cost of travelling to away games the team folded for the 1928-29 season. The club had debts of £24 and a cash balance of just nineteen shillings. They returned to the game the following year, David Boyd as president, beating Benwhat Heatherbell 4-1 to take the Irvine Herald Cup. This final was forced to a replay, for it was discovered that Benwhat had fielded a player registered with Annbank. Three cups came to the club in the 1930-31 season - Ayr and District (beating Cumnock 2-1 at Rosebank), Ayrshire Consolation Cup (beating Ardeer Thistle 2-1 at Rugby Park, Kilmarnock) and the Irvine Herald Cup (by beating Kello Rovers 5-1 at New Station Park, Cumnock). They held onto the Ayr and District Cup the following season by beating Glenafton 2-1 at New Station Park. Fortunes for the team tumbled thereafter; they gave a poor performance on the field and had financial difficulties.

The team played in red and white in the 1934-35 season, but soon returned to the fans' favourite black and gold. In 1938 a Talbot Supporters' Club was formed to raise cash for the team and make improvements to Beechwood. One of its first donations was of a new strip.

With it the team beat Cumnock 7-1 to take the Ayrshire Cup at Rugby Park. It was their last trophy before the outbreak of war, when most teams shut down and strong men went to fight for their country.

Lugar Boswell continued to play in the local league and challenge cups, but found trouble in 1910 and 1911. In 1910 they were due to play Glenbuck in a consolation tie but, despite thirty players on their books, were unable to raise eleven to form a team. In 1911, whilst playing in a Glasgow Shield game, there was a pitch invasion when Lugar scored against Catrine Thistle. One of the spectators grabbed the referee by the throat but the game went ahead, the score being three each. Catrine Thistle was subsequently banned from playing within a six mile radius of Catrine and their football pitch closed.

Lugar Boswell was reformed in 1926, having closed for a period. They began to play well, taking the Ayrshire Junior Challenge Cup in 1927-28 and again the year following, their first trophies for almost fifty years. They also lifted the Cumnock, Mauchline, Ayr and Coylton cups. In season 1929-30 they lifted the Irvine and District Cup.

Cronberry Eglinton played in the leagues, winning the Mauchline Cup in season 1917-18, but seems finally to have folded around 1932. They had won the Ayrshire Junior League in 1927-28 and came second in 1928-29, but dropped to bottom position in 1929-30. Nevertheless, they went out in style, beating all opposition to take the Ayrshire Junior Challenge Cup in 1930. Cronberry played in an all-white strip and their most famous player for a time was the great Bill Shankly who was capped for Scotland thirteen times between 1938 and 1943 and who went on to be a notable manager at Liverpool Football Club.

Auchinleck Bowling Club was founded in 1901 following a public meeting. A committee was formed and it identified land at Beechwood Park as a possible site for a green. However, Mr Angus suggested a site in Market Place. This was acquired on 6 September 1901 from Auchinleck estate and on which a new bowling green was laid. There was some opposition to using this site, as the tinkers often camped there and children played there. Locally, it was thought that Lady Boswell had gifted the ground as a playground, resulting in disruption in the village and the resignation of all but three of the committee. They continued to pursue the site, despite other residents burning effigies of them! Laid with Silloth turf, the green was formally opened on 17 May 1902 by Mrs Wilson, wife of the first president, William Wilson JP of Larchville. The original pavilion was designed by R. S. Ingram and erected at a cost of £700. A bazaar was held in 1903 to raise funds to clear the debt of the club, opened by Mr Angus and Sir William Arroll. The club had some early success, winning the Eglinton Cup in 1913. In the same year the club won the Rink Championship of Scotland.

A bowling green was created at Lugar in in 1924, the ground gifted by William Baird. In July that year a light railway was laid to allow material excavated from the site in the Store Park to be removed. Lugar Bowling Club was formed on Tuesday 17 March 1925, the first president being R. L. Angus. The green was opened on Saturday 13 June 1925 by J. T. Forgie, manager of Bairds. The pavilion erected at the time measured 24 feet by 12 feet.

Across the railway from Auchinleck bowling green was the quoiting pitch, operated by Auchinleck Quoiting Club. Another club was the Common Quoiting Club, which existed at Commondyke. Their old rink was located near to Commondyke pit but in 1911, when Common Thistle took over the site as part of their new football pitch, the club had to find a new location. A new rink was created at the old hearth of Dykes Pit in 1911, but it was noted that the rink was very cold and windy. The club was still in existence in 1925. Gasswater Quoting Club existed in 1903, playing in Cumnock & District League.

The Merlin Loch was still the scene of a few curling matches, but that sport was dying and few people followed it. Auchinleck Anglers Curling Club survived into the new century, in the winter of 1906-7 being successful enough to win the Eglinton Jug with T. Scott as skip. Auchinleck Curling Club won the jug in 1918, the winning rink comprising of Oliver MacConnell, John P. Smith, Peter Devlin and Hugh Alexander (skip). Hugh Alexander of Fore Rogerton was to complete 25 years as president of the club in 1921. In the winter of 1927-28 Auchinleck was to win the coveted trophy for the third and last time, with D. MacLeod as skip.

On Wednesday 21 April 1915 Auchinleck Golf Club opened its new course on the lands of Back Rogerton. The first president of the club had been John Henderson FEIS, but he died before the club was able to open its course. The course was nine holes in length. During the war the course was closed, reopening again in 1920. In 1922 a new course was opened on lands of Fore Rogerton, using fields of Orchard Knowe and Mill. Access to the course was from the back of the gas works. In 1923 the club moved to Blackston farm on Rigg Road. The course there had nine holes

6.24 Auchinleck Curling Club, Eglinton Jug Winners, 1927 *(Neil Sands)*

over 2,490 yards, laid out by A. W. Butchart and Mr Bryce, captain of Barassie Golf Club. The club was disbanded in April 1924.

Auchinleck Homing Club was formed in 1925. Other clubs in existence in the village in the 1920s included the Co-op men's and women's guilds. An indoor badminton club was formed in 1928.

The YMCA had premises in the Main Street near to the Clydesdale Bank. The Women's Temperance Association and Auchinleck Debating Society held regular meetings. The Auchinleck Silver Band played at numerous concerts and events but on New Year's Day 1914 the band was £7 in debt. The bandmaster, Mr Etherington, planned to raise subscriptions and the band's future depended on the result.

On 6 October 1906 a local branch of the Masonic Lodge was established, called Lodge Boswell St James (No. 1011). The first meetings were held in the Cross Keys Inn hall, which could seat 200 people. The Right Worshipful Master was William Wilson JP. The lodge acquired premises in Main Street in 1922 in which a Masonic Temple was established. The cost of purchase and conversion was £1,200, a bazaar in 1922 raising £700 towards the cost.

A branch of the Unionist Association was formed in the village.

The 42nd Ayrshire (Auchinleck) Scouts were founded in April 1911 following a public meeting held on Tuesday 7 March 1911. Rev James Hill took the chair, and the troop was set up soon after, attracting a good support amongst the lads of the village. Twenty-nine boys enrolled under Scoutmaster John Wilson. On 30 September 1911 the Scouts were presented with a set of colours by Lady Talbot at Auchinleck House, the boys marching from the village to the house. By this time Scoutmaster Mitchell was in charge.

Other Scout groups existed at Darnconner (in the early 1900s). Lugar Scouts were founded in 1940, meeting at the Institute.

A company of Boys' Brigade had been formed in 1900 but died out around three years later. On Friday 3 October 1941 the 1st Auchinleck Company of the Boys' Brigade was founded with Harry H. Russell as captain. Affiliated to both the Barony and Peden churches, they met in the Barony Church Hall. On 3 October 1942 the local Home Guard presented the company with its first set of colours, the ceremony taking place in the Picture House.

In Lugar a further company of Boys' Brigade existed, having 40 boys under the command of Captain Andrew MacSorland in 1926.

The British Order of Ancient Free Gardeners had branches in various communities. A branch of the Free Gardeners existed in the village in 1926, known as Auchinleck Blossom, Number 408. The Heatherbell Lodge was based at Darnconner, existing in 1911. The Craigston Lodge of Free Gardeners existed in 1935.

In September 1933 the Auchinleck and District Male Voice Choir was formed under the Presidency of Robert Waddell and the Honorary Presidency of Dr Henry MacLean. The first performance took place at the Old Folk's Party in December 1933. The choir took part in events across Ayrshire, and soon won second place in the Glasgow Music Festival, making their mark. In 1934 the choir had 36 members. For the next 25 years the choirmaster was James H. Yates. The choir became well known throughout Britain, particularly following their winning of the Palette Trophy at the 1938 Empire Exhibition Festival in Glasgow. In 1939 they won the Glasgow Music Festival, beating the top choirs from Glasgow and Ireland.

A significant new development took place in 1913 when the Auchinleck Picture House was opened. Work commenced in August 1913 at a site in Main Street, designed by Messrs James Balderston Whyte & William Gordon Galloway, of architects Whyte & Galloway, Bath Street, Glasgow. Built of brick, the street part of the building was faced with cement. Italian renaissance in style, the cinema had an entrance hall, vestibule, manager's office, fireproof operator's room, ladies' and gents' toilets, and a main hall for 585 patrons. A gallery over the entrance hall had seating for a further 115 patrons. The large hall was often full as the various feature films were shown. The picture house opened (in an unfinished but useable condition) on Saturday 29 November 1913, showing as its first film 'Alraune, the Gipsy'. Seats in the auditorium cost four pence at the front, sixpence at the back and nine pence on the balcony. The first manager was Herbert W. Morton (until 1916, when he moved to manage Cumnock Picture House) followed by Thomas

6.25 Auchinleck Picture House *(Author's Collection)*

Steele (from 1918), Kenneth MacCrae in 1923, followed by Malcolm Ross in 1924. The hall was also used for vaudeville shows, when the building was known as Auchinleck Theatre and Picture Playhouse.

The Literary and Debating Society was reformed in Auchinleck in September 1911, the first President being William Wilson JP. Perhaps as a result, Auchinleck Public Library was resuscitated in 1925.

In 1901 Darnconner Airds Moss Burns Club was established, becoming federated on the roll of Burns clubs in the Burns Federation as number 122. The next club to be federated was the Boswell Burns Club, also established in 1901, number 123.

Lugar and Cumnock branch of the Loyal Orange Lodge (No. 175) was formed in 1929. There was a branch of the Conservative and Unionist Party in the village, which held an annual social and dance in the institute, often presided over by Robert L. Angus, until the Second World War.

A branch of the Order of the Eastern Star was instituted in the Public Hall on 24 January 1925, number 250. An Auchinleck branch of the British Women's Temperance Association existed in 1928. At Cronberry the Jolly Ramblers existed in 1911.

SONS AND DAUGHTERS

Euphans Helen Strain, a noted female Scottish novelist of the late nineteenth and early twentieth century, died on 11 March 1934 at the age of 83. She had been born in the parish, daughter of James MacNaughton of Smithfield, a contractor and engineer, who had been responsible for building some of Ayrshire's railways. She married John Strain in 1874, civil engineer, son of a Glasgow coal-master, at Standalane in Stewarton. E. H. Strain, as she signed herself, wrote a number of novels set in Scotland, including *A Man's Foes* (published in 1895), *School in Fairyland* (1896), *Elmslie's Drag-net* (1900), *Laura's Legacy* (1903) and *A Prophet's Reward* (1908). She had travelled extensively throughout the world, and on one occasion had the honour of meeting Robert Louis Stevenson in Samoa. The last 37 years of her life were spent at Cassillis Castle, near Maybole, leased from the Marquis of Ailsa, where she was noted for her gardening interests.

Charles Howatson of Dornal, born 1833, had in 1867 exhibited a blackface ram at the Royal Highland Show, winning the supreme championship. It went on to win the Prince of Wales Gold Medal and Paris Show championships. His fortunes increased thereafter, and he built up a considerable estate in eastern Ayrshire. He lived for a time at Daldorch House, near Catrine, before moving to Glenbuck House, which he had erected in 1880 to the plans of John Murdoch of Ayr. In 1900 Howatson owned Dornal, Greenside, Shawfield, Whiteholm, High Glenmuir, Laigh Glenmuir, Duncanziemere, Hillhead and Wallaceton within Auchinleck parish. He died on 24 January 1918 and was buried in the parish kirkyard. His only son,

Captain Charles Nile Howatson of Glenbuck died March 1924 aged 34 and was buried in Auchinleck.

Every period in history breeds its characters, and the twentieth century was no exception. In Auchinleck dwelled 'Specky Murdoch' who ran a small bookselling business. He travelled round the local villages with his bags of books, selling them to those who could afford them. He was noted for books on natural subjects, even producing small volumes of his own.

At Birnieknowe Francis Collins lived in the small thatched cottage known as Habbie's Howe. His sister had married a Roman Catholic and set up home in the High Row, Commondyke. She told her brother that she did not want to be buried as a Catholic. She predeceased Francis, but a Catholic funeral was arranged by her husband, so Collins went to her house and asked for her corpse to be given to him. The priest requested that he be allowed to bury her, but Collins threatened the priest with his gun and demanded the corpse, which he got. For years afterwards he and his family were known in the district as 'Steal the Coffin'. The cottage at Habbie's Howe was to suffer in a fire and was then demolished.

The engineman at Common Pit, William Clark (1842-1914), was seriously injured in an accident there and did not work again. He turned his hand to poetry and contributed a number of verses to the *Cumnock Chronicle* under the pen-name 'Amateur Poet'. Most of these were on subjects to do with the mines, such as 'The Auld Big Engine Pit' or verses written on the breaking for scrap of the Common Big Engine in January 1903. Clark died at his home at Templeton on 12 August 1914 and is buried in the old kirkyard.

A number of sons of the parish were trained as ministers and served in parishes elsewhere. Among these was Rev William Smith, second son of William Smith of Thirdpart. He was ordained at Lerwick and served for three years. He then became assistant minister at Carradale in Argyll, assistant at St Thomas' Parish Church in Glasgow, and thence back to Shetland, where he served at Nesting. He retired as minister around 1910, returning to Treeshill, where he died on 30 January 1927, aged 58.

WORD WAR II

The lifestyle of the parish changed drastically with the outbreak of war in Europe in 1939. Windows had to be taped up to prevent them blowing out should a bomb land, lights on cars were virtually blacked out, just narrow slits pointing down left open, light from houses had to be prevented from shining outside at night, lest bombers spot them, and so black-out curtains were required. At Lugar School and elsewhere the windows were blacked out and baffles erected in case of blasts.

Within a few months the village was home to a number of evacuees from Glasgow and Clydeside. Some were made welcome and virtually became members of the family, others were seen as unwelcome guests, to be put up with whilst the war lasted. A weekly allowance of fourteen shillings per child, issued at the post office, was paid to those taking in evacuees, but in 1942 three people in Auchinleck were fined for claiming the allowance for evacuees no longer living with them.

In December 1939 an air raid practice was carried out in the village, with 'casualties' from fake bombs being treated by the local services in the town hall.

The army's presence was soon felt in the district, with the establishment of Pennylands Camp by the War Office, from where soldiers carried out military exercises. The camp occupied about twelve acres, acquired from the Marquis of Bute. Numerous Nissen huts were erected to which soldiers, around 750 in number, arrived for training sessions lasting up to six months before being sent to the front line. The expeditions took them onto Airds Moss for manoeuvres and a few unexploded shells and mines were later found there. Around 1943 the camp was converted to a prisoner of war centre. The German prisoners of war were taken on foot either to Barony or Highhouse pits where they were given a wash in the pithead baths. Some of them could make items like rings or toys, or decorate mirrors, in order to raise money with which to buy cigarettes. In 1945 some prisoners were used to convert Beechwood Park to an ash playing surface, but this proved to be unsuccessful and it was changed back to grass.

It was not just soldiers who were to suffer death, John C. Kavanagh (aged 13) was killed and three of his friends were injured on 26 July 1942 when an anti-tank hand grenade exploded. They had found it on a local moor following an exercise and had been playing with it that Sunday in the garden at 9 Lambfair Gardens.

In School Road there was a Decontamination Centre, run by the Secretary of State for War. At Auchinleck House a number of Free French, Canadian and Polish commandos were billeted and they were responsible for the bullet holes which exist on an outside wall.

Some of the men too old to join the armed forces, or else were in reserved occupations, formed branches of the Home Guard in Auchinleck, Lugar and Cronberry. Known throughout Britain as 'Dad's Army', the local platoons did live up to their amateur image for a time until rigorous training brought them up to a reasonable standard.

Humorous tales abound of incidents which occurred during the early days, such as the time a bullet, long believed to be a blank and used for practice, was accidentally fired off in Lugar Institute! Fortunately no-one was injured.

The Auchinleck platoon on one occasion planned to defend the village from an attack by the Cumnock Guard. Arranged on the slopes between the two communities, hiding behind trees and along the Auchinleck Burn, the Auchinleck men awaited the attack from Cumnock. However, the men from Cumnock marched up Barrhill Road, caught the train and arrived safely at Auchinleck station, behind 'enemy' lines and right in the centre of the village!

To improve the conditions of the servicemen and prisoners of war from the district, an Auchinleck War Work and Comforts Party was established. One of their major events was a drumhead service, held in Dumfries House policies on Sunday 31 May 1942. The service was conducted by Revs D. W. Ross and C. Johnston, and an address was given by Lord Inverclyde. In the years up to the time of the service, the party had raised £2,525 16s 0d. There were notices of 253 male parishioners serving in the forces, plus a further 11 women. The party had sent 2,142 parcels, and 1,557 postal orders. The fund placed money in the bank for each man serving abroad, rather than risk it being lost in transit, so that they would benefit from it later. In addition, the fund contributed £184 to the Red Cross, £45 to the Prisoners of War Fund, £20 to the West of Scotland Emergency Hospital, £25 in 'Aid to Russia', £40 to Mrs Churchill's Fund and £20 to buy equipment for a local first aid post.

Though the war was a serious time when many locals suffered death and injury in the struggle against Hitler, a great community spirit prevailed. A football match was arranged at Beechwood between a Davie Dunbar (ex-Talbot) select and a team of Polish Guards from the camp at Pennylands. Another game in May 1942 was arranged between the local Home Guard and an Army XI, the proceeds going towards the war effort. Numerous other fundraising events were organised, including many dances, some being held in the open-air at the school playground or else in the tennis courts behind the Peden Kirk, laid out in 1939. The Quoiting Club organised a large tournament in July 1942 to which 131 entries were made from all over Ayrshire. The profits raised were given to the Tommies' Postal Order Fund.

The names of 22 servicemen who died in the war were added to the memorial in the kirkyard, their names appearing on an additional bronze plaque. These are:

- Sergeant William G. Arthur, No. 137182, Flight Engineer, Royal Air Force Volunteer Reserve, 427 (RCAF) Squadron. Son of Gillian Milligan, Auchinleck. Died 25 June 1943 aged 23. Buried at Rotterdam (Crooswijk) General Cemetery.
- Private James Byrne, London Scottish Regiment.
- Stoker First Class Thomas Cairns, No. D/KX105483, Royal Navy, HMS Niger, lost at sea, 6 July 1942, aged 25. Son of George and Elizabeth Mitchell Cairns, Auchinleck. Also commemorated on Plymouth Naval Memorial.
- Lance Corporal Robert Calderwood Campbell, No. 2700811, Scots Guards. Attended 1st Battalion Welsh Guards. Died on 7 September 1944 aged 21. Buried at Groesbeek Memorial Cemetery. Son of William and Agnes Campbell, Auchinleck.
- Sapper Andrew Colvin, No. B/28364, 33 Field Company, Royal Canadian Engineers. Died 19 April 1945 aged 43. Buried at Groesbeek

Canadian War Cemetery. Son of William and Margaret Colvin, Auchinleck.
- Lieutenant Robert Gray, Royal Naval Volunteer Reserve.
- Private Andrew Hazel, No. 3132890, 2nd Battalion Gordon Highlanders. Died 28 August 1944 aged 25. Buried at St Desir War Cemetery.
- Private William Kelly, Royal Scots Fusiliers.
- Private David Finlay Strachan Judge, No. 3318778, 4th Battalion Black Watch (Royal Highlanders). Died 10 June 1940 aged 20. Son of Brown and Euphemia Judge, Auchinleck.
- Lance Corporal John Judge, No. 3133591, 6th Battalion Gordon Highlanders. Died 6 May 1943 aged 26. Brother of the above. Buried at Thibar Seminary War Cemetery, Tunisia. Husband of Elizabeth Nisbet, New Cumnock.
- Pilot Officer Robert Murphy, M. A., No. 172485, 141st Squadron Royal Air Force Volunteer Reserve. Killed 6 July 1944 aged 23. Buried at Longuenesse (St Omer) Souvenir Cemetery, France. Son of John Ross Murphy and Mary J. Murphy, Auchinleck.
- Private William MacCombe, Royal Scots Fusiliers.
- Private Archibald MacFadzean, No. 7372405, Royal Army Medical Corps, Died 6 December 1942 aged 24. Buried at Brookwood Memorial Cemetery, Surrey.
- Stoker First Class David MacKie, Royal Navy.
- Lance Corporal John MacLelland, No. 2697100, 1st Battalion Scots Guards. Died 29/30 January 1944 aged 26. Buried at Anzio War Cemetery, Italy.
- Guardsman Wilson MacLellan, No. 270068, 2nd Battalion Scots Guards. Killed 12 June 1943 aged 32. Son of William and Margaret MacLellan, Auchinleck, husband of Ruby MacLellan, Auchinleck. Buried at Enfidaville War Cemetery.
- Private Robert Pendergast, Royal Scots Fusiliers.
- Private George Templeton, No. 3133347, 7th/10th Battalion Argyll & Sutherland Highlanders. Killed 25 October 1942 aged 25. Buried at El Alamein War Cemetery.
- Warrant Officer Lawrence Tommie, No. 1125388. Wireless Operator/Air Gunner, 103 Squadron Royal Air Force Volunteer Reserve. Killed 26 July 1944 aged 21. Son of Mary Tommie, Girvan.
- Driver James Weir, Royal Artillery.
- Sergeant John Wilson, Royal Air Force.

- Stoker First Class, John Young, Royal Navy, HMS Belmont. Died 31 January 1942 aged 22. Commemorated at Portsmouth Naval Memorial. Son of James and Annie Young, Auchinleck.

In addition to those named on the war memorial in Auchinleck old churchyard, the following people with connections to the parish suffered in the war:

- Corporal W. L. Anderson, Royal Scots Fusiliers, No. 3127117, died 5 June 1940. Military gravestone in kirkyard.
- William Begg, 9th Royal Air Force, killed September 1944.
- Lance Bombardier Dick Fleming RA, died of wounds received in Sicily, 6 August 1943, aged 39.
- Joseph MacTurk, killed in action in Burma, 10 June 1944.
- Dan Mitchell, B.E.F., killed on active service, May 1940. Buried at Licques, near Calais.
- Sergeant Pilot George Stevenson, killed in flying accident, 21 July 1941 aged 25.

William Begg of Lugar served with the 9th Squadron of the Royal Air Force in the Second World War. His Avro Lancaster plane was hit by German gun-fire and crashed near Zuna in Holland in September 1944. Begg was only 21 years of age. The remains of the plane were buried, even although only three bodies were recovered. In October 2006 the body of Begg was recovered with the other bodies and they were reburied in a cemetery at Wierden on 18 August 2008.

CHAPTER SEVEN

THE GOLDEN YEARS (1945-2000)

VILLAGE LIFE

The immediate post-war years, and the 1950s in particular, were something of a boom time for Auchinleck village. By 1945 most of the old mining communities had been abandoned and a fair number of the rows demolished. The inhabitants of these had been rehoused in new schemes built onto Auchinleck or Cumnock, or else in new communities like Netherthird or Craigens. At Birnieknowe both the High and Store rows were demolished in 1943; most of Darnconner had been cleared in the mid-1930s, the church there abandoned in 1939, though it stood for forty years thereafter; the last of the rows in Cronberry and Gasswater were cleared, leaving only Riverside Terrace.

The population of the village increased considerably with the erection of new houses in Back Rogerton and elsewhere. By 1991, according to the Census, the village population was 4,116.

At Pennylands in 1947 the prisoner of war camp was converted into a Polish Repatriation Centre, one of a group in Ayrshire. Many Poles passed through the camp and tales abound of them eating virtually every dog or cat in the district! Some of the Polish Resettlement Corps who died at Auchinleck were buried in the new cemetery, along with soldiers who served at the camp, where their gravestones are quite distinctive. These were Lt. K. Dulczewski (died 1949), Col. K. Golachowski (1948), L. Cpl. E. Szwertner (1948), Cpl. J. Machaj (1948), Ul. J. Pyszny (1943), Pte. H. Bremer (1957), Plt. L. Bartkowial (1942), W. O. I. C. Polak (1947), Szer. J. H. Hopa (1946), Sjt. L. Cholewa (1947) and Z. Szczepanak (served as Plt. Z. Nowak, died 1945). A few Poles decided to settle in the parish and married local women. In some cases they adopted either their wives' surnames, converted their Polish name into a close Scottish equivalent, or else proudly retained their own surname.

From 1948 onwards the camp, abandoned by the authorities, was occupied by squatters, rising to 120 families in 1951, making a population of 380 (122 men, 115 women and 143 children). The camp was a lively place, the residents having a committee which oversaw the community and which ran the recreation hut. From January 1950 onwards a Sunday school was operated jointly by the Peden and

Barony churches, having a roll of 36. Most residents at Pennyland were noted as being decent and law-abiding, having converted their huts into reasonable homes, with fireplaces, closets and running water. However, there were some who were little more than tramps, living in squalid conditions. In 1949 a young boy, Robert Kennedy, found a gun and ammunition hidden behind plasterboard in one of the abandoned huts. It was thought to have been placed there by a Polish resident who quit the camp in 1948. During the 1950s, as new houses were erected in Auchinleck, the residents were gradually rehoused and the camp closed, the site of it now covered with trees.

In April 1947 99 temporary prefabricated (Uni-Seco) houses were erected in Auchinleck to alleviate the housing shortage and assist in the clearance of old mining houses, long-since out of date. These prefabs had a lifespan of ten years, but were still occupied until 1971 by which time they suffered from severe dampness. They were demolished that year, having stood in Back Rogerton Crescent (51), Talbot Drive (2), Judge Avenue (12), Barbieston Road (14), Milne Avenue (2) and Berryhill Drive (18).

In 1950 one hundred proper houses were erected by Ayr County Council, as well as 24 by the Scottish Special Housing Association. Most of these were located in the new Back Rogerton housing scheme. In 1950 it was noted that the village contained 1,508 dwelling houses, but of these 455 were below acceptable standards and around one third were overcrowded. The Highhouse Rows were demolished in February 1959 and the Dalsalloch Rows in April 1964. Easton Place was demolished in 1967. New houses were erected on greenfield sites at Back Rogerton, others in gap sites in the old village. 44 houses were built in Ballochmyle Avenue in 1959, others in Coal Road, Quarryknowe and three old folks' houses opposite the Railway Hotel in 1963. In Main Street, opposite Currie's, new homes were built in 1964 and two houses fitted into a large garden in Lambfair Gardens in 1965. Four old folks' houses were built in Church Avenue in 1966 and 6 houses (122- 132) in Ballochmyle Avenue the same year. Eighteen houses were erected in Coal Road in 1968. In 1972, 43 houses were erected on the site occupied by the prefabs. In 1971, according to the census returns, the village had a population of 5,554, made up of 1,689 households. 144 people owned their own homes, the council having 758 houses let.

In 1951 the *Third Statistical Account of Scotland* was published, at which time we find the village had, in addition to the Co-op, three bakers, four butchers, four grocers, five drapers, two chemists, one ironmonger, one drysalter, a glass and china merchant, seven fruiterers, six fish and chip shops and four newsagents. There were also five public houses, one of which (the Railway Hotel) had a seven-day hotel licence. Of the shops, Stewart's Grocery was long-established, having been founded in Kilmarnock in 1911, moving to Auchinleck (83 Main Street) in 1930 before moving to 153 Main Street in 1946. Maider's news agency closed in June 1959. John MacLean had taken over the small chemist shop of David Taylor in 1935 and ran it until 1961 when new larger premises were constructed at 178 Main Street. The business went from strength to strength, branches being opened in Cumnock. The firm was later purchased by Ayrshire Pharmaceuticals. A new large shop was erected at the corner of Main Street and Park Road in 1962 for Maider's furniture store. Many of the shopkeepers were members of the Auchinleck Merchants Association, but this organisation became defunct in 1965. The parish cemetery in Main Street was extended in 1958 and in 1977 a new refuse coup was created at Common.

In Main Street, where once stood Easton Place, a new Health Centre was opened in December 1975. Within it were two doctors' surgeries, a dentist, chiropodist, midwifery centre, district nurse centre, baby clinic and dietician, the last two covered by visiting specialists. A clinic under the National Health Service formerly existed at 97 Backrogerton Crescent. A Social Work sub office was located at 22-28 Aird Avenue.

The former co-operative building and butcher's shop at 156-160 Main Street was converted into a nursing home in 1989, named Nightingale House, by Mohammed Shafique.

In 1982 the United Kingdom became engaged in a conflict with Argentina over the Falkland Islands. A task force was sent to the southern Atlantic islands, where two locals died in the fighting. They were Sergeant Wallace M. M. Lawrie, Royal Electrical and Mechanical Engineers, and Staff Sergeant James Prescott CGM, Royal Engineers Regiment, and their names were added to the village war memorial.

TRANSPORT

The advance made in motor transport, and with ever-increasing private car ownership, resulted in a need to make improvements to the local road infrastructure. Most of this was undertaken by Ayr County Council. In 1959-60 the twisted roadway from Lugar to Cumnock was realigned, and a new bridge was erected across the Lugar water. The cost of the project was £70,000. Further upgrading of the A70 took place east of Boghead in 1963, when a new bridge and road realignment was undertaken to either side of the Boghead Burn, and at Cronberry road-end in 1964. In Auchinleck the Main Street was closed at the railway bridge for a time in March 1960, when alterations were being made to the structure. The first traffic lights in the district were commissioned in August 1966 at the railway bridge on the Runnels Road. In November 1963 the first fence was erected round what was claimed as common ground at the Runnels cross-roads. In 1963 that part of Rigg Road between Rigg Toll and Rigg farm was realigned, the old road which met the A 76 at the Toll Cottage being covered with soil, the new route opening in July 1963.

The road from Ochiltree towards Auchinleck was realigned in the early 1960s, avoiding the circuitous route over the Lugar Bridge. A new roadway, which was considerably wider than the old roadway, was formed, continuing in a straight line from Mill Street. The Lugar Water was crossed by a new steel girder bridge, erected in 1960-62. The contractors for the work was Murdoch MacKenzie Ltd. The roadway, by now in the parish of Auchinleck, then swings to the left and rejoins the old road. In total, 2,200 yards of new roadway was created. The old bridge was closed to traffic.

At Lugar a new way through the Bello Path was made from 1971 to 1973, including a new bridge over the Bello Water, which was partially diverted.

In the late 1950s the first plans were mooted for a by-pass road to avoid both Auchinleck and Cumnock. The cost of this meant that the date of construction was repeatedly put back, and work did not commence until spring 1990, by contractors W. & J. Barr. The roadway, engineered by Strathclyde Regional Council (W. S. MacAlonan, Director of Roads), began at the Dippol Burn where a bad corner, scene of numerous accidents, was realigned. A cutting was made through the knowe at Darnlaw and a roundabout was formed at Templeton. Running parallel with the Runnels Road, the new road bridges the Barony Road and descends past the Pennyland plantation, across Manse Glen to a new bridge across the Lugar Water to Terringzean Castle. A second roundabout was constructed at Dettingen Mount, Cumnock, and the by-pass continues on past Shankston Wood and Caponacre to Skerrington Mains roundabout on the New Cumnock road. The road was completed in 1991.

Death on the roads increased as cars became more popular and speeds increased. In 1947 two miners, H. Reynolds, Highhouse Rows, and A. Smart, Old Avenue, were killed on Barony Road by a small van. In August 1959 Martha MacNab (wife of Archibald MacNab of the Eagle Inn) was killed in the Main Street. Agnes Richard (74) was killed near her home at Rigg cottages by a car in February 1960. George Reid, aged two years, of Dalsalloch Rows, was killed by a van in the same month a year later. In October 1963 H. Walton, of Nottingham, was killed in a car accident near Darnlaw. On 22 August 1967 Brian Dorrans, aged 22 months, was killed by a mobile shop at Quarry Knowe.

In 1960 Stewart Given, a mental health patient at Ailsa Hospital, was given weekend leave to visit his relatives. On 30 October 1960 his body was found decapitated on the railway near Coal Road bridge. In August 1965 there was an attempt to murder Mrs Jean MacHallum at Auchinleck. Her assailant gave himself up at Ochiltree Police Station two hours later.

On the railways services began to decline, and branch lines were retained only to serve the mines, the passenger stations being closed. At Auchinleck the station-masters after the war were R. Reid (to 1958), C. Arnott (1958-61) and John Gray (from May 1961). During his time as stationmaster the station won third place in the Best Kept Station in Britain competition for 1961. When he retired in July 1965 he was not replaced, for the station was closed on 6 December that year as part of Dr Beeching's national cuts.

The line from Cumnock to Muirkirk was closed to passengers in 1951 (Commondyke Station was closed on 3 July 1950) and in 1964 its rails were lifted. This left only the branch from Auchinleck to Cairnhill Pit in operation, which was abandoned when that colliery closed and the line was later dismantled. On 30 January 1967 a train crashed on the line from Muirkirk near Coal Road. It was a 120 ton diesel engine pulling 24 waggons of coal from Kames Colliery bound for Ayr. Brake failure was blamed.

In 1984 Auchinleck Station was reopened to passengers, but was unmanned. The old station house was demolished in 1990. In 1991 there were plans to relay the line from Auchinleck to Powharnal (near Boghead) where a coal transportation plant was proposed to be built in order to reduce the number of coal lorries travelling through the local towns and villages. This did not come to anything.

LUGAR

The institute at Lugar continued in use after the war, buts its decline had set in. The swimming pool had been covered over and converted to a dance hall, where Lugar Boswell held regular Sunday dances. Below the floor the instruments of Lugar Brass Band were stored, ever since its last official performance on King George VI's Coronation Day in 1936. The billiard tables were in a poor condition and the library books out of date. A local badminton club used the hall. However, by 1965 the institute was closed following the erection of an IFE wing at Logan Primary School, and in May 1966 it was leased by the Falmer clothing company as an advance factory, prior to establishing a factory in Cumnock. Over 200 applied for the first thirty jobs. Falmers grew for the next twenty years, a second factory opening in Cumnock and one in Patna, Lugar remaining in use. However a downturn in Falmers' business resulted in the closure of the Lugar plant. The institute, a listed building, remained empty thereafter, but plans to demolish it in 1985 were refused.

The old school was leased to Hollybush Knitwear on 13 November 1964, an enterprise started in Auchinleck earlier that year by James M. Murdoch. From beginnings within the old Peden Church the company grew rapidly, employing 130 in 1966 and having a third factory at Crookedholm, Kilmarnock. In 1966 the Lugar school building was bought by Hollybush for £750. The Hollybush Knitwear Company folded in 1971. The school was later used by Kintyre Knitwear, but it too closed and the building was converted into dwellings.

The Lugar Co-op remained in Baird's ownership until 1947 when the mines were nationalised. However the National Coal Board did not wish to take over the Co-op so it was run by a local committee, along with the branches at Skares, Glengyron, Commondyke and Cronberry. Glengyron and Commondyke closed soon thereafter. This committee transferred the running of the surviving branches to Auchinleck Co-operative Society. The store at Lugar remained in business until 1966 when it was closed, having been superseded by a new branch in Logan. It had supplied general groceries, bakery foodstuffs and had a boot-repairing service. The store at Lugar was then demolished and within the year a new petrol station was erected on the site by William Conn. The Valley Service Station opened in August 1966, selling BP petrol twenty-four hours per day, seven days per week. A café attached to it opened shortly after. In 1965 an application to build a hotel and petrol station at Rosebank had been refused.

Work began on demolishing the old rows at Lugar. One of the village's oldest, Craigstonholm Row, was pulled down in September 1958 and in November 1961 the Brick and Front rows were knocked down, the occupants rehoused at Logan. The Crescent, only one house of which had running water in 1951, was demolished around the same time. The Post Office was demolished in 1962, the last postmaster being David Reid, serving from 1939 to 1961. He was the son-in-law of the previous postmaster, Archibald Rankin. Mrs Reid ran the office until November 1961. The Post Office advertised for a new postmaster, but he would have to provide his own premises. As a result a wooden hut was erected on the same site, lasting until the 1970s when it was closed due to lack of use.

At Bello Mill a new police station had been erected in 1914, replacing the old premises in the rows, Constable David Grant being last to serve the village, from 1958 until 1967. As with most of Lugar's services, the station was closed and a new office erected at Logan that year. To help link the two villages a footbridge was erected across the water by the county council in 1964. Some new houses were erected at Lugar on the site of the rows in 1972 – twenty-two in River View and fourteen in Braehead Place. In 1971 the first Lugar Re-union was held at Logan.

At the former ironworks the National Coal Board formed workshops, offices, research and development sections and machinery maintenance shops. The former ironworks chimney was demolished in 1955. In 1951 a total of 200 people were employed there, including those making Eglinton briquettes. In 1957 this plant produced 21,000 tons of briquettes and remained in production until it was struck by fire in the late 1980s. After a period of rebuilding, the briquette plant recommenced production. However, it was closed in the early 1990s.

George Kirkwood was appointed manager of the workshops in 1954 and remained until his retiral in December 1962. This marked a significant change in the Coal Board's operations in Ayrshire. The former West District offices at Prestwick were closed and new whole-Ayrshire offices were established at Lugar, former home of the East District offices. The 500 staff at Lugar were then joined by 600 from Prestwick, the new manager being R. D. Glass. In 1964 the offices were extended. The workshops closed in 1985. These were later leased to Coylebank Fabrications but this company went bankrupt. Plans for a charcoal manufacturing plant, using peat from Airds Moss, were refused due to environmental problems. In 1990 a new casting company was established at the works.

The former NCB offices were let to Cumnock and Doon Valley District Council, and conversion of these to municipal use was carried out to plans by Douglas Buchanan. A timber-lined council chamber was created, and various departments were located in the building. Over a period of years most of the departments were transferred to Lugar from smaller offices in old premises in Cumnock, such as planning, library headquarters, etc.

At the old spout at Hollowsholm Bridge, Cumnock District Council formed a small garden and seat, the work completed in 1974. The opposite bank was likewise improved, but the NCB claimed ownership and the garden was abandoned by the council. In August 1985 Scottish Gas commissioned a study into the possibility of creating a museum at Bello Mill dedicated to William Murdoch. Paterson & Associates, architects, produced a hideous scheme to cover the ruined mill in a £360,000 glass-house, but this plan was never pursued. Ironically, despite Murdoch having invented gas lighting, mains gas did not reach Lugar until 1988.

In the post-war years, some residents of Lugar and Cronberry formed a branch of the Labour Party.

CRONBERRY

After the war Cronberry went into decline. The rows were gradually emptied and demolished and the occupants were rehoused, mainly in Logan. By the time of the *Third Statistical Account* of Scotland, which was published in 1951, the three 'Tarry Rows' had been removed. In the same year the railway line from Cumnock was closed. The population was then 490, living in four old rows, the newer Riverside Terrace, and a few other cottages. The old rows had outside toilets, water pumps and ashpits, and internally were lit by paraffin lamps. Within a few years electricity was supplied to the newer houses. The former school, used since 1931 as a meeting hall for social nights, men's club and church, was in the late 1940s closed, as was the football clubhouse.

The branch of the Lugar Ironworks Co-operative operated under Baird's control until 1947 and then by committee. The manager was Mattha Begg. It was later taken over by the Auchinleck Co-operative Society but was closed down as the population declined.

A group of women formed the Cronberry Women's Rural Institute on 22 October 1947, meeting in the new school. They held regular meetings and social nights, but when most were rehoused at Logan the Rural moved with them in 1965, though retained the Cronberry name. The roll in 1991 was over 50. The Co-op Women's Guild also used the school for meetings, as did a Youth Club. Further education classes in various crafts and first aid were also offered.

The remaining rows were demolished in the mid-1960s. Riverside Terrace alone survived, with a few other cottages. At Dunena cottage Mrs Duncan ran the post office until 1990. Many of the Riverside Terrace houses became empty and were put up for sale by the Coal Board. In 1990, only six of the 28 Riverside Terrace houses were still occupied, but work commenced in rehabilitating the remaining houses in 1991 by Massinghomes, a private developer. The terrace was renamed Riverside Gardens, the houses re-divided into variously-sized flats and plans for private bungalows were made. At Logan the first Cronberry Re-union was held in 1970, when ex-residents met to look back with fond recollections of the rows.

LANDOWNERS

John Patrick Douglas Boswell succeeded to Auchinleck House in 1948 as the 15th Laird. He was born in Edinburgh on 4th March 1910 and educated in England followed by a military career, being a member of the Royal Company of Archers (the King's Body Guard for Scotland) from 1935. During the Second World War he served with the 7th Battalion of the King's Own Scottish Borderers. Boswell married Comtesse Lucie Catinka Christiane Julie, the daughter of Count Curt Ludwig Haugwitz-Hardenberg-Reventlow, of Korinth, Fyn, Denmark, by whom he had three sons and one daughter. These were John Robert Douglas Boswell (born 5 November 1937); James Alexander Douglas Boswell (born 1 October 1945); Patrick Charles Douglas Boswell (born 1948, died 20 October 2006); and Annabell Margaret Douglas Boswell (died 1942).

The marriage of John Douglas Boswell and Lucie was annulled by divorce in 1954 and he subsequently married Mary Patricia Sinclair Scott. Boswell spent many years in Australia where he learned farming, running a farm in Dumfriesshire before inheriting Auchinleck. At first he bred the Auchinleck Pedigree Ayrshire herd, but changed over to an Aberdeen Angus beef herd.

Auchinleck House was by this time in a rather derelict state. Internally the plaster was crumbling, rot had set in and the house had to be abandoned in favour of the smaller house at the home farm. Despite attempts to restore the building, the family did not have the money required, and the house became gradually worse. Windows were broken, lead stripped from the roof and damage was done internally by vandals. The Historic Buildings Council granted Boswell £15,000 with which to have the roof repaired and the dry rot eradicated. However, as work progressed it was soon discovered that the damage was greater than at first thought. The rooms were stripped of their wooden panels, and the remaining plasterwork removed. Work stopped on the death of John Boswell on 22 May 1966, not to be resumed for twenty years.

James Boswell, John's second son, succeeded as 16th of Auchinleck. He began looking into new ways of having Auchinleck House restored. A temporary home was sited behind the house and John Campbell, a retired postmaster, looked after the building. In 1978 Boswell engaged the noted English architect, Quinlan Terry, to survey the building and suggest a suitable programme for restoration, but again found that funds were limited and grants insufficient. The idea of obtaining funds from America did not materialise.

Eventually, in August 1986, Auchinleck House was sold to the Scottish Historic Buildings Trust for £50,000, along with the Front Park, The Lawn and part of the Braid Wood, totalling 35 acres. The money for the purchase came from the National Heritage Memorial Fund, and the keys were accepted on the trust's behalf by its chairman, Charles Elliot Jauncey, Hon. Lord Jauncey, QC, BA, LLB. Another architect, Simpson & Brown of Edinburgh, had the building surveyed, and this time work commenced. The roof was first to be repaired, followed by the woodwork, including the windows. Then the masons began replacing those stones which were suffering from erosion. Originally, the trust hoped to use the house as a museum and centre for eighteenth century Scottish studies.

However, a more productive use was to lease the house to the Landmark Trust, a charity founded in 1965 to restore historic buildings and let them as holiday accommodation. The trust took over the house in 1999. An appeal launched in May 2000 raised £3.7 million within eighteen months, allowing work on the restoration to commence, returning the house to its original condition. Further renovations commenced internally, with funds from the Royal Oak Foundation of America, Historic Scotland and the Heritage Lottery Fund.

James Alexander Douglas Boswell married Alexandra Elizabeth Pattinson (born 5 April 1952) and set up home at Auchinleck. His wife, known as Aly, was active in establishing the Auchinleck Horse Trials in 1984, which still attracts competitors from all over Britain. She was also involved in running Treadlers Ltd from 1994-99, a fabric retailer in Ayr. In 1972 the estate covered 700 acres and was for a time run by the Auchinleck Farming Company. By 2015 the estate had been reduced in size to around 500 acres, of which 350 were arable, or grazing land, the remainder woodlands. In 1988 planning permission was granted to create an 18-hole golf course on the estate, complete with clubhouse, swimming pool and leisure centre. The development, which was to cost £3 million, would also include 22 self-catering cottages and 37 houses, but it never came to fruition. In 1991 James Boswell was selected as the Conservative candidate for South Ayrshire, or Carrick, Cumnock and Doon Valley as the constituency was renamed, but was not elected.

James and Aly Boswell have three children – Harry Alexander Douglas Boswell, born 25 February 1983, who serves in the forces with the Royal Logistics Corps, Virginia Lucie Douglas Boswell, born 1 August 1984, and Rory James Douglas Boswell, born 5 October 1987.

CHURCHES

The parish church minister, Rev David Ross, was replaced by Rev George Alexander MacCutcheon. He was born on 18 January 1919 at Gourock, son of Alexander MacCutcheon and Ann Campbell Bain. He was educated at Paisley's John Neilson Institution from 1924 until 1931, followed by Glasgow High School (1931-36) and the University of Glasgow (1926-29 and 1946-48). He graduated as a Master of Arts in 1946. During the war he served in the forces from 1939-46, after which he was appointed Student Assistant Minister at Paisley Orr Square Church (1946-47), followed by Glasgow St George's Road Church (1947-48). Licensed by the Presbytery of Glasgow on 10 April 1948, he was ordained and inducted to Auchinleck on 30 September 1948. He remained until 14 March 1967 when he was translated to Clackmannan Parish Church.

On 30 August 1945 Rev MacCutcheon married Janet Todd (b. 1 July 1919), daughter of John Alexander Todd and Janet Watson. They had two children, Janet Ann, born 2 July 1951, and Alexander Hugh, born 25 March 1955. Rev MacCutcheon served as Clerk to the Presbytery of Stirling from 1985-94. He retired as minister at Clackmannan on 31 March 1984.

New stained glass windows were inserted in the church in 1947, the Solomon and Moses and Charity windows being designed by Gordon Webster.

Average morning attendance at the parish church in 1950 was about 200. Evening services were held jointly with the Peden Church, alternating between buildings. The Sunday school had an attendance of 200; with 50 Boys' Brigade members in the Bible Class. In 1963 a new font stand of light oak was presented to the church at Easter by John Shaw, Brycefield, Auchinleck, to hold the silver bowl presented by Lady Boswell.

7.1 Parish Church and Boswell Mausoleum in 1990 *(Dane Love)*

The church was used on 4 November 1962 to film 'Songs of Praise' for the BBC. This was to celebrate the 21st anniversary of the Boys' Brigade. On 1 December 1963 the morning service came from the Barony Church. Four Peden Church services were recorded in August 1962 for transmission on the Light Programme on radio. To accommodate this, the time of the services were changed from 11.00 a.m. to 12.00 noon.

On 28 September 1967 Rev Daniel MacCallum Robertson was translated from Camelon Trinity Church, Falkirk, where he had been ordained on 6 September 1960, to Auchinleck Barony Church. Dan Robertson was born in Bathgate on 20 April 1935, the son of Thomas Gray Robertson and Margaret Meta MacKay MacCallum. He was educated in Bathgate from 1940 to 1953, jointly winning the dux medal, followed by Edinburgh University, where he graduated as a Master of Arts in 1956. He served for a time as a student assistant minister at Broughton Place Church in Edinburgh (1958-59), and then as a probationary assistant at St Cuthbert's Church in Edinburgh (1959-60). He was licensed by the Presbytery of Bathgate on 16 April 1959 and soon after (on 4 July) married Anne Moffat Affleck (b. 27 December 1938), a fitting name for his future charge. She was the daughter of William Affleck and Elizabeth Agnes Tennant. By her he had four children, Mark Thomas (b. 11 May 1960); Garry William (b. 28 October 1962), married to Annette Elizabeth Wilson; Wendy Anne (b. 5 January 1966); and Iona Affleck (b. 25 May 1970), married to Allan MacDonald. Under Mr Robertson the parish church went from strength to strength, serving the community, and celebrating the centenary of the kirk building in 1989. He retired from the ministry on 7 May 2000 and died on 22 December 2006. A memorial headstone was erected in the kirkyard to commemorate him.

The first proposals for a new Peden Church had been made in 1939, but it was not until 1951 that work commenced on a new building. A site at the south-eastern end of Church Avenue had been designated for religious purposes and it was there the building was erected. The architect was James Andrew Carrick of Ayr, and he came up with a hall-church type of building, the main hall being used as a church on Sundays, and as a meeting hall for other organisations during weekdays. A lesser hall adjoining was named the Spence Hall in memory of Rev Prof James Spence. The church was built to accommodate a congregation of 400 and had cost over £16,000 to build.

The dedication ceremony of the new church took place on 14 January 1953, performed by the Rt Rev George Johnstone Jeffrey, Moderator of the General Assembly of the Church of Scotland.

The ministry was continued by Rev Charles Livingstone Johnston, who had been ordained and inducted on 26 March 1941. Born on 30 October 1913 in Glasgow, the son of Andrew Johnston and Catherine Dickson, Johnston was educated at Whitehill Secondary School (1926-31) and the University of Glasgow (from 1932), where he graduated as Master of Arts in 1935. He continued studying at the university until 1939. Johnston served as a student assistant then assistant minister at Glasgow Chalmers Church from 1936-41. He was licensed by the Presbytery of Glasgow in 1939. Rev Johnston served with the Church of Scotland Huts and Canteens in Germany from 1945-46.

Rev Johnston was married on 19 August 1955 to Jane Elizabeth Highet (b. 4 March 1929), daughter of William Highet and Catherine Rowan, by whom he had two sons, Charles Andrew (b. 28 November 1956) and Colin David (b. 26 March 1960). In 1957-58 he served as Moderator of Ayr Presbytery and from 1972 to 1991 was the presbytery clerk. Rev Charles Johnston died on 26 April 1996. Just prior to moving to its new building the Peden kirk had a membership of 270, with an average attendance of 120, and 115 Sunday School members. There was also a Women's Guild, Bible Class, Men's Guild and Youth Club. In the 1960s there was an active Dramatic Club and Badminton Club.

7.2 Former Peden Church in 2015 *(Dane Love)*

In 1964 plans were drawn up for an extension to the church, membership continuing to grow. This addition was to have been an octagonal shaped building, with seating for over 400, located in front of the existing building. The cost then would have been around £27,000. However, the Church of Scotland nationally began its readjustment policy for two-church communities and in 1980 the Peden Church was linked with the Barony Church, Rev Daniel Robertson taking charge. The Peden kirk was closed as a church on 4 September 1983, when it and the Barony kirk were united as Auchinleck Parish Church, the church services held in the Barony church, the Peden church becoming the new parish halls. The old Barony Church Hall was closed and put up for sale. It was bought by developers who demolished the building and erected six flatted dwelling houses on the site.

The Barony and Peden churches jointly were sponsors of the 1st Auchinleck Company of the Boys' Brigade. The captain until 1954 was Harry H. Russell followed by Craig MacMillan (1954-55, then 1964-75), who became a member of the Brigade Executive. On 25 October 1959 an ex-members' association was founded. This group presented a new Queen's colour on 2 October 1966, Sam MacMillan presenting a new Company colour. Other captains were J. Wilson Connell (1955-1964), William Garven (1975-85 and 1986-88) and George Devlin (1988-2004). The company celebrated its silver jubilee in 1991, but more or less closed in 2004 due to falling numbers.

LUGAR

Rev Andrew MacBride MacKirdie was translated to Lugar Church on 10 May 1944 from Schaw Kirk (Drongan) and he remained eight years. Rev MacKirdie had formerly preached at Clydebank West Church, until his translation to Glasgow Union Church on 28 October 1930. He was demitted on 11 January 1938 and was introduced to the Schaw Kirk, Drongan, in July 1940. In 1950 the church had a membership of 320, but found its work limited by the lack of hall accommodation. The Sunday School had 110 members, and 60 were in the Bible Class. Two services were held in the church on a Sunday and a Women's Guild existed. Rev MacKirdie demitted his charge on 31 March 1952 and died on 8 March 1953.

Rev James MacLeod was ordained and inducted to Lugar on 30 July 1952. He was born at Helensburgh on 14 November 1920, son of Alexander MacLeod and Mary Rodger. He received his education at Dalmuir (Clydebank) from 1925-29, followed by Dumbarton West Bridgend School from 1929-32. He then attended Dumbarton Academy for two years until 1934. MacLeod then served in H. M. Forces in the Middle East, Crete and Germany throughout the Second World War, although he spent 1941-45 as a prisoner of war. He was to return home and studied at the University of Glasgow and Trinity College from 1947-52. He graduated with a Master of Arts degree in 1950. He began working in churches as a missionary assistant at Clydebank St James's Church Linvale Mission (1951-2) and was licensed by the Presbytery of Dumbarton on 16 April 1952. He moved to Lugar in 1952. MacLeod was married on 23 June 1945 to Janet (b. 14 September 1914), daughter of Hugh MacTurk and Janet MacIntyre of Maybole, by whom he had two sons, Alexander James (born 29 March 1946) and Angus Hugh (born 12 June 1951). He was translated to Boddam (Aberdeenshire) on 27 November 1957 and thence to Kilfinichen and Kilvickeon parish (Argyll) in 1961, where he retired in 1964.

The pulpit at Lugar was filled by Rev Iain MacDonald Tweedlie who became a much-liked minister. Tweedlie was born in Detroit, USA, on 23 November 1928, the son of Robert and Mary Tweedlie. He was educated at the MacCulloch, Durfee and Cass Technical School from 1933-1947, followed by Wayne University from 1947-51, where he graduated with a Bachelor of Science degree, and MacCormick

Theological Seminary (where he obtained his Bachelor of Divinity) from 1951-54. He then moved to Scotland, studying at St Andrews University for two years until 1956. He was admitted to the status of licentiate by the General Assembly in 1956 (having been licensed by the Presbytery of Detroit in 1954). He worked as an assistant minister at Edinburgh Richmond Craigmillar Church from 1956-58. He was licensed by the Presbytery of Edinburgh on 12 November 1957. On 16 October 1958 Rev Iain Tweedlie was inducted to Lugar and within a year married Agnes Mitchell Brodie (born 23 October 1938), by whom he had two sons and two daughters – Stephen (born 12 November 1960); Paul (born 27 March 1962); Carol (born 8 June 1964); and Diane (born 17 December 1969).

Because of the movement of population from the old miners' rows to the new community erected on Logan Estate, ground was purchased in 1958 at Glenmuir Road for a new church. Only a hall was ever built. Logan Church Hall was dedicated on 24 February 1959 by Rev George Paterson. A Youth Club attached to the church began meeting in the hall, and a Dramatic Club was formed in 1960.

A falling roll led the Presbytery to link the churches of Lugar with Old Cumnock St Ninian's (Netherthird) on 20 December 1960. The new linked charge was under the care of Tweedlie, who moved to the manse at Netherthird. The manse adjoining the church at Lugar was sold off as a private house.

Iain Tweedlie was an active member of the Campaign for Nuclear Disarmament and during a march in George Square, Glasgow, followed by a campaign at the Holy Loch, he was arrested. Ordered to pay a fine of £5, Tweedlie refused and was sent to Barlinnie Prison for 30 days in August 1962. News of the minister's imprisonment brought the country's attentions to Lugar, but halfway through his term of imprisonment his fine was paid by well-wishers.

Lugar Church celebrated its centenary on 18 October 1967, when 350 members packed the building. A number of former ministers were in attendance. In 1974-75 Iain Tweedlie was Moderator of Ayr Presbytery. He died on 27 July 1988.

On 26 February 1989 Lugar church was separated from St Ninian's Church at Netherthird and linked with Old Cumnock Old Church. At Lugar Tweedlie was replaced by Rev Martin James MacKean who had been ordained and inducted to Old Cumnock Old Church on 13 December 1984. Martin MacKean was born on 3 October 1957, the son of James Black MacGillivray MacKean and Estelle Margaret Mair. He received his education at John Watson's in Edinburgh from 1962-74. He trained as a valuation surveyor from 1974-77. He then attended the University of Edinburgh from 1977-83, graduating with a Bachelor of Divinity degree and Diploma in Ministry. He was licensed by the Presbytery of Edinburgh on 3 July 1983. He was appointed as assistant minister at Glasgow St John's Renfield Church and served from 1983-4. He was married on 23 April 1988 to Audrey Margaret Beat (b. 16 June 1961), daughter of David Beat and Elizabeth Mathieson. They had two children – Ross Martin MacKean (b. 12 May 1989) and Rachel Elizabeth MacKean

(b. 17 November 1990). In 1990 the congregation was shocked to discover the church had been broken into and valuable silver stolen. On 30 June 1993 Rev MacKean was translated to Balerno Church, Edinburgh.

The next minister of Lugar Parish Church was Rev John William Paterson, who also served at Old Cumnock. Born on 7 June 1954 at Kelloholm, Kirkconnel, John Paterson was the son of William Paterson and Doris Craik Halliday. He attended school in that village, followed by Sanquhar and Dumfries academies (1959-72). He then studied at Stirling University from 1972-76, graduating with a BSc and DipEd, followed by the Royal Military Academy, Sandhurst (1976-77), where he was Cadet of the Year. From 1990-93 he studied divinity at the University of St Andrews (St Mary's College), graduating with a Bachelor of Divinity degree. He was awarded the Samuel Rutherford Prize for theology there. He worked overseas on mission work for a number of years, being the principal of a private school in Pakistan from 1984-90. He was licensed by the Presbytery of Dumfries on 4 July 1993 and was appointed as assistant minister at Largo Newburn with Largo St David's Church from 1993-4. Rev Paterson was married on 23 July 1983 to Margery Grace Macaulay (b. 1 June 1956), daughter of Francis Macaulay and Muriel Wilson. Rev Paterson was ordained and inducted to Lugar with Old Cumnock Old Parish on 15 June 1994.

OUR LADY & ST PATRICK'S R. C. CHURCH

After the war the members of St Patrick's chapel at Birnieknowe began fundraising by organising dances, concerts and drives in the Auchinleck hall. The Society of St Vincent de Paul was founded, which was active in looking after the needs of the poor. In 1946 the status of the school was changed, from being a junior secondary to primary school. Thus pupils left Birnieknowe and went either to St John's Junior Secondary in Cumnock or to St Joseph's Senior Secondary in Kilmarnock, depending on whether they passed the Primary Promotion Examination. In 1947 school dinners were introduced, central heating had been installed, and in 1950 electric lighting supplied. The hall in Auchinleck was extended in 1949, so that a sanctuary could be included, allowing mass and other services.

Father Maxwell moved from Auchinleck to Annbank, where he served from 1950-55. This was followed by work in Stevenston parish, from 1955 until his death there on 13 March 1976.

In 1950 Rev Matthew Littleton took up the post and he remained at Auchinleck for three years. He was born in Ireland and ordained at Glasgow in 1929. In 1946 he took up the position of priest at Ardrossan, thus moving into Galloway Diocese, remaining there until he moved to Auchinleck. Father Littleton was transferred to Kilmarnock in 1953, serving at St Joseph's Chapel until his death on 9 August 1977.

The next priest at Auchinleck was Rev Michael Rynn, who served the parish from 1953-61. Irish by birth, he was ordained in Glasgow Archdiocese in 1928.

Prior to coming to Auchinleck he served at Kilbirnie (1933-48) and Kirkconnel (1948-1953). Following Auchinleck, Father Rynn moved to the church at Beith where he remained until 1966, retiring to Clonakilly in Ireland. He died there on 22 February 1978.

Whilst the number of Roman Catholics in the parish remained high, a number of assistant priests helped out at Birnieknowe. These were James Manning (1949-53, died 1980), James Bannon (1953-56, born 1915, died 1986), Michael Lynch (1956-59) and Francis D. Crowley (1959-62, born 1932, died 1982).

The condition of the church at Birnieknowe continued to deteriorate, having never been fully maintained since the onset of war. Fundraising was now aimed at building a new church adjoining the hall in Auchinleck. The congregation became smaller with the erection of St Joseph's in Catrine in 1948, and the appointment of its first priest. The school had 190 pupils in 1955, rising to 220 in 1958, its catchment area including Catrine and Mauchline.

In 1961 Father Daniel Brennan was appointed to Auchinleck. Born in Glasgow in 1917, he was educated at St Aloysius' College, followed by St Peter's. He was ordained in 1942, serving at Saltcoats, Kilmarnock, Whithorn, Castle Douglas and Annbank before coming to Auchinleck. He remained here until 1970. Father Brennan was active in promoting the erection of the new church, work on which began in 1963. The architect was Charles William Gray of Edinburgh. On 29 June 1964 the new chapel of Our Lady of Lourdes and St Patrick was opened by the Bishop of Galloway, with some items brought from Birnieknowe, including the Stations of the Cross, Sanctuary Lamp, the font, and the pews.

The social activities of the church declined, the Men's Guild, Altar Society, Children of Mary, Knights and Handmaids of the Blessed Sacrament, Legion of Mary, Young Men's Society and Knights of St Columba all folding, leaving just the Union of Catholic Mothers and the St Vincent de Paul Society still active. In 1977 an old stained glass window from Birnieknowe church was saved from the demolition contractors and presented to the church by Gordon Hoyle. It was re-erected in the sanctuary. In 1986 the hall was refurbished, the ceiling lowered, walls plastered, new roof constructed and a large meeting room erected.

On 22 July 1966 the centenary of St Patrick's Church was celebrated, the guest speaker being Joseph MacGhee, Bishop of Galloway. Father Brennan moved to the chapel at Beith in 1970, but died in London on 29 January 1974.

Father Brennan was followed by Rev Sean Murphy, a native of Ireland, who entered the Salvatorians with the religious name, Bonaventure. He was ordained in 1948 and came to the Diocese of Galloway in 1953. He served at Troon, Hurlford, Saltcoats, Newton Stewart and Waterside before coming to Auchinleck in 1970. He died here on 2 October 1975.

The vacancy was filled by Rev James Coyle, who served for two years before his death on 25 February 1977 aged 58. He is buried in the new cemetery. Father Coyle was born in Ayr in 1919. Following his education, he was ordained in Dumfries in 1942. He served in a number of chapels – Waterside, Stranraer, Annbank, Dumfries, Stranraer for a second time, Saltcoats and Muirkirk prior to his arrival at Auchinleck.

The next priest was Rev John Kane, who served from 1977 until 1985. Born in Stevenston in 1921, he received his education at Glasgow University, followed by Blairs College and the Scots College in Rome. He served at St Joseph's in Kilmarnock from 1952-57, after which he worked as a professor at Blairs College until 1964. He then served as priest at Dalry, Maybole and Waterside, before arriving in Auchinleck. He moved on to Galston.

The next priest was Father Thomas Joseph Murphy, appointed in 1985. Murphy was born in Kilmarnock in 1919 and was educated at St Joseph's Academy there. He attended St Aloysius' College in Glasgow, followed by Blairs College. He was ordained in 1943. His first ten years were spent at St Margaret's in Ayr, followed by seven years in Dalbeattie and four years in Dalry. A couple of years at Prestwick followed, and from 1966 until 1985 he served at St Mary's in Irvine. He was elevated to the Cathedral Chapter of Canons of the Diocese on 15 February 1986.

At Birnieknowe the chapel, presbytery and school were demolished, leaving just the convent, converted into a private house. In the 1980s the ground was used as a small caravan site, but in January 1990 the convent, renamed Laurienne, was purchased by the Butterfly Foundation, a charity based in Kilmarnock which cared for cancer sufferers. The building was converted into a hospice, but was only used for three months before financial difficulties led them to close it. After sitting empty for a few months, the building was gutted by fire on 22 November 1990, leaving a roofless shell.

OTHER DENOMINATIONS

In the 1950s a number of Jehovah's Witnesses arrived in the district and a group of converts joined them. In 1950 there had been no Witnesses in Cumnock and district but by 1959 there were 50. They acquired an old building at 107-111 Main Street for £100 and set about converting it into a Kingdom Hall. The building was reroofed, using timbers from buildings recently demolished. The ceiling of the main hall was raised from eight to twelve feet high, and 80 seats were obtained from an old picture house. Most of the work was carried out by the members themselves and following eighteen months' work they were delighted to welcome Don Ward, the Scottish Supervisor of Witnesses, to officially open the hall on 11 April 1959.

In Park Road the Christian Brethren had 60 members in 1950 with 200 children attending the Sunday afternoon Bible Class. Membership fell gradually to 41 in 1981 and 25 in 1991.

The Auchinleck Christian Union was regarded as a focal centre of the community, having weekly tea meetings at their Well Road hall. James McConnell was president of the group, followed by John Nisbet from 1953 to 1959 whereupon James McConnell was re-elected. The children's meetings were discontinued in 1961 and in 1962 it was considered whether to close the mission all together. At a meeting held on 23 May 1963, at which six of the seven members attended, it was agreed to sell the hall, close the Auchinleck Branch and donate the proceeds to the Ayr Branch of the Christian Union. The hall was purchased by R. D. Hunter of Cumnock for £10,000 and was subsequently used by the Auchinleck Scouts.

The Pentecostal Assembly of God had a hall at 117-119 Main Street which was opened in 1970, the building having been bought from Liptons, being previously a grocery. The first church business meeting was held on 15 August 1970. The two main founders were Frank Smith and Robert Lockhart, with about ten other members in the first year, rising to around eighteen. Frank Smith acted as pastor until 1977 when he was replaced by Maimie Simpson, who served until 1987, followed by Alwynne Pearson. Membership rose to 30 in 1978, but fell again to eighteen by 1990. Services were held twice on a Sunday, on Thursday evenings, and there was a children's meeting on Saturdays. The church was eventually closed, and the building subsequently demolished.

EDUCATION

In 1950 Auchinleck Junior Secondary School had a roll of 750 pupils, aged between five and fifteen. Of these, 600 pupils were in the primary department, the remaining 150 pupils housed in the Main Street secondary department. John Allan was still the headmaster, with 26 teachers. Each year around twenty pupils left Auchinleck primary school to attend the academy at Cumnock where languages were taught. Teaching at Auchinleck for a time was J. Campbell Kerr, who became well-known throughout Scotland as the artist who painted the cover of the weekly *People's Friend* magazine. In 1958 James W. Armour became the new headmaster, remaining until his death in April 1961. That year the school had 771 pupils and in August 1962 new temporary huts were erected at both sites to accommodate the increase in numbers.

There was some difficulty in getting teachers to fill vacancies at Auchinleck at this time and the county council erected two houses in an attempt to attract them. In August 1961 John Finlayson became the new headmaster, transferring from Bank School at New Cumnock. He, too, died in office on 16 January 1970, to be replaced by Alexander Nelson, who retired in 1991. He was succeeded by Danny Easton. The school had to be extended again in August 1966 by the erection of another hut containing two classrooms. Accommodation eased with the opening of the new Academy in 1971, when the old infant school was converted to a nursery school for the pre-fives.

John Strachan continued as headmaster at Lugar Primary School. Immediately after the war the roll had dropped to 170, having fallen steadily since 1900. In

September 1948 the first two pupils from the new houses at Logan were enrolled. It was decided that pupils from Logan should be allowed to pick from Lugar or Cronberry which school to attend. As Logan was being built the roll at Lugar increased again, to 187 in 1949. In that year John Strachan moved to Kilmarnock and Alexander A. Rowan was appointed headmaster. He had previously taught at Lugar, but had returned to his home area of Girvan and Barr in between. The roll increased to 214 in 1953 when a new classroom hut was erected. In 1958 the projected roll indicated that Lugar School would not cope with the numbers.

7.3 St Patrick's Primary class, c. 1961 *(Moira Frize)*

At the same time as the new Roman Catholic chapel was erected in Auchinleck, the education authority commenced building a replacement St Patrick's Primary School in May 1966. Located off Well Road, it was opened on 29 May 1967. In 1958 plans to erect the new school at Dalsalloch had been abandoned due to mining subsidence. Thomas A. O. Milgrew MA was the headmaster, along with a secular teaching staff, for the Sisters of the Cross and Passion had decided to leave on 12 July 1965. In 1971 the school suffered some damage, as did a few houses in Quarryknowe, due to mining subsidence. Mr Milgrew retired in 1974 and died on 26 May 2006, aged 91. He was succeeded as head teacher by Miss Witherington and then by Mrs Amy Kinnaird.

As Logan was growing, and Lugar's population diminishing, it was decided to erect a new school in the former community. Lugar School's final day was on 3 July

1963 when the closing ceremony was held in Lugar Church. Prizes were presented by Mrs Hunter, formerly Miss Jean MacCardel of Craigston House, the dux being won by David MacKillop. When Logan Primary School opened on 18 August that year the roll was 235, including children admitted from Cronberry. Alex Rowan continued as headmaster until 1976. Logan School had been built at a cost of around £90,000.

At Cronberry Junior Secondary School Sam MacQuaker retired as headmaster in spring 1946, to be replaced by Alec M. Sloan. The school served Cronberry and district, with some pupils moving on from Dalblair Side School to it, and in some cases travelling from Logan to Cronberry, if the family rehoused in Logan had originally lived in Cronberry. In 1947 the roll was 80 rising to 100 in 1951. Some pupils at Lugar attended Cronberry for part of the week for some practical subjects. From 1948 to 1951 some of the school's excess rooms were used by local miners as a training centre. From 1951 onwards these rooms were used by primaries 4, 5 and 6 of St John's Roman Catholic school in Cumnock, due to overcrowding in the old school at Bank Avenue. This continued until 1961 when the new St Conval's High School was opened. Similarly, in 1952 the infant class from Cumnock school was based at Cronberry, as were some pupils from Cumnock Academy.

Two Cronberry pupils were to die at the end of 1949; one of them fell from the parapet of Logan Bridge, the other from the Black Rock in the Bello Path. On a happier note, Eric Caldow signed for Glasgow Rangers at Cronberry School in 1951. In the 1960-61 season he became team captain and captain of Scotland. Alec Sloan left Cronberry in 1955 to become headmaster at Coylton Primary school. He was a Justice of the Peace, and wrote a book of memoirs entitled *Those Were the Days*, privately published. The next head was P. D. Anderson, who saw great changes.

In the late 1960s the school was converted into a special school, the ordinary pupils being transferred to Logan. These special pupils, with physical and mental handicaps of various types, were joined in 1972 by pupils from Garrallan School in Old Cumnock parish which was closed that year. The school continued as a special school until it was replaced by Hillside School, erected at Drumbrochan in Cumnock in 1991.

Another special School was erected at Easton Place in Auchinleck. The headmistress was Margo MacFadzean (until 1991). In 1991 the school was closed, the pupils transferring to the new Hillside School in Cumnock.

The Public School at Dalblair was what was known as a 'side school', or school attached to another main school. Dalblair served pupils from the upper Glenmuir, and some went on to attend Cronberry, to which school it was associated. Miss Helen D. Campbell was the school's teacher, retiring in July 1950. When Dalblair was closed it had the distinction of being the last side school in the country. The building survives, converted into a dwelling house.

7.4 Auchinleck Academy in 2015 *(Dane Love)*

There had been plans for a new secondary school at Auchinleck for a number of years previous to work commencing on Auchinleck Academy. The school was built on fifteen acres of land purchased from Robert Smith Drummond of Dalsalloch. The new school was designed jointly by Clark Fyfe (Ayr County Architect) and his assistants, C. Toner and W. Kerr, and the head architect of Messrs Crudens Limited, which company had won the contract to build it. The first pupils made their way to the school in January 1971, the official opening ceremony being held on 31 March 1971, performed by William Paterson JP, Convener of Ayr County Council. Also in attendance was J. I. Wallace, Director of Education, Thomas MacIntyre, Education Convener, Jim Sillars, M. P. for South Ayrshire, and William Goudie, Vice Convener of Ayr County Council. The cost of construction was £1,138,465 and the academy comprised of four main buildings with five surrounding playing fields. There was a large assembly hall with stage, lecture theatre (its external mural somewhat distinctive), two dining halls, games complex with hall, gym and swimming pool, library and, of course, numerous classrooms. The first rector appointed was William M. Crichton MA, former head of Muirkirk Secondary School. On his retiral he was replaced by James Aitken. He in turn was superseded by Colin MacLean. Six hundred pupils were enrolled in the first year, with a projected roll of 1,750, making it the largest comprehensive school in Ayrshire. The roll subsequently fell, however, to around 900 in November 1990.

The Lyon Office was petitioned on 26 August 1970 for a coat of arms for the new school. The arms granted were: Argent, a bend Vert surmounted of three bars

Sable, the middle bar charged with three cinquefoils of the First. The motto, 'A Just Weight', was taken from Proverbs, chapter 11, verse 1. The arms are recorded in the Lyon Register, Vol. 50, p. 107.

INDUSTRY - COAL-MINING

After the war there were just four mines still operating in the parish, all owned by Bairds and Dalmellington. Barony, Highhouse, Lugar and Cronberry Moor pits produced a total of 622,000 tons of coal in 1947. In that year the mines were nationalised, the National Coal Board taking over numerous pits in Britain. At the time there were 1,763 workers employed in the parish mines, 1,357 of which worked underground.

Cronberry Moor colliery produced 62,000 tons of coal in 1946, 67,000 tons in 1947, falling to 60,000 tons in 1951. In 1946 there were 162 men working below ground, plus a further 48 on the surface. The pit was closed in March 1957 due to exhaustion of the reserves.

Lugar employed 67 men in 1947, 54 of which worked below ground. Output was 8,000 tons per year, rising to 20,000 tons in 1951 when 100 men were employed. On average, there were 116 men employed at the mine, peaking at 130. Its biggest output occurred in 1949. On the surface was a screening plant, but coal had to be taken to Cronberry Moor for washing. There were neither baths nor canteen for the miners. The pit was closed in 1953 and abandoned in 1954.

In 1950 Mortonmuir pit was developed by the NCB. Located north-east of Cronberry, this pit did not last long due to serious water problems and was closed in 1954, never having produced any amount of coal. Another small pit, Powharnal (east of Boghead farm) was developed in the 1950s by the National Coal Board but proved to be unprofitable and was closed in 1959. Also at Boghead in 1950 an open cast mine was opened, producing around 900 tons per day at that time.

In 1956 a new coal-mine was sunk at Gasswater, named Cairnhill Pit, by the National Coal Board. It was to work seams left by the old Gasswater Coal Pits. The baths were erected that year and by 1957 the pit produced 350 tons of coal per day. A new way of 'continuous mining' was then being experimented with at Cairnhill and proved to be a suitable method in the correct conditions. On 23 October 1958 there was a small subsidence at the mine but there were no casualties. In 1959 a new coal preparation plant was erected, capable of handling 75 tons per hour. In 1971 Cairnhill mine won the NCB National Safety Competition for the best improvement in accident avoidance, due mainly to the improved lighting at the pit. At the time there were 245 employees, producing 2,000 tons per week, most of which went to the power station at Yoker. The pit continued to operate until 1976 when it was closed.

After hostilities ended, work resumed in 1946 on the sinking of Barony's No. 3 shaft. This shaft, used for transporting men, materials and coal, was 2,052 feet deep, 21 feet 7 inches in diameter, lined with concrete. New winders of 1,500 hp and 1,100 hp were installed, and the winders on shafts 1 and 2 replaced. A new treatment plant was erected, the first operational Dense/Medium plant in Scotland. It was also the largest in Britain at the time and treated coal from Whitehill and Hindsward pits as well as Barony. When work on the third shaft was completed in 1950, it could take four cages of four decks, capable of accommodating a 2½ ton capacity mine car on each deck. At this time 1,128 men were employed in the pit, of which 856 worked below ground. The parish of Auchinleck produced 645,000 tons of coal per annum, and it was reckoned that 80% of the population was supported either directly or indirectly by mining.

7.5 Barony Colliery from the air *(Author's Collection)*

In 1946, when the pit was taken over by the National Coal Board, there were 804 miners working below ground in the mine, with 247 men working on the surface. In 1947 production was 412,000 tons of coal.

At the beginning of 1947, half an hour before the day shift was ready to ascend No. 2 shaft, one of the cages broke loose and fell 1,500 feet to the pit bottom, sinking into 60 feet of sludge. The master ring, which connected the cage to the winding cable, had broken. The cage was loaded with four hutches of coal and fortunately no-one was injured. The pit was idle for two days afterwards, losing 1,500 tons output. Production in 1950 was around 380,000 tons per annum, expected to rise with the completion of the new head-frame of No. 3 shaft in 1954, an 'A' shaped horrals of 180 feet in height.

There was quite a bit of redevelopment at the Barony in 1958. Output increased with new horizons of 238 and 289 fathoms worked. A new preparation plant was built, capable of cleaning 450 tons per hour, new electrical winders installed over shafts 1, 2 and 3, and a new canteen created. For a couple of days in February, some of the men went on strike over a wages dispute.

At the start of the 1960s there were 1,600 employees, but on 8 November 1962 a serious incident occurred when No. 2 shaft collapsed and the winding frame partly fell into the hole. It proved to be a disaster for the whole district, the culmination of three lesser subsidences which had thrown the future of the pit into doubt. At 2.15 on Thursday morning an inrush of debris fell 1,400 feet down No. 2 shaft, trapping four men. The Mines Rescue Brigade went into swift operation, with support from similar stations at Highhouse, Whitehill and Kilmarnock, but it was soon realised that there was no hope of getting the men out alive. Indeed, following the collapse of the head-frame, weighing 1,200 tons, into the hole on Wednesday 14 November, attempts to recover the bodies were suspended.

The men who lost their lives were not of the parish – they were Henry Green (aged 44) of Netherthird, John MacNeill (49) of Drongan, George Wade of Carluke, and Thomas Fyvie of Ayr, the latter two employed by Andrew Kyle Ltd of Galston. On 16 November a memorial service to the dead men was held in the community centre, conducted jointly by Rev G. A. MacCutcheon and Rev C. L. Johnston, and attended by 1,200 men. Eleven hundred of the pit's 1,614 workers were laid off, almost 200 men were redeployed to other pits, and over 300 were kept on to carry out remedial work.

Shafts 1 and 2 were filled in, leaving just No. 3 shaft in operation. There were many tales saying that the pit would be closed down, but Lord Robens insisted that Barony had a future. No coal came from the pit for four years while rehabilitation work was undertaken and a new shaft, No. 4, was sunk. Work commenced in October 1963. During construction, on 14 January 1964, James MacIntyre, aged 55, from Doncaster, was killed near to the shaft. When it was completed in September 1966, following the spending of £2,000,000, coal was once again produced. No. 4 shaft was 1,672 feet deep, 18 feet in diameter, and concrete lined. In September 1969 the new pit canteen was completed. Robert Johnston, manager at Barony, left in 1970. In 1973 the pit had 1,025 employees, producing 320,000 tons of coal. In 1980 there were 849 men working below ground, 157 above. By 1985 there were around 700 workers in the pit, dropping to 390 in October 1988. This figure gradually decreased until the pit was finally closed in 1989. Demolition work commenced, most of the surface buildings being removed. The older buildings were retained for a time, being of architectural importance, but eventually they, too, were demolished.

In 1946 output at Highhouse was 135,000 tons produced by 337 miners plus 98 surface workers. This rose to 185,000 tons in 1951. In 1959 a new winding engine was constructed at the pit and 'Auld Ben' was dismantled and taken to Heriot-Watt College in Edinburgh, the last working machine of its type in Britain. It was later transferred to the Scottish Mining Museum in Midlothian. The numbers of miners employed in the pit decreased gradually until 1980 when 254 men worked below ground, 47 above. In 1983 the pit was closed down and work commenced on dismantling some of the machinery. Some artefacts were taken to the museum at Waterside, near Dalmellington, though the headframe remained in situ, acting as a monument to the lost mines and miners of the district.

The miners at Highhouse and Barony went on strike on numerous occasions, often just for a day, at other times for a week. A few strikes only can be detailed – 3-4 September 1958 over ventilation at Highhouse; in September 1959 a strike at the same pit occurred over a dispute concerning wages. After three days more than 1,500 tons of coal production was lost; 5-11 June 1962 over a sacking at Barony; 31 October 1967 over six men given notice to transfer at Barony. On 21 December 1958 600 miners attended a protest meeting against pit closures at which Emrys Hughes gave a speech. Active on that day was the Barony Branch of the National Union of Miners. The miners nationally had gone on strike in 1972 for seven weeks and downed tools again n 1974. With the threat of pit closures in 1984 they went on strike again (from 9 March). This strike proved to be the final act by the miners in the parish, for it lasted until 5 March the year following, though by then a number of miners had become demoralised and returned to work. Killoch Colliery, west of Ochiltree, was closed within two years, some miners transferring to Barony, but when it closed the National Coal Board, or British Coal as it had been renamed, no longer operated any coal mines in the Ayrshire coalfield.

Of miners killed in local mines from 1945 onwards the list is long, and includes the following:

Highhouse:
Hugh Reynolds and Andrew Smart, 17 August 1947
Robert Mitchell Harvey, 14 December 1954
Daniel Gibson, 8 August 1962

Barony:
Vinces Azbraitis, 14 July 1950
B. MacCluskie, 1954
James 'Clinks' MacLean, 27 September 1957
Richard Murray, 1958
Josef Turzyck (41), 23 March 1959. Fell down shaft.
Antonio Cano (38), 1 April 1959. Fell 700 fell down shaft. Italian.
John Harkness (22), 27 August 1962, from Catrine, struck by mine car.

Frank Young, 6 November 1962, fall from roof.
James MacIntyre, 14 January 1964

Another small mine existed in the parish in the 1950s/1960s, although being located at Penbreck it was more often associated with Kirkconnel or Sanquhar. The mine operated for a short time and was run by a small firm from Sanquhar.

To service the mining machinery from across Ayrshire, new workshops were erected at Lugar. The National Coal Board also erected new offices, designed by the board architect, Egon Riss. Erected in the 1950s, the offices were extended in 1963.

With the demise of deep mining, the workshops at Lugar were becoming increasingly under-utilised and eventually they were closed in June 1985. In 1984 there had been 140 workers there, but this number had dropped to 40 by March 1985.

Although the deep mines were gradually all closed, mining by open cast means became the norm for the next period in the parish's mining history. A number of open cast mines were established across much of the countryside in the parish to the east of the village, and sites were developed at Darnconner and Common farms (the former from 1985, the latter from 1990). Birnieknowe was open cast from 1994 onwards, the land being returned to agricultural use within a few years.

The open cast mine at Darnconner produced over 600,000 tons of coal before 1991. Darnconner was also used for the extraction of clay for brick-making. Brick-making collapsed, and so the site became abandoned. It was sold to a waste management company for landfill purposes, planning permission for it being granted in 1996. However, the site was never used and permission for dumping expired. The hole had also filled with water, creating a lochan of around 30 acres in extent. The site was subsequently subject to a variety of semi-restoration schemes, whereby the loch would be retained and the surrounding mounds landscaped to reduce their impact on the countryside.

When Highhouse Pit was closed an industrial estate was formed, some of the units located in surviving miners' rows or former pit buildings. New factory units were also erected and the estate was officially opened in January 1990 by Sir David Nickson, chairman of the Scottish Development Agency. Work at the site had been funded jointly by British Coal Enterprises Ltd, Scottish Development Agency, Cumnock and Doon Valley District Council, Strathclyde Regional Council and the European Economic Community. Thirty small industrial units were created.

Work in the Barytes mines continued. Between 1940 and 1965 the mines produced a total of 500,000 tons of barytes, about one-fifth of the total output from British mines, of which Gasswater barytes was regarded as one of the purest to be obtained. The ore was used extensively in the rubber industry, paint manufacture and in the manufacture of linoleum.

The owners, Wrentnall Baryta Company Limited, were taken over by the Anglo-Austral Mining Company in 1947, following which new development work took place. Four mines operated in total, the first, the Gasswater Mine, being located furthest west. From it an aerial ropeway extended just short of two miles down to the treatment plant at Gasswater village, where a row of six houses for employees existed. The ropeway carried buckets which held around five hundredweight of barytes, emptied by an operator into bins of different coloured mineral. The waste material was then separated by the gravitation method and the dressed ore sent by rail to Messrs Ores Zinc White Ltd at Widnes, near Liverpool, for reducing.

The mine offices were at first located at Gasswater village, next to the dressing plant, but were later transferred to the Gasswater mine. From it a narrow gauge railway extended for 1¼ miles eastward, past the former Central and Southern mines to the Burnside Mine, the last mine to be developed. Mining of barytes differed to that of coal in that the barytes veins were vertical, varying in width from one to three feet. Mining was carried out in an upward fashion, a shaft sunk to a level, the roof of which was blown down. The ore was cleared away, rubble filled in below, thereby raising the floor, and the new roof was again blown. Levels of around 100 feet difference proved to be the most satisfactory distance for operations. At Gasswater Mine the levels were 81, 112, 212, 312, 412, 512, and 612 feet deep.

7.6 Gasswater Barytes Mine *(Author's Collection)*

Though different to coal mining, a number of colliers found employment in these mines, but most of the managerial positions were filled by men brought up from England, from the mining regions of West Yorkshire. The greatest number of employees was just short of 100. The period from 1950 to 1965 was the mines' best years in terms of output, but by then the quality had dropped considerably. Around 15,000 tons of ore were excavated each year during that period. In 1956 the old horrals at Gasswater was removed and replaced by a larger winding frame brought from Cowgreen pit in England. Anglo-Austral merged with Rio Tinto Zinc in 1962, but with quality dropping as the mines deepened it was decided to close down in 1965. Seventy men lost their jobs. A two-day sale of equipment took place on 29-30 April that year. By this time the mine was owned by the Imperial Smelting Company, which also owned the barytes mine near Lochwinnoch, Renfrewshire. Around 1980 the bings at the barytes mines were riddled to obtain ore which had previously been overlooked.

7.7 Gasswater Barytes Treatment Works *(Author's Collection)*

Deaths in the barytes mines were less frequent than in the coal mines, but they still occurred. Alexander Paton was accidentally killed there on 25 November 1948 at the age of 47 years. He was buried in Auchinleck cemetery.

Soon after the nationalisation of the electricity generating industry on 1 April 1955 it was announced that a new power station was to be built in Ayrshire which could generate electricity from waste colliery washery slurry. Commissioned by the

South of Scotland Electricity Board, the burning of coal slurry to produce power was a new idea and thus Barony Generating Station was the first of its kind in Great Britain. The slurry was dried and swept into the furnace by fans. Twenty-four and a half acres of land of Thirdpart farm was acquired adjacent to the Barony Colliery and work commenced on what was to be the largest structure in Auchinleck parish. Two cooling towers of reinforced concrete 200 feet high were built by Bierrum and Partners, the 265 feet chimney by Tileman and Company. John Laing was responsible for the foundations and buildings, whilst the Colville Construction Company erected the steelwork. Other work was constructed by Babcock and Wilcox Ltd. The old mill dam at Ochiltree was rebuilt and used as a source of water for cooling. The first two 30,000 kW generators were formally commissioned on 11 October 1957 by the Secretary of State, John S. MacLay, who described the generating station as a 'modern alchemist's dream come true'.

7.8 Barony Power Station and Barony Colliery *(Dane Love)*

Pits in a fifteen mile radius were used as sources of washery slurry, of which 150,000 tons per annum were required. The output, as well as providing power to Barony Colliery, was sufficient to supply a town of 50,000 inhabitants. The cost of construction, £10,500,000, was more than twice the original estimate.

The Barony Generating Station continued to operate until 1982 when washery slurry became more difficult to get. The two large cooling towers were blown up in 1983, the chimney in 1986 and the site cleared thereafter.

The old bings of the parish were used as road-metal or for brick-making. In 1950 the Common Brickwork was erected. A fair-sized set up had a chamber kiln, machine building and other ancillary works. The chimney was a prominent feature on the moor. The works produced bricks until 1976, when it closed. Originally owned by A. Kenneth & Sons of Dreghorn, it was latterly part of the Scottish Brick Company. The kiln was demolished in the winter of 1980-81. In 1965 the Cronberry Slag Company was formed to work the old slag bings on Airds Moss for road bottoming, housing infill and other uses. The company was owned by Andrew Wilson of Coylton and William Anderson of Mauchline.

7.9 Barony Power Station *(Author's Collection)*

After the war the Auchinleck Gas Company kept on growing, and by 1950 was serving around 1,000 households in the village. The gasworks at the bottom end of Main Street, occupying a site of two acres, had a gas-manager's house, workshops and two cylindrical gasometers. Gas managers included William Forsyth. The Act of Nationalisation of the many small gas companies was passed in 1949. It took many years to bring a gas grid to the various villages and so the local gas works continued to produce their own gas. A new gas main from a large works at Kilmarnock was laid to Auchinleck and on to New Cumnock in 1958. In April that year the local gasworks at Auchinleck, Catrine, Old and New Cumnock were closed, but a gasometer was retained at each station, to store a limited supply of gas in case the Kilmarnock works failed in some way. In the 1970s the Kilmarnock works were closed, when the supply was changed from coal gas to Natural Gas piped in from the North Sea.

Currie and Company began to expand following the war. At first lorries were scarce, so ex-service vehicles were bought and used to distribute bottles of lemonade in the district. Sugar was still rationed, and it was not until it was de-rationalised in 1953 that the process of expansion commenced. In 1954 Currie's bought over the Minford lemonade company of Hamilton, followed by Johnstone-Hill of Dumfries in 1968, Arnison of Wigtown and Carey's of Ayr. Production of lemonade at the other plants was ended and they (except for Ayr) were used as depots for distributing lemonade made at Auchinleck. Further depots were established at Earlston (sold 1990), Stranraer and Ardrossan. In 1990 McDougall's of Bonhill was taken over. Though the production of lemonade was switched to Auchinleck (using the McDougall recipe), it was still sold in Dunbartonshire with McDougall labels.

In 1950 Currie's opened an ice-lolly factory which operated until 1965. One of the better known lollies was the 'Treble Chance', sold for three pence, which had an ice-cream centre surrounded by raspberry and orange flavoured ice. Production of lemonade continued to grow, and extensions to the factory were made in 1957 and 1959. In the latter year Currie's patented a new method of producing lemonade which prevented the growth of bacteria. A means of doing this had long been sought by many multi-national soft-drink companies. Currie's used carbon-dioxide to fill the gap in the tanks above the liquid sugar syrup which was used in the manufacture at that time, and which had to have a bacteria count within a specified legal limit. With Currie's new method no bacteria could live in the carbon dioxide. In 1959 Currie's produced 4,800 bottles per day, at peak production using 4,000 gallons of syrup. A newly-introduced flavour was Bitter Lemon. Using 160 gallons of milk per day they produced 3,000 dozen ice lollies and from 300 to 400 gallons of ice cream.

On 2 November 1959 Currie's was taken over by the Metallic Manufacturing Co. Ltd. of Ardrossan (owned by Morton of Dunure). The last surviving MacMichael brother, Robert, retired to a farm near Ayr. Production continued to grow; in 1977 65 people were employed at the plant, rising to 75 in 1990. In 1989, to improve distribution in Dumfriesshire and Galloway, a joint company, Dunn and Currie, was formed, with Dunn and Moore Ltd. Production in 1990 was around twelve million units (bottles of various sizes). When the old houses of Jamieson Place were demolished a new wider entrance to the factory was created from Main Street, and the flower beds and lawns planted. In 1990, following a time of discoloured water from Glen Afton, a private well was sunk within the yard, from which the factory obtained its water for a time. Water from this well was also sold as Auchinleck Spring Water for a few years.

In 1993 Currie's was sold to Dunn and Moore, who subsequently transferred production to their own factory. Auchinleck was wound down and used as a depot for some years before being completely closed in 1998. The site was sold to Tesco.

Other industries included a small knitwear factory opened in 1947 at Auchinleck. In 1960 a hosiery factory was formed in Park Road.

7.10 Selection of different bottles produced by Currie's of Auchinleck *(Dane Love)*

A new company was set up in Auchinleck in 1994 to manufacture aerosols, known as Barony Universal. Located at the Barony Road Industrial Estate, the firm was established by Stewart Shaw. It made own-label products for various shops and retailers. Stewart Shaw was born in Buckie, Banffshire, in 1952. He was educated at Robert Gordon's College in Aberdeen. From 1976 until 1988 he worked in sales and marketing in Australia. From 1989 to 1993 he was the sales and marketing director of Sanmex, an aerosol manufacturer based in Rutherglen, prior to establishing Barony Universal.

In 1998 the new Egger Barony factory was opened and the manufacture of chipboard commenced. Using timber from Scottish forests, and beyond, in addition to recycled wood, large chipboard sheets were made. Most of this was transported to the Egger factory at Hexham in Northumberland for surface veneering and other finishing.

Other smaller businesses operating in the parish included Vycon Plastics Ltd, which manufactures special plastic ring binders, document wallets and boxes for a variety of uses. The business is located in the former Peden Church. At Lugar Adelphi Engineering and Construction Ltd. was established in 1998 by partners James Davie and Samuel Abercrombie. The firm makes bespoke staircases in steel and other products. Also at Lugar Pollock Farm Equipment Ltd was established in 1997 by James Moran McGhee and Euphemia McGhee. They had purchased the former Pollock agricultural machinery business which had been established in Mauchline in 1867.

COMMERCE
With the ever-growing popularity of the motor-car, businesses were set up to cater for their needs. At the former Bridgend Smithy Bridgend Garage Ltd. was established in 1947 by John Allardyce. The business was continued by Thomas Allardyce. At the opposite end of the village the Merlin Park Service Station was opened in 1942, operated by Alan MacFadzean. The business was transferred to Gordon Hamilton then Murray Blackwood. In 1998 a new building was added alongside for Discount Tyres and Components, run by John McGinn. This business was established in 1988, operating for the first ten years in Cumnock.

The Auchinleck Co-operative Society continued to grow in the immediate post-war period, reaching a membership of 4,000 in 1950. The dividend was 12½% on purchases made, and motor vans took provisions and other goods out into the county for five miles around. The society coal merchant continued to thrive, as did the laundry division. During the 1950s the former Lugar Ironworks Co-operative Society was taken over and this increased the membership. In 1954 the old Peden Church was purchased for use as a store, and in 1956 the society enlarged the Hamilton Place shop in Cumnock. In 1958 there were 5,760 members, buying an average of 49s 6¾d worth of goods per week each, and earning a dividend of 1s 10d in the pound. In 1960 the Church Avenue branch was extended and in 1964 a new food store was erected in Cumnock's Glaisnock Street. In January of that year Harry Russell replaced Mr Brown as the society president.

In 1966 there was a total annual sale of £677,000, soon to be increased when the Catrine Co-op Society was taken over. Membership in 1967 stood at 6,692 though the average weekly purchase per member had fallen to 42s 7d, earning a dividend of 1s 3d in the pound. On 16 September 1967 the laundry, which employed 45 men and 15 women, was closed. Harry Russell had been its manager for the previous 29 years.

In 1971 the Auchinleck Society was taken over by the Ayrshire Regional Co-operative Society (ARCOS) and the dividend (for which members had to remember their number) was replaced by Co-op stamps. This was the beginning of the decline in support for the society, and in 1991 only the Church Avenue branch in Auchinleck was still open, plus the Hamilton Place branch in Cumnock.

A number of coal merchants existed in the parish, one of the longest lasting being MacPherson of Lugar.

James Hill Stewart was the postmaster in Auchinleck from 1976 until August 1991. The position was then filled by John Malcolm Brown.

The Eagle Inn continued to serve thirsty drinkers for many years after the war. In 1981 the proprietor was Bob Hunter. The inn was closed in 1990 when the business went into administration, one of the partners at that time being Anita Stageman. The inn was redeveloped as housing thereafter.

The Market Inn continued to be owned by David and Alex MacLeod until 1964. It thereafter passed through a number of hands, including Knox and Margaret Alexander; Andy and Norma Garrity; George and Anne Heggie; George and Margaret Marshall; John MacPheators (1983-88); and James and Jean Hartley (1988-93). Known locally as the 'Mad Hoose', previous by-names for it were 'The Library' (during the Marshall years) and 'The Manger' (after a short ownership of three months by a couple named Mary and Joseph). The Market Inn was bought by John Kyle on 16 June 1993.

The Boswell Arms became the property of a brewery company and it was leased and managed by a variety of people over the years, including Walter Craig in 1976, Robert and Nan Holland and Tommy Kane. Janey Dowds managed it until 1993, when Douglas Aitken bought the inn and renovated it.

At the Railway Inn the various owners included Robert Dick (a retired policeman), Daniel Sinclair (when it was renamed the Sinclair Arms) and Jim Small. In 1992 the inn was purchased by John Campbell and the Railway Hotel name was revived.

AGRICULTURE

On the farms much time and effort was put into draining fields and improving production. The Scottish Milk Marketing Board ensured a ready market, and so dairying was generally practised, in 1950 the average farm having from 30 to 40 milk cows (mostly Ayrshires) on from 40 to 250 acres, averaging at 140 acres. As the years passed and farm became more mechanised, the amount of labour required fell and the farms grew in size, one farmer buying out another. Thus some farming 'pairs' were formed – Fore and Back Rogerton, Carbello and Sunnyside, Roadinghead and Dixton, to name but a few. A number of steadings were abandoned, a few becoming ruinous, or used, like Stonebriggs, for other uses – a haulage-contractors' garage. From 56 farms in 1950 this figure fell to around 30 units in 1990. Most are owner-occupied, but a few farms belonged to Dumfries estate (in the Glenmuir area), Dunure estate (Boghead) or British Coal. Cropping diminished even more, surviving only in small acreages at the west end of the parish, the rest used for grazing, mainly beef or sheep. The making of hay was largely superseded by silage.

Some of the more remote farms were abandoned and the ground sold off for forestry, notably Penbreck and Auchtitench, or else part of the rough grazing planted with trees - Craigstonhill Plantation, Lugar, being planted in 1959 (30 of the 90 acres were burnt in 1962), Darnconner and High Glenmuir plantations were formed in the early 1980s. Many farmers started secondary businesses to bring in additional income, such as Robert Duncan at Blackston farm, who started R. S. Duncan plant hire in the 1960s, the business being continued after his retiral in 2000 by his son, John Duncan.

LEISURE

Following the war Talbot took a couple of years to rebuild their team, failing to win a trophy in their first two seasons. During this time Beechwood Park witnessed a spectacle when Glasgow Rangers took on a district select, in which three Talbot players took part, to raise money for charity. To improve support and the financial condition of the club, Talbot and Auchinleck Juveniles merged in 1945. The first post-war trophies were won in the 1947-48 season, when Talbot won the Western League Cup for the first time. Other trophies that season included the Moore Trophy, the West of Scotland Cup, the Irvine District Cup and the League Trophy.

The year following the club reached their highest point in their history thus far, winning the Scottish Junior Cup. The opposition in the final was Petershill, favourites before the game but, in front of 68,837 spectators at Hampden Park, Talbot beat the Glasgow side 3-2. The team was Patrick Burns, Scott, MacFadzean, Finnan, Kelvin, Len Loneskie, MacKie, James Robertson, James Galloway, Fraser and Hugh Goldie. The team returned to a village celebrating in carnival style, the Main Street seething with folk bedecked in black and gold wanting a glimpse of the team in the open-topped bus.

Around this time improvements were being made to Beechwood, the funds being raised by a Building Committee (founded 1948) which organised dances, concerts, bingo nights, and other events. One of their first improvements was a concrete and metal barrier round the pitch and a corrugated iron boundary wall. In 1949 they transported 1,200 tons of slag from Highhouse bing to form terracing. In the season following the ground held 9,000 spectators, a record to date, but they witnessed the home team being knocked out of the Scottish Cup. Gates slumped in the years following, and Talbot failed to perform in a way which would attract a greater support. In 1954 a Talbot Social Club was formed to raise money for the team, and with the Supporters Club organised a sale of work in the British Legion Hut which raised over £62. Glory returned to the club again in 1955 when it won the Vernon Trophy, beating Glenafton. In 1956 they beat Irvine Meadow to take the Ayrshire Cup and in 1957 the Western League Southern Section. Fundraising events continued to be organised, Beechwood being the venue in 1956 for an American baseball game with Field Day which raised £116. However the funds were quickly used up when the clubhouse went on fire in July 1956 causing £200 worth of damage to the roof.

Talbot's fortunes on the field tumbled, and they did not win a trophy again until 1977. In 1957 the club almost closed, but bingo games helped to support the team financially. In 1959 Beechwood got floodlights to help in evening training, but in the same year vandals struck. The clubhouse was repeatedly broken into, floorboards ripped up, balls stolen, the floodlights broken, and finally the clubhouse burned down again. The building committee bought a replacement building which was blown over in a storm. It was re-erected in 1960. In 1968 the committee organised the first 'hop' or disco in the community centre, to where the bingo games were moved in order to get a bigger audience. The clubhouse was again broken into, the team's three balls stolen. In 1971 a plan to buy the laundry garage and convert it into a social club fell through.

The 1972-73 season was the club's worst ever, the clubhouse again being burned down, and the team suffering its worst-ever defeat against its auld enemy, Cumnock Juniors, eleven goals to nil. An emergency meeting was held, to which the public were invited, and this seems to have formed a turning point in the club's fortunes.

A new brick clubhouse was erected and in 1975 Talbot scored their greatest win to date, 15-0 against Whitletts. At Beechwood in January 1975 a riot took place in a game against Kilbirnie, spilling out onto the Main Street and resulting in eighteen arrests. In 1977 Willie Knox became the club's new coach and earned the nick-name of the 'Patron Saint of Auchinleck'. Their first trophy was the Jackie Scarlett Cup, won in November 1977, and the Ayrshire League Trophy followed in 1978. In 1979 a new Social Club building was erected, opened in 1980, but a lack of support resulted in its failure.

In 1986 Talbot again won the Scottish Cup, beating Pollok 3-2 at Hampden. The year following they won the cup again, beating Kilbirnie 1-0 at a replay at Rugby Park, Kilmarnock. In 1988 Talbot won for the third successive season, a Scottish record, and the defeated side were none other than Talbot's first final opposition, Petershill. The scorer of the only goal was Talbot's Tom MacDonald. Players who took part in the three finals were:

Alistair Wilson, Brian Lannon, William Young, Sam MacCulloch, Albert Morrison, Ross Findlay, Bert Ferguson, Jimmy MacMillan, Jim O'Donnell, Bobby Dickson, George Gemmell, Tom MacDonald, Kenny Paterson, Tom Dowdells, John MacCool, Derek MacDicken, Dougie Chisholm, John Coughtrie, Gordon Mills, William Russell, Hugh Lyden, Hugh MacDonald and Alec Wilson.

In the New Year's Honours List of 1989 William Knox was awarded the British Empire Medal for his services to football. The clubhouse was again burned down in 1986 and the club took over the former social club building.

On Sunday 19 May 1991 Talbot won through to the Scottish Junior Cup Final for the fifth time, beating Newtongrange Star 1-0, to equal a record set by Parkhead, Petershill and Cambuslang Rangers. The game was played at Brockville Park, Falkirk, in front of thousands of supporters. In the 66th minute Sam MacCulloch headed the ball into the net to score the only goal of the match. The team comprised Wilson, Gemmell, Young, Findlay, MacCulloch, Macdonald, Pirie, Lyden, Mills, Paterson, Thomson, with Frew and Mains as substitutes.

Talbot was to reach the Scottish Junior Cup Final again in 1992. The game was played against local junior enemies, Glenafton Athletic F. C., from New Cumnock. Auchinleck were to win by four goals to nil.

In season 1994-95, Talbot won the First Division, Super Cup and Cumnock & Doon Valley Cup. In the following season they lifted the Ayrshire Cup. In 1996-97 the honours were the Division Champions, Ayrshire Cup, District Cup and East Ayrshire Cup. In 1997-98 they won the Scarlett Cup and in the following season lifted the East Ayrshire and Super cups. In season 1999-2000 Talbot won the Ayrshire Cup.

At Rosebank Lugar Boswell continued to play well, winning the Western League in 1954 and 1956, the Consolation Cup in 1950 and 1954, the Land o' Burns Cup in 1951, the Moore Trophy in 1950, 1951, 1952 and 1956, and the Irvine Cup in 1949. Lugar also held the Western League championship in 1953-54 and 1955-56. In 1956 they reached the final of the Scottish Junior Cup for the first and only time, but were defeated by Petershill 4-1. There were 64,000 spectators present at Hampden to witness the game, played by Fraser, Love, Cathie, MacEwen, Baird, Donnelly, Bingham, Collins, Sharp, Neil and Wilkie. Alexander Sharp was Lugar's goal scorer.

Apart from Beechwood Park, sport was played at the Merlin Park, created on the site of the old Merlin Loch. This loch had been formed in a hollow by building a sluice to prevent water escaping. In addition, the base of the pond was lined with clay to prevent water draining naturally. This was to prove troublesome in the years ahead, for the field was often flooded. Various improvements to the drainage were made from 1958 onwards, though not all were successful - some even claimed the drains were made to flow the wrong way. All throughout the sixties and seventies various plans to drain the park were put into operation, but it still flooded after heavy rain. The park, which has various pitches and recreation areas, was augmented by a new pavilion.

The old playing field at Highhouse was taken over in December 1958 by the Barony Miners' Welfare Club, which planned to form a sports stadium. The council sold the tennis courts to the Miners' Welfare Association and the Barony Harriers Athletic Club put it to good use.

The Picture House was acquired by H. W. Morton, owner of Cumnock Picture House, and continued to show feature films until 29 February 1964 when it was closed. It was still used for bingo until 1974, but this too was terminated and it stood empty for many years until demolition in February 1991.

The Auld Affleck Burns Club was formed in 1947 and joined the Burns Federation that year as club number 649. Though active in its early years, the membership fell and it was wound up in 1952.

The Bowling Club went from strength to strength. In 1962 Joe Devlin represented Scotland. In 1963 the club obtained a drinks licence and set about extending the pavilion to the west, opened in May 1965. A second extension to the east was opened on 16 September 1967. Membership in 1950 was around 100. In 1991 a new wall was erected round the green at the same time as Market Place was improved.

Auchinleck Curling Club did not survive very long after the war. A special meeting was held in the Market Inn on 3 November 1946 when it was agreed to wind the club up. The trophies owned by the club were presented to the Bowling Club, and the small funds held were gifted to the Old Folks' Cabin.

The Angling Club had around 400 members in 1950, one of the highest in Ayrshire. It did a power of work in restocking rivers. Membership fell to 100 in January 1961. A Homing Pigeon Club existed, with its headquarters in a converted railway carriage near to the railway station. Near it was a hut belonging to the Affleck Wheelers Cycling Club. This club became defunct in 1963. One of its members, Bill Houston, achieved fame in the district from his accounts in the *Cumnock Chronicle* of cycling trips all over the world. Farther afield he became known following a BBC Television documentary film entitled *Look, Stranger* which featured him and which has been shown a number of times since. A new hall was erected in Station Road to house the Army Cadet Force.

Guilds of various sorts existed, two of which were sponsored by the Auchinleck Co-operative Society, one for men, the other for women, both held in the Toll Branch Hall. The Men's Guild held an annual Open Forum of Opinion at which numerous topics were debated. The Women's Guild celebrated its fiftieth anniversary on 24 November 1970. Another discussion group met weekly in the school.

Both parish churches had women's and men's guilds and a youth club for children. Older men had a wooden hut or cabin next to the bowling green erected by the Boswell St James Masonic Lodge. The Masons themselves were to obtain property at 104-108 Main Street which was converted into a Masonic Temple.

The Auchinleck and District Male Voice Choir continued to find fame outwith the district under the guidance of James Yates, who died on 27 December 1970. In 1948 the choir was chosen to represent Scotland at the Miners' Festival in London. It celebrated its Silver Jubilee by holding a concert in the Barony Church Hall on 5 March 1958. However, interest in the choir began to wane and it was wound up in 1961, despite a meeting being called in November that year to try to entice new members to join. In April 1965 the choir was reformed for a short time to provide music for the BBC film *In a Mining Parish* which was made about the collapse of the Barony shaft and its effect locally. The film was televised on 12 September that year. Women singers could join the Boswell Ladies' Choir, men the Barony Singers, conducted by Craig MacMillan. In August 1961 a new music shop was opened at 185a Main Street by Mr Morrison who founded the Thistle Accordion Band in 1962. Those who were not musical could appreciate the art of others by joining the Auchinleck and District Recorded Music Society.

The British Legion had a hut in Well Road which was used for various social events, as well as billiards, table tennis, darts and carpet bowls. In the late 1960s and 1970s the Affleck Week gala was a popular event of merry-making in the village. Various socials were held during the year to raise funds for this.

Auchinleck Scouts continued to operate, the first Queen's Scout being George Clark, who gained his badge in 1958. Many of the villagers had an interest in politics, the biggest number being followers of the Labour Party, of which an Auchinleck branch existed with premises at 221 Main Street. There was also a Cronberry, Lugar and Logan branch. Conservatives were fewer, as were Liberals and Communists. The Auchinleck branch of the Scottish National Party was formed in November 1967. On the local council George Morrison represented the folk of Auchinleck from 1953-1971, followed by Jean Allan, who was elected to Cumnock District Council in February 1966. When she died Anna Boyd was elected.

Norberto Sanchez Donis and Peter Devlin were the two main forces behind the formation of the Greyhound Stadium which was created on a three acre site at the west end of Merlin Park. Work on the project commenced in 1956, taking four years to complete. A special meeting took place on 21 April 1959 to consider the application for a betting licence which was granted. Stands were erected for spectators, of which 700 could be accommodated in the field, and an elevated judges' box was situated in the centre. The first day of races took place on 21 May 1960, over 230 and 425 yards. A special feature of the track was that it had an underground 'blanket' of electric cables which could be used in frosty conditions. A new stadium was erected in 1965. Gerry Donis took over the running of the course and in 1970 a bar was added. Support fell as the years passed, and the track held its last race meeting on Sunday 15 October 2000.

The sport of carpet bowling had for many years been popular in a number of the village's halls. Clubs attached to the Peden and Barony churches existed, and one associated with the British Legion. Following the creation of Cumnock and Doon Valley District Council in 1975, plans were mooted for an indoor bowling stadium. Many claimed it would prove to be a 'white elephant', but the council made inquiries and reckoned it would attract 3,000 members. Work commenced on a red-brick building in Well Road, on the site of the laundry, designed by Rennie, Watson and Starling. The principal architect was Angus Allan James Starling (b. 1939). Comprising eight fourteen feet rinks, upstairs and downstairs lounges, the building cost £750,000 to erect and was leased from the council by the Auchinleck Indoor Bowling Club, the first President being H. Richmond. The stadium was officially opened on 29 August 1980 by Councillor Jean Allan, 1,500 people joining. Despite a fall in membership to around 800 in 1990, the club proved itself nationally, the Scottish Singles Cup being won in 1987 by Neil McGhee and in 1989 by Steven Rankin. In 1988 Hugh Duff won the World Indoor Singles championship. In 1993 Kate Adams won the Ladies' World Championship.

The Auchinleck Boswell Society was founded in January 1970 by three men desirous to see some form of memorial to the great biographer, James Boswell. John MacCulloch, station-master at Auchinleck, John Paterson (1919-1982), session-clerk of the Barony Church, and an in-comer from Yorkshire, Gordon P. Hoyle (1899-1987), who ran a drapery business in the Main Street, each donated £1 and thus the society was founded. The first president was Mrs Patricia S. Boswell. John Paterson quickly persuaded the kirk session to donate the ruins of the old church, and thus the society had something to aim for - the restoration of the building as a museum. The adjoining mausoleum was donated by Joyce, Lady Talbot de Malahide. There had previously been a plan to restore the old church as a small hall, for use by the kirk session and church choir, and for the 'Kirk Nights' which at the time were popular. In 1965 Thomas Wallace, architect, prepared plans for the church's restoration, costing around £5,000, which would have provided a hall capable of holding about 120 persons. The 'Kirk Nights' were Wednesday night meetings at which members met to be entertained, to listen to lectures and to get involved in the discussions which followed. The restoration plans of this time failed to come to fruition.

The Boswell Society in 1976 had half of its 160 members from America and, with donations from interested parties all over the world, work began by volunteers in restoring the old church. The architect, Robert S. Wallace of Troon, drew plans for the work. The walls were stabilised and the roof replaced. In the mausoleum internal lighting was installed. In October 1976 the Manpower Services Commission (a Government-backed organisation) paid for the employment of three skilled workers and six labourers for a period of one year. The museum was opened on 19 August 1978, Lord Ross, a judge and former Dean of the Faculty of Advocates, performing the ceremony. In March 1986 James Watt College (Greenock) presented a seventeen inch model of William Murdoch's steam engine to the society for display in the museum. This was as exact a copy of the original as was possible, and was accepted on the society's behalf by the chairman, Sheriff Neil Gow. However, by the summer of 1987 the museum was closed, due to falling visitors. These had dropped to as low as twenty per year.

At Birnieknowe, the old convent had become a private house. In 1979 Donald MacDonald obtained planning permission to establish a small caravan site and craft shop there, the latter not being created, but the grounds were used as a caravan site for a number of years.

For recreation the people of Lugar continued to support the bowling club, the pavilion of which was extended and rebuilt. Membership in 1951 was 40, falling to 20 in 1962, but this rose again when the club obtained a drinks licence. In September 1970 the Ladies' Rink of the club won the Scottish CISWO title. The Lugar and Cumnock Loyal Orange Lodge held its thirtieth anniversary social in March 1959. The Lugar Christian Union continued to operate for a number of years after the war. The Lugar Scouts (65th Ayrshire) had 30 members in 1951, plus 40 girls in the Guides. In October 1958 plans were made for a new Scout Hut at Logan, for which two huts were bought from Monkton airport at a cost of £50. The hut was opened on 3 May 1960, though the Lugar name was maintained.

COMMUNITY SERVICES

A new Community Centre was built in Well Road at a cost of £35,000, formally opened on Saturday 11 October 1958 by Dr Henry C. J. MacLean of Auchinleck. Funds for the construction were met jointly by the council and the Coal Industry Social Welfare Organisation. In the same year similar centres were opened at Netherthird and New Cumnock, followed by Dalmellington. The centre was run by Auchinleck Community Association, which had been established following a meeting held in the old Town Hall on 29 March 1956. The first president was Harry Holland, Rev G. MacCutcheon was vice president, J. Russell as Secretary and J. Paterson as treasurer.

The building erected in Auchinleck comprised a large hall, snooker room, canteen, old men's cabin, and adjoining library. It was run by a Community Centre Committee, appointed by Auchinleck Community Association. The library, run by the county council, opened in December 1958, with a stock of 5,000 books, 3,000 of which had been transferred from the old library in Main Street, the remainder supplied by the county library service. The first librarian in the new premises was Miss Margaret Milne. Within a short time the local newspapers reported that virtually every society in the village had moved its meetings to the new centre, being more conveniently located than the town hall, where attendances plummeted.

A number of notable acts and groups played at the centre, including the then unknown Beatles in 1960. When they asked to return in 1962 the committee turned them down! Other popular groups playing there included Freddie and the

Dreamers, The Troggs, Cat Stevens and the Tremeloes. The local group, Merry Macs, were regulars. The Scottish National Orchestra also played at Auchinleck Community Centre in April 1960 and October 1965 and ballets were also performed. On 20 April 1967 a new five-day centre for handicapped adults was opened, an addition to the community centre. Work on it had commenced on 2 May 1966.

On the site of the old Dalsalloch Rows Ayr County Council erected a new residential home for the elderly, called Affleck House, in 1972. This building had thirty beds, four of which were kept as respite beds to give individuals a break from caring for the elderly. The home had residents from all over the district and was officially opened on 17 April 1973.

William MacCombe Court was named after an Englishman who had a second-hand shop next to the Post Office. In Judge Avenue, Carrick View hostel for mentally handicapped adults was opened in May 1979. This hostel took twelve residents plus one emergency resident. Running it were one officer-in-charge, one depute, one senior, one full-time and one part-time worker plus two temporary domestics. In 1990 a new training house was opened where three clients could learn to look after themselves in the community. One senior and two part-time workers ran this section.

At 154 Main Street was the Auchinleck District Office for birth, marriage and death registration.

Auchinleck had three police constables in 1951. In January 1963 work began on a new Police Station in Well Road to replace the old building in Main Street. The new premises, which had two cells and a police house attached, was opened on 14 May 1965. The old building was converted into a probation centre and base for the youth service. It latterly became the office of the Community Education service.

In 1963 170 men in the village formed a Working Men's Club and engaged William Nimmo, architect, of Wishaw, to design premises which were erected on a 2/3 acre site at the junction of Coal Road with Barbieston Road, from August 1963. The contractor was Bryce & Co. of Wishaw. The building was declared open on 5 May 1964, having a large lounge which could hold 350 people, a small lounge capable of holding 110, a games hall, kitchen and ancillaries. The club existed for many years thereafter, but a falling membership and lack of attendance resulted in its closure in the 1990s. The building was demolished on 1 July 1998.

Following the opening of the Community Centre, attendance at the Town Hall fell dramatically as a number of organisations moved to the larger premises. A public meeting was called in 1961 to see what could be done to improve matters, but it was very poorly attended. On 20 September that year another meeting took place and despite the controversial topic only 32 people turned up, including members of the Public Hall Trust. Following a vote (15 to 14) it was agreed that the trust should be wound up and the hall was closed. It remained empty until 1964 when the Lugar and Cumnock Loyal Orange Lodge acquired the premises and the Star of the West Social Club opened on 8 October 1966. This club closed in 1974, the hall remaining empty thereafter, finally being demolished in 1979-80 after which three houses were built on the site.

SONS AND DAUGHTERS

The parish continued to breed literary figures. Though not actually born in Auchinleck, Iain Finlayson spent much of his early life in the village, his father being headmaster of the junior secondary school. Born in 1945, Iain was educated at Cumnock Academy followed by Edinburgh University where he graduated in Scots Law. However the solicitor's life did not appeal to him and he left to join the Home Office. This lasted for four years before he decided on a journalistic career, writing articles for newspapers like the *Scotsman*, *Daily Telegraph*, *Sunday Times* and magazines like *Harpers & Queen*, *Tatler* and *Cosmopolitan*. His first book was published in 1984, *The Moth and the Candle*, a biography of James Boswell, which was received with literary acclaim. Written at his mother's home in Ayr, the book was dedicated to his father who died in 1970. Finlayson followed it up with *Writers in Romney Marsh* (1986) and *The Scots* (1988).

Another writer was Rev Dr James Richmond, who was born at Darnconner. His book, *Faith and Philosophy*, was published in 1966 by Hodder and Stoughton.

Achieving fame in a different field was Tom Watson who became a well-known Scots actor. Born in the village, he went on to appear in a number of films and television programmes, including *Your Cheatin' Heart* and *The Govan Ghost*.

Characters of the post-war period seem to be fewer in number, though many folk will recall 'Setterday Sanny' who was in the habit of giving his bonnet a turn after drinking a pint in the pubs. 'Charlie the Darkie' was a well-known tramp who lived at Highhouse.

CHAPTER EIGHT

TWENTY-FIRST CENTURY

VILLAGE LIFE
As the new millennium dawned, the population of Auchinleck village had grown to 3,512, according to the 2001 Census. Estimates made in 2006 saw a slight increase to 3,650.

Auchinleck Community Council and East Ayrshire Council were delighted to officially unveil the new Millennium Clock on 6 December 2002. The clock is a four-sided tower in the shape of pit winding gear, which is also a tribute to the area's heritage and history. Former chair of the community council, Arthur Burley, conceived the original idea for the project in 1998 and the Council's Technical Services Department designed the clock tower. The cost of the clock was funded by the Minerals Trust, East Ayrshire Coalfield Area Social Inclusion Partnership, Scottish Coal, East Ayrshire Council and Barr Environmental.

In 2004 Auchinleck Community Development Initiative was established as a company and charity with the intention of making improvements to the village. A number of initiatives were completed within the first ten years of its existence, including constructing the community garden and geodomes in Aird Avenue, forming a trim trail within the woodlands off Cameron Drive, starting the Alive and Kicking music festival, forming decorative garden areas, and increasing activities for the youth of the community. The geodomes were officially opened by the Provost of East Ayrshire Council, Jane Darnborough, on Tuesday 18 March 2008. The trim trail was opened on 6 September 2008.

A new festival of arts and entertainment was established in 2010 known as Alive and Kicking. Taking place in August of each year, the festival continues to run, with live music of different types taking place in venues throughout the village. Some of the music events were held at the Barony A-frame.

The old Barony Colliery had been demolished, leaving only the massive A-frame standing on the site. The frame had been listed by Historic Scotland as being unique in Britain. The Barony A-Frame Trust was founded in 2003 with the intention of saving the frame. Funds were received from a variety of bodies, including the Coalfields Regeneration Trust, Heritage Lottery Fund, Historic Scotland and East Ayrshire Council. Work commenced in October 2006. The site was developed as a heritage site, the frame standing next to a new parking area with picnic and playground. At the frame information boards were erected, telling the story of the mineworkers. The new facility was opened to the community on

8.1 Millennium Clock *(Dane Love)*

Saturday 14 June 2008. The official opening was performed by His Royal Highness, Prince Charles, on 21 January 2008.

In 2011 the Friends of the Barony A-Frame Trust was formed, allowing supporters of the project to become more involved. A 'token' board, similar to that used by the miners, was created, commemorating larger donations. In 2014 the grounds at the access to the A-Frame were redesigned, with the addition of a couple of 'hutches' on rails and other works.

8.2 Barony A Frame *(Dane Love)*

Two winding wheels from the Number 4 shaft of Barony Colliery were erected on the grass near to the Templeton roundabout on 18 June 2013 to form the Auchinleck Mining Heritage Monument. They had been at Dunaskin museum prior to this. This was undertaken by the Auchinleck Community Development Initiative, and the memorial was dedicated to 'all the Auchinleck Miners and their families who serve the industry and their community.' The wheels were lit at night from November 2014. The memorial was officially unveiled on 13 November 2014.

Another mining relic, the Highhouse winding frame and engine-house, was kept at Highhouse Industrial Estate. However, in 2015 the owner of the estate,

Highhouse Estates Ltd., proposed demolishing the frame and engine-house due to vandalism.

In August 2011 plans were passed for a new community centre that was to be built on the site of the old community centre, demolished that year. The new centre has a local council office, day-care centre and library located within an L-shaped building. Work commenced in the spring of 2012. The new centre cost £4.9 million to build and it was officially opened on 29 September 2013 by Councillor Douglas Reid, Leader of East Ayrshire Council. The new centre was named the Boswell Centre, after the famous diarist, James Boswell. Within the new centre is the branch library for Auchinleck, plus a learning centre, interview rooms, two community halls, three multi-purpose rooms, and other facilities. The day-care centre is also located within the building.

8.3 Barony Winding Wheels *(Dane Love)*

The old Carrick View Hostel was deemed to be unsuitable for modern care and so in April 2008 a new centre was erected at the corner of Back Rogerton Crescent with Barbieston Road. Named Berryknowe, this care home houses ten adults with learning difficulties and is operated by East Ayrshire Council.

On the road to Cumnock, but within the parish, the lands of Knockroon were developed as a model community from 2011. The lands were acquired as part of Dumfries House Estate by the Great Steward of Scotland's Dumfries House Trust and were to be used for development in order to fund renovations on the estate and pay for the acquisition of the house and contents. The first building was constructed at the corner of Auchinleck Road and the Kirk's Alarm, the foundation stone being unveiled by His Royal Highness, Prince Charles, Duke of Rothesay, on Tuesday 31 May 2011. At first, this was used as a visitor centre, but in May 2014 it opened as a café and pizzeria. The first block of houses was completed in 2015, comprising buildings facing onto Auchinleck Road, The Kirk's Alarm, Pottery Row, Darsie Brae and Jimmy Boyd Walk.

8.4 The Boswell Centre *(Dane Love)*

At Lugar East Ayrshire Council moved out of the office block at Lugar and this was demolished early in 2014.

In 2011 the residents of Cronberry were shocked to discover that two of its residents were murdered by a third resident. Former soldier Thomas Bennie Smith (aged 26) had previously been imprisoned for sexual assault and on his release moved to live at Cronberry. He became friends with the Fallon family, but he was to murder Holly Fallon, aged ten, and dump her body in the Bello Water. He then went on to torture and kill her mother, Diane Fallon (aged 43). Smith was apprehended by the police, and after some searching Holly's body was discovered. Smith was found guilty of both murders and was sentenced to a minimum of 32 years for the double murder.

Road improvements continued on a small scale across the parish. On the A70, east of Cronberry, the road was realigned to either side of the Welltrees Bridge in 2006-7, a new bridge replacing the older one. In 2011-2012 the railway bridge in Main Street was partially rebuilt. Having been hit a few times by tall vehicles, it was felt that some additional reinforcing was required. Accordingly, new bumpers were added to each side, and the opportunity was taken to reduce the width of the bridge, part of the northern side being removed.

8.5 Knockroon *(Dane Love)*

LANDOWNERS

The lands belonging to Dumfries House Estate within the parish were partially sold to a consortium led by His Royal Highness, the Prince Charles, Duke of Rothesay, on 27 June 2007. This comprised the lands west of the village, along the Barony Road, as far as the Egger chipboard factory. Prince Charles was active in redeveloping the estate as a visitor attraction, and although most of the important work was located on the south side of the Lugar Water, within the parish of Old Cumnock, a number of improvements were located on the Auchinleck parish side of the river.

Near to Pennylands a new outdoor centre for youth groups was erected in 2012-13. Known as the Tamar Manoukian Outdoor Centre, the centre was officially opened on 5 April 2013 by Prince Charles. In 2014 a new drill hall was erected on the north side of the outdoor centre, in a similar style. This was opened by Prince Charles on 29 April 2015.

The walled garden associated with Dumfries House, which occupies the site of the old Waterside House, was redeveloped from 2011-14 as part of the greater development of Dumfries House Estate as a visitor attraction. The walled garden extends to around five acres, and thus is one of the largest in Scotland. It is surrounded by a tall brick and stone wall on three sides, the southern, Lugar Water facing side, being open. The Fife-based landscape gardener Michael Innes was influential in providing a design to emphasise the heritage, but also to allow the introduction of new ideas. Around 450 yards of wall were rebuilt, using 47,000 new bricks. The first section of garden to be completed was the western end, where a small bothy was built in the centre. The Summer House was built by craft apprentices of the Prince's Foundation for Building Community, 2012. It was named the Kauffman Summerhouse and Education Garden. Around the bothy, radiating at angles, are pathways which represent the shape of the Union Flag. At the north end of this garden, adjoining the northern wall, is the Pierburg Building, which contains rooms used as educational classes and laboratories. The education centre was opened by Prince Charles on 14 June 2013. It was designed and built by Hope Homes of Drongan.

The eastern end of the walled garden was developed in 2014, new terrace walls being erected and flower beds created. The design was the work of Michael Innes, and within it is a small pool and fountain in the shape of a thistle, designed by the sculptor William Pye. The garden was named the Queen Elizabeth Garden and officially opened by H. M. The Queen Elizabeth on Tuesday 1 July 2014. On that day the Queen, the Duke of Edinburgh, Prince Charles and the Duchess of Cornwall were present. The garden contains a number of walled terraces, steps, garden areas, borders, parterres and orchards. Within the Queen Elizabeth garden are a number of greenhouses, used for growing vegetables, and young plants, as well as a display greenhouse, built on the site of a Victorian vinery.

8.6 The Queen Elizabeth Garden, Dumfries House Estate *(Dane Love)*

Within the garden is an ancient sycamore tree which is thought to be at least 400 years of age. This is all that remains of the old policies of Waterside. The sundial was made by Armillary Spheres of Cornwall. It is adorned with an inscription commemorating the opening of the garden by the Queen.

At the north-east corner of the garden is a new Gothic belvedere, constructed in the main of red bricks. This octagonal building was designed by the Duke of Rothesay. On the exterior walls are ornate gargoyles, based on the wyverns from the Crichton coat of arms. There are also bas-reliefs depicting the thistle emblem that is used across Dumfries House. On the floor inside it a carved stone lion, representing the Duke of Rothesay, echoed on the weather vane on the top of the roof.

Between the garden and the Avenue Bridge an arboretum was created, where numerous specimen trees and shrubs were planted, complete with a shelter and ponds. Funding for this came from the Maguire Charitable Trust and this was officially opened by H. R. H. The Prince Charles, Duke of Rothesay, on 2 July 2014. In the centre of this a garden folly was built, comprising of a shelter built of timber by students of the Prince's Foundation for Building Community.

In 2013-14 the Avenue Bridge, which crosses the Lugar Water from the Auchinleck side to Dumfries House, was restored at a cost of £400,000. The Temple gateway was restored in 2014-15 at a cost of £268,000. A new avenue of trees was laid between the Temple and the arboretum folly in 2015.

The Boswell family retained the core of Auchinleck estate into the twenty-first century. On 14 April 2014 the former home farm courtyard was opened as a café and gift shop, known as Boswell's Coach House, the restoration of the buildings partially funded by European Union agricultural diversification grants. The business was established on 8 December 2011 as Boswell's Coach House Ltd. The Auchinleck Horse Trials continue to attract competitors from across Britain, the June 2014 event having around 300 competitors.

Auchinleck House itself was covered in scaffolding from 2000-1 to allow repairs to the fabric. Fallen urns were replaced or restored and the plasterwork and masonry renovated. The work was completed in late 2001 and the house was let to holiday tenants soon thereafter. The cost of works undertaken by the Landmark Trust was in excess of £2 million. The refurbished house was opened by Allan Wilson, Scottish Deputy Minister for Sport, the Arts and Culture.

CHURCHES

On 7 September 2008 a memorial plaque was unveiled in the Parish Church to commemorate the long service of two former ministers of the Peden and Parish churches, Rev Charles Johnston and Rev Daniel Robertson who, between them, served from 1940 until 2000.

At the parish church Rev James Sloan MA BD was accepted as sole nominee on 16 January 2001 and was inducted as minister on 15 January 2002. Born in Glasgow, he emigrated to Canada where he lived most of his life until deciding to return to Scotland, taking up the post at Auchinleck. He also served at Catrine

Parish Church, the two churches being linked under the same minister in August 2002. Rev Sloan retired on 4 March 2005. He died in Canada on 23 June 2013.

Rev Steven Frank Clipston was inducted as minister on 7 December 2006. He had served as a locum minister at the church for a short period of time. Steve Clipston was born at Gillingham in Kent on 31 July 1955, the son of Raymond Frank Clipston and Jessie Ogilvie Thomson MacIntosh. As a child, he moved to Stonehaven in Kincardineshire. He was educated at Mackie Academy in Stonehaven from 1967-73, followed by the University of Glasgow from 1973-76. He graduated with a Master of Arts degree. He continued his studies, until 1981, graduating with a Bachelor of Divinity degree. He was licensed by the Presbytery of Glasgow on 30 June 1981, being assistant minister at St David's Knightswood Church in the city from 1981-82. He was married on 24 July 1978 to Elaine Margaret Jack (b. 7 June 1955), daughter of David Ronald Jack and Eleanor Craig Lumsden Clark, by whom he had six children. They were later divorced. Their children are David Andrew (b. 19 May 1979); Joanne Ruth (b. 1 August 1980); Euan Philip and Alasdair Stephen (twins, born 5 January 1982); Morag Elizabeth and Jonathan Alexander (twins, born 17 December 1984). He was ordained and inducted as minister at St John's Parish Church, Galashiels, 24 September 1982 where he served for 22 years before resigning in February 2005. He was married for a second time to Moira McLennan

8.7 Interior of Parish Church *(Dane Love)*

on 19 November 2010. In 2011 Auchinleck Parish Church had 350 members, of which 120 were communicant. In March 2013 the church guild celebrated it ninetieth anniversary.

Lugar Parish Church continued under the ministry of Rev John Paterson, linked with Old Cumnock Old Church. He has been Chieftain of the Caledonian Society. He served as Moderator of Ayr Presbytery of the Church of Scotland from 2008-9.

The chapel of Our Lady and St Patrick's underwent considerable refurbishment in 1999-2000 at a cost of £40,000. The Very Rev Thomas Joseph Provost Murphy served the parish until he died on 3 December at the age of 85 years, being the oldest serving priest in the Diocese of Galloway. The church was served by priests from Cumnock for a time, before Rev Graham Bell was appointed in 2007. He remained until 2010, when he moved to Our Lady of the Star and Sea at Ardrossan. He resigned from the priesthood in 2015. Rev Stephen G. McGrattan BSc PhL STB was installed as the priest in 2010. To mark fifty years of worship in the church an anniversary mass was held on 29 June 2014, to which past priests attended.

The Christian Brethren meeting in the gospel hall in Park Road changed their named to Auchinleck Christian Fellowship, and the members carried out some restoration work to their church.

The old Kingdom Hall used by the Jehovah's Witnesses was damaged by fire in 2007. The group had to meet elsewhere for a time, but set about arranging to build a new hall. This was erected in May-July 2009. The main construction took place over four days, 25-28 June 2009. Over 50 Auchinleck members plus 200 friends from all over Scotland came to assist. The new hall can seat 120 worshippers. Membership in April 2011 was 56, the hall serving the surrounding parishes, including Mauchline, Sanquhar, Muirkirk, Old Cumnock and Ochiltree.

EDUCATION

A new primary school and nursery school building was erected on the site of the old rows at Dalsalloch and this was opened in 2000, the official ceremony taking place on Thursday 15 June, performed by Councillor Thomas Farrell JP, Chair of the Education Committee of East Ayrshire Council. The plans for the school, erected 1998-2000, were prepared by the builders, Barr Construction. The old school building in School Road was retained for a number of years, with proposals to convert it into industrial or commercial premises. However, these plans came to nought and the building was demolished in February 2006.

Danny Easton continued as headmaster until he retired in August 2010. He was replaced by Mrs Pamela Wilson, who had previously been head teacher of Crossroads Primary School. Mrs Wilson served from 2010 until 2014, when she moved on to Dunlop Primary School. The head teacher's job was filled by Mrs Jacqueline Hanlon from August 2014. The roll at that time was 230.

At the Academy, education continued under the headship of Colin MacLean. The school roll in 2004 was 1,109 pupils. This gradually diminished over the years, dropping below 1,000 in 2010 for the first time, at 983. By 2014 the roll had fallen further to 867 pupils, with an occupancy rate of just 54% for the size of the buildings. Colin MacLean retired at the summer of 2011, shortly after the school celebrated its fortieth anniversary, and he was replaced by Peter Gilchrist. The school received some major upgrading, the lecture theatre being demolished on 27 December 2007 and the sports facilities upgraded in 2010. In 2012-13 a new all-weather football pitch was constructed on the north side of the school. In 2015 East Ayrshire Council set out proposals to replace Auchinleck Academy, Cumnock Academy and two primary schools in Cumnock with a new purpose-built school, located at Broomfield in Cumnock.

8.8 Auchinleck Primary School *(Dane Love)*

St Patrick's continued to offer primary education for Roman Catholic pupils in the area. Head teachers at the school were Mrs Amy Kinnaird, Mrs Maureen Bradley, and Catriona Gray. From 2010 Catriona Gray held the joint responsibility of St Patrick's and St John's Primary in Cumnock. Numbers on the roll gradually decreased until in 2012-13 the school was operating at 39% capacity. In October 2013 pupils from St John's Primary School in Cumnock re-enrolled in St Patrick's when the former school was closed, Catriona Gray remaining as the head teacher. The roll in 2014 was 108 pupils.

INDUSTRY

In 2007 Barony Universal aerosol manufacturers was partially sold to Questbridge, which acquired an 85% stake. In 2009 the firm filled more than 56 million cans of deodorant, hairspray and other propellants, with a turnover of £19m. By 2013 over 65 million units were filled. In 2009 there were 106 people employed at Barony's plant in Auchinleck. In 2010 the company launched a £14m international expansion, and purchased the former Simclar computer plant in Irvine for £3m in order to increase production. This expansion was expected to create a further 100 jobs, tripling capacity. The Auchinleck plant was to be changed to produce household products, such as polish. In 2014 the business became 100% owned by the Arnet Group. The factory in Auchinleck was closed in the summer of 2015.

At Egger Barony Ltd. the manufacture of chipboard continued, with just over 100 employees at the site in 2014.

The excavation of coal continued in the parish on a large scale. Deep mining has long-gone since the closure of the Barony Colliery, to be replaced by surface mining using the open cast method. A number of surface mines have been created in the parish, particularly in the Darnconner and Common areas, as well as on the road to Muirkirk.

The Powharnal open cast coal mine was established at the east end of the parish, on the border with Muirkirk parish. The site was operated by Scottish Coal Ltd. and employed 110 workers in 2010, producing around 550,000 tons of coal (worth £32m) per annum. The mine was being restored in 2012 but Scottish Coal went into administration, leaving the site unfinished.

The open cast mine at Dalfad was operated by Scottish Coal from 2011-2013 as an add-on to its former Gasswater and Powharnal sites.

The Laigh Glenmuir Open Cast Coal Mine was opened in 2007, operated by ATH Resources. It was extended into ground on Duncanziemere farm.

LAW Mining carried out surface mining at various locations in the parish. In 2003 the firm suffered financial difficulties and was taken over by ATH Resources. The price of coal dropped considerably in the first few years of the second decade of the century, and in 2013 Scottish Coal and ATH both went into administration. A number of open cast sites were abandoned, the financial bond that was supposed to restore them in such circumstances being discovered to be woefully inadequate.

The Duncanziemere open cast mine had been opened in August 2011 by ATH Resources. After the firm went into administration in May 2013, Duncanziemere was taken over by Hargreaves, saving around 60 jobs, in 2014. The site was extended to the east and a restoration plan created in 2015. This would allow a further 400,000 tons of coal to be extracted and the site restored over three years. However, with the low price of coal, Hargreaves decided to close the site in September 2015, with the loss of 57 jobs.

Thomas French (b. 1946) started a business at Stonebriggs farm in 1967 transporting goods. The company grew over the year, joined in 2000 by T. French & Son (Earthwork) Ltd followed by T. French & Son Ltd in 2005. By 2013 the company ran 80 lorries, employing 150 people, and transported coal, grain for whisky, stone, sand and gravel, as well as feedstuff to farmers across much of Scotland and the northern half of England. Directors in 2015 were Thomas John French and Elizabeth Ann McMenemy.

The Highhouse Industrial Estate was taken over by Highhouse Estates Ltd in 2012. The site was cleaned up and in 2014 all units were occupied. Most of these were small businesses, including Ayrshire Memorials, Ayrshire Granite, Autographic vehicle graphics, Just Jeans clothes, Carpet King floorings, K. P. welding services, Cube laundry and upholstery, George Murphy & Son, plumbers, Highhouse Motors, Boanerges car maintenance, R. & M. Heys, sewing manufacturer, S. B. road surfacing and the Highhouse Café, to name a few.

COMMERCE

At the Post Office John Malcolm Brown was the postmaster from 1991 until 2010. The position was then filled by Sheila Richmond. On 15 January 2015 the post office was transferred to the Auchinleck News premises, at the corner of Main Street with Well Road, Maqbool Ahmed becoming the new postmistress.

MacPherson the coal merchant in Lugar was taken over by William Morris & Son Ltd. and continued to supply coal to the few homes that retained a coal fire. The yard was later cleared and the buildings demolished.

The site of the former Currie's lemonade factory was cleared and on 3 April 2000 a new supermarket, operated by Tesco, was opened on the site. In 1999 some archaeological investigations were carried out prior to the development, but nothing of any interest was found.

The Boswell Arms was owned by Douglas Aitken until 2008, when it was taken over by Robert Beatson. The Market Inn continues to be owned by John Kyle. The Railway Hotel was still operated by John Campbell and was considerably renovated and extended to the rear, forming a large function suite.

Liddell's Coaches continues to thrive, operating buses and mini-buses from their bases at 1 Mauchline Road and garages adjacent. The old toll branch of the co-operative had been used by Charles Houston as a furniture store and then a builder's merchant before being acquired by Liddell in 1987. In 2015 the firm employed around 50 people, running school contracts, bus tours and other services.

AGRICULTURE

Farming continued in the parish, with sheep, dairy, and beef cattle being the principal form of income. With the introduction of farming quotas for milk in 1984, many farmers closed their small dairies and converted into beef and sheep rearing.

Crops, other than grass for silage, became almost non-existent, and the growing of barley has reduced to almost nothing.

A number of agricultural holdings, or their land, were sold and, using grant money available at the time, the ground was planted in trees, both for amenity value, but also for the growing of timber. Farms planted in this way included Dalsalloch and parts of Glenshamrock, Darnconner (planted 2005), and High Glenmuir.

Many farmers and their families began to diversify, finding other means of income to supplement a falling return from agriculture. Examples include John Duncan at Blackston farm, who expanded his father's plant hire business, with diggers of various sizes for hire. In addition, with a fall in demand for construction works during the recession of 2007 onwards, he established the 'Dig-a-day' experience, where visitors can try operating an excavator for themselves. Also on the farm are Clydesdale horses, which visitors are invited to ride or groom, and various endangered species. Blackstone Clydesdales was formed in 2011.

Hugh Spittal (1901-1996) of Berryhill farm established a business as a supplier of coal to local households, but with the arrival of natural gas to the district, demand for household coal fell. Around 1990 he moved into supplying potatoes and vegetables, building up a family business. Originally he had been a vegetable distributor in Clackmannanshire and Fife, based at Boghall farm, Dollar, prior to moving to Mauchline around 1953 where he had a milk distribution business, based at High Street Dairy. By 2015 Spittal of Berryhill employed seventeen staff, their lorries and vans distributing vegetables across south west Scotland, from Dunbartonshire and Cumbernauld in the north, south to Galloway and Carlisle.

LEISURE & RECREATION

At Beechwood Park Auchinleck Talbot F. C. continued to attract good crowds of supporters and played well in many competitions. In season 2001-2002 they won the East Ayrshire Cup. In the following season they took the Kerr & Smith Cup. In 2004-2005 the team won the Ayrshire Cup. Season 2005-2006 was to be significant once more, for the team won the Premier Division of the league and were to reach the final of the Scottish Cup once more, when they faced Bathgate. In the game they won by two goals to one. In May 2006 the heritage mural was painted on a wall around the park, the work of Auchinleck Youth Arts Project and East Ayrshire Council.

In 2006-2007 and 2007-2008 the club's honours were the League Cup. A trip to glory occurred again in season 2008-2009, when in the Scottish Cup final Auchinleck Talbot F. C. beat Clydebank F. C. two goals to nil to take the title for the seventh time.

A lean year followed, but Auchinleck Talbot F. C. reached the Scottish Cup final once more on 29 May 2011, facing Musselburgh Athletic F. C. at Rugby Park in Kilmarnock. Auchinleck played in front of a crowd of 6,026, winning two goals to one after extra time. In that year they also added the Ayrshire and League cups to their trophy cabinet.

8.9 Auchinleck Talbot Scottish Junior Champions, 2011 *(Hazel Love)*

Talbot were to reach the final once more in 2012, playing Shotts Bon Accord at Braidwood Stadium, the home of Livingstone F. C. Unfortunately, Talbot were beaten two goals to one by a team that was regarded as the underdogs.

In 2012-2013 the local team managed to win the Premier Division of the Stagecoach Super League after a record-breaking season, gaining 62 points, winning every away game and scoring 64 goals. They also progressed to the final of the Scottish Junior Cup once more, playing Linlithgow Rose at the Braidwood Motor Company stadium, Livingston, on 2 June. On this occasion Talbot were to achieve the cup, beating Linlithgow Rose by one goal to nil, David Gormley scoring the goal. They had now lifted the trophy ten times, a Scottish record. It was to be Linlithgow's first defeat in 51 matches.

In 2013-2014 the club were league champions once more, and they won the West of Scotland Cup, beating Troon by two goals to nil. Scorer for Talbot was Graham Wilson. They also lifted the Evening Times Cup.

Auchinleck reached the final of the Scottish Cup for the thirteenth time in 2015, beating Hurlford United in the semi-final. The final was played against Musselburgh Athletic at Rugby Park, Kilmarnock, on 7 June 2015, before 5,186 spectators. Auchinleck won by two goals to nil, Dwayne Hyslop and Gordon Pope scoring for Auchinleck. The win made the club winners of the trophy eleven times, a Scottish record. Manager, Tommy Sloan, had now equalled Willie Knox's record of leading the team to five Scottish Cup victories. The club had already won the league title for 2014-15.

Lugar Boswell F. C. continued to play in the junior ranks, though never with as much success as their near rivals. Usually placed in a lower division, Lugar played in many Ayrshire games, and on occasion showed their mettle against larger teams. Support for the club waxed and waned, and on a number of occasions the committee and organisers felt that their work was in vain, with a change of manager, coach and president being a regular occurrence. In April 2015 the club faced the threat of folding once more but managed to pull through.

At the Merlin Park a new changing pavilion was erected to replace an older building. The park was used for minor football games, as well as recreation by locals.

At Auchinleck Academy the football fields were redeveloped into new all-weather pitches in 2013 and, with an improved swimming pool (reopened in 2011), became known as Auchinleck Leisure Centre. The new facilities were reopened by local referee, Charlie Richmond, on 24 October 2013.

At the Indoor Bowling Green club member Stewart Anderson became World Indoor Bowling Champion in January 2013 after beating Paul Foster from Troon. He had previously been runner-up in three finals. He was the fifth World Champion to come from the Auchinleck club in the past 30 years. Carrie MacLean became world under-25 champion in 2013 at the age of 15.

The Brother James McCombe Lodge (number 205) of the Loyal Orange Institution of Scotland was founded in 2004. The lodge leased the former Johnston Hall at the Peden Church and converted it into an Orange hall in 2008. The lodge celebrated its tenth anniversary in 2014. There is also a 'Sisters of Peden' Ladies Orange Lodge associated with it.

A new book festival, named the Boswell Book Festival, was established in 2011, the first event taking place over the weekend of 20-22 May. Held on the lawn in front of Auchinleck House, most talks and lectures were based on the theme of biography, with many celebrities attending to discuss their books. The event was started by the Boswell Trust, which was founded in 2010 to restore the Boswell burial aisle in Auchinleck, and to establish a visitor attraction in the adjoining old church. In 2015, the festival having grown, it was decided to move the principal venue to the grounds of Dumfries House, but retaining the children's part at the Boswell community centre in Auchinleck, plus visits to Auchinleck House and the Boswell mausoleum.

The Auchinleck Boswell Society was re-established as the Boswell Society in 2003, and the artefacts remaining in the old museum building in Auchinleck were re-housed either at Auchinleck House or else in the Ayrshire Archives. The chairman of many years, Sheriff Neil Gow Q.C., retired in 2004. The new Boswell Society was founded by a group of interested former members, principally under the guiding hand of David Rutherford Boswell of Auchinleck, heir male of the Boswells of Auchinleck. The society organises four meetings per annum across the country, including at Auchinleck House, with speakers on a variety of Boswell subjects.

8.10 Boswell coat of arms – David Rutherford Boswell *(Author's Collection)*

APPENDIX I

FARM AND SMALL LAIRDSHIPS

1899 - dates in Roman type are known dates.
1900 - dates in Italic type are known, but are not necessarily terminal.
c.1895 - indicates approximate dates.
Ordnance Survey six-figure Grid References are shown after the farm name to indicate its location.

Auchinleck Mains (Auchinleck Home Farm) (NS 503227)
1795-1809   Auchinleck Estate - Andrew Dalrymple (1742-1809)
1941   Auchinleck Estate -

Auchtitench (NS 719181)
1793   James Swan
c.1800   - John Lambie
c.1850-c.1875   Dr Dugald Hamilton of Beechgrove (Mauchline) -
                   Mary Henderson
1899   Major James Wallace Dunlop Adair, Bath -
1923-1926   Major William MacCall of Dalwhat - James Hope (d. 1926)
1934-1941   Major William MacCall of Dalwhat -

Barglachan (NS 573227)
192 acres in 1925.
       -1621   Auchinleck Estate - George Boswell (-1621)
       -1782   Auchinleck Estate - Alexander Gibson (1710-1782)
       -1823   Auchinleck Estate -
1851   Auchinleck Estate - Archibald Boswell (1815-   )
1875-1878   Auchinleck Estate - Archibald Boswell (-1878)
1899-1911   Auchinleck Estate - Charles Gibb (1826-1911)
1911-1926   Auchinleck Estate - Hugh Hastie
1926-1945   Auchinleck Estate - James Templeton (d. 1947)
1945-1947   James Templeton (d. 1947)
1947-1965   James Templeton (1914-1965)
1965-1967   Mrs Annie Clark Campbell Murdoch Templeton, nee Collins
1967-*2015*   James Templeton (1947-   )

Bello Mill (NS 598216)
Bellowmilne in 1691.

1728	Craigston Estate -
C1758-	Auchinleck Estate - John Murdoch
-1848	Auchinleck Estate - George Mearns (1755-1848)
1848-	Auchinleck Estate - William Stewart
1875	Auchinleck Estate - Thomas Stewart & John Stewart
c.1880s-1922	Auchinleck Estate - David Millar
1922-1952	Thomas Laird (d. 1955)
1952-1955	Thomas Laird (d. 1955) - Alexander Robertson
1955-1972	William Laird (1911-1978) - Alexander Robertson
1972-1978	William Laird (1911-1978)
1978-1995	Sarah Laird (d. 1995)
1995-*2015*	William and Sadie Craig

Berryhill (NS 561228)
Incorporated Houstonhall from at least 1875. 93 acres in 1962. 48 acres sold to Scottish Woodlands.

1875	Auchinleck Estate - James Miller
1899	Auchinleck Estate - Andrew Wallace
1925-1941	Auchinleck Estate - Elizabeth M. Wallace Welsh
c.1957	John Stevenston
-1962	Neil Thomson
1962-1996	Hugh Spittal (1901-1996)
1996-*2015*	Alistair Spittal (1938-)

Birnieknowe (NS 570222)
138 acres in 2015.

1875-1901	Auchinleck Estate - John Begg (1827-1901)
1911-1919	Auchinleck Estate - Thomas Baird
1929-1947	John Baird
1947-1956	Robert Wardrop
1957-1961	James Purdie (1909-1994)
1961-*2015*	John Purdie (1938-)

Blackfauldhead (NS 512226)

1774	Auchinleck Estate - Andrew Dalrymple

Blackston (NS 567214)
Also known as 'The Row' or 'Raw' historically. Sometimes spelled Blackstoun and Blackstone. Latterly included Longpark.
1795	Auchinleck Estate - James Murdoch
1875-1880	Auchinleck Estate - John Lamont (1803-1891)
1890-1920	Auchinleck Estate - Thomas Kerr (1842-1920)
1920-*1934*	Auchinleck Estate - John Henderson
c.1935-*1941*	Robert S. Duncan trustees - John Syme Duncan (1883-1960)
c.1965-	Robert Duncan (1938-)
2000-*2015*	John Duncan

Bogend
1875	Auchinleck Estate - John Picken of Mansfield Mains, New Cumnock

Boghead (NS 635247)
Included Welltrees from at least 1899.
1793	James Swan
1899	Auchinleck Estate -Andrew Picken of Knockrivoch
-1923	- Mrs Rennie
1923-*1925*	A. D. & W. Mitchell of Hazelside -
1941	A. D. & W. Mitchell of Hazelside -Thomas Mitchell
-c.1960	John Sproat
c.1960-	Robert Morton -
1971-1981	David Howat
c.2000-c.2015	Scottish Coal - Alexander Blackwood
c.2015-	Alexander Blackwood

Bogside (approx. NS 630248)
1793	James Swan -

Braehead of Craigston (NS 599218)
1728	Craigston Estate -
1875-1899	Auchinleck Estate- John MacCormick (1818-1899)
1925	John Osborne MacCormick
1934-c.1955	John Osborne Johnstone
c.1955-	Robert Currans
-*2015*	Jeannie Currans

Braehead of Knockroon (NS 557207)
1899-1925	Dumfries House Estate - Matthew Martin (1849-1925)

1934   Dumfries House Estate - Jane MacMillan

Bridgend Mill (NS 554213)
c.1750-c.1758   Auchinleck Estate - John Murdoch
   -1800   Auchinleck Estate - William Smith (1739-1800)
                Auchinleck Estate - Andrew Gibb (1798-1874)
1899   Auchinleck Estate -Joseph Smith
1925-1934   Auchinleck Estate - Hugh Alexander

Broomfield (NS 563202)
1875-1919   Dumfries House Estate - John Kennedy (1841-1919)
1921-*1934*   Dumfries House Estate - David Scott
1941   Dumfries House Estate

Broomhouse (NS 502222)

Burnside of Craigston (NS   )
Demolished when Lugar was created.
1728   Craigston Estate -

Carbello (NS 611229)
Carbellow in 1691.
   -1755   - John MacKerrow (d. 1755)
   -1784   - Robert MacKerrow (1720-1784)
   -1857   - John Harper (1789-1870)
1857-1906   Auchinleck Estate - Robert Harper (1813-1900) & James Harper
                (1841-1916)
1908-1922   Auchinleck Estate - Hugh Sloan (c.1856-1932)
1922-*1928*   Auchinleck Estate -
1934-1964   Auchinleck Estate - William Smith
1964-2013   Thomas Laird (d. 2013)
2013-   Thomas Laird (1949-   )

Common (NS 582229)
   -1831   - Hugh Murdoch (1744-1831)
1837   Ballochmyle Estate -
   -1873   Ballochmyle Estate - James Clark (1829-1873)
1873-1902   Ballochmyle Estate - James Clark of Carskeoch JP (1866-1926)
1902-1926   James Clark of Carskeoch JP (1866-1926) -
                Alexander Dalziel (d. 1937)

1926-1946	Christina Gordon of Carskeoch - Alexander Dalziel (d. 1937) & William Dalziel (d. 1983)
1946-1983	William Dalziel (d. 1983)
1973	William Dalziel & Son - Alexander Dalziel (1933-)
-2015	William Dalziel & Son - Alexander Dalziel (1933-), Janet Dalziel (1933-) & John Dalziel (1966-)

Commondyke (NS 577225)
44 acres in 1925.

	- Robert Murdoch (1712-1792)
	- James Murdoch (1750-1846)
1810	Auchinleck Estate - William Murdoch (d. 1833)
1875-1918	Auchinleck Estate - Hugh Miller (1832-1918)
-1925	Hugh Miller
1925-*1940*	James MacKerrow
	Mrs Auld and David Auld
1941	John B. Hunter
c.1950-1964	J. K. Campbell - George Campbell
1964-*2000*	Hugh Young
	Malcolm Smith
-2015	William Stakem

Craigston (NS 590212)
Farm demolished and site occupied by Craigston House when Lugar Ironworks were developed.

1601	George Reid
1728	Craigston Estate -
C1760	Auchinleck Estate -
1792	Auchinleck Estate - William MacKerrow (1733-1807)
-1845	Auchinleck Estate - James Brown

Cronberry (NS 605231)
In 1844 extended to 1,040 acres, including Cronberry Tileworks and grouse moor. Farm originally located at NS 611239. Present Cronberry farm was actually called Mortonmuir.

-1822	Charles Howatson (1757-1822)
1844	William Howatson
1847	William Baird & Co. -
1875-1882	William Baird & Co. - William Howatson (1808-1882)
1899	William Baird & Co. - Donald John MacFarlane
1923-1925	William Baird & Co. - Thomas White

1934-1941	Bairds & Dalmellington Ltd. - George H. White
	National Coal Board - James Fleming
2015	Helen Fleming

Dalblair (Low) (NS 646192)

1733-1767	James Gibb
1767-	James Boswell of Auchinleck (1740-1795) -
1779	James Boswell of Auchinleck (1740-1795) - Andrew Howatson
1847	David Limond of Dalblair -
1873	Dumfries House Estate - John Weir (1846-1927)
1875-1899	Dumfries House Estate - William Latta & Robert Latta
1923-1925	Dumfries House Estate - Robert Latta
1934-1941	Dumfries House Estate - William Latta
-1989	Dumfries House Estate - Ian Latta
1989-	Dumfries House Estate - James Blackwood

Dalblair, High (NS 671198)

1899	Dumfries House Estate - William Latta & Robert Latta -
1915-1916	Dumfries House Estate - John Borthwick
1925	Dumfries House Estate - Robert Latta - James Gilchrist
1934	Dumfries House Estate - Robert Dryfe

Dalfad (NS 621222)

1831	- Robert Baird
c.1850	- Hugh Gibson
1899-1922	Auchinleck Estate - John Gibson
1925	A. D. & W. Mitchell of Hazelside -
1934-1941	A. D. & W. Mitchell of Hazelside - James Mitchell

Dalsalloch (NS 549225)

1844-	- Findlay
1875	Auchinleck Estate - Alexander Findlay & Robert Findlay
1899	Auchinleck Estate - Robert Findlay (1842-1917)
1913-*1928*	- David G. Findlay
1934-1941	David G. Findlay
1970	Robert Smith Drummond
c.1975	Andrew Lees
c.1985	James Messenger

Darnconner (NS575239)
400 acres in 1929.
1687	Waterside Estate - Hugh Gibson
1760-1764	James Lennox
1837-1875	Ballochmyle Estate - James Clark
1899	Ballochmyle Estate - James Clark
1911	Ballochmyle Estate - William MacFadzean
1925-1928	- Andrew Murdoch
1934	Christina Gordon of Carskeoch - John Murray & Alexander Duncan
1941	Christina Gordon of Carskeoch - Alexander Duncan James Duncan (d. 2009)

Darnlaw (NS 539226)
Dernlaw in 1691-1875.
-1777	Auchinleck Estate - John MacGavin (1695-1777)
1777-1783	Auchinleck Estate - James MacGavin
1875	Auchinleck Estate - John Samson & David Samson
1899	Auchinleck Estate - Janet & Margaret Samson
1934	John Brown trustees -
1941	Mary Downie
-1963	John Downie
1963-1978	Robert Sloan
1978-*2015*	Bryce Sloan (1955-)

Dickston (NS 583210)
Dickston in 1691; Dixton in 1841.
1728	Craigston Estate -
-1841	- George MacKerrow (1770-1841)
1864	- James MacKerrow
1875-1899	Auchinleck Estate -William Fraser
1924-1934	William Craig
1941	William Arthur Craig
c.1958	George MacKerrow
c.1990	George MacKerrow

Dippolburn (NS 534231)
Dippelburn in 1691. In ruins before 1856.
1774	- James Farquhar

Dornal (NS 633195)
Dornhill in 1691. 140 acres in 2015.
1703	Dornal Estate - John Beg
1875	Dornal Estate - David Hastings of Cloyntie, Kirkmichael
c.1880-1913	Dornal Estate - Alexander Struthers (1844-1913)
1916	Dumfries House Estate - David Struthers
1923-1925	Dumfries House Estate - Alexander Struthers
1921-	Dumfries House Estate - Andrew Struthers
1934-1938	Dumfries House Estate - Andrew Struthers
1938-*1941*	Dumfries House Estate - Adam & John C. H. C. Gordon
-1999	Dumfries House Estate - Adam Gordon
1999-*2015*	Dumfries House Estate - Thomas Anderson (1961-)

Duncanziemere (NS 613217)
420 acres in 1926.
1601	John Boswell
1683	- Boswell - Andrew Brown
c.1760	David Boswell
c.1765-1781	Alexander Milliken (1721-1781)
1781-*1785*	John Reid
-1851	John Robertson WS - David Blair (1790-1851)
1875-1883	Alexander Hamilton Robertson - James Dalgliesh
1896-1916	Dornal Estate - James Findlay (1855-1916)
1925	Dornal Estate - David Findlay & William Findlay
1934-1941	Capt. Charles N. Howatson trustees - David Findlay
-1973	David Aird Findlay (1885-1973) (bd. Muirkirk cemy.)
	- Gavin Paterson
	- Alistair Clark

Dykes (NS 572216)
Dicks in 1691. 140 acres in 1926. 180 acres in 2015.
c.1800	- David Kay
	- William Dalgleish (1829-1914)
1875-1915	Auchinleck Estate - John Alexander
1915-1926	Auchinleck Estate - William Hunter
1926-	Robert Dalgleish Hunter
1934-1964	John Tannock
-1971	Robert Craig Weir
1971-1981	John Weir
1981-1993	James Hodge (1937-)
1993-*2015*	James Hodge (1966-)

Gibston (NS 513219)
1875   Auchinleck Estate - Mrs. Jamieson

Glenhead (NS 538219)
c.1770   - Hugh Reid (1717-1796)
1843   - William Smith

Glenmuir, High (NS 623207)
1875   Major General Francis Claude Burnett of Gadgirth, Coylton - Daniel Craig
1899-1908   Dornal Estate - Gavin Struthers
   -1908   -   Woods
1908-1915   - A. Semple (-1915)
1915-
1921-   -   - John Craig in Guelt
1923-1929   Dumfries House Estate - John T. Weir
1934   Dumfries House Estate - William Prentice
1941   Dumfries House Estate - Thomas L. Thorburn
                    Dumfries House Estate - James and Hugh Howie
                    William Buchanan
2015   John Lancaster

Glenmuir, Laigh (NS 617204)
Previously known as Whitestoneburn, Hallglenmuir (1774-1864) and Glenmuirhall. 947 acres in 1864.
1774-1779   Alexander Mitchell
                    Hugh Logan of that Ilk -
1847   David Limond of Dalblair -
1875   Major General Francis Claude Burnett of Gadgirth, Coylton - John Samson
1899-1900   Dornal Estate - Georgina Grant
   -1919   Dornal Estate - James Blane (-1919)
1925   Dumfries House Estate - D. W. & H. Blane
1934-1941   D. W. & H. Blane
c.1955   James Cowan
c.1980   James MacLanachan

Glenmuirshaw (NS 695199)
1875   Dumfries House Estate - James Wilson
1899   Dumfries House Estate - John Latta Senior
1916   Dumfries House Estate -   Wilson

1923-1925	Dumfries House Estate - Robert & John Latta
1934-1941	Dumfries House Estate - Jacob S. Murray of Dalgig
	Dumfries House Estate - Latta
	Dumfries House Estate - Hugh Blackwood

Glenside (NS 538216)
Glensid in 1691.

-1761	Auchinleck Estate - James Smith
	Auchinleck Estate - Margaret Peden
1774	Auchinleck Estate - Robert Smith (son)
c.1820	Auchinleck Estate - James Smith (1768-1834)
-1856	Auchinleck Estate - Jacob Smith (1805-1856)
1875-1912	Auchinleck Estate - William Smith (1843-1930)
1912-	- Watson
1925-1929	Dumfries House Estate - Thomas Baird
1934-c1961	Dumfries House Estate - Gilbert Baird
1987-2005	Dumfries House Estate - John Kirkland
-2013	Dumfries House Estate - Morrisons -
	Andrew Robinson (1968-)
2013-*2015*	Dumfries House Estate - Morrisons -

Greenside (NS   )

1875	Dornal Estate - James MacCrone
1899-1900	Dornal Estate - Alexander Struthers in Whiteholm -
1925	Dumfries House Estate -

Hapland (NS 536216)
80 acres in 1840.

1681	Auchinleck Estate - John Templeton
c.1723	Auchinleck Estate - James Templeton (c. 1696-)
1755-1792	Auchinleck Estate - John Templeton (c. 1725-)
	Auchinleck Estate - James Templeton (1757-)
	Auchinleck Estate - Andrew Templeton
1774-1795	Auchinleck Estate - John Templeton (d. c. 1800)
-1852	Auchinleck Estate - George Templeton (1774-1852)
1852-1854	- William Templeton (1817-1854)

Highhouse of Auchinleck (NS 551216)

-1782	Auchinleck Estate - Jean Barry (c.1682-1782)
1875	Auchinleck Estate - David Morton

1899	Auchinleck Estate - William Baird & Co.
1925	William Baird & Co.

High Shaw (NS 710208)

Hill of Auchinleck (NS 547219)
c.1750   - John Mitchell (1687-1772)

Hillhead (NS 617214)
1875	Alexander Hamilton Robertson - James Dalgleish
1900	Dornal Estate -
1918	Dornal Estate - Andrew Hutchison
1925	Dornal Estate - David Findlay & William Findlay
-1926	for sale

Houston Hall (NS   )
Attached to Berryhill from at least 1875.

Knagshill (NS 534225)
McCnaigshill in 1691, Naigshill in 1783, Knaigshill in 1875.
1774-1783	- William Templeton
-1832	- David Auld (1778-1832)
-1844	- James Kennedy (d. 1844)
1832-	- William Auld (1818-1876)
1875	Auchinleck Estate - Sarah Wales
1899-1918	Auchinleck Estate - Alexander Findlay
1925-1941	Robert Sturgeon
2015	James Shankland

Knockroon (NS 553211)
Knockcroon in 1691.
	Dumfries House Estate - John Samson
c.*1850-1899*	Dumfries House Estate - William Samson (1814-1882)
-1915	Dumfries House Estate - James Samson (1844-1915)
1915-*1941*	Dumfries House Estate - William Samson (1855-1944)
-c. 1980	Dumfries House Estate - John Auld

Knowe (NS 517223)
170 acres in 1921. 200 acres in 2015.
1774-1794	Auchinleck Estate - Alexander Peden (1708-1794)
1794-	Auchinleck Estate - William Peden

1823	Auchinleck Estate - Peden
1875	Auchinleck Estate - William Peden (1800-1882)
1890-1920	Auchinleck Estate - George Templeton (1852-1920)
1920-1921	Auchinleck Estate - George Templeton
1921-*1925*	George Templeton
-1968	George Templeton (1901-1968)
1968-c.1990	George Templeton (1933-2004)
c.1990-*2015*	George Templeton (1961-)

Kyle (NS 651192)
Also known as Castle Kyle.

	- Robert Latta
1875	Dumfries House Estate - William Latta & John Latta
1882-c.1895	Dumfries House Estate - John Latta (1825-1906)
c.1895-	Dumfries House Estate - Robert & John Latta
1916-1925	Dumfries House Estate - Robert, William & John Latta
1934	Dumfries House Estate - Robert Latta trustees
1941	Dumfries House Estate - James Latta & John Latta
	Dumfries House Estate - Hugh Blackwood

Langholm (NS 506218)
Latterly included Loganston. New farmhouse erected 1887. 150 acres in 1981.

-1748	Auchinleck Estate - William Templeton
1748-*1774*	Auchinleck Estate - William Lennox
1839-*1875*	Auchinleck Estate - Mungo Lennox
1899-1920	Auchinleck Estate - John Jamieson JP (1856-1940)
1920-	Auchinleck Estate - Mrs Jamieson
1925-*1941*	Auchinleck Estate - Mungo L. Jamieson
-1981	Richmond Douglas
1981-*2015*	George Templeton of Knowe -

Laurenceknowe (NS 618242)
Also known as Laurence Knoll, Lauchlan Knoll in 1875.

1875	William Baird & Co. - James Mair
1899	William Baird & Co. - Donald John MacFarlane - William Stewart
1923	- Thomas White

Loganston (NS 512215)

1774	Auchinleck Estate - Alexander Gibson
1792	Auchinleck Estate - James Gibson

1875	Auchinleck Estate - John Weir

Merlinhill (NS 548218)
Demolished 1894 to allow construction of Highhouse Pit.
1875	Auchinleck Estate - William Campbell

Mill Affleck (NS 521209)
Also known as Mill of Auchinleck, or Milne of Auchinleck. Latterly included Weilside. 120 acres in 1921. 134 acres in 2015.
Auchinleck Estate - Donald MacAlexander
1706-	Auchinleck Estate - Samson
-1780	Auchinleck Estate - George Samson (1705-1780)
1795	Auchinleck Estate - William Samson
1774	Auchinleck Estate - George Jamieson
1851-1860	Auchinleck Estate - James Jamieson
1875-1921	Auchinleck Estate - William Hettrick
1921-*1928*	Auchinleck Estate - William Hettrick
1933-1945	Auchinleck Estate - Hugh Brown Howat (1892-1969)
1945-1969	Hugh Brown Howat (1892-1969)
1969-	John Howat Jardine Howat (1939-)
2011-2015	Hugh Howat (1964-)

Mortonmuir (NS 605231)
Mortonmuir farm was renamed Cronberry farm (qv).

Mosshouse (NS 603223)
1875	Auchinleck Estate - John Pearson

Mosside (NS 515226)
1774	Auchinleck Estate - William Wallace

Oldbyres (NS 529216)
Old Byers in 1775.
1660	Auchinleck Estate - John Murdoch
1774-1795	Auchinleck Estate - James Peden
-1857	Auchinleck Estate - James Peden (1814-1857)
1857-1883	Auchinleck Estate - John Peden (1817-1883)
1883-1910	Auchinleck Estate - John Peden (1854-1910)
1925	- William J. Houston

Orchard (NS 559215)
In ruins before 1911
1797 - Robert Wallace

Pathhead (NS   )
Site no longer known, roughly Lugar.
1728 Craigston Estate -

Penbreck (NS 724194)
Penbreak in 1691.
1847	William Brown (Broom)
	William Broom of Dalwhat
1875	Margaret Broom of Dalwhat
1899	Margaret MacCall of Dalwhat
1923-1925	Major William MacCall of Dalwhat - William Kirk & Robert Kirk
1934-1941	Major William MacCall of Dalwhat -

Rigg (NS 560212)
60 acres in 1844.
1756	Cochrane
-1782	
1782-1794	Rev John Dun (1724-1794)
1794-*1800*	William Samson
-1839	George Samson (1786-1839)
1844-1875	James Templeton, Ayr - Robert Wardrop & Patrick Wardrop (1820-1913)
c.1885	James Templeton, Ayr - Patrick Wardrop (1820-1913)
1899	James Templeton, Ayr - William & Thomas Wardrop
1925-1941	William D. Wardrop
	Douglas Kennedy
	Alexander Houston

Roadinghead (NS 578211)
Roddenhead in 1691. 188 acres in 1922.
-1778	Auchinleck Estate - Johnston (d. 1785)
1778-1807	Auchinleck Estate - William Murray (1714-1807)
1807-1829	Auchinleck Estate - James Murray (1748-1829)
1875-1884	Auchinleck Estate - David MacKerrow (1792-1884)
1899	Auchinleck Estate - David MacKerrow Jr.
1920-1922	Thomas MacKerrow

1922-	Alexander MacKerrow
1925	Jeanie MacKerrow
1934-1941	Jeanie MacKerrow - George MacKerrow
-2012	George MacKerrow (19 -2012)
2012-*2015*	Gordon Sloan (1965-)

Rogerton, Back (NS 558222)
10 acres in 2015.

1791	Auchinleck Estate - Andrew Dalrymple
1875-1881	Auchinleck Estate - Andrew Mitchell (1806-1881)
1881-1902	Auchinleck Estate - James Mitchell (1834-1902)
c.*1902-1922*	Auchinleck Estate - Helen Mitchell (-1922)
1923-	Auchinleck Estate - Mr Mitchell Jr, Creoch
1925	Auchinleck Estate - Thomas Mitchell & Hugh Mitchell
1928-1934	Auchinleck Estate - John Young Craig
1941	Auchinleck Estate - James Craig
	James Pearson
	Alexander Watt
	Andrew Lees
	David Wardrop
2015	Robert McClure

Rogerton, Fore (NS 562219)
Incorporated Orchard since at least 1875.

-1861	Auchinleck Estate - William Alexander (1781-1861)
1875	Auchinleck Estate - James Alexander
1896-1928	Auchinleck Estate - Hugh Alexander
1934	Auchinleck Estate - Agnes Alexander
1941	Adam Wardrop
2012-*2015*	Mungo Wardrop

Shawfield (NS 654208)

1900	Dornal Estate -
1923-1925	Dumfries House Estate - Alexander Struthers

Springhill (NS 641199)
Includes Dornalhill.

c.*1880-1913*	Dornal Estate - Alexander Struthers (1846-1913)
1916	- Ferguson
1923-1941	Dumfries House Estate - Alexander Struthers
2015	Dumfries House Estate - Alastair Struthers of Boylston -

Stevenston (NS 517216)
Steinstoun in 1691.
1690	Auchinleck Estate - George Caldow
1795	Auchinleck Estate - late James Caldow
	Auchinleck Estate - William Caldow (d. 1801)
-1873	Auchinleck Estate - Alexander Jamieson (1839-1873)
1873-1875	Auchinleck Estate - Heirs of Alexander Jamieson
-1911	Auchinleck Estate - Elizabeth Jamieson (1824-1911)
1899-1922	Auchinleck Estate - John Howat
1922-1925	John Howat
1941-1963	William Hettrick Howat (-1963)
1963-2015	Mungo Brown Howat (1932-)

Stonebriggs (NS 625239)
Stonebridge in 1796, 1876, 1913.
1601	George Reid in Craigston -
-1796	- William Gibson (1714-1796)
	- Alexander Gibson
1875-1876	Auchinleck Estate - Hugh Gibson (1812-1876)
	Auchinleck Estate - David Gibson (1864-1916)
1899	Auchinleck Estate - John & James R. Gibson (1873-1941)
-1922	- Alexander Gibson (1850-1924)
1922-	- John Gibson
1925	A. D. & W. Mitchell of Hazelside -
1941	A. D. & W. Mitchell of Hazelside - Thomas Mitchell
1945-	A. D. & W. Mitchell of Hazelside - John French (d. c. 1950)
	Robert Morton - John French
	Robert Morton - Thomas French (1946-)
1964-2015	Thomas John French (1973-)

Sunnyside (NS 610219)
184 acres in 1924.
-1868	- Thomas Pearson (-1868)
1868-1882	Auchinleck Estate - Mrs Anne Pearson
1899-1921	Auchinleck Estate - Thomas Pearson
1921-1924	Thomas Pearson - Alexander Pearson
1924-1928	Thomas Pearson - William Dinning (1876-1928)
1941	Thomas Pearson trustees - Alexander Pearson
	Gilbert MacWhirter
2010-2015	Thomas Laird of Carbello

Tarrioch, Nether (NS 634269)
Tareoch in 1691.
	Duke of Portland -
1875	James Baird of Cambusdoon - John Hamilton in Nether Wellwood
1899	J.G.A. Baird of Adamton - James Hamilton in Nether Wellwood
1925	Edith C. Broun Lindsay -
1934-1941	Dumfries House Estate - Hugh Anderson in Nether Wellwood

Tarrioch, Upper (NS 646268)
In ruins by 1860
Duke of Portland -

Templand Mains (NS 573207)
-1854	- Hugh Dalgliesh (1782-1854)
1873-1875	Auchinleck Estate - Robert Dalgleish
1899	Auchinleck Estate - Thomas Hunter
-1915	Auchinleck Estate - William Hunter
-1917	Auchinleck Estate - John Dixon (1848-1917)
1920-1928	Auchinleck Estate - William Hunter
1934-1941	Robert Dalgliesh Hunter - William Hunter
1967-1989	Ian Andrew
1989-*1993*	Lakshman Welikanna

Templandshaw (NS 597249)
Templeshaw in 1875. 137 acres in 1920.
-1837	John Harvey (Harvie) (1748-1837)
1875-1890	William Harvey (1805-1890)
1890-*1899*	John Harvey
1909-1920	William MacMurray of Minnivey & Thomas MacIlwraith MacMurray
1925	William MacMurray - Adam Gordon
1934-1941	William MacMurray - Thomas MacIlwraith MacMurray
1946-1957	Thomas Dumigan
1957-1961	William Allison Leckie
1961-1961	Robert Mathieson Cockburn
1961-1966	Robert Valentine Armstrong
1966-1971	John Lindsay
1971-1973	Major Bruce Bingham Kennedy of Doonholm (d.1984)
1973-1976	John Binnie
1976-*2012*	Michael & Pamela J. Poole

Thirdpart (NS 525215)

1774-1791	Auchinleck Estate - John Reid
1791-	Auchinleck Estate - William Smith
1793	Auchinleck Estate - David Murdoch
1875-1880	Auchinleck Estate - James Smith (1803-1880)
1880-c1902	Auchinleck Estate - William Smith (1836-1906)
	Auchinleck Estate - William Smith (1872-1925)
1906-1925	Auchinleck Estate - John Peden Smith (1871-1945)
1934	John Peden Smith (1871-1945)
1941-1962	Bairds & Dalmellington Ltd. - John Peden Smith Jr. (-1962)
1962-1996	National Coal Board - Alexander Anderson and James Anderson
1996-1999	Alexander Anderson and James Anderson
1999-*2015*	Mungo Howat of Stevenston

Townhead of Auchinleck (NS 519227)

Tounheade in 1691.

1706	Auchinleck Estate - Robert Pedine
1774-1791	Auchinleck Estate - George Paton
1798-1836	Auchinleck Estate - John Sloan (1773-1836) (buried Ochiltree)
1875	Auchinleck Estate - William Sloan (1811-1884)
	Auchinleck Estate - Hugh Sloan (1860-1891)
1899	Auchinleck Estate - Mrs Sloan
-*1915*	Auchinleck Estate - Sloan
1915-1920	Auchinleck Estate - John Sloan (1851-1920)
1920-1921	Auchinleck Estate - Bryce Nairn Sloan (1885-1969)
1921-1954	Bryce Nairn Sloan (1885-1969)
1954-1993	Robert T. Sloan (1928-)
1993-*2015*	Gordon Sloan (1965-)

Treeshill (NS 526228)

	- George Sloan (1818-1882)
1875	Auchinleck Estate - James Smith & William Smith
1899-1906	Auchinleck Estate - William Smith (1836-1906)
1934	John Peden Smith - William Smith
1941	John Peden Smith
-2012	- [William] Douglas Smith (-2012)
2012-*2015*	Alastair Smith
2015	Egger - Mungo Howat of Stevenston

Underwood (NS 558205)
Underwoodholm in 1875.
c.1850-c.1871	- William MacLanachan
1875	Dumfries House Estate - John Hayman
1899	Dumfries House Estate - Agnes Hayman & Margaret Hayman
1925-1941	Dumfries House Estate -Thomas Hayman

Wallaceton (NS 603215)
170 acres in 1924.
1609-1616	William Wallace (d. 1616)
1616-	James Wallace
-1678	James Wallace (d. 1678)
1732-1740	James Wallace
	John Wallace
	William Wallace
1807-1817	Hugh Wallace
-c.1850	Wallace
c.1850-	other family
1875	Alexander Hamilton Robertson - William Fergusson & Robert Fergusson
c.1890s	Dornal Estate - James Armstrong (-1906)
1899	Dornal Estate - Robert Armstrong
-1913	- James Armstrong
-1924	Thomas Pearson
1934-1941	Thomas Pearson - Matthew Tannock
	Nairn
c.1980	George
2015	Thomson

Weilside (NS 514212)
Became part of Mill Affleck.
1774	- Adam Caldow
1875	Auchinleck Estate - John Gemmell

Welltrees (NS 630242)
Walltrees in 1691. In ruins by 1860.
1601	Leifnoreis Estate -
1829	- James Weir
c.1880	- George Johnstone (c.1848-1918)
1899	Auchinleck Estate -Andrew Picken of Knockrivoch - Thomas Weir

1925   A. D. & W. Mitchell -

Whirr (NS 515230)
1774   Auchinleck Estate - James Murdoch

Whiteholm of Dornal (NS 625199)
Whytholme in 1691.
   -1859   - James MacKerrow (1828-1859)
c.1850   - Hugh MacKerrow (1810-1886)
1875-1900   Dornal Estate - Alexander Struthers (1844-1913)
1916-   Dornal Estate -   MacLauchlan
1925-1934   Dumfries House Estate - D. W. & H. Blane - John Todd
1941   D. W. & H. Blane - William Arthur
                  William Anderson
1980   Dr Graham Hunter
                  Robert Laird

Whiteholm of Kyle (NS 655186)
c.1880   Dumfries House Estate - William Ferguson
1899   Dumfries House Estate - Robert Latta & John Latta -
1916   Dumfries House Estate -   Murdoch

Woodside (NS 531216)
In ruins by 1856.
1661-   Auchinleck Estate -   Templeton
1792   Auchinleck Estate - James Templeton
                  Auchinleck Estate - William Templeton
1840   Auchinleck Estate - James Templeton (1757-   )

Woolmill (NS 561214)
In ruins before 1911.
1899   James Templeton, Ayr - Mrs Blain

APPENDIX II

MINES

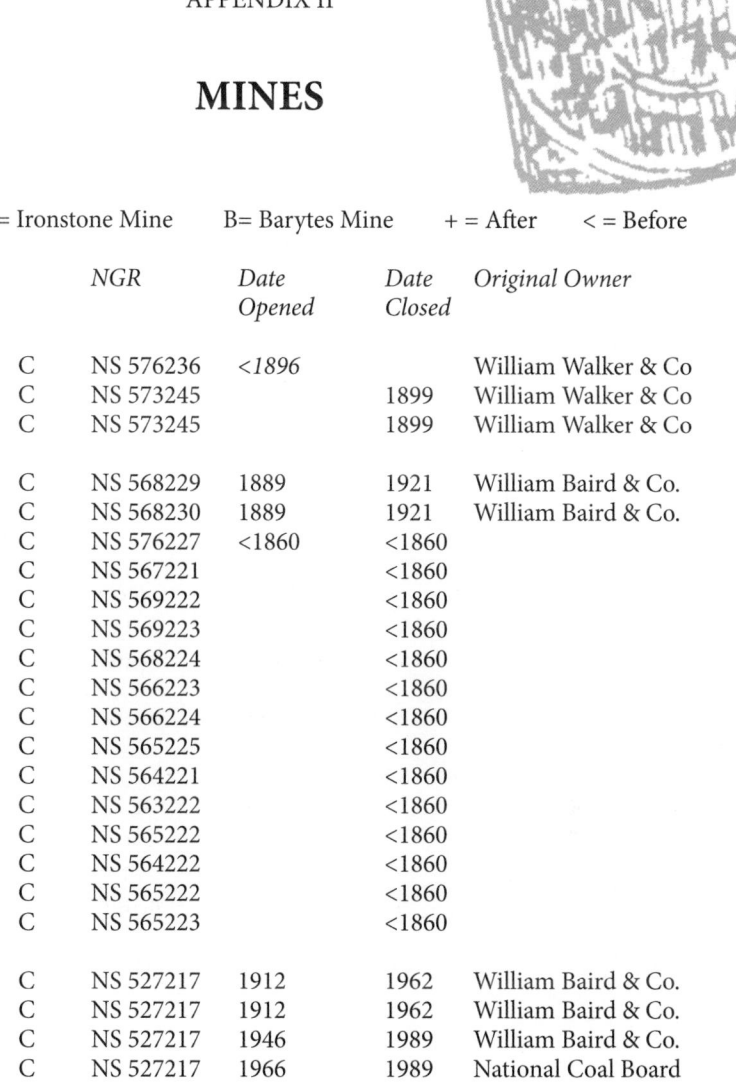

C = Coalmine   I = Ironstone Mine   B = Barytes Mine   + = After   < = Before

Name		NGR	Date Opened	Date Closed	Original Owner
Ballochmyle No. 2	C	NS 576236	*<1896*		William Walker & Co
Ballochmyle No. 7	C	NS 573245		1899	William Walker & Co
Ballochmyle No. 8	C	NS 573245		1899	William Walker & Co
Barglachan No. 1	C	NS 568229	1889	1921	William Baird & Co.
Barglachan No. 2	C	NS 568230	1889	1921	William Baird & Co.
Barglachan No. 30	C	NS 576227	<1860	<1860	
Barglachan a	C	NS 567221		<1860	
Barglachan b	C	NS 569222		<1860	
Barglachan c	C	NS 569223		<1860	
Barglachan d	C	NS 568224		<1860	
Barglachan e	C	NS 566223		<1860	
Barglachan f	C	NS 566224		<1860	
Barglachan g	C	NS 565225		<1860	
Barglachan h	C	NS 564221		<1860	
Barglachan i	C	NS 563222		<1860	
Barglachan j	C	NS 565222		<1860	
Barglachan k	C	NS 564222		<1860	
Barglachan l	C	NS 565222		<1860	
Barglachan m	C	NS 565223		<1860	
Barony No. 1	C	NS 527217	1912	1962	William Baird & Co.
Barony No. 2	C	NS 527217	1912	1962	William Baird & Co.
Barony No. 3	C	NS 527217	1946	1989	William Baird & Co.
Barony No. 4	C	NS 527217	1966	1989	National Coal Board
Barytes - Gasswater	B	NS 655219	1917	1921	Hedworth Barium Co. Ltd.
Barytes - Central	B	NS 663214	1923	1965	
Barytes – South	B	NS 657217		1965	
Barytes - Burnside	B	NS 673212	1931	1965	
Benalt a	C	NS 671191		<1860	
Benalt b	C	NS 673189		<1860	

Berryhill No. 1	C	NS 554229	1876	1881	(In Sorn parish)
Berryhill No. 2	C	NS 558227	1900	1925	
Berryhill No. 3	I	NS 564231	1901	1925	
Birnieknowe		NS		1865	
Blackston No. 1	I	NS	1879	1886	
Blackston		NS	1873	1881	
Braehead No. 1		NS	<1896		William Baird & Co.
Braehead No. 2		NS			
Braehead No. 3		NS			
Braehead No. 4		NS			
Braehead No. 5		NS			
Also known as 'Auld Carbello'					
Braehead No. 6	C	NS 593223	*1883*		
Braehead No. 7	C	NS 592222			
Braehead	CI	NS	1888	1897	
Braehead a	I	NS 600221	<1856	+1856	
Braehead b	I	NS 595216	<1856	+1856	
Cairnhill	C	NS 627231	1956	1976	National Coal Board
Carbello No. 1	CI	NS	1873	1906	
Carbello No. 2	I	NS		1880	
Common No. 1	C	NS 586229	1850	1905	Known as Maid Pits
Common No. 2	I	NS 586229	1850	1905	Known as Maid Pits
Common No. 3	I	NS 575244			
Common No. 4		NS			
Common No. 5	I	NS 586234			
Common No. 6	I	NS 581231	<1896	<1911	William Baird & Co.
Common No. 7	C	NS 582242	<1911	+1911	
Common No. 8	C	NS 589227		<1860	
Common No. 9		NS 586227			
Common No. 10	C	NS 586234	<1896	+1911	William Baird & Co.
Common No. 11	C	NS 594230	*<1896*	*+1911*	William Baird & Co.
Common No. 12	I	NS 582242	*<1896*	*<1911*	William Baird & Co.
Common No. 13		NS			
Common No. 14	I	NS 590240	<1883	+1911	William Baird & Co.
Common No. 15	I	NS 573237	*<1896*	*+1911*	William Baird & Co.
Common No. 16	C	NS 571237	*<1896*	*+1911*	William Baird & Co.
Common No. 16½		NS	<1916	1925	
Common No. 17	C	NS 594232			
Common a	I	NS 595229		<1860	
Common b	I	NS 596234		<1860	
Commondyke 1	I	NS 576223	1878	1881	
Commondyke a	C	NS 578221		<1860	

Commondyke b	C	NS 577223		<1860	
Craigston No. 1	I	NS 591216	<1856	+1856	William Baird & Co.
Craigston No. 2		NS			
Craigston No. 3		NS			
Craigston No. 4	I	NS 589224		1886	
Craigston No. 5	CI	NS	*1865*	1876	William Baird & Co.
Known as Roadinghead pit					
Craigston No. 6		NS 593224			
Craigston No. 7	I	NS 593224		1887	
Craigston No. 8		NS			
Craigston No. 9		NS			
Craigston No. 10		NS			
Craigston No. 11		NS			
Craigston No. 12		NS	*1849*		
Craigston No. 13		NS			
Craigston No. 14		NS			
Craigston No. 15		NS			
Craigston No. 16		NS			
Craigston No. 17	C	NS			
Craigston No. 18		NS			
Craigston No. 19		NS	*1853*	*1857*	
Craigston	I	NS	1878	1881	
Craigston a	C	NS 579214		*<1857*	
Craigston b	C	NS 586213		*<1857*	
Craigston c	I	NS 578209		1857	
Craigston d	I	NS 585220		<1860	
Cronberry No. 1	CI	NS 599235	1864	1893	William Baird & Co.
Cronberry No. 2	I	NS		1880	William Baird & Co.
Cronberry No. 3	C	NS 599234		1876	William Baird & Co.
Cronberry No. 4	CI	NS		1886	William Baird & Co.
Cronberry No. 5	CI	NS		1886	William Baird & Co.
Cronberry Moor	C	NS 624249	1922	1957	William Baird & Co.
Dalblair	C	NS 645197			
Dalfad a	C	NS 628220		<1856	
Dalfad b	C	NS 624223		<1856	
Dalfad c	C	NS 627229		<1856	
Dalfad d	C	NS 624223	<1856	1860	
Darnconner	I	NS 575244	<1858	+1860	
Dickston a	I	NS 585214	*<1857*	<1911	
Dickston b	I	NS 582216	<1860	<1911	
Dickston c	C	NS 581215		<1860	
Dickston d	C	NS 581218		<1860	

Dickston e	C	NS 579219		<1860	
Dykes a	CI	NS	1876	1888	
Dykes No. 2	C	NS 578220	1889	1894	William Baird & Co.
Dykes b	C	NS 577220		<1860	
Gasswater a	C	NS 621233	<1860	1861	
Gasswater b	C	NS 624233	<1860	1861	
Highhouse No. 1	C	NS 549216	1894	1983	William Baird & Co.
Highhouse No. 2	C	NS 549216	1894	1983	William Baird & Co.
Holm	I	NS 576206	+1857	<1911	
Lugar No. 1	C	NS 589216		1880	
Lugar No. 2	C	NS 588216	1943	1954	Bairds & Dalmellington Ltd.
Mortonmuir	C	NS 625248	1950	1954	National Coal Board
Mosshouse a	I	NS 608225	<1856	+1856	
Mosshouse b	I	NS 608225	<1856	+1856	
Mosshouse c	I	NS 608225	1873	1877	
Mosshouse d	I	NS 601221		<1856	
Mosshouse e	I	NS 601219		<1856	
Powharnal a	C	NS 648249	<1860	<1860	
Powharnal b	C	NS 645249	1950s	1959	National Coal Board
Roadinghead a	C	NS 579214		<1860	
Roadinghead b	I	NS 578208	<1860	+1860	
Roadinghead c		NS 574209			
Roadinghead d		NS			
Roadinghead No. 5	I	NS 574209			
Rosebank	I	NS 598216			
Stepends No. 1	I	NS 566204			
Stepends a	C	NS 567204	1848	1892	
Stepends b	C	NS 566203			
Stepends c	C	NS 565203			
Templand No. 1	I	NS 569207	1873	1878	
Welltrees a	C	NS 629238	<1860	<1860	
Welltrees b	C	NS 629235	<1860	+1860	

BIBLIOGRAPHY

REFERENCE BOOKS

Statistical Account of Scotland - Chapter on Auchinleck Parish by Rev John Dun, 1792.
New Statistical Account of Scotland - Chapter on Auchinleck Parish by Rev James Chrystal, 1837.
Third Statistical Account of Scotland: Ayrshire, by John Strawhorn and William Boyd, Oliver & Boyd, Edinburgh, 1951.
Burke's Landed Gentry - various volumes.
Dictionary of National Biography - various volumes.
Pigot & Co.'s National Commercial Directory, J. Pigot & Co., London, 1837
Scottish Biographies 1938, E. J. Thursdon, London, 1938.
Fasti Ecclesiae Scoticanae, volumes 3, 8, 9, 10, 11.
Register of the Great Seal of Scotland, (11 volumes).
Scotland - Owners of Lands and Heritages, HMSO, Edinburgh, 1874.
Imperial Gazetteer of Scotland
Ordnance Gazetteer of Scotland, edited by F. H. Groome, 6 volumes, 1882-1885.
Valuation Rolls for Auchinleck Parish, various years, 1875-1974.

OTHER PUBLISHED WORKS

Baird, John George Alexander, *Muirkirk in Bygone Days*, W. Shaw Smith, Muirkirk, 1910.
Blind Harry the Minstrel, *The Acts and Deeds of Sir William Wallace*, 7th Book, Chapter III.
Boswell, Sir Alexander, *Songs, Chiefly in the Scottish Dialect*, Manners & Miller, Edinburgh, 1803.
Boswell, James, *Life of Johnson*
Boswell, James, *Journal of a Tour to the Hebrides*, Charles Dilly, London, 1785.
Boyd, A., *The Biography of John Smith, Ayrshire Geologist and Naturalist*, Arthur Guthrie & Sons, Ardrossan, 1930.
Boyle, Andrew M., *The Ayrshire Book of Burns Lore*, Alloway Publishing, Darvel, 1985.
Brady, Frank & Pottle, Frederick A., *Boswell in Search of a Wife*, Heinemann, London, 1957.

Brook, Alexander J.S., *Communion Tokens of the Established Church of Scotland*, Neill & Co., Edinburgh, 1908.

Burns, Robert, *The Complete Letters of*, (Edited by James A. Mackay), Alloway Publishing, Darvel, 1987.

Cameron, I. B. & Stephenson, D., *British Regional Geology - The Midland Valley of Scotland*, H.M.S.O., Edinburgh, 1985.

Chalmers, John, *Duel Personalities: James Stuart versus Sir Alexander Boswell*, Newbattle Publishing, Edinburgh, 2014.

Cowan, Ian B., Mackay, P. H. R., & MacQuarie, Alan, *The Knights of St John of Jerusalem in Scotland*, Scottish History Society, Edinburgh, 1983.

Daiches, David, *James Boswell and His World*, Thames & Hudson, London, 1976.

Dickson, Neil T. R., *Brethren in Scotland 1838-2000*, Paternoster, Milton Keynes, 2002.

Dunlop, A. Ian, *The Kirks of Edinburgh*, Scottish Record Society, Edinburgh, 1989.

Finlayson, Ian, *The Moth and the Candle*, Constable, London, 1984.

Fowler, James J. *The Presbytery of Ayr: Its Schools and Schoolmasters*, Ayrshire Archaeological and Natural History Society, Ayr, 1961.

Fullarton, Col. William, *General View of the Agriculture of the County of Ayr*, John Paterson, Edinburgh, 1793.

Griffiths, John, *The Third Man: the Life and Times of William Murdoch*, Inventor of Gaslight, Andrew Deutsch, London, 1992.

Haldane, A.R.B., *Three Centuries of Scottish Posts*, Edinburgh University Press, 1971.

Hannan, Thomas, *Famous Scottish Houses*, A. & C. Black, London, 1928.

Haws, Charles H. *Scottish Parish Clergy at the Reformation*, Scottish Record Society, Edinburgh, 1972.

Johnson, Christine, *Scottish Catholic Secular Clergy, 1879-1989*, John Donald, Edinburgh, 1991.

Johnson, Dr Samuel, *Journey to the Western Islands of Scotland*, W. Strahan & T. Cadell, London, 1775.

Kirkwood, Rev John, *The United Presbyterians in Ayrshire*, Arthur Guthrie & Sons, Ardrossan, 1900.

Lindsay, Maurice, *The Burns Encyclopaedia*, Robert Hale, London, 1959.

Lockhart, John Gibson, *Memoirs of the Life of Sir Walter Scott*, Robert Cadell, Edinburgh, 1845.

Lorimer, Hugh, *A Corner of Old Strathclyde*, Andrew Spence, Glasgow, 1952.

Lustig, Irma, & Pottle, Frederick A., *Boswell: The Applause of the Jury*, Heinemann, London, 1982.

MacAulay, James, *The Classical Country House in Scotland*, Faber & Faber, London, 1987.

MacAuley, James, *The History of Auchinleck Talbot*, New Cumnock, 1989.

McClure, David, *Tolls and Tacksmen: Eighteenth Century Roads in the County of John Loudon MacAdam*, Ayrshire Archaeological and Natural History Society, Ayr, 1994.
Ayrshire in the Age of Improvement, Ayrshire Archaeological and Natural History Society, Ayr, 2002.
MacGibbon, David & Ross, Thomas, *The Castellated and Domestic Architecture of Scotland*, (Vol. 3), David Douglas, Edinburgh, 1889.
MacIlvean, John Gardiner, *The Birth of Football in the Burns Country*, Cumnock, 1982.
Mackay, James A., *The Complete Works of Robert Burns*, Alloway Publishing, Darvel, 1986.
MacKelvie, Rev William, *Annals and Statistics of the United Presbyterian Church*, Oliphant & Company, Edinburgh, 1873.
MacKerrell, Thomas, & Brown, James, *Ayrshire Miners' Rows 1913*, Ayrshire Archaeological and Natural History Society, Ayr, 1979.
Moore, John (ed.), *Among Thy Green Braes*, Cumnock & Doon Valley District Council, Lugar, 1977.
Morrison, Alex., *The Bronze Age in Ayrshire*, Ayrshire Archaeological and Natural History Society, Ayr, 1978.
Morrison, Alex; & Hughes, Isobel, *The Stone Ages in Ayrshire*, Ayrshire Archaeological and Natural History Society, Ayr, 1989.
Nisbet, Alexander, *A System of Heraldry*, T. & A. Constable, Edinburgh, 1984.
Paterson, Barbara E., *Social and Working Condition of Ayrshire Mining Population 1840-1875*, Ayrshire Archaeological and Natural History Association, Ayr, 1972.
Paterson, James, *History of the Counties of Ayrshire and Wigtownshire, with a Genealogical Account of the Families of Ayrshire*, (2 volumes), John Dick, Ayr, 1847 and 1852.
Pottle, Frederick A., *Boswell's London Journal*, Heinemann, London, 1950.
Boswell in Holland, Heinemann, London, 1952.
Boswell on the Grand Tour: Germany and Switzerland 1764, Heinemann, London, 1953.
Boswell in Search of a Wife, 1766-1769, Heinemann, London 1957.
James Boswell: The Earlier Years, 1740-1769, Heinemann, London, 1966
Reed, Joseph W., & Pottle, Frederick A., *Boswell, Laird of Auchinleck*, McGraw Hill, London, 1977.
Robertson, T; Simpson, J; & Anderson, J., *The Limestones of Scotland*, HMSO, Edinburgh, 1949.
Robertson, William, *Ayrshire: Its History and Historic Families* (2 volumes), Dunlop & Drennan, Kilmarnock, 1908.

Ryskamp, Charles A. & Pottle, Frederick A., *Boswell: The Ominous Years*, Heinemann, London, 1963.
Shaw, James Edward, *Ayrshire 1745-1950*, Oliver & Boyd, Edinburgh, 1953.
Sloan, Alec M., *Those Were The Days*, Privately Published, Ayr, 1988.
Small, Rev Dr Robert, *History of the United Presbyterian Church from 1733 to 1900*, David Small, Edinburgh, 1904.
Smith, John, *Prehistoric Man in Ayrshire*, Elliot Stock, London, 1895.
Smith, Robert Howie, *The Poetical Works of Sir Alexander Boswell*, Maurice Ogle & Company, Glasgow, 1871.
Steven, Helen, *Auchinleck - Its History and Associations*, Dunlop & Drennan, Kilmarnock, 1898.
Strawhorn, Dr John, *The New History of Cumnock*, Cumnock Town Council, Cumnock, 1966.
Swain, Margaret, *Ayrshire and Other Whitework*, Shire Publications, Princes Risborough, 1982.
Thomas, John, *Regional History of the Railways of Great Britain - Scotland: The Lowlands and the Borders*, David & Charles, Newton Abbot, 1971.
Thomson, Rev John Henderson, *The Martyr Graves of Scotland*, Oliphant, Anderson & Ferrier, Edinburgh, n.d.
Todd, Adam Brown, *Covenanting Pilgrimages and Studies*, Oliphant, Anderson & Ferrier, Edinburgh, 1911.
Urquhart, Robert H. J. & Close, Rob, *The Hearth Tax for Ayrshire 1691*, Ayrshire Records Series, Volume 1, Ayrshire Federation of Historical Societies, Ayr, 1998.
Warrick, Rev John, *The History of Old Cumnock*, Alexander Gardner, Paisley, 1899.
Weis, C. MacC., & Pottle, Frederick A., *Boswell in Extremes*, Heinemann, London, 1971.
Whatley, C. A., *The Finest Place for a Lasting Colliery*, Ayrshire Archaeological and Natural History Society, Ayr, 1989.
Wimsatt, W. K. & Pottle, Frederick A, *Boswell for the Defence*, Heinemann, London, 1960.
Wodrow, Rev Robert, *The History of the Sufferings of the Church of Scotland, traced from the Restoration to the Revolution* (4 vols.), Blackie & Son, Edinburgh, 1839.

PERIODICALS

The Auchinleck Newsletter (various editions)
Ayr Advertiser (various editions)
Ayrshire Post (various editions)
Cumnock Chronicle (various editions)
Kilmarnock Standard (various editions)

JOURNALS
Discovery & Excavation in Scotland:
   MacFadzean, H. M. & D., *Glenmuirshaw, agate implements, waste flakes, chipping floor*, 1984.
   Baker, L., *Gasswater Open Cast Coal Scheme, Cronberry*, 2000.
Proceedings of the Society of Antiquaries of Scotland:
   Christison, D., *The Prehistoric Forts, &c. of Ayrshire*, Vol. 27, 1893.
   Fairbairn, Archibald, *Notes on excavation of prehistoric and later sites at Muirkirk, Ayrshire, 1913-1927*, Vol. 61, 1927.

BOOKLETS
Adam Wilson & Sons: The History of a Firm of Timber Merchants, Adam Wilson & Sons, Ayr, 1980.
Auchinleck Co-operative Society Limited 1890-1940, Auchinleck Co-operative Society, Auchinleck, 1940.
Barony Generating Station, S.S.E.B., Glasgow, 1958.
Our Lady of Lourdes and St Patrick's, 1867-1967, Centenary brochure.

MAPS
Timothy Pont's *Coila Provincia*, 1654.
H. Moll's *The South Part of the Shire of Air*, 1725.
General William Roy's *Military Survey*, 1750.
A. & M. Armstrong's *Map of Ayrshire*, 1775.
Ordnance Survey 25" 1st edition, various sheets, 1855-82.
Ordnance Survey 6" *County Series*, 1860.
Ordnance Survey 1" *Map*, sheets 14 and 15, 1902.
Geological Survey of Great Britain, *6" Map*, Sheet No. NS 52 SE, 1965.

UNPUBLISHED SOURCES
Auchinleck and the Boswells, Gordon P. Hoyle, Burns Monument Centre, Kilmarnock.
Auchinleck Kirk Session Baptism Register 1858-1927, Burns Monument Centre, Kilmarnock.
Auchinleck Kirk Session Baptism Register - Darnconner Church 1882-1937, Burns Monument Centre, Kilmarnock.
Auchinleck Kirk Session - Proclamation of Banns 1855-64, 1865-93, 1893-1925, Burns Monument Centre, Kilmarnock.
Auchinleck Kirk Session Minute Books, 1752-1819, 1819-1854, 1853-1886, 1886-1947, 1922-1964, Burns Monument Centre, Kilmarnock.

Auchinleck Original Secession Church - Session Minutes 1837-40 (with Baptisms 1837-57 and lists of members 1811, 1827, 1837, 1848.), Burns Monument Centre, Kilmarnock.

Auchinleck U. F. Church/Peden Church Minute Book, 1922-1981, Burns Monument Centre, Kilmarnock.

Ayrshire Christian Union - Building Fund Book 1922-1929, James Tanner, Cumnock.

Ayrshire Christian Union - Minute Book 1947-1963, James Tanner, Cumnock.

Census of Scotland 1851-1921.

Corrins, R. D., *William Baird and Company, Coal and Ironmasters 1830-1914*, Strathclyde University Thesis, 1974.

Lugar School Log Book, Two Volumes, 1876-1963, Logan Primary School, Logan.

McCombe, James L., *A History of the Auchinleck Assembly*, 1981.

Moyes, Andrew, *A History of Agricultural Liming*, Strathclyde University Thesis, 1976.

Ordnance Survey Card Index of Antiquities on Maps

Richmond, Henry, *Diary 1823-1824*, held at Burns House Museum, Mauchline.

Smith, Frances M. M., *Life in Miners' Rows -Auchinleck Parish (East) 1860-1935*, Thesis, St Andrews College of Education, 1983.

Tombstone Inscriptions from Auchinleck Kirkyard and other on-site examinations.

INDEX

Figures in **bold** type refer to illustrations

Adelphi Engineering, 279
Aerated waters, 174, 226, 277-8
Affleck House, 288
Agriculture, 11-12, 48-9, 64, 105-7, 109, 130, 159-61, 280-1, 302-3
Airds Moss, 11-13, 15, 53-5, 129, 150, 166, 243, 253, 276
Airds Moss, Battle of, 53-4
Aitken, James, 267
AKHB, *see Boyd, Rev Andrew*
Alexander of Ballochmyle, 87, 103, 108-9, 130, 133, 154, 183, 185-6
Allan, John, 215
Angus, Robert, 125, 137, 149, 163, 178, 194, 201, 203, 211, 236-7, 241
Auchinleck – meaning, 12
Auchinleck Academy, **267**, 267-8, 300, 305
Auchinleck Arms, 105
Auchinleck burgh, 30-1
Auchinleck Castle (new), 28, 37, 39-40, **40, 41, 42**, 73, 107
Auchinleck Castle (old), 11, **18**, 18-20, 22, 28, 35
Auchinleck Christian Fellowship, 299
Auchinleck House, 50, 60, 63, **65**,
69-70, 72, 74-5, 81, 83, 103, 117, 123, 131-2, 200-1, 239, 243, 254-5, 297, 305-6
Auchinleck Mains, 307
Auchinleck of that Ilk, 20-5
Auchinleck of that Ilk, James (I), 22
Auchinleck of that Ilk, James (II), 23
Auchinleck of that Ilk, John, 21-2
Auchinleck of that Ilk, Sir John (I), 23
Auchinleck of that Ilk, Sir John (II), 24-5
Auchinleck of that Ilk, Nichol, 20
Auchinleck parish – extent, 11
Auchinleck Press, 76
Auchinleck Talbot 233-7, 281-3, 303-5
Auchinleck, Lord, *see Alexander Boswell*
Auchtitench, 12, 34, 47, 143, 281, 307

Back o' Hill, 49
Baird of Wellwood, Col. John G. A., 13
Baird, William, ironmasters – *see Bairds & Dalmellington*
Bairds & Dalmellington, 124-8, 133,

337

INDEX

135, 145-6, 148-55, 157, 163-4, 171, 174, 178, 181-3, 186, 211, 216, 218, 220, 222-4, 237, 251, 253, 268

Ballochmyle Pits, 128, 147, 154, 185, 227, 327

Ballochmyle Rows, 128, 142, 144, 154, 158, 183, 185-6, 209, 224, 227

Bands, 131, 142, 162, 176, 207, 211, 230, 234, 238-9, 251, 285

Bank Viaduct, 130

Banks, 158, **159**, 230

Bannatyne of Kames, 34, 44

Barglachan, 58, 129, 149-50, 155, 174, 180, 185, 201, 233, 307

Barglachan Pits, 149-51, 153, 217-8, 327

Barnsdale, 76

Barony A-Frame Trust, 290, 292

Barony Colliery, 218-20, 223, 243, 268-71, **269**, 275, 285, 290, 292, 327

Barony Power Station, **275**, 274-6, **276**

Barony Universal, 278, 301

Barytes mining, 12, 224-5, 272-4, **273**, **274**, 327

Bello Mill, 11, 108, 112, **112**, 114, 147, 160, 175, 230, 252-3, 308

Bello Path, 15, 54-5, 57-8, 107, 109, 250, 266

Bells, 50, 95

Benalt, 12, 103, 146, 327

Berryhill, 216, 303, 308

Berryhill Pits, 149, 216-7, 327-8

Berryknowe care home, 293

Birnieknowe, 48, 101, 103, 124, 127, 139-142, 146, 148, 150, 201, 206-9, 233, 242, 247, 261-3, 272, 287, 308, 328

Black Bull Inn, 105

Blackfauldhead, 308

Blackston, 45, 149, 151, 237, 281, 303, 309, 328

Bogend, 309

Boghead, 34, 37, 44, 53, 107, 109, 155, 159-60, 249, 251, 268, 280, 309

Boghead Moor, 11

Bogside, 42, 159, 309

Boswell Arms Inn, 61, **77**, 81, 123, 158-9, 230, 234, 280, 302

Boswell Book Festival, 305

Boswell Centre, 293, **294**

Boswell Museum, 28, 286-7

Boswell of Auchinleck, Alexander, Lord Auchinleck, (VIII), 60, 62, 65-70, 88, 92, 109-10, 117

Boswell of Auchinleck, Sir Alexander, 1st Baronet (X), 12, 72, 75-83, 103, 131

Boswell of Auchinleck, David (II), 31-3

Boswell of Auchinleck, David (V), 39, 42, 44, 50-1, 56

Boswell of Auchinleck, David (VI), 42-4, 87

Boswell of Auchinleck, James (IV), 38-40

Boswell of Auchinleck, James (IX), 28, 62, 66-7, 69-75, 85, 87, 89-93, 99, 108-9, 110-1, 117-8, 130

Boswell of Auchinleck, James (VII), 64-5, 85, 89

338

Boswell of Auchinleck, Sir James, 2nd Baronet (XI), 106, 130-1, 133, 135, 147, 160
Boswell of Auchinleck, John (III), 32-3, 44, 47, 201
Boswell of Auchinleck, Thomas (I), 24, 29-31
Boswell of Craigston, David (III), 85
Boswell of Craigston, Mungo, 47
Boswell of Duncanziemere, John, 47
Boswell of Knockroon, John, 74, 87, 95, 99
Boswell of Knockroon, William, 44, 55
Boswell Society, 286-7, 305-6
Boswell, Captain John, 38
Boswell, James Douglas (XVI), 254-5
Boswell, James, 83-4
Boswell, John Douglas (XIV), 188, 200-2, **202**
Boswell, John Douglas (XV), 254-5
Boswell, Robert, 74-5
Bowling, 176, 236-7, 284-7, 305
Box-making, 103-4
Boyd, Rev Andrew (AKHB), 94, 135, **165**, 165-6
Boyd, Rev James, 82, 93-4, 165
Boys' Brigade, 239, 256-7, 259
Braehead of Craigston, 29, 49, 85, 235, 309
Braehead of Knockroon, 309
Braehead Pits, 129, 146, 149, 151-23, 328
Brennan, Rev Daniel, 262
Brethren, Christian, 142, 171, 208-9, 263, 299

Brick-making, 154, 182, 275
Bridgend Mill, 61, 63, **63**, 91, 105, 112, 131, 156, 160, 174, 310
Briquette manufacture, 147, 153, 252
Bronze Age, 13, 15
Broomfield, 132, 161, 310
Broomhouse, 310
Brown, Rev Benjamin, 137
Brown, George Douglas, 127
Brown, James, MP, 178, 207-8,
Burnhouse, 143
Burns, Robert, 78, 88, 90, 117-8
Burns Clubs, 241, 284
Burnside of Craigston, 310

Cairn Hill, 15
Cairnhill Pit, 15, 251, 268, 328
Cairns (Bronze Age), 13-14
Cameron, John, 152
Campbell, Rev John, 59
Campbell, Rev Joseph, 205
Cameron, Rev Richard, 53-4, 163
Cameron's Stone, 13, 15, **54**
Campbell Place, 123, 169
Carbello, 49, 124, 129, 133, 149, 151, 155, 183, 222, 280, 310
Carbello Pits, 328
Carrick View Hostel, 288, 293
Cell or cille, 27
Chapel Knowe (Lugar), 14, 34-5
Choirs, 207, 239, 285
Christian Union, 142, 208, 263-4, 287
Chrystal, Rev James, 94, 106, 123, 133-4, 137, 143, 145, 202-3
Churches, 35-6, 49-51, 62, 87-97, 133-42, 202-9, 256-64, 297-9

INDEX

Cist, 14
Clark, William ('Amateur Poet'), 242
Clelland, Rev John, 136
Clipston, Rev Steven, 298-9
Cochrane of Waterside, John, 43-4, 86
Collins, Francis. 242
Commerce, 105, 157-9, 227-31, 248-9, 279-80, 302
Commercial Inn, 158-9, 169, 226, 230
Common, 87, 103, 128, 133, 146, 155, 163, 186, 211, 231, 233, 237, 249, 272, 301, 310
Common Brickworks, 275
Common Pits, 122, 128-9, 146, 149-50, 153, 186, 217, 222, 242, 328
Common Thistle, 233
Commondyke, 114, 121, 124, **128**, 128-9, 138, 140, 144, 146, 149, 155, 183, 185, 211, 237, 242, 251, 311
Commondyke Pits, 328
Commonloch, 128, 144, 185-6
Communion tokens, 12, 89, **89**, 96
Communion vessels, 65, 89
Community Centre, 287-8
Connor Hill, 15
Cooper, Rev David, 88-9
Co-operative society, 126, 157-8, 180, 182, 226-7, 229-30, 249, 252-3, 279, 284
Council housing, 171-3, 247-8
Covenanters, 42-3, 51-9, 86, 95, 116, 204
Coyle, Rev James, 262-3
Craighead, 48
Craigston, 30, 47-9, 85-6, 109, 125, 129, 137, 145-7, 149, 151-2, 159, 162-3, 178, 194, 266, 311, 329
Crauford, Rev Robert, 96-7
Crichton, William, 267
Cronberry, 17, 42, 44, 87, 103, 121, 124, 126-7, 129, 133, 143-6, 149, 152, 154, 163, **180**, 181-3, 187, 211, 214-6, 218, 220-2, 224, 231-2, 241, 243, 247, 249, 251, 253-4, 265-6, 268, 276, 285, 294
Cronberry Brickworks, 154, 182
Cronberry Eglinton, 232, 234-6
Cronberry Moor Pit, 146, 218, 222, 268, 329
Cronberry Pits, 329
Cronberry School, 145
Cronberry Viaduct, 129
Cross Keys Inn, 158, 226, 239, 311
Curling, 112, 131, 161-2, 237, **238**, 284
Currie's Lemonade, 226, 277-8, 302

Dacre Terrace, 116, 123
Dalblair (Low), 11, 34, 47, 87, 107, 109, 132, 146, 155-6, 214, 266, 312, 329
Dalblair, High, 103, 144, 155, 312
Dalblair School, 214, 266
Dalfad, 129, 146, 153, 155, 301, 312, 329
Dalrymple of Glenmuir, 86
Dalrymple, Rev Andrew, 51-2
Dalsalloch, 43, 171, 173, 181, 248, 250, 265, 267, 288, 299, 303, 312
Dalziel, John, 169, 171, 174
Darnconner, 58, 87, 99, 103, 121, 124,

127-8, **128**, 130, 133-4, 136-7, **137**, 143-6, 149, 153-4, 158, 163, 169, 171, 182-7, 202, 204, 206, 210-1, **212**, **213**, 215, 229, 233, 239, 241, 247, 272, 281, 289, 301, 303, 313, 329
Darnconner Britannia, 233
Darnconner Parish Church, 136-7, **137**
Darnconner School, 145
Darnlaw, 61, 109, 114, 158-9, 173, 227, 250, 313
Diack, Rev William, 206
Dick, Robert (Covenanter), 54
Dickston (Dixton), 85, 129, 146, 162, 280, 313, 329
Dippolburn, 313
Dornal, 16, 34, 37, 47-8, 87, 91-2, 108-9, 130, 133, 143, 155, 202, 214, 241, 314
Dornal Moat, 16-17, **17**
Douglas of Pennyland, 33, 43
Doyle, Rev Martin, 207
Dumfries House, 43, 54, 69, 89, 110, 244, 293, 295, 297, 305
Dumfries House Estate, 157, 280, 293, 295
Dumfries, Earl of, 11, 44, 47, 55, 69, 86, 92, 103, 109-11
Dun, Rev John, 18, 63, 70, 73, 89-93, 118
Dunbar Cottage, 62
Duncanziemere, 27, 32, 37-8, 47, 49, 85, 99, 109, 133, 143, 241, 301, 314
Dykes, 146, 314
Dykes Pit, 146, 149, 237, 330

Eadie, Rev William, 206
Eagle Inn, 158-9, 162, 174, 230, 250, 280
Easton Place, 123, 248-9, 266
Easton Place School, 266
Easton, Danny, 264, 299
Education – *see schools*
Egger Barony, 278, 295, 301
Enclosure, 15
Evacuees, 216, 242-3

Fairbairn, Archibald, 13
Fairs and markets, 30-1, 161, 176-7
Fergusson of Knockroon, 86
Finger ring, 13, **13**
Finlayson, Iain, 289
Finlayson, John, 264, 289
Football, 162-3, 232-6, 244, 281-3
Fowler, Captain John (Covenanter), 54
Fryer, Rev George, 204-5

Gasswater, 12, 29, 101-2, 121, 124, 126-7, **127**, 129, 143-4, 148, 155-6, 168, 182, 199, 222, 224-5, 237, 247, 268, 272-4, 301, 330
Gasworks, 156, 174-5, 226, 276
Gemmel, John (Covenanter), 54
Gibston, 315
Gilmilnscroft, 27, 47-8, 147, 153-4
Glenhead, 315
Glenmuir, 11, 33-4, 47, 86-7, 108, 145, 155-6, 202, 214, 266, 280
Glenmuir, High, 103, 155-6, 241, 281, 303, 315
Glenmuir, Laigh, 33, 47, 49, 108, 146,

155, 160, 214, 241, 301, 315
Glenmuir Limeworks, **102**, 155-6
Glenmuir School, 143, 146, 209, 214
Glenmuir Viaduct, 130
Glenmuirshaw, 15, 47, 108, 132, 144, 214, 315
Glenside, 316
Golf, 237, 255
Grant, Rev John, 88
Gray, James (Covenanter), 54
Greenfoot, 28, 40
Greenside, 316
Gregg, A. Baird, 116-7
Greyhound Racing, 285
Greymare Stone, 15
Grose, Francis, 19
Guthrie, James, 212-5

Halbert, William, 68, 99, 108-9
Hallglenmuir, 33, 99, 315
Hamilton of Newton, Sir William, 34
Hamilton, John (Covenanter), 54
Hapland, 119, 160, 316
Health Centre, 249
Health, 62, 122, 249
Hearth Tax, 37
Henderson, James, 209-10
Higgins, Rev Andrew, 204
Higgins, Rev James, 137
High Shaw, 317
Highhouse, 153, **173**, 173, 177-8, 201, 221, 224, 232-4, 248, 250, 281, 284, 289, 292-3, 302, 316
Highhouse Colliery, 149, 153, 177-8, 218-21, **219**, 243, 268, 270-2, 292, 329

Highhouse Rangers, 232-4
Highland Host, 52-3
Hill of Auchinleck, 317
Hill, Rev James, 134, 202-3, 209, 217, 239
Hogan, Rev Joseph, 206
Holm Pit, 330
Holmhead, 122, 153, 160-1
Home Guard, 239, 243-4
Houston, Rev David, 56-7
Houston Hall, 308, 317
Howatson of Dornal and Glenbuck, Charles, 87, 130, 133, 143, 202, 241-2
Hume, William, 145, 211-2
Hyslop, James, 145, 214

Industry, 251-2, 301-2
Inglis, Rev John, 36
Ingram, James, 94-5
Ingram, Robert Samson, 123-4, 135, 137, 143-5, 164, 202, 209, 211-2, 237
Inns, 105, 158, 230
Ironworks, 100-1, 103, 121-2, 124-5, 129, 133, 135, 145-6, 149-151, 153-6, 164-5, 176, 178, 180, 223-5, 252

Jamieson, James, 94, 133
Jehovah's Witnesses, 263, 299
Johnson, Dr Samuel, 19, 66-7, 71-4, 84, 118
Johnston, Rev Charles, 244, 257-8, 270, 297
Jougs, 50

INDEX

Kane, Rev John. 263
Keithstoun, 30-1, 60
Kirkland, 49, 121
Knagshill, 317
Knockroon, 11, 32, 44, 55, 74, 85-7, 95, 99, 109, 132, 172, 201, 293, **295**, 317
Knowe, 317
Kyle, 318
Kyle Castle, **25**, **26**, 25-7, 29, 33-4, 47, 87

Lady Boswell's School, 143
Lamb Fair, 161, 176-7
Landmark Trust, 255, 297
Langholm, 48, 159-60, 201, 318
Langside, Battle of, 29, 32
Lapraik, John, 34
Laurenceknowe, 318
Laurienne, Sister, 140-1
Lawrie, Rev John, 87-8
Lead, 12
Leisure, 112, 161-3, 231-41, 281-7, 303-6
Library, 124, 241, 251, 253, 287, 293
Liddell's Coaches, 231, 302
Limestone and limeworks, 12, 69, **102**, 102, 106, 124, 129, 146, 152, 155-6, **156**
Limond of Dalblair, 87, 107, 130, 155
Lindsay, Rev John, 82, 93
Littleton, Rev Matthew, 261
Logan of that Ilk, Hugh, 87
Loganston, 318
Longpark, 309
Lugar, 12, 14-15, 29, 34-5, 49, 57, 103, 108, 113, 121-2, 124-7, **125**, 129, 133, 142-56, **147**, 158-60, 162-4, 168, 173-5, 178-81, **179**, 187, **187**, 194-200, **197**, 205-6, 208, 211-3, 215, 218, 221, 223-5, 228, 234-7, 239, 241-3, 246, 249-53, 259-61, 264-6, 268, 272, 279-81, 283, 285, 287, 289, 294, 299, 302, 305
Lugar Boswell Thistle F. C., 162-3, 235-6, 251, 283, 305
Lugar Institute, *see Weir Institute*
Lugar Ironworks – *see Ironworks*
Lugar Mine, 223, 268, 330
Lugar Parish Church, 135-6, **136**, 205-6, 209, 259-61, 266, 299
Lugar School, 145
Lugar Workshops, 272

MacCabe, Rev William, 138
McCree, William, 213-5
MacCrone, Guy, 200-1
MacCrone, Robert, 200
MacCutcheon, Rev George, 256, 270, 287
MacDerment, Rev Peter, 97
MacGavin, William, 95-6, 114-6, 166
MacGinnis, Rev John, 139
McGrattan, Rev Stephen, 299
MacIntyre, William, 214
MacKean, Rev Martin, 260-1
MacKerrell, Thomas, 178, 181, 183
MacKirdie, Rev Andrew, 259
MacLean, Colin, 267
MacLeod, Rev James, 259
MacQuaker, Samuel, 266
MacTurk, Matthew, 168

Manses, 36, 51-2, 60, 73, 89, 94-7, 122, 133-4, **135**, 137, 165, 187, 202, 204, 260
Market Inn, 158, 230-1, 280, 284, 302
Mary Queen of Scots, 29
Masonic Lodges, 239, 284
Maxwell, Rev Joseph, 207
Merlin Loch, 161-2, 237, 283
Merlin Park, 279, 283, 285, 305
Merlinhill, 61, 111, 153, 201, 319
Mesolithic finds, 15
Milgrew, Thomas, 265
Mill Affleck, 12, 160, 201, 319, 325
Millennium Clock, 290, **291**
Milne, Rev Walter, 136, 205
Mining, 101-3, 146-7, 149-54, 216-23, 268-274
Mitchell of Glenmuir, 87
Mortonmuir, 311, 319
Mortonmuir pit, 268, 330
Mosshouse, 124, 129, 146, 149, 152, 319, 330
Mosside, 319
Mounsey, George, 131-2
Murdoch, 'Specky', 242
Murdoch, John, 101, 108, 112, 166, 168
Murdoch, William, 112-14, 147, 166, 171-2, 175, 253, 286
Murphy, Rev Patrick, 139-41
Murphy, Rev Sean, 262
Murphy, Rev Thomas, 263, 299

Nelson, Alexander, 264
Neolithic period, 12
Netherholm, 48

New Statistical Account, 64, 97, 100, 103-6, 155

O'Dwyer, Rev John, 138-9
O'Neil, Rev John, 139-41, 206
Ochiltree Castle, 22
Oldbyres, 319
Open cast mining, 29, 49, 168, 214, 224, 268, 272, 301
Orange Lodges, 126, 241, 287, 289, 305
Orchard, 130, 160, 171, 237, 320, 321
Our Lady of Lourdes and St Patrick's R. C. Church, 138-42, **139**, 209, 261-3, 299

Paisley Abbey, 21, 27-8, 34, 36
Paterson, James, 19, 24, 33, 130
Paterson, Rev John, 261, 299
Paterson, Robert ('Old Mortality'), 50, 58
Paterson, Robert (Covenanter), 54
Paterson, William, 267
Pathhead, 320
Peden Church, 204-5, 239, 251, 256-9, **258**, 279, 305
Peden, Rev Alexander, 55, 166, 204
Penbreck, 34, 47, 155, 272, 281, 320
Pennyland, 13, 23, 33, 43-4. 47, 107, 109, 250, 295
Pennylands Camp, 243-4, 247-8
Pentecostal Church, 264
Picture House, 176, 239, **240**, 240-1, 284
Planned village, 60-2
Police, 122, 128, 174, 179, 181-2, 185,

252, 288
Pollock Farm Equipment, 279
Population, 50, 60, 63, 121-2, 124, 126-7, 155, 169, 173, 178, 181-3, 185, 247-8, 253, 290
Post Office, 105, 126, 158, 169, 182, **228**, 228-9, 243, 252, 254, 280, 302
Powharnal open cast mine, 301
Powharnal pit, 268, 330
Prehistoric Man in Ayrshire, 12, 101, 165
Proceedings of the Society of Antiquaries of Scotland, 16

Quarrying, 12, 94, 101, 138, 155, 157, 168, 173-4, 177-8
Queen's Sheuch, 29
Quoiting, 162, 237, 244

Railway, 121, 129-30, 146-7, 154-5, 168, 174, 223, 237, 241, 249-51, 253, 273, 294
Railway Inn, 129, 157-8, 223, 230, 280, 302
Ramsay, Rev Alexander, 51
Rattray, W., 214-5
Rechabites, 163, 185, 192
Reformation, 35-6, 51, 97, 138
Reid of Pennyland, 33, 43-4
Richmond, Andrew (Covenanter), 52
Richmond, Rev Dr James, 289
Rigg, 87, 91, 95-6, 107, 122, 160, 249-50, 320
Roadinghead, 146, 152, 159, 280, 320
Roadinghead Pits, 330
Roads, 107-11, 172-3, 249-50, 293

Robertson, Rev Daniel, 257-8, 297
Rocking Stone, **14**, 15
Roger, Rev George, 97, 138
Rogerton, 30, 34, 44, 201
Rogerton, Back, 221, 237, 247-8, 280, 293, 321
Rogerton, Fore, 160, 162, 237, 280, 321
Roman period, 16
Rosebank Pit, 330
Ross, Rev David, 203-4, 244, 256
Row, The, 308
Rowan, Alexander, 265-6
Rynn, Rev Michael, 261-2

St Patrick's Church – *see Our Lady and St Patrick's*
St Patrick's Primary School, 139, 207, 216, 261, 265, **265**, 300
St Vincent's Chapel, 28, 35
Schaw of Glenmuir, 33, 47, 86
Schaw, Rev John, 50-1, 98, 166
Schools, 97-100, 142-6, 209-16, 264-8, 299-300
Scott, Rev A. D., 137
Scott, Sir Walter, 38, 50, 58, 67, 74, 77-8, 82-3
Scouts, 239, 264, 285, 287
Searle Terrace, 123, 169
Secession Church, 95-6, 138
Shawfield, 321
Shiloh Terrace, 123, 169
Shirt making, 226, 229
Simpson, Patrick, 77
Sloan, Alec, 266
Sloan, Rev James, 297-8

Smith, John (antiquary), 12, 16, 101, 149, 164-5
Smith, Rev Robert, 96
Smith, Rev William. 242
Spence, Rev Prof. James, 138, 143, 257
Springhill, 321
Stations, 129, 174, 181-2, 250-1, 286
Statistical Account, 11, 18, 63, 91-2, 99, 101, 104
Stepends, 107, 122
Stepends Pit, 153, 330
Steven, Rev Robert, 92-3
Stevenston, 159-60, 322
Stobbs, Rev Simon, 136
Stone Age, 12-13
Stonebriggs, 15, 48, 109, 280, 302, 322
Stoner, Villiers Stanley, 172
Stony Hill, 12
Strachan, George, 215-6
Strachan, John, 216, 264-5
Strain, Euphans Helen, 241
Sunnyside, 160, 280, 322

Tait, Matthew, 116
Talbot de Malahide, Lord, 131, 174, 200-1, 203, 234
Tarrioch, 11, 34, 36, 44, 47, 53, 100-1, **100**, 155, 159-60, 323
Taylor, Rev Edward, 206
Templand Mains, 35, 44-5, 73, 109, 130, 143, 323
Templand pits, 149, 330
Templandshaw, 11, 35, 150, 159, 323
Templars (Knights), **28**, 28, 34-5
Temple, 109-11, **111**, 297
Templeton, 35, 121-2, 124, 142, 169, 177, 208, 231, 242, 250, 292
Templeton, John, 119-20
Tenshillingside, 55, 74
Thatch, 17, 29, 50, 62, 76, 96, 116, 122, 124, 160, 169, 171, 174, 177, 242
Third Statistical Account, 248, 253
Thirdpart, 242, 275, 324
Threeshire Education District, 144, 214
Threeshire Stone, 11, 12
Tolls, 107-8, **108**, 122, **161**, 227, 249
Town Hall, 123, **123**, 142, 144, 157, 162, 164, 217, 243, 287-9
Townhead of Auchinleck, 231, 324
Transport, 107-11, 172-3, 249-50
Treeshill, 324
Tweedie, William, 127, 145, 210-1, 215
Tweedlie, Rev Iain, 259-60

Underwood, 325

Vallance, John (Covenanter), 54
Vignoles, Rev Reginald, 206-7
Vycon plastics, 279

Walker, Rev George, 39, 49-50, 166
Walker, William (coal-master), 128, 147, 154
Wallace, Rev James, 205-6, 209
Wallace, Rev Thomas, 138
Wallace, Sir William, 20-1
Wallace's Cave, 20
Wallaceton, 12, 14, 45, 86, 95, 101, 108, 109, 133, 146, 159, 241, 325

Wallaceton Preaching Society, 95-6
War Memorial, 149, 187, **189**, 188-196, **197**, 205, 244-5, 249
Wardlaw Hill, 12-13, 15, 87, 224
Water supply, 121-2, 174
Waterside, 11, 43-4, 58-9, 86, 92, 99, 107, 109, 295-6
Watson, Rev John, 52, 59
Watson, Thomas (Covenanter), 54
Watson, Tom, 289
Weaving, 60-1, 63-4, 104, 114, 145-6, 162, 168
Weilside, 325
Weir Institute, 124-5, **126**, 149, 175, 243, 251
Wells, 19, 40, 121, 168, 182, 277
Welltrees, 44, 47-8, 101, 129, 159, 294, 325
Welltrees Pits, 330
Whirr, 326
Whirr Loch, 48, 112

White Heart Inn, 158
Whiteholm of Dornal, 14, 47, 87, 214, 241, 326
Whiteholm of Kyle, 326
Whitestoneburn, 33, 37, 47, 315
Wightman, John, 169, 171
Wilson & Sons, Adam, sawmill, 156-7, 174, 176, 225
Wilson, William, 157-8, 176, 225, 237, 239, 241
Women's Rural Institute, 253
Woodside, 326
Woolmill, 160, 326
Working Men's Club, 288
World War I, 158, 187-200, 205, 207
World War II, 207, 229, 242-246, 254, 259
Wright, Rev Patrick, 139

Young, Rev James, 205